D1094348

UNDER THE AXE
OF FASCISM

UNDER THE AXE
OF FASCISM

by

GAETANO SALVEMINI

NEW YORK

Howard Fertig

1969

First published in 1936

HOWARD FERTIG, INC. EDITION 1969
Published by arrangement with The Viking Press, Inc.

Library of Congress Catalog Card Number: 68-9589

PRINTED IN THE UNITED STATES OF AMERICA
BY NOBLE OFFSET PRINTERS, INC.

To

ALVIN JOHNSON

SINE GRATIA AUT AMBITIONE,
BONAE TANTUM CONSCIENTIAE
PRETIO

Preface

THE "march on Rome" of October 28, 1922, marked the advent to power of the Fascist party in Italy under the leadership of Benito Mussolini. This seizure of the government through a coup d'état was justified by the claim that Italy had to be rescued from the imminent danger of a Bolshevist revolution. Before the eyes of a world horrified by the tragedy of Russia, Italian Fascism assumed the role of the knightly Saint George who had slain the red dragon of communism. The legend appealed to the imaginations and soothed the fears of all the good people of Europe and America. It became the sacred myth around which was woven the early Fascist propaganda.

Meanwhile Fascist institutions were developing in Italy, and at the end of 1926 the personal dictatorship of Mussolini emerged. Dictatorship was not a new political system, nor did it enjoy a high reputation in the records of history. Mussolini did not relish the idea of passing down in history as a mere imitator of old discredited experiments. Therefore a new and greater myth had to take the place of the early anti-Bolshevist myth, if the existence of what was now the Fascist state was to be justified. Fascist "thinkers" abandoned the anti-Bolshevist myth, which had outlived its usefulness, acknowledged that in 1922 Italy had been neither on the verge of ruin nor under the menace of a communist revolution,[1] and clothed Fascism in a brand-new mantle, the mantle of the "corporative state." Fascism was no longer to be regarded negatively, as a mere measure of defence against communism in Italy, but positively, as a new

---

[1] Volpe, *Storia del Movimento Fascista*, 1932, p. 81: "We must acknowledge that during the second half of 1921 and much more during 1922 conditions in Italy, or some of them, had begun to show improvement. There were encouraging signs of economic recovery. The people of Italy were back at work. Infatuation for Russia and its Bolshevism was disappearing: credit for this must be given also to those Socialist leaders who had paid a visit to Russia to see with their own eyes the conditions prevailing in that country. . . . The Italians were finding themselves again. . . . All this can and must be acknowledged. . . . But while many even among the Fascist sympathizers thought that the time had come for Fascism to disarm . . . Fascism to the contrary pushed forward the mobilization of its forces. The main target was now the government, or, we may say, the parliamentary regime." Signor Volpe is the official historian of the Fascist regime.

social system—the "corporative" system—destined not only to supersede the outmoded institutions of democracy in Italy, but also to lead the whole world to a higher form of civilization.

The new myth has been advertised all over the world by a propaganda which equals, if it does not excel, in efficiency the elaborate organization which Soviet Russia employs for similar purposes.

As a result of this wonderfully organized propaganda, the Fascist "corporative state" has awakened curiosity, hope, and even enthusiasm. Italy has become the Mecca of political scientists, economists, and sociologists, who flock there to see with their own eyes the organization and working of the Fascist corporative state. Daily papers, magazines, and learned periodicals, departments of political science, economics, and sociology in great and small universities, flood the world with articles, essays, pamphlets, and books, which already form a good-sized library, on the Fascist corporative state, its institutions, its political aspects, its economic policies, and its social implications. No details are omitted, no problem concerning its origins and sources is left unexplored, no connexion or comparison with philosophical and economic systems is overlooked. The Italian corporative state is hailed as "the most amazing creation of Fascism for the solution of the thorny problem of the relations of capital and labour," and as "an extraordinary achievement, worthy of the closest study and admiration." [2]

Yet, strange and amazing as it may seem, it was only on November 10, 1934, with the formal inauguration of the "corporations," that "the wheels of Premier Mussolini's new Corporative State started turning" (*New York Times*, November 10, 1934). And when the wheels started turning, all saw that they were turning to no purpose. As has been observed by an English scholar, who has known how to seek and to discover the realities behind the words, "the term 'corporative' has been used, if not invented, to rouse a sense of wonder in the people, to keep them guessing, to provoke inquiry, and to contrive, out of the sheer mystification of an unusual word, at once to hide the compulsion on which the Dictatorship finally depends and to suggest that a miraculous work of universal benevolence is in the course of performance. . . . The 'corporate state' is a tool of propaganda." [3] From 1926 to 1935 the sole reality in Italian political life was the dictatorship of a man

---

[2] Professor P. M. Brown of Princeton, in *Current History*, May 1931, p. 163.
[3] Finer, *Mussolini's Italy*, p. 499.

and his party. But side by side with this reality a new myth had grown to gigantic proportions—the myth of the "corporative state."

To be sure, not all writers were so blind as to fail to perceive that the Fascist corporations existed only on paper. But in most cases the writers who claimed first-hand knowledge of the Italian situation were either superficial observers without much time at their disposal, who were satisfied with the official explanations given by the Fascist guides to whom they appealed for assistance, or propaganda agents whose purpose was not to make an objective study of the subject, but to sing the praises and benefits of the dictator who was maintaining them at the expense of the Italian taxpayer. On the other hand the Fascist terminology itself seems to have been invented for the purpose of spreading confusion and misinformation. The associations of employers, the unions of employees, and the associations of professional classes are called either "syndicates" or "corporations" or "guilds." The term "syndicate" is of French origin and is applied in French only to the unions of employees. It has no such significance in English. The terms "corporation" and "guild" in English do not denote anything resembling the "syndicates" or "guilds" of Fascist terminology. Moreover, the term "corporation" is used by the Fascists to indicate not only the associations of employers and the unions of employees but also those bodies which are supposed to stand above the associations and the unions and to co-ordinate their activities. It is easy to understand how chaos may be engendered in the mind of a non-Italian reader when all these terms are used without any clear definition.

Add that the Fascist legal documents often are obscure and inconsistent. In most cases, the legislator himself either had no clear idea of the institutions he was creating, or he purposely left room for misunderstanding. When from juridical texts one passes to political and philosophical treatises the confusion becomes even worse confounded. As a Fascist high personage, Signor Farinacci, has said, "each one vies with the others to create interpretations and philosophies always more and more in contradiction with one another; the multitude of those who have an average culture—without speaking of the workmen who also have some right to understand something—ends up by not understanding anything." [4]

The result of such ambiguities and confusion is that even a person

---

[4] Speech made in Florence June 21, 1925.

who is thoroughly conversant with Italian finds himself between the horns of a dilemma when he tries to translate the Italian text into another language. If he seeks to make intelligible the thought of the original text, he adds something that is not there, substituting an undesired clarity for an intentional ambiguity. If, on the other hand, he makes a literal translation, he runs the risk of being unfair to the author by making him seem to be a fool, whereas in actual fact he used ambiguous language not because he was a fool, but for the purpose of fooling others. Or the foreign reader, behind the equivocal words which are handed out to him, will see institutions which have nothing in common with those which function in actuality.

Finally, very seldom do Fascists go beyond a mere formal description of institutions and vouchsafe definite information concerning the effects of those institutions upon the conditions of the Italian population. And when they do advance such information, it is usually a fabrication out of whole cloth.

Only in this way can one explain the presence of so much misinformation and confusion in the literature concerning Fascism.

In the present book the reader will find hard facts, not vague legal formulæ; concrete realities, not abstract doctrines. Its purpose is to provide the English-speaking public with accurate information not about the whole economic, social, and political system of the Fascist dictatorship, but about one single phase of it, i. e., those institutions through which Fascism claims to have solved the problem of the relations between capital and labour.

As the reader will discover for himself, the sources used in our study have been almost exclusively Fascist sources: official documents and statistics, speeches and writings of Fascist leaders and "thinkers," and news taken from Italian Fascist daily papers and periodicals. We have as a rule reproduced the original texts, making no changes except the occasional elimination of superfluous words and the placing of passages in italics in order to catch the reader's attention. Except where otherwise specified, italics in quoted matter indicate our emphasis.

We have always indicated our sources with the greatest possible exactitude, except where it was a question of documents, such as Mussolini's speeches or interviews with the press, legal texts, parliamentary debates, etc., which may easily be traced, by reference to the date, in any Italian daily paper or in official collections. The reader will be able to check our statements if doubt should arise in his mind.

We have also made an extensive use of the literature on the subject. In some cases we have strengthened our statements by quoting those few non-Italian scholars who have investigated Italian institutions with care and without bias. In most cases, however, we have exposed the inconsistencies and falsehoods of those writers who, either by careless observation or by a dishonest habit of mind or by a fanatic admiration of Fascism, have misled the public. The broad dissemination of this inaccurate literature and the misinformation which it has spread in the English-speaking countries have made it imperative for us to pay to these publications more attention than they would otherwise have deserved. Since we are writing for an English-speaking public, we have confined ourselves to calling the reader's attention to misstatements published in the English language. But we assure our Anglo-Saxon readers that the alluvion of propaganda is no deeper in his country than elsewhere.

Dr. David Fellman of the University of Nebraska, Dr. Max Ascoli of the Graduate School of Political Science, New York, and Professor George La Piana of Harvard University have read the manuscript and given us the benefit of their valuable criticism and advice. The officers of the Widener Library, Cambridge, Mass., have been unsparing of their assistance. We ask them all to accept our most sincere thanks.

G. S.

Cambridge, Mass.
November 30, 1935

Table of Contents

Part One

THE "CORPORATIVE STATE"

I

The Origins of Fascist "Syndicalism"

DURING the half century of free government in Italy, associations of every sort sprang into being: clubs for political, religious, philanthropic, sporting, educational, and recreational purposes; societies for mutual aid; co-operative societies of consumers and producers, co-operative buying associations; building societies; trade unions; associations of industrialists, landowners, bankers, professional men, civil servants, priests, teachers, and students; associations of ex-service men, disabled soldiers, etc. Some of these associations were grouped in national organizations, others remained unaffiliated, but all competed freely under the most varied political and religious banners.

Unfortunately, no reliable statistics on these associations have ever been compiled. The only figures available are those for the trade unions and the co-operative societies. Towards the end of 1920, at the moment when Italian trade-unionism reached its greatest expansion, there were 2,300,000 trade-unionists who formed a national organization called the General Confederation of Labour under Socialist leaders, while 1,800,000 belonged to the Italian Confederation of Workers, associated with the People's Party (Partito Popolare) under a Christian-Democratic flag.[1] There existed also the Italian Syndicalist Union, run by revolutionary Syndicalists and Anarchists, and the Italian Union of Labour created by Socialists and Syndicalists who during the war had become also nationalist. No official figures of membership for these two bodies are available, but it was said that the former had about 500,000 members and the latter about 200,000 members. The co-operative movement had likewise achieved a high degree of development. In March 1921 government statistics gave the number of co-operative societies as 19,377.[2]

Today Mussolini and the Fascists can say with Molière's Sganarelle: "Nous avons changé tout cela."

---

[1] *Bollettino dell'Ufficio del Lavoro*, Dec. 1920, pp. 318, 320, 522.

[2] Riguzzi and Porcari, *La Cooperazione Operaia*, pp. 14, 22, 42. The Director of the British Institute of Florence, H. E. Goad, in *The Making of the Corporate State*, p. 75, states that prior to the advent of Fascism Italian workmen felt a "traditional reluctance to enroll themselves in any union."

At the end of 1920 the Fascists began methodically to smash the trade unions and the co-operative societies by beating, banishing, or killing their leaders and destroying their property. They made no distinction between Christian-Democrats and Socialists, between right-wing and left-wing Socialists, between Socialists and Communists, or between Communists and Anarchists. All the organizations of the working classes, whatever their banner, were marked out for destruction because they were "Bolshevist." The Fascists were provided with arms, ammunition, and means of transportation by the military authorities, and could almost always count upon the passive and frequently even the active connivance of the police. Their opponents were divided among themselves and hence incapable of united action, insufficiently furnished with arms or without any arms at all, and paralyzed by the pro-Fascist sympathies of the police, whose role in the struggle resembled that of Mephistopheles in the duel between Faust and Marguerite's brother. Under these circumstances, the Fascists had to fear only individual reprisals, necessarily unco-ordinated and inefficient. Their victory was inevitable.[3]

A single episode will suffice to give an idea of the nature of the civil war in Italy in 1921 and 1922. In a street fight that occurred in the city of Ravenna on July 26, 1922, seven persons were killed, among them a Fascist. This is the manner in which the leader of the Fascists in the "anti-Bolshevist" reprisals described his glorious exploits:

That night our storm-troops proceeded to destroy the vast headquarters of the Confederation of the Socialist Co-operatives of the province. . . . The old palace was completely destroyed. . . . We undertook this task in the same spirit with which we demolished the enemy's stores in war-time. The flames from the great burning building flashed ominously into the night. The whole city was illumined by the glare. We had to strike terror into the hearts of our opponents. Fascists are not slain with impunity. . . . Scarcity of water assisted the work of the flames. The large amount of provi-

---

[3] Those wishing to arrive at their own conclusions concerning the civil war which took place in Italy during 1921 and 1922 should compare the Fascist and the anti-Fascist versions. The former will be found in L. Villari, *The Awakening of Italy*, pp. 102–288; the latter in G. Salvemini, *The Fascist Dictatorship in Italy*, pp. 20–161. Signor Villari is attached to the Ministry of Foreign Affairs, his function being that of carrying on propaganda in English-speaking countries. He must not be confused with his father, Professor Pasquale Villari, who was a first-rate scholar and a high-minded man.

sions with which the building was stocked rendered the fire inextinguishable.
. . . I went to the chief of police and announced to him that I would burn
down the houses of all the Socialists in Ravenna unless he gave us within half
an hour the necessary means for transporting the Fascists elsewhere. I demanded a whole column of trucks. The police officers lost their heads, but
after half an hour had passed they told us where we could find trucks already supplied with gasoline. I had asked for these trucks on the pretext
that I wished to take the indignant Fascists away from the city. In reality, I
was organizing the "column of fire," as our opponents described it, in order
to extend our reprisals to the whole province. The march of the trucks began
at eleven o'clock yesterday morning, the twenty-ninth, and ended this
morning, the thirtieth. We had almost twenty-four hours of continuous
travelling, during which no one stopped for a moment's rest or food. We
passed through towns and villages in the province of Forli and the province
of Ravenna, destroying and burning all the centres of the Socialist and Communist organizations. It was a terrible night. Our passing was marked by
mounting columns of fire and smoke. The whole plain of Romagna up to
the hills was subjected to the reprisals of the outraged Fascists, determined
to put an end to the red terror. Innumerable episodes. Encounters with the
Bolshevist rabble, in open resistance, none. All their leaders were in flight.
The headquarters of the organizations, Socialist clubs, co-operatives—these
were practically deserted.[4]

While the civil war was going on, new Fascist unions were being
created which were called "economic syndicates." The first of these
"syndicates" arose on February 28, 1921, in the little town of San Bar-
tolomeo in Bosco in the province of Ferrara.[5] In November 1921 the
members of the "economic syndicates" numbered 64,000,[6] and by January 1922, 250,000.[7] Speaking of these early recruits on May 7, 1928,
Mussolini admitted that "a number of them had no clear idea of where
they were going." They were facetiously dubbed "prisoners of war."

In January 1922 a "syndical convention" was held, in Bologna, at
which it was decided that all Fascist "syndicates" should be grouped
into five "corporations": agriculture, industry, commerce, seamen, and
the middle and intellectual classes. The five "corporations" were to
form a "General Confederation of National Syndicates." Each "corpora-

---

[4] Balbo, *Diario, 1922*, pp. 102–10.
[5] Chiurco, *Storia della Rivoluzione Fascista*, vol. III, p. 90.
[6] *Stampa*, Nov. 9, 1921. Pantaleoni, *Bolscevismo Italiano*, p. xxxi.
[7] Chiurco, *op. cit.*, vol. IV, p. 33.

tion" was to "gather within itself all the professional, intellectual, manual, and technical activities." [8] Yet employers and workers were not
to be thrown indiscriminately into the same "corporation." The employers' and the employees' associations, while remaining distinct from
each other, were, however, to be subject to a common higher governing
body called a "corporation." For this reason the "corporations" were
also called "mixed syndicates." But the employers did not let themselves
be seduced by the Fascist sirens; they stuck to their own associations
and left the workmen, the artisans, the small landowners and farmers—
in short, the small man—to be regimented by the Fascists. [9]

Between January and June 1922 the number of organization members
rose from 250,000 to 459,284; [10] by August 1922 there were 800,000, [11]
and the same number in October of that year, when Mussolini seized
power. [12]

The budgets of these organizations as well as the salaries paid the officials were shrouded in mystery. It is scarcely too much to attribute the
larger portion of their income to subsidies from industrialists, large land-

---

[8] Chiurco, *op. cit.*, vol. IV, p. 33; vol. V, p. 337. Villari, *The Awakening of Italy*,
p. 235.

[9] R. W. Child, U. S. ambassador at Rome from 1921 to 1924, in *A Diplomat Looks
at Europe*, p. 217, described the Fascist organizations as "producers' co-operatives."
Goad, in *The Making of the Corporate State*, pp. 14–5, asserts that "under pressure
from the Fascists, the employers of patriotic workers agreed to keep open their factories even at financial sacrifice offering the best wages in the circumstances. The relative success of firms and factories that adopted the sensible policy of co-operation
brought into these Nationalist mixed Syndicates steadily increasing numbers both of
workmen and employers." All this is sheer invention, and could not be substantiated by
evidence of any kind.

[10] Chiurco, *op. cit.*, vol. IV, p. 125.

[11] *Industrial and Labour Information*, Oct. 30, 1922, p. 9; Beals, *Rome or Death*,
pp. 116, 261.

[12] Chiurco, *op. cit.*, vol. V, p. 457. We give these figures without guaranteeing their
accuracy. At the end of 1919 there were 17,000 Fascists according to the report presented to the Fascist Congress of Nov. 1921 (*Popolo d'Italia*, Nov. 8, 1921), but
"there were not even 10,000" according to a speech by Mussolini on March 9, 1924,
and were a mere 870 according to an official *communiqué* published in the *Popolo
d'Italia* on March 23, 1929. On May 22, 1921, Mussolini stated in an interview to the
Giornale d'Italia that there were "no less than half a million" Fascists; but on Nov.
8, 1921, the secretary of the Party announced that there were 230,000. In a speech on
March 23, 1924, Mussolini stated that in 1921 the Fascists were 248,936 in number;
while the official *communiqué* of March 23, 1929, said there were 299,867 at the end
of 1922. Is it possible that during a year of extraordinary good fortune, politically
speaking, the Fascists had increased only from 248,000 to less than 300,000? If the
statistics on the number of members in the political organization are thus unreli-
able, we are hardly justified in placing confidence in those concerning the "syndicates."

owners, merchants, bankers, and others who welcomed the violent destruction of the unions and co-operative societies.[13]

The chief organizer of the new Fascist unions was Edmondo Rossoni. After the fashion of Mussolini, Rossoni had been before the war a revolutionary Socialist of the extreme left. He had been a militant of the revolutionary-Syndicalist Industrial Workers of the World in the United States. On June 1, 1911, a group of "prominent" Italians placed a wreath on the monument to Garibaldi in New York. Following this "patriotic" demonstration the Italians of a revolutionary stamp staged one on their own account. The orator who held forth at the monument was none other than Rossoni.

Rossoni [we read in the paper *Il Proletario* for June 2, 1911] with a sonorous voice that vibrates in one's ears like the string of a taut bow, lashes out against the whole filthy crew of swindlers, exploiters, counterfeiters who need the cloak of patriotism to conceal their plunder. And after having declared that he assumes full responsibility of his act, amidst a delirium of applause he spits with might and main on the King's tricolor and on the wreath of the prominent citizens. Our protest has been made and we are satisfied. But not Rossoni, for he throws himself once more at the pedestal of the monument and proposes that each one of those present file before the wreath and decorate it with a conscientious spit, which everyone does, applauding.[14]

When the war broke out, Rossoni, like Mussolini, suddenly discovered that he too was a nationalist. He returned to Italy and in May 1918 with other Socialists no less revolutionary and no less patriotic than he, helped found the Italian Union of Labour with the programme of "war against the capitalist system and all the institutions upholding that system." [15] In 1919 and 1920 this organization adopted an attitude more revolutionary than that of the Socialist-controlled General Confederation of Labour, thereby hoping to win the working masses to the nationalist ideology, but it never succeeded in obtaining a wide influence. Rossoni was a general without soldiers when in 1921, after "secret travail" [16] similar to that which in 1914 had caused him to change allegiance a first time, he

---

[13] See note on p. 8 of the present chapter.

[14] The files of *Il Proletario* are available in the New York Public Library.

[15] Rosenstock-Franck, *L'Économie Corporative Fasciste*, pp. 12–4, 25–8. This is the best study up to the present available concerning the relations between capital and labour under the Fascist dictatorship.

[16] Malusardi, *Elementi di Storia*, p. 52.

left the Italian Union of Labour and threw himself body and soul into the Fascist movement.

The officials of the new Fascist unions were appointed by Rossoni.[17] The term "syndicates," by which the Fascist unions were designated, was the last remaining shred of the old revolutionary syndicalist banner under which Rossoni and several of his coadjutors had begun their careers as politicians.

NOTE

The amounts of the subsidies paid by Italian capitalists to Mussolini and other Fascist chieftains have never been and probably never will be published. But there is no lack of evidence to substantiate our statement.

The most active propaganda agent of Fascism in the English-speaking countries, Signor Villari, admitted in 1926 that "many adhered to the movement for selfish reasons—landlords and manufacturers who simply regarded it as a form of protection for the right of property." [18] It is quite improbable that these gentlemen asked to be admitted or were admitted into the Fascist organizations with empty hands.

The official daily of the Vatican, the *Osservatore Romano*, in its issue of October 9, 1921, published a circular of a "fascio" (local Fascist Party organization) in the village of Cadelbosco di Sopra, province of Reggio Emilia, dated September 10, 1921, in which the property owners of the village were invited to contribute to the movement "in proportion to their financial means"; "each contribution should not be less than two hundred lire."

A Florentine Fascist wrote in 1922:

One saw on arriving at the Fascist headquarters the well-known surly and rapacious faces of the war profiteers. These gentlemen were shabbily clothed

---

[17] A group of dissident Fascists wrote in 1924: "The organization of this voluntary army was necessarily improvised due to the absence of experienced leaders. We admit that at first dictatorial methods were necessary to cope with the sudden creation of an exceptional organism at an exceptional moment in history."—Avarna di Gualtieri, *Il Fascismo*, p. 128.

[18] *Encyclopædia Britannica*, supplement of 1926, under "Fascism," p. 16. Speaking on "The Economics of Fascism," at the Williams College Institute of Politics during the summer of 1931, Signor Villari said: "The movement was at first accepted by the employers who saw in it a defense of their own interests against anarchy. But later they began to regard it with suspicion."—*Bolshevism, Fascism, and Capitalism*, p. 71.

and shod, but all had the inevitable diamond on their finger—and we were obliged to accept their money because we needed it to stifle an evil worse than they.[19]

In the general election of 1924 the Italian Association of Joint-Stock Companies obliged each one of its dependent companies to contribute to the Party's campaign fund one fifth of one per cent of its capital.[20]

In October 1924 the organization representing the agricultural employers in the province of Ravenna decided that all sugar-beet producers must pay to the provincial Fascist Federation ten centesimi for every quintal of sugar beets harvested that year.[21] It may be assumed that these practices existed since the origin of the Fascist movement, although not in the systematic form they took in later years. At the beginning of 1921 it was especially the agricultural employers in the Po valley who dug into their pockets, thereby setting an example to other employers elsewhere in Italy.

A Fascist organizer, Signor Cuzzeri, declared in a public speech in March 1925:

The industrialists are greatly mistaken if they think that Fascism, having accepted their subsidies in 1919, 1920, and 1921, has given up protecting the workers.[22]

The official historian of the dictatorship, Professor Volpe, admitted in 1928 that to the early Fascist movement "members of the bourgeoisie . . . contributed their personal support and their money"; and also that "war profiteers and frightened bourgeois were ready to give money in lieu of blood."[23]

Goad, in *The Making of the Corporate State*, p. 71, affirms that the Fascist movement "was not backed by financiers"!

---

[19] Banchelli, *Memorie di un Fascista*, p. 12.

[20] The circular was published by all the anti-Fascist newspapers in the spring of 1924 and its authenticity was never denied. There is an allusion to it in Chiesa, *La Mano nel Sacco*, p. 103.

[21] Avarna di Gualtieri, *Il Fascismo*, p. 149.

[22] Quoted in Hautecoeur, *Le Fascisme*, p. 145.

[23] *Lo Sviluppo Storico del Fascismo*, pp. 8, 10. In the latest form of this study, *Storia del Movimento Fascista*, published in 1932, Professor Volpe prudently suppressed these statements.

II

The Vidoni Palace Pact

AFTER the "march on Rome" (October 1922) the violent destruction of the Socialist and Christian-Democratic unions by the Fascists continued on a larger scale.[1] At the same time the provincial prefects[2] were suppressing anti-Fascist associations of all kinds. They made use of Paragraph 3 of the Local Government Act, which empowered them in case of emergency to adopt any measure necessary to preserve public order. From 1860 to 1900 this article had been applied only in exceptional circumstances to dissolve associations regarded by the government as subversive. After 1900 it fell entirely into desuetude. Not even during the World War was it applied. The Fascist government revived it and made extensive use of it.

On January 24, 1924, the king signed a decree, without previous discussion or approval by Parliament, by which all "associations of whatever nature, maintained by the contributions of workers," were placed under the surveillance of the prefects:

> Should there arise any suspicions of abuse of the public confidence, of illegitimate expenditure, of misuse of funds to the detriment of the members, or for ends other than the economic and moral welfare of the workers, the Prefect of the Province may institute inspections, or make inquiries into the affairs of such associations, revoke or annul their decisions, dissolve their executives, and entrust to a state commissioner the administration of their estate.

A year after the appointment of a state commissioner, the prefect was empowered to liquidate the property of the association, "applying any assets, at his own discretion, to the furtherance of the economic and moral ends pursued by the dissolved association." The best way to

---

[1] Compare Villari, *The Fascist Experiment*, pp. 56–100 and 136–61, with Salvemini, *The Fascist Dictatorship in Italy*, chapters III–V.

[2] The office of prefect has no exact counterpart in the English-speaking countries. The prefect is the executive head of a province, but unlike the American state governor, he is not elected by the voters, being instead the appointee of the Minister of the Interior, to whom he is responsible for the administration of his province.

employ the assets was to hand them over to a Fascist organization.[3]

By an act of November 26, 1925, all associations were obliged "to communicate to the police, whenever required, the names of their responsible officials and of their members, and any other information concerning their activities." The decimation of the associations not in good odor with the party in power became systematic after the enactment of this law.

By October 1926 in thirty-three out of the seventy-three Italian provinces nothing remained of anti-Fascist organizations. On November 6, 1926, a new "public security" law ("legge di pubblica sicurezza") was enacted whereby associations were defined as "parties, groups, and in general all political organizations, even of a temporary nature" (Article 218). The prefects were empowered to dissolve all associations whose activities were "contrary to the national order of the state" (Article 215), i. e., to Fascism. By virtue of this law a Napoleonic *communiqué* to the press on November 11, 1926, announced:

All political parties, all anti-Fascist political organizations, and others of a suspected character have been dissolved. Government commissioners have been placed in charge of economic organizations whose leaders gave cause for doubts.

A law passed on November 25, 1926, enacted that:

Anyone reconstituting under new names the associations dissolved by the police shall be liable to from three to five years'.imprisonment; anyone belonging to these illegal associations or carrying on propaganda for the doctrines, programmes, or methods of action of such associations, shall receive from two to five years' imprisonment.

Thus disappeared in Italy the last traces of non-Fascist associations. The only associations permitted to exist were those which submitted to the supervision of the Fascist Party, whose leaders chose their presidents, councillors, and secretaries.[4]

---

[3] See the memorandum of the General Confederation of Labour in the Transactions of the International Labour Office, *Compte rendu provisoire*, May 31, 1926, p. x.

[4] Signor Pitigliani, in *The Italian Corporative State*, p. 16, makes no effort to inform his readers of the illegal violence and of the laws by which existence was rendered impossible for any organization in Italy that refused to accept the supervision of the Fascist Party. He writes merely: "In the regime of political *exclusiveness* which Fascism in arriving at power had *uncompromisingly* created, the Fascist Syndical Associa-

Meanwhile, in 1923 and 1924, Rossoni tried to gather into a single national confederation all the organizations of employers, employees, and professional classes that were on good terms with the Fascist Party or had accepted its supervision. Naturally, the president of such an all-inclusive confederation would have been Rossoni.

The landowners reluctantly accepted Rossoni's proposals in February 1924. The industrialists refused. These gentlemen were subsidizing the Fascist movement in order that the Fascist "corporations" might regiment the workers, not in order that their own hands should be tied in dealing with their employees. Mussolini decided in favor of the industrialists.[5] As a result, the workers' organizations and those of the employers remained distinct from each other.

This attempt having failed, Rossoni, during the autumn of 1924, proposed that legal recognition should be reserved for only one union in each trade or profession, such recognition to be granted only to Fascist unions, and to these all workers in that trade must belong. The committee appointed by the government to study the reform of the constitution rejected Rossoni's suggestions.[6]

While these discussions were going on, the Fascist unions protected the interest of their members by methods which may be guessed from the following instances:

1. A trial before the Court in Naples during June 1925 revealed the fact that during March 1923 Dr. Preziosi, a Fascist, had been called upon to represent the workers in a wage dispute with the Manifatture Cotoniere Meridionali (Southern Cotton Mills Co.). The agreement imposed by him on the workers was so outrageously unjust that the other Fascist leaders refused to sanction it. In April 1923 Dr. Preziosi was made editor of the newspaper *Il Mezzogiorno*, whose owner was the manager of the firm which Preziosi had favoured by his decision against the workers. The editorship of this paper, of course, offered a very respectable salary.[7]

---

tions were able to strengthen their organization. The political tendencies of opposing parties no longer hindered their technical improvements." At the international conference held in London in 1933 under the auspices of the International Institute of Intellectual Co-operation, Signor Rosboch was much bolder than Signor Pitigliani. He made the following statement: "We have not abolished the non-Fascist Unions" (*The State and Economic Life*, p. 283).

[5] *Industrial and Labour Information*, June 15, 1923, p. 535; Feb. 11, 1924, p. 27; March 17, 1924, p. 372. Rosenstock-Franck, *L'Economie Corporative*, pp. 33–7.

[6] Rosenstock-Franck, *op. cit.*, p. 40 ff.

[7] *Stampa*, June 23, 1925.

2. In *Avanti*, August 15–6, 1925, we read: "Busto Arsizio, August 14. A meeting took place between the representatives of the cotton trade and the Fascist union of operatives to examine a request for a rise in the bonus for the cost of living. After long discussion a revision of the rates of payment was agreed upon, but the task of determining the amount of increase for each branch *was entrusted to two employers*."

3. On the morning of November 20, 1925, each employee of the Trieste branch of the Banca Commerciale Triestina received a circular from the management notifying him that the existing agreement would terminate and be replaced on December 1 by another one already drawn up by the management. In the afternoon of the same day (note the close relationship of the two facts) the prefect of Trieste announced that the Trieste branch of the National Federation of Bank Employees had been placed under the authority of the secretary of the Fascist unions in that province. On November 28 the management of the bank called together the employees and announced the terms of the new agreement, which increased the bonus for the cost of living, but at the same time lengthened the working day by from half an hour to an hour, according to the grade of the employee, and reduced by half the overtime rates. The provincial secretary of the Fascist unions was present and informed the employees that they must accept the new terms without discussion or comment.[8]

No wonder, therefore, if the Fascist unions remained as uninhabited as the Sahara Desert. In June 1924 a Fascist organizer among the steel workers, Deputy Bagnasco, wrote in a memorandum to Mussolini:

The working classes, swept into Fascist unions by the Party, are now perplexed and sceptical as to the efficacy of our movement, without, however, losing their confidence in it. Thus unconsciously they swell the grey, inert mass of those who remain passive in the face of events. They do not help to shape our future through their action and their passion. Certain groups of our adherents, morally and technically mature, are now, as formerly, tempted by the Red [Socialist] Unions, not so much for political reasons as because the activities of our unions do not appeal to them.[9]

In March 1925 there was in Lombardy an opportunity for measuring the Fascist and anti-Fascist strength among the metal workers. The Fascist metal workers' union of Brescia was in conflict with the employ-

---

[8] Information about this incident was obtained by the author from one of the employees in the bank.
[9] Avarna di Gualtieri, *Il Fascismo*, p. 117.

ers. No agreement having been reached, the Fascists called a strike. At once the leaders of the Socialist F.I.O.M. (Italian Metal Workers' Federation)—one of the few workers' organizations which had not yet been dissolved—gave the order for the strike to be extended to the whole of Lombardy. This would have meant not only the extension of the strike but a united front by Socialist and Fascist unions. Taken aback by this unexpected action, the industrialists and the Fascist leaders hastened to come to an agreement. But on March 17, when the Fascists called off the strike, the leaders of the F.I.O.M. gave the order for it to be continued one day longer. They wanted to demonstrate that the great bulk of the workers were with them and not with the Fascists. The newspaper which published the order was confiscated by the police. Nevertheless the word went round. Out of the one hundred thousand strikers, eighty thousand continued the strike on March 18. In the city of Milan only 5697 out of thirty-five thousand workers obeyed the Fascist order. This manifestation having been made, the workers returned in a solid body.

Voting took place at Turin on April 4, 1925, among the eighteen thousand workers in the Fiat Motor Works, to elect the council of the Factory Benefit Society. Ninety-four per cent of the workers voted. There were no Fascist votes!

Sometimes it happened that the Fascist organizers, after making a fresh agreement with the employers in regard to labour conditions, called for a referendum among the workers to confirm or reject their arrangement. The agreement of March 1925 in the metal trades of Trieste was rejected by eighty per cent of the eight thousand workers in the San Marco shipyard, and unanimously by the Lloyd and Sant' Andrea yards. A referendum taken among the textile workers on the labour agreement of 1925 gave the following results:

Works	Total votes cast	Votes cast against the Fascist agreement
Biella: Simone Bros.	119	107
Successori Sella & Co.	178	172
Torelli, Viera & Bros.	88	87
Valli and Co.	252	252
Cartosti Ludovico	143	143
Schio: Cuzzola Works	438	414

Prior to the fall of 1925 the workers in many factories, especially in the metal trades, appointed annual "factory committees" to represent them in negotiating with the managers. These elections took place within the factories, where only the workers were allowed to enter. Not a single Fascist candidate was ever returned. If one sums up the results of the elections held between November 1924 and the spring of 1925 in twenty-four factories for which figures are available, one gets the following totals:

Fascist votes.......... 605

Anti-Fascist votes...... 8,887 [10]

The Fascists published statistics upon statistics to prove that their unions contained millions of members, but much light is thrown on the value of Fascist statistics by the following quotations (the reader must keep in mind that all of the Italian papers quoted here are Fascist):

Popolo di Lombardia, February 21, 1925: "We know quite well that these figures [two million members in the Fascist unions] do not correspond to the truth, and are exaggerated and fantastic. In dealing with trade unions it is not easy to bluff, as in poker; the bluff always recoils upon its perpetrators. The main categories of industrial workers are entirely absent from our unions: textile workers, builders, printers, seamen. If the agricultural unions are numerous and strong in the provinces of the Po Valley and Tuscany, there is a void elsewhere, as far as they are concerned."

Italia Nuova, March 30, 1925: "Our members are not numerous. Our unions have never wished and do not now wish to have with them the masses who cannot reason and who are willing to lap up the words of the Red demagogue."

MacLean (American commercial attaché at Rome), in *Labor, Wages and Unemployment in Italy,* p. 4: "A large membership is claimed by the Fascist Corporations, but it is generally admitted that their success has been decidedly limited and that they have not succeeded in obtaining the confidence of the workers. Thus, while the Confederazione del Lavoro [the Socialist-led General Confederation] has undoubtedly lost ground, it may still reasonably be considered as the leading representative of organized labour."

Idea Sindacalista, June 6, 1926: "If it is true that the unions have such great memberships, it is difficult to understand why they never have any

---

[10] These figures form a part of those collected in the memoir presented to the International Labour Office at Geneva by the General Confederation of Labour in the spring of 1925: *Conferences: 1925,* p. 617 ff. None of these figures was questioned by Signor De Michelis, the representative of the Fascist government.

funds. *Concerning their numerical standing the Head of the Government seems not to wish any more discussion. We understand the political reasons for this.* And out of the respect and devotion which we have always shown the Duce, we declare ourselves ready, in our turn, to accept these figures. But none the less, there exists in the unions nothing but emptiness. The members may exist, even to the number of two million. But these two million appear only when, in the secret voting inside the factories, they disapprove of the Fascist unions and give their votes to the Red parties. Either the members of the Fascist unions do not exist, or, if they do, they always vote against the programme of their unions, precisely when those unions have most need for their support.

The Fascists had succeeded in destroying the Socialist and Christian-Democratic unions, but not in seducing the working class from allegiance to their former leaders.[11] It was, therefore, necessary to think of other means for placing them under the control of the dominant Party.

Thus Rossoni's idea, which had been rejected in the autumn of 1924, triumphed in June 1925. The Fascist Grand Council decided that the monopoly of representation should be vested in the Fascist unions. The employees' associations accepted this principle. On October 12, 1925, the Confederation of Industrial Employers concluded with Rossoni an agreement known as the Vidoni Palace Pact, so called from the place where the Fascist Party had its headquarters and where the pact was signed. By the terms of this Pact the industrialists' confederation recognized the Fascist unions as being the only representatives of their workers, and promised to make no agreements with their workers except through the Fascist unions; the latter authorized the industrialists thenceforth to ignore the "factory committees" elected by the work-

---

[11] Signor Villari, in *The Economics of Fascism*, pp. 74–5, informs us that "while the Fascist syndicates [unions] were developing and expanding, the older trade unions continued to exist, although their membership was declining"; but he fails to give any reason for this last phenomenon. True, he admits that "not all the men who dropped out of the old unions joined the new syndicates"; for which he offers a highly original explanation: "the money put into the coffers of the old unions had evaporated with no tangible result, even when it was not pocketed by the leaders and secretaries"; consequently "the workers were chary of joining new unions which might go the way of the others." Signor Rosboch thought it expedient to give a different version of the same facts in the London Conference of 1933: "Up to 1925, the majority of our workers were organized in Socialist corporations [unions]. . . . It is the workers who went over by the million to the Fascist organizations. . . . They realized that the Corporative State defended their interests much better than the Socialist Party." (*The State and Economic Life*, p. 283.)

ers. On October 6, 1926, the Grand Council of Fascism approved the Vidoni Palace Pact, and decided that it should be consummated by the abolition of the right to strike. Thus the industrialists recognized the Fascist unions as the sole representatives of Italian labour and obtained in recompense the abolition of the factory committees as well as of the right to strike.[12]

All that now remained was to give legal shape to the new principles. This was the object of the act of April 3, 1926, and the regulation of July 1, 1926.

---

[12] The abolition of the factory committees was legalized by a decree-law of Nov. 15, 1925, which provided: "Any agreement to the contrary notwithstanding, all clauses in labour agreements providing for workers' representation entered into before Oct. 1, 1925, may be repudiated." Monsieur Rosenstock-Franck, *Economic corporative*, p. 36 ff., and Mr. Finer, *Mussolini's Italy*, p. 497, have made this point clear. Professor Schneider, in *Making the Fascist State*, p. 117, says that the factory committees "were supposed to defend labour interests"; but "they had really become pliant instruments in the hands of the employers." Evidently he obtained this information from a Fascist who deceived him. Goad and Currey, in *The Working of a Corporate State*, p. 34, dish up to their readers the following titbit of historical romance in the manner of Emil Ludwig: "A large number of workingmen's syndicates [unions] induced their employers to make collective contracts whereby both strikes and lockouts were abandoned, and brought these contracts to the government with a request for the recognition of them, and asked that courts should be created for the settlement of future disputes. The original agreement between the workers and employers is known as the Pact of the Vidoni Palace, dated Oct. 1925."

III

The Fascist Organizations

ACCORDING to these legislative measures,[1] only one organization of employers or employees can be legally recognized by the government for each trade in each city or town.

All the employers' associations for a given trade unite in one national body known as a "national federation," while all the employees' unions in the same trade likewise constitute a parallel national federation. These national federations in their turn are gathered into "national confederations."

In each of the ninety-two provinces of Italy each federation of employers and each federation of employees is represented by a provincial secretary, who directs all the organizations dependent on his federation in the province.

Employers and employees do not have the right to group themselves according to the economic affinities they spontaneously feel. Are tailors, for instance, industrialists or tradesmen? Should fishermen come under the confederation of seamen or under that of the industrialists? Are the million *mezzadri* (share-croppers), who not only cultivate the soil themselves, but also employ hired hands, employers or employees? Are the caretakers of private houses to be organized under the confederation of the unions in industry or under that of the unions in commerce?

The government, in its omniscience, resolves all these knotty questions and fixes the category under which each individual must range himself. Thus the caretakers form a branch of the confederation of the unions in commerce, heaven knows why.[2]

---

[1] To avoid confusion, we give here the meaning of the terms which we shall employ: 1, by "associations" we mean the organizations of the employers and professional classes; 2, the term "unions" refers to the organizations of the employees; 3, "organization" is a generic term including those of the employers as well as those of the employees and the professional classes; 4, by "corporations"—for lack of a more precise term—we mean those bodies above the associations and unions, which are supposed to co-ordinate the work of both in the interests of the community. When we reproduce an English text with terms that differ from the ones explained above, we shall always put our terms in brackets immediately after.

[2] Lachin, *La IVe Italie*, p. 228. Bottai, in *Il Consiglio Nazionale delle Corporazioni*, p. 24, says: "Our job these last two years has been to sort out the Italians according to

17

The newspapers of July 17, 1926, published the following statement by the industrialists' confederation:

> Reports concerning an association for the smaller industries have appeared recently in the press. The Confederation of Industry warns that such a scheme clashes directly against the policy pursued by the government. The Fascist Party has clearly stated that the exclusive right to represent Italian industrialists of every rank belongs to this confederation and that therefore no other organization can be recognized by the government. The confederation hence reminds the small industrialists that they must join their branch of the confederation.

The significance of this document is better appreciated if one recalls that the confederation is controlled by the great protected business men, for example the steel magnates. The smaller fry, if permitted to form an independent association, might ask for the free import of such raw materials as pig iron and steel.

According to the regulation of July 1, 1926, all the employees' unions formed a national super-confederation, of which Rossoni was the president-general. But on November 20, 1928, Mussolini with one stroke of his pen abolished this super-confederation, and Rossoni, left without an organization to preside over after having held the fate of Italian labour in his hands for three years, suddenly retired to complete leisure. According to the official explanation, this measure was dictated by the necessity of ending an excessive centralization which was impeding the functioning of the individual unions.[3] According to the stories related in Italy by persons who have "inside" information, Rossoni was looked at askance by the employers because he had not completely forgotten his ultra-revolutionary slogans and used them too often in his public speeches, particularly in those made at the time when he was obliged to grant the employers a wage-reduction; the employers were grateful to him for the reduction but were perturbed by his syndicalist fireworks. Mussolini, profiting by the fact that the employees' organizations were in a state of unbelievable chaos, suddenly dismissed Rossoni in response to the pressure brought to bear upon him by the employers.[4]

---

occupation or trade and distribute them to their respective organizations." (Address of March 3, 1929.)

[3] Spencer, *Government and Politics of Italy*, pp. 259–60.

[4] An echo of this has penetrated into Rosenstock-Franck's book previously cited, pp. 87–8, and Finer, *Mussolini's Italy*, pp. 508–9.

But whatever actually took place behind the scenes, the mode of the dismissal was characteristic of the system: the rank and file of the unions and the union officials learned of the *coup* through the newspapers.

The government draws up the charters ("statuti") which are to regulate the activities of the national, provincial, and local organizations. It examines their budgets, audits their accounts, and may modify or annul any of their decisions.

Presidents, directors, and secretaries, regardless of their rank, must give an "undoubted guarantee of national [i. e., Fascist] loyalty." They may be removed from office as soon as they give the slightest sign of not possessing a sufficient measure of "national loyalty." The government may also deprive an organization of its legal recognition if the Ministry of Corporations considers it necessary "for serious motives." There is no appeal from a decision of this sort.

In 1926 thirteen national confederations were established, six for the employers, six for the employees (industry, banking, commerce, agriculture, maritime and aerial transport, and inland transport), and one for the professional classes. In 1934 the confederations of employers in maritime and aerial transport and inland transport, together with the corresponding confederations of employees, were abolished as independent organizations and were annexed to the two confederations of industry. All Fascist organizations are born, live, are transformed, and die, not as a result of decisions made by their members, but according to the discretion of the government.[5]

The government frequently makes use of the decree of January 24, 1924 (see above, p. 10) and appoints commissioners extraordinary for national and local organizations. According to an official announcement of December 31, 1933, the presidents of all the confederations had presented their resignations to Mussolini. A strike? Not in the least. When Mussolini wishes to dismiss some minister or high official in the government, the Party, or the legal organizations, he has published in the press that So-and-so has resigned; the victim, after having in this manner been apprised of his eclipse, receives a resignation formula to be signed. In the present case the simultaneousness of the resignations proved even to the blind that they had been imposed by the Duce. Mussolini proceeded to

---

[5] Yet in the London Conference of 1933, Signor Righetti told his listeners: "We have autonomous Trade Unions [associations of employers and unions of employees] which may organize for each category *as they wish.*" (*The State and Economic Life,* p. 265.)

name commissioners to occupy the places of the resigned-dismissed presidents.

Naturally, when it was a question of applying the law to organizations already in existence, the government granted legal recognition to none but Fascist ones.[6]

Rossoni said in the Chamber of Deputies on December 9, 1925:

All those who are preparing to come into the Fascist trade unions, especially when they are the only recognized ones, must give up any illusion that they are coming to play the master. They will find us in the unions. The official unions are Fascist. It will never be possible to work in the unions against our regime and our Revolution.

Mussolini himself, in a speech delivered on July 31, 1926, proclaimed:

The economic organizations are recognized, guaranteed, protected within the Corporative State and live within the orbit of Fascism. They accept the Fascist doctrine and practice. They are directed by leaders who are invariably enrolled in the Fascist Party. It could not be otherwise.

The secretary-general of the Party, Signor Augusto Turati, asserted on February 21, 1927:

Not only in administrative and political life, but also in the economic organizations, black-shirts of tested loyalty shall everywhere be in the posts of command.

On the same day Rossoni reiterated in the *Lavoro d'Italia:*

It must not be believed that the organizations of employers and employees can ever free themselves from the control of the Fascist Party. We have always maintained that the selection of leaders for the economic organizations must be made by the Party. We reject the humbug of political neutrality.

On November 1, 1927, the Grand Council of Fascism promulgated sixteen guiding principles for the legal organizations, of which the third ran as follows: "The selection and control of the organization leaders

---

[6] Goad, in *The Making of the Corporate State*, p. 80, gives a very intelligent explanation of this policy: "Those syndicates [organizations] that were recognized were those that came forward first: it is obvious that there could not be more than one representative body for each category." Goad and Currey, in *The Working of a Corporate State*, p. 36, have discovered that the government "carefully respected, wherever possible, the previously existing groups, when they applied for recognition and showed their willingness to co-operate."

shall be conducted with increasing strictness." The Ministry of Corporations, by a circular of November 9, 1927, summoned the organizations to send in lists of all their officials, reserving to itself the authority to indicate where changes ought to be made. In a speech to the Chamber on March 15, 1928, Signor Bottai, then Under-Secretary at the Ministry of Corporations, made the following declaration:

We supervise the selection and purging of the directors of the legally recognized organizations, in co-operation with the Ministry of the Interior and the Secretariat of the Party.

On September 27, 1930, being Minister of Corporations, he made the following statement:

We want the leaders of the Fascist unions to be one hundred per cent Fascists because our constitution is typically and solely political. We demand that all leaders be Fascist in order to avoid in practice all those deviations which might lead to the creation of a trade-union order different from that which we wish to create.

On March 10, 1933, he said in the Chamber:

Concerning the selection of officials, I may say that the Ministry, with the political assistance of the Party, exercises great care and rigour.

In conclusion, no organization can obtain legal recognition and the privileges that result from it, unless it submits itself to the rules governing all associations under the Fascist regime, that is, unless it consents to be administered by men in the confidence of the Party.

"The Fascist unions," stated Mussolini on March 1, 1926, "form a great mass completely under the control of Fascism and the government: *a mass that obeys.*" One of the regime's jurists has offered the following explanation:

We must avoid a common error of interpretation by which the legally recognized organizations are regarded as representative of special interests distinct from those of the state. This point of view violates the basic requirement of the Fascist system which aims at centralizing and unifying. The unions are not bodies capable of autonomous life, but are mere disciplinary frames for the mass. The unions are the state hierarchies in the economic sphere. Mussolini has called the Fascist unions "instruments of the regime." [7]

---

[7] Costamagna, *I principî generali della dottrina fascista dello Stato*, p. 64.

Rossoni, one of the inventors of the system, tells us that "the Fascist unions are nothing but instruments of the Party, of the regime and of the Revolution." [8] The secretary-general of the Party delivered in 1930 the following lecture to the legally recognized organizations:

> It is true that you constitute the basis of the state, but not because the state derives its vitality from you, but only in so far as the state regulates your functions and your activities. Beyond this manifestation of the state, you do not exist. [9]

To remind any who by chance had forgotten, Signor Bottai repeated on August 29, 1931, that "the trade union is a political instrument of the authorities and consequently a Fascist political organ; the trade-union official is essentially a politician, who through his technical and administrative work can and does influence the political opinions of the masses." [10]

Senator Longhi, Attorney-General of the Supreme Court, when addressing that body on January 7, 1932, stated that "the legal organizations carry out the will, not of the membership, but of the state which makes use of the organizations." The state and the Fascist Party are in Fascist doctrine and terminology equivalent.

It would be vain to seek clear information on this point in the writings of those Fascists who purport to describe the institutions of the "corporative state."

Mlle. Lion, in *The Pedigree of Fascism*, p. 231, writes: "The new syndicates are to be of no political color at all."

Signor Muriello, in *Mussolini: His Work and the New Syndical Law*, p. 58, asserts that "it is not necessary that these syndicates [associations of employers and unions of employees] should be only Fascist syndicates; they can be non-Fascist." Signor Murriello professes to be unmotivated by any idea of "propaganda" and to be "without political bias."

Major Barnes, in *The Universal Aspects of Fascism*, p. 207, admits that the directors of the legal organizations must provide guarantees of "firm national faith." He justifies this necessity on the grounds that "it

---

[8] Haider, *Capital and Labor under Fascism*, p. 233.

[9] *Lavoro Fascista*, Apr. 19, 1930.

[10] *Industrial and Labour Information*, Sept. 14, 1931, p. 346. Goad, in *The Corporate State*, p. 786, assures us that "it is not the aim of the syndicates [unions] to keep the nose of the worker to the grindstone, but to widen his views as much as possible."

is not a question, as some would make out, of securing power indefinitely to the Fascist Party: it is a question of securing power indefinitely to those of high moral character, intelligence, and patriotism." Since a man like Benedetto Croce, for example, could not belong to the directory of an association of intellectuals, because, being anti-Fascist, he lacks "high moral character, intelligence, and patriotism," it is obvious that to secure power indefinitely to those who possess high moral character, intelligence, and patriotism, means to secure power indefinitely to the Fascist Party.

Signor Curcio, in 1930, had the effrontery to write:

The fact is that the syndicates [organizations] come to life spontaneously, that they lead an autonomous life of their own, and that they regulate their inner affairs according to statutes laid down by themselves.[11]

In the summer of 1931 Signor Villari assured his audience at the Institute of Politics at Williams College that "in actual practice there is very little interference on the part of the authorities in the activities of the syndicate [organization]." (*The Economics of Fascism*, p. 83.) In the review *Recovery*, August 25, 1933, p. 10, he stated that the legal organizations "are *autonomous* bodies regulated by their respective rules and only under *indirect* State supervision."

Sir Charles Petrie asserted before the Royal Institute of International Affairs at London that the corporative state "avoids the danger of excessive government control." (*International Affairs*, November-December 1933, p. 783.)

If we are to believe Mr. Goad, "syndicates to be recognized need not be in any sense Fascist syndicates." (*International Affairs*, November-December 1933, p. 785.)

In the official report on *The Relations between Capital and Labour* laid before the London Conference of 1933 one reads: "State control fetters in no way the free development of the interior and exterior life of the Trade Unions [associations of employers and unions of employees]." (*The State and Economic Life*, p. 378.)

Mr. Goad and Miss Currey, in *The Working of a Corporate State*, pp. 27 and 36, affirm that the Fascist organizations are "freely constituted"; they must consist of "absolutely spontaneous groups of men or employers"; "nothing proves the humanity and elasticity of the whole

---

[11] *Die geistige Grundlagen*, p. 403.

system more than the diversity of this grouping, which was not imposed on the workers and employers as a formal plan, but was gradually built up." The two authors assure their readers that "the background of their book is the outcome of many years of personal observation and study both in Rome and Florence" and that their book is "an objective description" (p. 10).

IV

The De Facto Organizations

THE act of April 3, 1926, provides that those employers and employees who do not wish to join their legal organization may form *de facto* organizations. These cannot acquire legal status and are subject to two conditions: 1, they can at any time be dissolved by the prefect of the province and have their assets confiscated, under the royal decree of January 24, 1924; 2, under the law of November 26, 1925, they must communicate the names of their members and officials whenever requested by the political authorities.

These *de facto* unions, even though truncated and exposed to every violence, even though muzzled and passive, might have become centres of anti-Fascist activities if a change had taken place in the political situation. The Fascists therefore made their existence impossible.

The most striking instance is that of the *de facto* union of Molinella, a town of fifteen thousand inhabitants, chiefly agricultural labourers, twenty miles from Bologna.[1] When the act of April 3, 1926, came into operation, five hundred and thirty-nine men and four hundred and sixty-nine women formed a *de facto* union. On April 7, 1926, five of those workers who had given their names to the *de facto* union were kidnapped by the Fascists and dragged to the former headquarters of the Socialist co-operatives, now commandeered by the Fascio. They were first questioned by a captain of the carabineers and the police commissioner. These authorities then having left the room, a squad of Fascists rushed in and bludgeoned the captives. By the time the carabineers put in an appearance, one of the workmen, Bagni by name, was lying unconscious on the floor, bathed in blood. On the night of April 7 police and Fascists searched a number of houses, arrested sixty-four working-men and dragged them off handcuffed to prison at Bologna. On the ninth, fifty-five of these men were released, nine, among whom were Bagni and the others beaten the previous day, were detained until the twelfth, the

---

[1] For a more detailed description of life in Molinella from 1922 to 1926 and of the events of 1926, see the author's *The Simple Annals of Fascismo* in *The Atlantic Monthly*, June 1927.

aggravating circumstance against them being the beating they had received. The *Avanti*, giving the news of this on April 10, asked whether the act of April 3, 1926, granted those who formed a *de facto* union the right to be bludgeoned and imprisoned. On April 10 the foreman of the marsh-reclamation works gave notice that on the twelfth all workers who had joined the *de facto* union would be dismissed. On May 6 the landlords of Molinella were summoned to the Fascio and ordered to give notice to leave to all families whose members had joined the *de facto* union. On July 1, 2, and 3 two hundred women were arrested for gleaning without the ticket of the Fascist union.

On October 1, 1926, the eviction of the tenants began. The London *Times*, October 2, 1926, wrote as follows:

Following this order of the Fascio, notices to quit were given, and the evictions, which were due to begin yesterday, will be carried out during this month. Some 234 families are affected, among them ex-combatants and war widows. About 60 families live in houses belonging to the municipality, and these also have received from the Mayor notices to leave their homes. In spite of this extreme measure, the resistance of the workmen of Molinella has not yet, after years of persecution, been broken. The first of those to be turned out will live with the families who are to be evicted at the end of the month. Afterwards the labourers hope to find asylum here and there among different families. As is known, the workmen of Molinella, having so far fought against entering the Fascist trade unions, have been unable to secure employment. A few of them had attempted to find work in other parts of Italy, but as soon as the Fascists found out the farmers who had employed them they compelled them under threats to cancel the contracts. A dozen or so applied for passports with the idea of proceeding to France to work, but their applications were refused. At Molinella the approach of winter is awaited with dismay, because the suffering will certainly be greater than in other years; but in spite of this, there is no sign of surrender to the will of the Fascists.

The evictions were ruthlessly carried out up to November 19. The evicted families with their household goods were crowded on military lorries and transported to the old customs-barracks of Bologna, which had been cleared for the purpose.[2]

---

[2] Many other cases, not so distressing as that of Molinella but likewise instructive, were enumerated by the General Confederation of Labour, or rather by the remnant left after its destruction, in the memorandum quoted above p. 15, n. 10, in the manifesto

The attempts to create *de facto* unions ceased in November 1926, when the police disbanded all organizations not controlled by the Fascist party, and after the act of November 25, 1926, which threatened anyone who should attempt to reconstitute organizations declared illegal by the police with from three to six years' imprisonment.[3]

The government inserted into the act of April 1926 Article 12, authorizing the existence of *de facto* unions, because Italy, as a participator in the International Labour Office at Geneva, was pledged to recognize "the principle of the freedom of association" (preamble to Part XIII, Treaty of Versailles). Article 12 was to demonstrate that freedom of association had never been suppressed in Italy; if there were no *de facto* unions, the reason was that the Italian workers preferred to join the Fascist unions.

To prove this theory there was the fact that the General Confederation of Labour, which was directed by Socialist leaders, had never been dissolved. But a "General Confederation" which was allowed to exist, while all its branches were forbidden to do so, was obviously nothing more than a hollow sham.

On January 4, 1927, those who formed the executive committee of this ghost of a General Confederation of Labour declared the organization dissolved, after pointing out in a manifesto that "an uninterrupted series of illegal acts of vandalism, the dissolution of trade unions for political and not for legal reasons, the promulgation of the new acts on public safety and for the protection of the realm, the continual pressure exercised by the Fascist trade unions to force the workers to join the official unions, the sentence of undisguised economic and political ostracism pronounced on workers who had remained faithful to the free organizations—all this constituted such a general record, and gave such slight ground for hopes in the future, as to prove that there was no room in Italy for unrecognized trade-unionism."[4] Seven of the signatories of

---

of Jan. 1927 soon to be mentioned, and in a memorandum presented to the International Labour Office of Geneva in June 1927.

[3] On May 27, 1928, eight persons received from the Special Tribunal for the Defence of the State sentences ranging from two to thirty years and aggregating seventy-two years' imprisonment, for an attempt to revive the old General Confederation of Labour.

[4] The Italian press reproduced only the last few lines of this manifesto announcing that "the work of the Confederation was at an end and its affairs had been wound up." The complete text was printed in *Industrial and Labour Information*, Feb. 21, 1927, pp. 294–5, under the somewhat humorous caption: "Voluntary dissolution of the Confederation of Labour."

this declaration announced that they felt it to be their duty to accept "what in principle may be accepted in Fascist trade-unionism"; but they themselves had to recognize that "the Confederation has been dissolved because there was no hope of the application of Article 12." [5]

The gist of this system of legal and economic pressure, by means of which the existence of any *de facto* union has been rendered impossible, was summarized in the following words by the *Lavoro d'Italia* on July 1, 1930:

> To permit today *de facto* organizations would mean interrupting the rhythm of the new social order. Such organizations, be they Catholic or verging on socialism, would sooner or later come into conflict with Fascist trade-unionism. *This would be a form of suicide.*

Thus, Fascist trade-unionism, in spite of all its legal privileges, would commit suicide, if it allowed the existence of *de facto* organizations, even though stripped of every legal privilege.

In 1931 the heads of the Catholic Action, taking advantage of the recognition accorded in 1929 to all associations working for religious ends under the supervision of the bishops (Article 43 of the Lateran Concordat), attempted to form on the margins of the Fascist unions, Catholic working-class organizations aimed at looking after the "spiritual development" of their members. In a speech delivered April 20, 1931, Signor Giuriati, Secretary-General of the Party, proclaimed that the Fascist organizations had the exclusive right to watch over the spiritual

---

[5] *Corriere della Sera*, Feb. 3, 1927. In 1929 Signor Villari described this affair in the following terms: "The G.C.L. rapidly lost importance, but continued to eke out a precarious existence as a *de facto* body, until early in 1927 the executive decided to close down. The executive realized that at the present time the Fascist syndicates offered the best prospects for the working classes. . . . In conclusion it decided on the dissolution of the G.C.L. itself." (*Italy*, pp. 278–9.) A year later, in the summer of 1931, speaking before the Institute of Politics at Williams College, Signor Villari gave the following version: "In 1927 the leaders of the Socialistic General Confederation of Labour came to the conclusion that under the Fascist syndical system its own postulates would be accepted and applied, and it consequently dissolved itself." (*Economics of Fascism*, p. 85.) Mr. Goad, in *Making of the Corporate State*, pp. 78–9, surpassed Signor Villari with the following interpretation: "The non-militant trade unions were not destroyed, they were gradually abandoned by their members who either joined the syndicates [Fascist unions] that made terms with their employers or remained outside all syndicates whatsoever. . . . Later, when these recognized syndicates were able to obtain the best possible [sic] wages that the industry could pay, having the influence of the government behind all the workmen in the category, there was no *raison d'être* for any other union. . . . Finally, in January 1927, the central committee of the old depleted unions transferred itself abroad."

as well as the economic interests of the workers. The Catholic working-men's associations were, therefore, forbidden, and as a matter of fact none of them exists in Italy today.

After the existence of all unions not controlled by the Fascist Party had been prohibited, could a workman at least remain peacefully in his little corner, paying the annual contribution to the legal union of his trade, but refraining from enrolling himself as a member? The law of April 6, 1926, says that membership in the legal organizations is free. But it must not be forgotten that in Fascist Italy, more than in any other country, there exists on the margin of the written law, and in many cases above it, an unwritten law, which supplements and frequently modifies the former, and without knowledge of which it is impossible to obtain an exact idea of realities. After the act of April 3, 1926, had assured the Fascist organizations of a monopoly over legal recognition, the Fascists began to insist that only workers belonging to their unions should be given work. Here are three documents chosen from among many:

1. On April 16, 1926, the Vicenza papers published the following notice:

All porters, carmen, and coal porters of the railway station are summoned to a meeting on Sunday next to constitute the Fascist union and appoint its officers. As we intend that all the station staff shall join the Fascist union, we give warning that any who do not come to the meeting will be replaced at their work by members of the union.

2. The following manifesto dated July 8, 1926, comes from Andria, province of Bari, in Southern Italy:

Landowners and employers must not employ workers who are not members of the Fascist unions, and must insist on their employees obtaining the Fascist membership card. Those who fail to comply with this will be reported to the higher authorities of the Fascist Party for rigorous measures to be taken against them. Let no one fail to give this proof of discipline required by the Duce of Fascism.

3. In a memorandum presented by the former leaders of the defunct General Confederation of Labour to the International Labour Office in June 1927 we read:

'There is in Milan an employment agency for the printing trades which is maintained by the contributions of the employers and employees. All the workers must pay their contributions but they do not enjoy equal rights. In June 1926 the General Confederation of Labour complained in the press that the agency boycotted those workers who were not inscribed in the Fascist unions. The *Popolo d'Italia*, Mussolini's organ, and the *Lavoro d'Italia*, organ of the Fascist unions, answered at once that "persons not inscribed in the Fascist unions were only allowed to work as a *generous concession* on the part of the leaders of the Fascist unions."

On March 2, 1928, the Minister of Transport ruled that in all contracts for railway construction, the contractors should pledge themselves, when engaging hands, to give preference to members of the Fascist Party and of the Fascist unions according to seniority. A few days later the act of March 29, 1928, concerning the labour exchanges, ordained that in the registers of the unemployed the members of the Fascist Party and of the Fascist unions, arranged in order of seniority, should be given precedence over the other unemployed. The employers were not obliged to select their men according to the order of precedence thus established; but if they merely asked for workers without indicating them by name, the labour exchanges were to follow this order.

The employers in industry have succeeded down to the present in keeping the right to choose such men as they please, even from outside the registers of the labour exchanges. In their own house, that is, in their factories, they must be master. But the employers in agriculture, who have less political influence than those in industry, have to choose their men from among those registered in the labour exchanges,[6] even if they are not obliged to follow the order of precedence. This order is strictly followed by agencies of the government and all institutions under the control of the Party.

It is easy to understand the importance assumed by this practice, in a period of growing unemployment, when many workers, unable to find employment in the private market, compete for employment in the public works.

Moreover, as we shall see in a later chapter, workmen who have a dispute with their employers must submit the case to the officials of the legal union in their trade, even if they are not members of that union,

---

[6] In June 1934, the Supreme Court ruled that forestry is an industrial and not an agricultural activity, and therefore the employer in forestry is not bound to choose his hands from among the unemployed registered by the exchanges. *Corriere della Sera,* June 14, 1934.

and the officials decide whether or not they will support the workman's case. It does not require a profound insight into human nature to realize that the workman will be wise if, before going to talk the matter over with the secretary of the union, he inscribes himself as a member of the union and procures a membership card. The Fascists point triumphantly to this fact as proof that the popularity of Fascist "syndicalism" is increasing from year to year.[7]

[7] Bottai, *Corporate State and N. R. A.*, p. 616.

V

How History Is Written

FROM the report on "Freedom of Association" in the *Studies and Reports* of the International Labour Office, 1927, Series A, No. 28, p. 20, we learn that in Italy, as in Belgium, Switzerland, etc., the constitution "expressly guarantees certain fundamental rights, including the right of association and of assembly," and that therefore "the right to combine for trade purposes is included in these rights." The compiler of the report refrained from ascertaining what was actually happening to the rights which the Italian constitution laid down. He did not go behind the letter of the law and examine the realities of the situation. The International Labour Office possesses no fact-finding instrumentalities of its own; it is merely a channel for such information as the various member governments vouchsafe to give it. Any government that pays its annual dues to the I.L.O. is entitled to add its propaganda to the alluvion of publications with which the I.L.O. deluges the world. The officials of the I.L.O. would soon get into hot water if they ventured to make an independent scrutiny of the information furnished them by the member governments.

Miss Haider[1] and Monsieur Rosenstock-Franck,[2] being neither officials of the I.L.O. nor agents of Fascist propaganda, understood that it would be utterly impossible for any *de facto* union to attempt to operate in Italy.

Signor Villari wrote in 1927 with his customary candid innocence:

The non-recognized unions may continue to operate as *de facto* organizations under the existing laws, provided of course that they abstain from revolutionary activity, which Fascism will in no case tolerate.[3]

Two years later he informed his readers:

In practice such syndicates [unions] have almost ceased to exist, or at all events, are wholly without importance; the advantages from the workers' point of view of the existence of a single union are obvious.

---

[1] *Capital and Labor under Fascism*, p. 236 ff.
[2] *L'Economie Corporative Fasciste*, p. 56.
[3] *The Fascist Experiment*, p. 156.

One of the advantages secured by membership was "the possibility of exercising greater influence on the policy of the syndicate." [4] The reader could thus believe that the workers who remained outside the union exercised a *great* influence on them, and that those who belonged exercised a *greater* influence. Naturally, Signor Villari made no effort to explain the obvious disadvantages which the attempts at creating *de facto* unions might have from the workers' point of view.

Signor Bottai asserted in 1927 that the Fascist law *"as was known,* neither prohibited nor opposed freedom of association." [5] In 1928 he went farther and affirmed: "Fascism has not suppressed the freedom of association: the law, in homage to the principle of liberty, admits the existence of organizations other than the recognized ones, as simple *de facto* bodies." [6] In 1932 he made the following statement:

The postulate of freedom of association is put into operation [in the official Fascist organizations] together with another of the postulates of modern trade-unionism: the unity of organization. In pre-Fascist unionism the thirst for unity had as its result the fact that the stronger unions, or those most favoured by the ruling political classes, exterminated the smaller unions, or those opposed to the interests of those classes. Unity was in conflict with liberty. Where the latter predominated, there was anarchy; where the other was supreme, there was tyranny. The great professional organizations of the Fascist corporative state were born of the conjunction of these two principles. By marrying each other, the liberty of trade-unionism and the unity of trade-unionism have become real liberty and real unity. Yet many foreign critics continue to ascribe to our legal organizations a principle of compulsion which is unknown to our legislation. [7]

It is obvious that Signor Bottai was convinced that in Italy the Fascist organizations had obtained no favors from the ruling political class and that Socialist and Christian-Democratic unions had never been exterminated.

Major Barnes harbours no doubts concerning the fact that "nonmembers equally share in the benefits received through any action of the associations." [8]

---

[4] *Italy*, pp. 274–5.
[5] *Trade Union Organization in Italy*, p. 816.
[6] *Civiltà Fascista*, p. 387.
[7] *Il diritto del lavoro*, Sept.–Oct. 1932, p. 505.
[8] *Universal Aspects of Fascism*, p. 208.

Mrs. O. Rossetti Agresti confidently assured the readers of the *Encyclopædia Britannica* (fourteenth edition, 1929, vol. IX, p. 104) that "unrecognized unions might continue to exist as *de facto* organizations."

Professor Volpe stated in 1928 that there did not exist in Italy one all-inclusive compulsory organization. There was no monopoly for Fascist organizations; Fascism counted upon freedom of association and on the initiative of minorities, *at least in theory:* "all are free to join whatever organizations they wish, *provided their purposes are permitted by law;* but the State recognizes only those which fulfil certain conditions." [9] In 1932 he wrote: "Fascism puts its faith *largely, if not exclusively,* in free initiative; all are free to combine into such organizations as they see fit"; the Fascist organization "is not compulsory and monopolistic for the various categories"; it is "the result of free associative life." [10]

From Signor Pitigliani we learn that Fascist legislation "does not refuse to admit the co-existence of *de facto* associations," side by side with the legal ones, but he remarks that this form of organization "has had no practical development." Socialist and Christian-Democratic unions "between 1922 and 1926 continually lost ground"; after the passing of the act of 1926, "there was no longer *logically* any possibility of co-existence" for them.[11] Signor Pitigliani made no effort to dispel the impenetrable mystery surrounding the acts of illegal violence and legal pressure which rendered that co-existence logically impossible.

Mr. I. S. Munro, Rome correspondent of the London *Morning Post,* on whom Mussolini has conferred the title of Commendatore della Corona d'Italia, assures us that "enrolment is not compulsory: the real inducement is that of personal interest." [12]

The British commercial attaché in Rome informs us that "apart from the syndical associations [official organizations of employers and employees], other trade associations *can and do* exist, but without power to bind non-members by collective agreements." He cites as examples of these *de facto* organizations the Italian Association of Joint Stock Companies, and the Italian Cotton-Spinners' Association; but he explains that the staff of the first is composed of men drawn from the national directorates of the employers' industrial and banking confederations,

---

[9] *Civiltà Fascista,* p. 27.
[10] Mussolini, *La Dottrina del Fascismo,* pp. 121, 129.
[11] *The Italian Corporative State,* pp. 20, 30–1.
[12] *Through Fascism to World Power,* p. 341.

and he might have added that it is merely a research bureau of these two organizations, and without autonomous life. As for the second, he informs us that it "existed until recently." With regard to the *de facto* organizations composed of workers, he says: "No workers' association [union] has survived the Fascist revolution, with the exception of certain mutual benefit societies." These latter, however, have been placed under the control of the Fascist Party, a fact evidently unknown to the British commercial attaché.[13]

The president of the Confederation of Agricultural Unions had the effrontery to publish in the press on June 28, 1933, a circular to remind the officials of the unions that "no coercive action of any sort may be brought to bear upon the workers" in order to make them join the unions: "The act of joining the unions should be a free and spontaneous adhesion on the part of the members." The circular was intended to serve—as it actually did—as a "hand-out" for the foreign journalists in Rome, for them to send home, thereby giving their readers the impression that membership in Fascist unions is optional for the Italian worker.

In the London Conference of 1933, Signor Righetti, one of the Italian representatives, was heroic enough to utter the following statements:

> The fact of recognizing only one trade union [association of employers and union of employees] does not imply that that trade union is not a free one. . . . Membership is free and optional.[14]

Signor Rosboch was even more heroic:

> We have complete trade-union liberty. *Socialist Unions can still be re-established today again,* for there is no restriction on the liberty to organize trade unions.[15]

Mr. S. A. Jones has discovered "that there is absolutely no objection to associations or unions being freely formed."[16]

But as usual, it is Mr. Goad, the director of the British Institute in Florence, who wins the prize for sheer inspiration. He asserts that according to the act of 1926 "other unions should share in the advantages obtained by those recognized"; "it goes without saying that in these

---

[13] Turner, *Economic Conditions in Italy: July 1933,* p. 158.
[14] *The State and Economic Life,* p. 265.
[15] *The State and Economic Life,* p. 283.
[16] *Is Fascism the Answer?,* p. 67.

industrial organizations there is no distinction between Fascist and non-Fascist workmen. It suffices that they be not anti-Fascists."[17] In his speech before the Royal Institute of International Affairs of London, in October 1933, Mr. Goad stated that "the syndicates [legal organizations] must be free and open, not exclusive nor monopolistic; they must be voluntary and, as it were, spontaneous." And to prove that all this was the unimpeachable truth he cited the fact that "other syndicates [unions] share in any advantage secured by the recognized syndicates"; "the advantages are the same for those who belong to other syndicates, to the old Catholic syndicates, for example"; "we know how English union men have protested against employment of non-union men. *These things cannot happen in Italy.*"[18]

Heaven knows the labour involved in ascertaining a single historical truth. Fantasies, however, may be invented in limitless quantities without the slightest effort. Hence, it is not surprising that Mr. Goad, in a letter published in the *Manchester Guardian* on January 12, 1933, revealed the following confidential information about the Fascist unions:

They [the organizations] constantly spring up quite "spontaneously" in this city [Florence]. If a new industry is started in Florence, the workmen usually form a new syndicate [union] of their own, or a category of workmen breaks off from a larger syndicate in order to make a new one. If a large number in a recognized syndicate are discontented with it for some reason, they are free to leave it and set up another, and sometimes they succeed in so depleting the old syndicate that it no longer embodies ten per cent of the workers of the category and thus becomes no longer entitled to "recognition." As all the advantages gained by the "recognized" syndicate are embodied in the model labour contract of the category, which applies to all its syndicates without distinction, and also to all independent workers, there is no practical advantage for a worker to belong to any particular syndicate, or indeed to any syndicate at all. That is what I meant when I said that the syndicates are not "monopolistic."

No Florentine paper, no Italian paper has ever printed any notice of unions being formed freely at Florence or anywhere else in Italy by workers who had broken off from the official unions. This phenomenon exists only in the imagination of the director of the British Institute of Florence.

---

[17] *The Making of the Corporate State*, p. 80.
[18] *The Corporate State*, pp. 776-8.

In a letter to the *Manchester Guardian*, January 22, 1934, Mr. Goad again defends his point "about the Italian syndicates [unions] being free, open, spontaneous and not monopolistic":

There is no distinction between those who belong to the recognized syndicates and those who are merely "represented" by each syndicate. With regard to employment offices, there is a formal regulation that where conditions are absolutely equal an employer should take an ex-soldier or a Fascist rather than another, but I am assured that this regulation is entirely a dead letter, as any employer who wishes to take on a man without these qualifications has only to say that he is better qualified for the work he has in mind for him to do.

Finally, in conjunction with Miss Currey, Mr. Goad writes as follows:

The personal liberty of the working-man to join or not to join a recognized syndicate [union] is assured by the fact that he enjoys all the economic benefits of membership under the collective labor contracts of his category. This prevents the syndicate from becoming monopolistic as regards the supply of labor, or exclusive as regards the admittance of new members.[19]

In May 1934 a "group of students of the Corporate State in Italy" made a discovery more extraordinary than any of those which we have enumerated in the preceding pages: they discovered that, in 1932, in a "new complementary treaty" which Pius XI and Mussolini had entered into for the interpretation of the Lateran agreements of 1929, Catholic trade organizations had been granted the right to exist, and "today the Catholic syndicates [trade organizations] exist precisely as before, with, in fact, greatly increased possibilities of development." [20] No one in Italy has ever heard of a concession of this sort made by Mussolini to Pius XI in 1932. Presumably we are here confronted with a secret "new complementary treaty," which Mussolini or Pius XI imparted in confidence to the "students of the Corporate State." And the Catholic trade organizations of which the "students" speak, must be clandestine organizations, for no newspaper has ever mentioned their activities and no one in Italy has ever suspected their existence.

Signor Bottai is convinced that "through legal organization the individual can realize the true self-determination which is synonymous

---

[19] *The Working of a Corporate State*, p. 34.
[20] *New Statesman*, May 26, 1934.

with liberty"; "individual members of a given occupational group are free to choose whether or not they wish to enroll in the appropriate organization"; "Italian law guarantees the voluntary character of syndicate membership." [21]

What is most offensive in these gentlemen is not the fact that they are convinced Fascists, but the fact that they do not have the courage of their convictions. They trick the public with vague, equivocal, or mendacious statements. Those who write for an Italian public commonly resort to reticence and ambiguous statements rather than to actual mendacity: people living in Italy know how things stand, and too barefaced a lie would simply discredit the writer. In books destined for a non-Italian public all regard for truth vanishes. "Machiavellian" Latins are George Washingtons in comparison with certain representatives of Anglo-Saxon respectability.

In the discussions which take place every year at the International Labour Office concerning the validity of the credentials offered by the delegates of the Italian "workers," the labour delegates from all countries vote against recognizing them, while the employers' delegates consistently vote in favour of recognition, maintaining that the I.L.O. does not have the right either to contest the validity of the credentials officially issued by governments or to examine whether the governments do or do not respect the freedom of the labour organizations. The representatives of the governments remain as silent as oysters, but as a rule consistently vote with the employers. When some of them vote otherwise or abstain from voting, it is a sign that their governments are using this method to bring pressure to bear upon the Italian government in order to blackmail it in regard to some other question then pending. Hence, the "labour" delegates from Italy are always accepted.

---

[21] *Corporate State and N.R.A.*, p. 616–8.

VI

The Officials of the Legal Organizations

B Y whom and by what procedure are the presidents, secretaries, and directors designated for the local and provincial organizations and the national federations and confederations?

Under the Fascist regime "democratic" methods, such as the election of executive committees by the members, are dispensed with; "authority comes from above."

In the case of important national organizations the executive committees are chosen by the secretary-general of the Fascist Party. Take for instance the following, reported in the *Corriere della Sera* on June 23, 1928:

> The executive committee of the Milan Aero Club has resigned in accordance with the regulation of the Fascist Party that the appointment of the directors of all Fascist organizations rests with the superior authorities of the Party and not with the members of the associations.

It is not an uncommon occurrence for a provincial secretary of the Party to select on his own authority a "commissioner extraordinary" to administer an association.[1] When such "revolutionary" interference does not take place, the executive committees of the associations are "elected" by the members. The word "election" does not, however, have the same significance in Fascist terminology as that to which we are accustomed in democratic regimes, namely, a secret balloting on competing lists of freely nominated candidates. The "elections" as a rule consist of simple "acclamations." The secretary of the Party in the province or the city, according to the importance of the association, indicates officially the names of those who must compose the executive committee, or even intervenes personally in the election meeting and announces the list of

---

[1] The provincial secretary of the Fascist Party in Rome made the following statement in the course of a trial on Feb. 13, 1931: "Having learned that in the sporting club Roma there had arisen discord, I determined to bring about peace. Consulting first the higher authorities, I proceeded to dissolve the Council of Administration and to appoint as commissioner extraordinary a person who was acceptable politically as well as from the point of view of sport."

"candidates." The members are invited to "acclaim." Anyone raising any objections would thereby immediately brand himself as "anti-national." Everyone therefore "acclaims"—and the election is over.

In fairness it must be admitted that sometimes there is actually an election by ballot. The voter is given a ballot paper prepared by the men at the top and deposits it in the urn. Nobody checks the number of votes, the personal identity of the voters, or the work of the tellers. The latter invariably announce that the official list has been elected by a unanimous vote.

Fairness likewise compels us to concede that there are occasions upon which there is even a real election with the secret ballot. But if the official list is not returned, the election is invalidated. There is the interesting case of the election in the Teamsters' Co-operative of Massa Lombarda, province of Ravenna, which took place in October, 1928. This organization had been founded by the Socialists in the liberal era, and had been "co-ordinated" (*fascistizzata*) after the establishment of the dictatorship. The provincial secretary of the Party attended one of the co-operative's meetings and announced that the election of the new executive committee would take place in complete liberty, since the Duce now had faith in the Italian people. The members applauded and prepared to elect their old Socialist administrators, previously eliminated by the Fascists. Having got wind of this "plot," the local Fascist secretary became infuriated, and ordered the members to elect the candidates whom he had selected. The members, fortified with the declaration of the higher authority, held firm and voted for the original list. The local secretary annulled the election and denounced the candidates elected to the police as "anti-nationals." The unfortunate candidates invoked the testimony of the higher authority, who upheld them and had them freed from arrest. A new election was held, in which the local secretary, upon orders from the provincial secretary, demanded that the members should elect those men upon whom he had shortly before put his veto. This time it was the candidates who refused. Again there were threats from the local secretary and more calls for the police. Finally, the candidates accepted office after having obtained the assurance that this time they would not be branded as "anti-national."

Matters do not always end in such a good-humoured manner. On February 23, 1931, the *Corriere della Sera* gave a rather confused account of disorders in the village of Busnago twenty miles from Milan:

two persons were said to have been killed by "criminals who succeeded in escaping without leaving traces." The actual facts are as follows. Before 1922 the Socialists in this village had founded a consumers' co-operative, which the Fascists took over, forcing the Socialists in charge to resign. On the morning of February 22, 1931, the annual election meeting was held. The members were asked to elect the Fascist list, as usual the only one permitted. But on counting the votes, the Fascists discovered that practically every one had cast a blank voting paper; the Fascist list had not even obtained as many votes as there were candidates. The Fascists of the surrounding villages, called together by telephone, invaded the village in the afternoon. Every one found on the streets, men, women, and children, were beaten. Of the two Socialists who were suspected of having engineered the demonstration of the blank voting papers, one, Angelo Ripamonti, was stabbed to death in his shop while selling some sugar, while the other, Carlo Veneroni, was killed by a dagger-thrust in a tavern whither he had gone to hide. The Fascists who composed the *squadre* (storm troops) were known to everybody, but according to the unwritten law of the "new era" they remained "persons unknown" to the police and the press.

The "elections" in the legal associations of employers and in the unions of employees fall under analogous rules. The act of April 6, 1926, provided merely that the presidents and secretaries may be "either elected or appointed." The regulations of July 1, 1926, did not clear up the point. The charters given by the government to the local organizations [2] would have us believe that the secretaries and directorates are "elected" by the members. But what the charters call an "election" is not a genuine election. Someone in the election meeting, in collusion with the outgoing officers and the local Fascist leaders, proposes the names of those who are to be "elected," and calls upon the meeting to "elect" them. "The dissentients can dissent at home!" [3] Upon rare occasions secret balloting is permitted—and these occasions are pointed out as exceptional proofs of the leaders' confidence in the fidelity of the organizations. But the voters have no chance to meet in advance of the election and discuss possible candidates; when they go to vote

---

[2] The *Gazzetta Ufficiale* and the *Bollettino del Lavoro*, beginning with the issues of July 1926, have printed these documents. The charters of the workers' organizations have been amended many times, the last editions being those of 1932.

[3] Finer, *Mussolini's Italy*, p. 506.

they receive the list of candidates already concocted by those higher up. Their sole function is to place this list in the urn.[4] On the other hand no opposition would be of any use. If any person were "elected" who was not furnished with the necessary dose of "undoubted national loyalty," the ministry would annul the "election" and the "elected" person would be dispatched to some penal island.

In the provincial meetings the members do not even serve to "acclaim," since only the local secretaries attend them. Employing the methods already described, these gentlemen "elect" a directorate for their provincial organization. This directorate has only a consultative capacity. He who makes and executes decisions is the provincial secretary; and he is not "elected," by either a real or a mock election, but is appointed outright by the national authority of the organization.[5]

The provincial secretaries, in their turn convened in the national congresses of the federations and confederations,[6] "elect" the presidents and

---

[4] Signor Rocca, an official in the confederation of industrial workers, boasted to the Chamber of Deputies on May 16, 1930 (Official Records, p. 2727), that he had had the hundred or more representatives in each department of the Borsalino works in Alessandria elected by their co-workers "with the secret ballot and in absolute freedom." The exceptional character of this instance is shown, as the speaker explained, by his having had to obtain beforehand "the assent of the confederation," and by his having "wished to perform such an *important and interesting experiment,* which turned out very successfully, because he wanted to demonstrate that the workers were really worthy of the confidence of the regime." Signor Rocca neglected to explain that the ballots had been prepared in advance and consigned to the voters only at the last minute by men in his confidence.

[5] Instead of reproducing several pages of newspaper notices concerning these "elections," let a single example suffice. In the *Lavoro* of July 18, 1933, is a summary of the proceedings of the Conference of the Industrial Unions in the province of Genoa held on July 16. The conference is called the "general assembly of the workers" ("assemblea generale dei lavoratori"), but only union officials participate. The president of the National Confederation of Industrial Unions presides, there being also present the prefect of the province, the provincial secretary of the Party, the podestà of the Commune of Genoa, and other similar dignitaries. The government's commissioner, who hitherto has directed the provincial unions, reads "a long and detailed report," which "is received at the end with hearty applause." Then the provincial secretary of the Party takes the floor, and his address "is accorded an enthusiastic ovation." One of the delegates thereupon delivers a panegyric on the commissioner who has been directing the unions, and moves that the conference "as an expression of the gratitude of the working class, elect him by acclamation to the general secretaryship of the industrial unions in the province of Genoa." The motion is "passed by acclamation."

[6] Until Oct. 1928 the provincial organizations were represented at the national congresses by delegates "elected" especially for that purpose at provincial conferences by the secretaries of the local unions; but even this procedure seemed dangerous, and therefore a decree of Oct. 18, 1928, provided that henceforth the provincial organizations would be represented by their own secretaries. *Industrial and Labour Information,* Dec. 17, 1928, p. 357.

directors of the national organizations by "acclaiming" a list of candidates already selected by the outgoing officers and the Party leaders.[7]

This system has been described by a French writer, anything but hostile to Fascism, in the following terms:

> In the Fascist legal organizations, which are supposed to represent employers, employees, and professional classes, the key man, the one to whom it is necessary to go in order to stipulate labour contracts, is the secretary. Now this secretary is not elected by the members but appointed directly by the government. Let us add that the delegates of the organizations to the national council of the federation are these same secretaries of the inferior organizations. In his turn the secretary of the national federation is appointed by the president of the national confederation, who in his turn is appointed by the government. On each new rung of the ladder, for each important position, is a creature of the government or of the Party who is designated for office.[8]

Towards the end of 1927 several Fascists timidly asked that free elections for the choosing of secretaries be allowed, declaring that there no longer was any danger that men hostile to the Fascist Party would be able to get hold of the workers' organizations. The secretary-general of the Fascist Party, Signor Augusto Turati, rejected the petition. In an address to Mussolini, dated January 1, 1928, he recorded as one of the signs of the "revolutionary consciousness" of the Party, the fact that "all the leaders were appointed from above, according to our anti-electionistic and anti-democratic doctrine." [9] And in an address delivered at Milan, where the "electionistic" movement was most strongly intrenched, he repeated:

> The method of appointing the leaders from above is a fundamentally Fascist one. It has produced good results by suppressing all remains of democratic mentality. We are an army of believers, not a mass of associates.[10]

On January 28, 1928, the *Lavoro d'Italia*, the official organ of the Fascist unions, remarked that on the agenda of a conference called by the National Federation of Sugar Beet Workers, there stood the items: "resignation of the president" and "election of the president." The pa-

---

[7] See, for example, in *Lavoro*, June 10, 1933, the "acclamation" by which the president of the Confederation of Inland Transport Unions was elected.

[8] Robert Aron, "Les fausses sorties" in the review *L'Ordre Nouveau*, June 1, 1935, p. 21.

[9] *Corriere della Sera*, Jan. 2, 1928.

[10] *Ibid.*, Jan. 22, 1928.

per marvelled greatly that there were still under the Fascist regime people who spoke of elections:

> We thought that these electoral methods had been relegated to the scrap heap of old and obsolete regimes. But we see that they are still the backbone of organizations living in the sixth year of the Fascist era.

In the book *La Carta del lavoro illustrata e commentata* (pp. 71–3) published in 1929 under the auspices of the secretary-general of the Party and Signor Bottai, we read:

> The Party cannot leave the organizations to themselves until all the remnants of Socialism have disappeared, and these are still numerous among the urban working classes. The Party's supervision over the labour organizations seems indispensable. Only when a universal Fascist mentality has been created, will it be possible to fuse the political system with the social.[11]

Dissatisfaction nevertheless continued to manifest itself covertly. On April 1, 1930, Signor Bottai asked the Grand Council to pass on the request that the manner of designating officials "take on a more representative character" by means of "elections with several steps"; which would appear to signify, given the plural number of steps, that the members of the local organizations would have elected, not the officials, but the electors, who in their turn would choose the real electors of the officials. The Grand Council found even this elaborate mystification dangerous, and on April 8 decided that "no modification should be made in the system for designating the officials; their choice, in accord with the spirit of Fascist corporative legislation, must reconcile the need of the economic groups for representation with the political exigencies of the regime." Reconciliation was obtained by sacrificing "representation" to "exigencies."

Two months had not yet elapsed after this declaration by the regime's highest political body, when Deputy Rotigliano in a speech to the Chamber on May 14, 1930, asked that the offices in the unions be made elective and that the elections take place "under conditions of freedom and absolute independence":

---

[11] In 1935 Signor Bottai, *The Corporative State and N.R.A.*, p. 615, stated that each organization has the right "to appoint delegates" whenever representation is required, but he did not make clear who does the "appointing."

Let the life of the union become real for the worker, above all by abandoning the system of choosing the leaders by appointment from above and returning to the elective system, which undoubtedly, in spite of all its defects, is the one which best fulfills the principle of representation by category.[12]

Touched to the quick by Signor Rotigliano's words, the union officials protested vigorously. Signor Clavenzani, president of the Confederation of Industrial Unions, was greatly amazed that Signor Rotigliano should be ignorant of the fact that Articles 10, 11, 12, 13, 14, 15 of the charter of the provincial organizations had already rendered union offices elective. His opponent interrupted him, asserting that elections took place only "on paper." Clavenzani would, however, exclude the elective method in the choice of "provincial secretaries and other leaders, upon whom is dependent the management and co-ordination of the unions"; "projects of such a sort, if carried out, would only bring about chaos." [13] Another union official, Signor Rocca, declared that in the Confederation of Industrial Unions "all offices are filled by the elective system"; but this falsehood was so enormous that he was obliged to add that "only the secretaries of the provincial organizations and the national federations were named from above, these posts carrying not only an administrative responsibility, but above all a political one." [14]

At the sitting of the Chamber on March 10, 1933, the under-secretary at the Ministry of Corporations stated that "the categories meet frequently, discuss their problems, *choose their leaders*." But there was no reality behind these words. In fact, the speaker added: "The government and the Party—which is present and always close to our activities—can extract from this intensification of collective life a better understanding *upon which to base the choice of leaders*." The choice, then, still lay with the government and the Party.

In 1934 the farce of "election" was abolished as far as the presidents of the confederations were concerned. They are now "appointed" directly by Mussolini. The farce is still going on where the other officials are to be "elected."

In the conference of the Institute of Intellectual Co-operation held in London in 1933, Signor Rosboch, one of the official representatives of the Fascist Government, asserted that the object of the corporative

---

[12] *Atti Parlamentari*, May 14, 1930, p. 2641.
[13] *Ibid.*, May 15 and 20, pp. 2697, 2714.
[14] *Ibid.*, May 16, 1930, p. 2727.

state was "to put the forces of capital and labour on the same footing, under conditions of perfect equality." [15] As a matter of fact, if one looks only at legal formulæ, there is no difference between the organizations of the employers and those of the workers in respect to the "elections" of their officials. All officials alike are "elected" by the same method. But the same legal formulæ and methods, applied to different social groups, in practice yield different results.

Among the employers we must distinguish between the big and the little. The big industrialists, the big merchants, the large landowners, the more important bankers, choose in their private gatherings the men who are to be "elected" to run their associations and encounter no difficulty in arranging the matter with the Fascist leaders; they call these up on the telephone, give them the name, and the "election" is "in the bag." Consequently the employers' associations are always staffed with presidents, secretaries and directors who enjoy the confidence not only of the Party bosses but of the employers most influential in each economic group. The industrialists' confederation and the bankers' confederation until December 1933 had as their national presidents and secretaries the same persons that held those offices before 1926.[16] Even when the employers' associations are directed by new men, these always possess the complete confidence of the capitalists who control the bigger enterprises in that field.

If we were to take, for instance, the persons "elected," in January 1932, to constitute the national directorate of the Confederation of Industrial Employers for the triennium 1932–5, and place under their names the list of the corporations of which they are chairmen (*presidenti*), managers (*consiglieri delegati*), directors (*consiglieri d'amministrazione*), or overseers (*sindaci*), we should have to fill three or four pages of this volume. Let us, therefore, limit ourselves to some examples. Signor Antonio Stefano Benni, president of the Confederation of Industrial Employers and member of the Chamber of Deputies, was also:

1. Chairman of the Banco di Roma
2. Chairman and manager of the Società Ercole Marelli e C.

---

[15] *The State and Economic Life*, p. 217.

[16] Rossoni wrote in the *Gazzetta del Popolo* on June 28, 1930: "The employers' associations have at all times and regardless of political climate remained unchanged in their form and in their attitude."

3. Chairman of the Fabbrica Italiana Magneti Marelli
4. Director of the Società Generale Italiana Edison di Elettricità
5. Director of the Società Romana di Elettricità
6. Director of the Società Generale per l'Industria Mineraria e Agricola (Montecatini)
7. Vice-Chairman of the Istituto Imprese Italiane all'Estero
8. Director of the Società Italiana per le Strade Ferrate
9. Director of the Società Istrumenti di misura C. G. S.
10. Director of the Istituto di Riunione Adriatica di Sicurtà
11. Director of the Società Telefonica Internazionale Piemontese (Stipel)
12. Chairman of the Società Idroelettrica dell'Isarco
13. Chairman of the Società Trentina di Elettricità
14. Director of the Società Elettrica Italo-Albanese
15. Vice-Chairman of the Società Auto-Strade
16. Chairman of the Società per la Sede delle Associazioni Industriali
17. Chairman of the Società Vanossi
18. Director of the Agricola Somala
19. Director of the Immobiliare Automobile Club
20. Chairman of the Immobiliare Sabauda

Among the other directors of the confederation let it suffice to mention Signor Agnelli, manager of the Fiat Motor Company, and Signor Donegani, manager of the Montecatini Chemical Trust. It is evident that these gentlemen were perfect representatives of the interests of Italian big business. On December 30, 1933, Mussolini dismissed Signor Benni from office and appointed as commissioner extraordinary Signor Pirelli. Here is a list of the capitalistic corporations in which Signor Pirelli is interested:

1. Manager of the Società Pirelli e C.
2. Director of the Società Dinamo
3. Director of the Strade Ferrate Meridionali
4. Vice-Chairman of the Società Elettrofonica
5. Director of the Società Innocente Mangili
6. Director of the Filatura Mako
7. Director of the Imprese e Manutenzioni-Telefoniche
8. Vice-Chairman of the Assicuratrice Industriale
9. Director of the Ippodromo Trento
10. Chairman of the Trasversale
11. Chairman of the Immobiliare Lampugnana
12. Director of the Società Le Capannelle

In September 1934 Signor Pirelli disappeared. His place was immediately taken by Count Volpi, who fifty years ago started out without a penny and who now, after a business career that has always been closely linked with politics, is one of the richest men in Italy. From Benni to Pirelli, from Pirelli to Volpi—why should Italian business become uneasy? It has lost nothing by such changes. If we pursued our investigation down through the federations to the provincial and local associations, we should find that the important places are always occupied by the largest capitalists or their trusted lieutenants. We should come to the same conclusion, were we to explore all the other employers' confederations.[17]

He who has no influence is the middle-sized or small-scale employer, whose *raison d'être* seems to be to pay his dues and wish he were one of the big fellows.

Among the workers there exists no distinction between big and small. All are small. Unlike the capitalist class, the working class has no nuclei of richer and more influential persons, who can pull strings from behind the scenes in accord with the Fascist leaders. A big capitalist can always jump on a train for Rome, with the assurance of being received immediately and respectfully by the officers of his organization or by the Party hierarchs; but the hundreds and thousands of those who work for him cannot take the train and be received by the dignitaries in Rome. The masses are too numerous; and not being permitted freely to organize a collective voice, they are condemned to silent passivity.

When the legally recognized organizations were created in 1926, the old Socialist and Christian-Democratic unions were a heap of ruins, and the new Fascist unions existed on paper only. Mussolini appointed as commissioner to build up the legal organizations of all the workers' categories, Rossoni, who during his life has followed every trade but that of an "authentic labouring man." Rossoni appointed the secretaries of all the national, provincial, and local organizations, choosing his men "at least ninety per cent from among the ranks of the Fascist storm

---

[17] The *Lavoro Fascista* of Feb. 14, 1935, states that on the lands surrounding Lake Fucino, which belong to Prince Torlonia, the association of agricultural employers does not admit any interference of the union in the relations between Prince Torlonia and his tenants. Until 1934 the latter were organized under the Confederation of Agricultural Unions. In 1935, by command of the government, they passed under the Confederation of Agricultural Employers. "The president of the Provincial Association of Employers is the owner of the lands [Prince Torlonia]. What, the tenants ask, will become of our interests?"

troops." [18] Thus was handed down from above the hierarchy aimed at regimenting the Italian working class. Consequently, the persons who direct the workers' organizations in no way represent the mass of their members; they are officials who govern the central and local organizations in accordance with the commands they receive from the government and the Party bosses.

---

[18] Speech of Deputy Begnotti to the Chamber, March 9, 1933. The storm troopers (*squadristi*) were members of the Fascist squads that kept the country in a state of terror from 1921 to 1926. See Salvemini, *The Fascist Dictatorship in Italy*, chapter II and ff.

VII

Company Unions, Nazi Unions, and
Fascist Unions

IN the so-called "company unions," which have been fostered by employers in the United States during recent years, the union officials are appointed directly by the employers. In Nazi Germany there are no longer employers and workers: there are "leaders" (the employers) and "followers" (the workers); and the Nazi unions are called "shop communities." Each "shop community" is administered by a "council," the members of which are nominated by the "shop cell," that is, by those "followers" who are members of the Nazi Party, after consultation with the "leader." Voters cannot propose other candidates, but have the right to scratch off the ticket names to which they object. If the "followers" do not give a majority to any name, the Council is nominated by one of the "labour trustees" (*Treuhändler*), to whom the government entrusts the function of keeping up the standard of "social honour" in the German shops. All this is as clear as daylight. Everyone understands what the secretary of a company union is in America today, and what the council of a "shop community" is in Germany. Everyone knows that in these organizations "the bosses sit on both sides of the table."

The Fascist unions do not stand out so clearly. The Italian Fascists do all they can to confuse people's minds on what is manifestly an essential point for a comprehension of the true nature of Fascist "syndicalism": by whom and by what method are the officials of the local, provincial, and national organizations "elected"?

When the French journalist, Monsieur Lachin, told the president of industrial employees, Signor Cianetti, "You are appointed by the government. You were not chosen by the working-classes," Signor Cianetti neither protested nor contradicted him; he began talking about something else.[1] Another Fascist official, Signor Capoferri, admitted that the general secretary of the unions in each province is appointed by the president of the confederation, but he stated that he is assisted by the

---

[1] *La IVᵉ Italie*, p. 195.

secretaries of the different provincial branches of the unions. "Who appoints these secretaries?" Monsieur Lachin asked. "They are elected"—thus the answer ran—"by the workers of the capital city of the province and by the secretaries of the unions existing in the different towns and cities of the province." M. Lachin insisted: "Who appoints these local secretaries?" The colloquy continued:

"They are elected."

"The affirmation has been made to me, however, that they are appointed by the secretary-general in the province."

"Of course the secretary-general in the province is called upon to ratify the choices. He can veto them for political reasons. As a matter of fact, the elections take place after the central bureaus have approved the designation of the candidates made by the provincial secretary. It is also true that we favour certain nominations." [2]

If Monsieur Lachin had insisted, Signor Capoferri would have had to admit that the "elections" take place neither by a secret vote nor on competitive lists; the president of the meeting announces the nominations and the assembly applauds. If he had pushed his inquiry still further, Monsieur Lachin would have learned that the workers of the provincial capitals are merely present at the acclamation, and that the local secretaries alone, and not the workers, participate in the acclamation; furthermore the workers as a rule stay away from these meetings. But Monsieur Lachin did not insist. Another official, the secretary-general of the union in industry in the province of Turin, told Monsieur Lachin:

Why should I not tell you? It is true that I exercise a rather weighty influence in the election of the directors of the provincial branches of our organization. . . . But the names we choose have not always been ratified by the assemblies convoked for that purpose. . . . It would be incorrect to say that we have not consulted the workers, but it would also be incorrect to say that we allow an entirely free choice, since we attach to each nomination certain conditions which one may regard as involving political partisanship but which we consider indispensable. [3]

That loyal Fascist would have been unable to give the place and date of a single assembly which had refused to ratify a choice made by the superior authorities.

---

[2] *La IVᵉ Italie*, pp. 197–9.
[3] *Ibid.*, pp. 201–2.

The president of the bankers' confederation stated that the presidents of the confederations were appointed by the government, but only after they had been nominated in meetings in which, however, not more than thirty persons took part (p. 240). He was careful not to reveal that during the summer of 1934 Mussolini had abolished the preliminary designation, and himself appointed the presidents, and that even when the preliminary nomination was in effect, it was a farce in which the thirty persons, all officials appointed by the president in charge, acclaimed the names announced by the president or by some men in the confidence of the president.

The non-Italian apologists for Fascism do their best to increase the confusion. In 1928 Sir Frank Fox perceived the truth:

> The representatives, apparently, may ultimately be elected by the associations [associations of employers and unions of employees] by the votes of their own members, but at present they are to be chosen, in some [?] cases at any rate, by the government. The reason given for this is that in many of the associations, being newly formed, no machinery exists for election; but, as one repeatedly observes, Fascism has a dislike for elections.

Having made this concession to truth, Sir Frank proceeded to forget about it, and went on undauntedly to speak of "representatives" of the organizations.[4]

Mlle. Lion writes in her own peculiar English:

> As for the moment there are no such qualified people to be had, and people are not yet used to choose their representatives according to their value in the trade and common sense, they are appointed by the government. And this is one weak point of the organization, although it is obviously a temporary one.[5]

---

[4] *Italy Today*, pp. 168 and 176. Sir Frank discovered that the British trade unions, "before they became involved in the Socialist political movement," "contained the germs of the Italian Fascist system. . . . They had no policy of class war. Their aim was, by fair collective bargaining with employers, to improve the lot of the workers in matters of wages, hours, and conditions of labour." Thus Sir Frank made no distinction between a trade union whose secretary is elected by the members, is responsible to them for his acts, and can be deprived of his office by them, and a trade union whose secretary is appointed by the Party in power, is responsible to no one but the Party in power, and may be dismissed alone by the Party in power. The only distinction he was prepared to recognize was that between unions which had or had not become involved in the Socialist political movement, with the consequence that the British trade unions before they became involved, etc., belonged to the same species as the Fascist unions.

[5] *The Pedigree of Fascism*, p. 232.

The assertion that the "weak point" was "obviously a temporary one" rested upon no firmer ground than Mlle. Lion's intuition.

Let the reader be warned against expecting any enlightenment on this point in the articles published in the *International Labour Review* for September 1926 and June 1927 by Professor Arias and Signor Bottai, or in Major Barnes' book *The Universal Aspects of Fascism*, or in Dr. Einzig's book, *The Economic Foundations of Fascism*. Anyone reading the writings of these "experts" on Fascistology, without having been informed in advance as to how Fascist organizations actually operate, would imagine that they elect and dismiss their officials, as they do in France, England, and the United States. This deceptive reticence is easily understood in the cases of Professor Arias and Signor Bottai. Major Barnes's case is also comprehensible, the major being completely absorbed in his contemplation of the "universal aspects," or as he says, the *Weltanschauung* of Fascism, and consequently unable to bother about such an unimportant detail as the method whereby union officials are "elected" in Italy. Dr. Einzig's reticence is incomprehensible, since he opens his book with a statement deploring the fact that "most people outside Italy have only vague, and frequently distorted, notions of what is going on in Italy." Nor did the British commercial attaché at Rome, when in 1933 he described "some points of difference between the Fascist syndical organization and the trades-union system," see fit to offer any information on the manner in which officials are appointed or elected.[6]

There have, however, been Fascist "doctors" who were less discreet. Signor Rossoni, in his maiden speech at the conference of the International Labour Office at Geneva on June 3, 1927, had the temerity to declare:

I am elected by the congress. It is not quite correct to say that our unions are run by officials. It is rather the contrary. Read the statutes of my organization. There it says that the directorates and the executives of all unions are elected by the members. This is our system. As for the officials, it is I who nominate them. This is because I need collaborators capable of working on the lines laid down by the national congress.[7]

Professor Volpe, in his *Sviluppo storico del Fascismo*, published in

---

[6] Turner, *Economic Conditions in Italy: July 1933*, p. 158.
[7] I.L.O., *Transactions*, 1927, vol. I, p. 81.

1928, stated that the leaders were "designated" by the organizations,[8] and let the matter rest at that simple word, uttered casually, as the most obvious thing in the world. In the latest edition of this study, issued in 1932 under the title *Storia del Movimento Fascista*, even this word was prudently omitted.

Mrs. O. Rossetti Agresti, in the *Encyclopædia Britannica*, fourteenth edition, 1929, vol. IX, p. 105, states that "the federations and confederations appoint their own officials." Signor Villari asserts that the officials "are chosen by the members of the organizations" and "are elected according to the statutes of each syndicate." [9]

In 1931 Major Barnes condescended to interrupt his Platonic contemplations long enough to note a mundane detail of Italian Fascism by referring to the "elected representatives" of the organizations.[10]

Sir Charles Petrie likewise assures us that "the members elect their own president and secretary"; [11] Sir Charles, like Dr. Einzig, is scandalized by the "gross ignorance" which prevails in England "of everything for which Fascism stands" (p. 128) and has written his book to remedy this situation.

The *Enciclopedia Italiana*, vol. XI, p. 463, states that the directorate is "always to be elected by the members."

Commendatore Munro states that "in the syndical units employer and employee are on equal representative footing throughout." [12]

In his address in the autumn of 1932 at the Fabian Society of London, Mr. Bernard Shaw stated that "in the experiments which have been made in Italy with its new Corporate State and in Russia with its new communist State we see, to begin with, the people *electing representatives*." [13] Let us hope that upon the new Communist state in the U.S.S.R. Mr. Shaw is a little better informed than he is upon the new Corporate State in Italy.

Signor F. Pitigliani, "doctor in economics and in law, formerly research fellow at the Brookings Institution, Washington, D. C.," in *The Italian Corporative State*, pp. 35–7, says that "the assembly nominates the members of the directorate, the secretary, and the president of the

[8] *Civiltà Fascista*, p. 28.
[9] *Italy*, p. 275. *The Economics of Fascism*, p. 83.
[10] *Fascism*, p. 176.
[11] *Mussolini*, p. 136.
[12] *Through Fascism to World Power*, p. 353.
[13] *In Praise of Guy Fawkes*, p. 175.

association": "the principle which inspires the choice of the directing bodies is that of election." On the other hand he cannot refrain from adding that "up to the present, it is true, the syndical associations [associations of employers and unions of employees] have not had a precise policy in this matter":

> There is no doubt that the election of those who direct the occupational associations [organizations of employers and employees] must be *scrupulously maintained*, if it is desired to give to the members of the syndical associations faith in the association to which they belong. . . . It is necessary that the fullest electoral guarantees should be granted in the choice of the persons who manage the association, in order that the persons in charge shall not act as individuals completely independent of the association to which they belong.

From which the reader concludes that the directing bodies are "elected," that this principle is contested by someone and therefore it has not yet become definitive, but it is to be hoped that it will be "scrupulously maintained." Signor Pitigliani purports "to give as accurate a description as possible of the organization of the Corporative State as regards the relations between Capital and Labour" (p. xi).

Whoever ventures as far as pp. 203–4 in Professor Schneider's opus, *Making the Fascist State,* will find the following confused account:

> At present it is difficult to tell whether the internal structure of the syndicates [official organizations] is democratic or not. In their origin and general spirit the syndicates are highly bureaucratic. The whole movement was directed from above by a few leaders who imposed their representatives on the local units. . . . On the other hand, according to the new constitutions, in all the confederations, employers' as well as workers', the president is elected by the congress, which is composed of representatives chosen by [!] the members of local syndicates. So that on paper, at least, the syndicates have representative government. . . . Of course all elections and nominations are subject to the approval of the government, and the Fascist Party can interfere with syndicalist procedure at any point and at any time. But this is Fascist procedure rather than syndical, and it has already been restricted somewhat by decree [!] and the tendency is not [!] in the direction of arbitrary control by the government. . . . So far as the syndicate constitutions go, the decisive [!] power would rest with the mass of electors [!] in the syndicates, but in practice and under the present regime the Italian Government could have its way, if it chooses to interfere.

This confusion is completely dispelled in the volume of Professor

Schneider and Mr. Clough, *Making Fascists*, p. 22, from which we gather that the Fascist organizations are "the only institutions left in which there is any democracy":

> The delegates to the provincial councils are elected by balloting [!] in the syndicates [employers' associations and workers' unions], and the Provincial Councils in turn elect the members of the National Councils, which in turn elect the directors. This is in striking contrast to the organization of the party and the bureaucracy. This situation is bound to change soon, and then either the Fascist regime will feel the power of democratic syndicates or else the Fascist party will disregard the syndicate constitution and will include the whole syndical machinery in the dictatorship.

It would seem easier for a camel to go through the eye of a needle than for two Anglo-Saxon professors to pass safely through the fog of Fascist propaganda.

The director of the British Institute at Florence, Mr. Goad, when addressing the Royal Institute of International Affairs in London on October 17, 1933, was asked: "To what extent does the worker choose the representatives who speak in his name?" He made the following meaningless reply:

> The peasants are generally represented by some educated man who has been among them and sympathizes with them, and the working-men are mostly represented by middle-class people.

Another person in the audience insisted: "How are the representatives chosen? Is there any definite method of electing them?" To which Mr. Goad replied:

> Except in the primary syndicates [local unions] it is not by show of hands. A number of candidates are put forward by common consent and the choice is made between them.[14]

Obliged to return to this subject once again in the course of a letter published in the *Manchester Guardian*, January 12, 1934, Mr. Goad made another revelation:

> As to the method of election of officials, each local syndicate is free to use the method it prefers—ballot, or show of hands, or otherwise. The only stipulation made is that the official chosen should be efficient and capable of fulfilling his task, and neither criminal nor opposed to the system he has to

---

[14] *The Corporate State*, p. 788.

work with—a stipulation which seems to affirm a very large measure of freedom.

Foreseeing that doubts might arise as to the veracity of his assertions, he invited all who wished to go to Florence and inspect the Fascist organizations. One would have to be a doubting Thomas, not to be convinced by such an argument.

Having thus provided definitive proof of his discovery, Mr. Goad, in collaboration with Miss Currey on a new book, *The Working of a Corporate State*, could calmly declare that "the local syndicates [legal organizations] *choose* men possessing ability, character and public spirit and enjoying the confidence of their fellows" (p. 97).

Mr. Jones, in *Is Fascism the Answer?*, p. 145, has also discovered that "in Italy the right of employees . . . to choose their own representatives, rights of self organization and other concerted activities are all *expressly* provided for."

The "students of the Corporate State in Italy," in the *New Statesman* of May 26, 1934, assert that the national conventions which "elect" the presidents of the confederations are "composed of the *elected* heads of the provincial sections," and that when the president is "elected" the Ministry of Corporations "has only to see that the *candidate* possesses the qualifications required by the law, namely, that he is competent to hold the position, both in ability and in character."

In an address delivered before the Institute of Public Affairs at the University of Virginia, on July 3, 1934, Dr. De Ritis had the temerity to assert that "each member of a syndicate organization of employers or employees casts a ballot in the election which creates its directive body." Dr. Nicholas Murray Butler, president of Columbia University, took it upon himself to reproduce Dr. De Ritis's address in the monthly pamphlets of the Carnegie Endowment for International Peace, January 1935, n. 306, pointing out that Dr. De Ritis is the Director of the Institute of Italian Culture at Malta. One can only feel concern as to the standards of this institute.

The International Labour Office in the *Année Sociale 1934–35*, I, 19, lets us know that the directors of the federations are "elected" by the "assemblies of the organizations."

The author of the report on *The Economic and Financial Position of Italy*, published in the spring of 1935 by the Royal Institute of Interna-

tional Affairs, maintains a discreet silence on this point. The only difference which he notices between Fascist and Social-Democratic unions
is that "in the latter the class-struggle and internationalism take precedence over national interests," while "in the former the nation comes
first." There are, he admits, other differences, but he does not trouble
himself to expound them (p. 5).

Besides Monsieur Lachin the only persons who have presented this
problem in its true features are Miss Haider,[15] Monsieur Rosenstock-
Franck,[16] Mrs. Dean,[17] Mr. Elwin [18] and Mr. Finer.[19]

---

[15] *Capital and Labor under Fascism*, pp. 109, 166–7, 221–5, 277; *Do We Want Fascism?*, pp. 19, 21.
[16] *L'Economie Corporative*, pp. 89–97.
[17] *The Economic Situation in Italy: the Corporative System*, p. 295.
[18] *Fascism at Work*, pp. 186–7.
[19] *Mussolini's Italy*, p. 505.

VIII

Labour Agreements

THE official of an organization, when supported by the leaders of the Party, is a miniature Mussolini within the limits of his jurisdiction. He "directs and represents the organization, is responsible for it, and exercises disciplinary powers over its members." No one may enter the organization without his permission. The official may expel, without appeal, any members who, in his opinion, are "undesirable from a moral or political point of view." Whoever criticizes the official organizations is guilty of disparaging an institution of the state.[1]

No one is forced to join the legal organization of his economic group; but everyone must pay his annual dues to it. This is nothing more nor less than a personal tax, collected by the tax-collector.[2] Those who consent to become members of the legal organizations are subjected to a special admission fee and to an annual "supplementary" contribution, the amount of which is fixed from year to year by the national executive committees of the confederations. These extra contributions are likewise paid to the tax-collector. The officials of the organizations have no need to work themselves to death in order to keep up their memberships. They have merely to sit at ease in their offices, while the taxgatherer rakes in their salaries.[3]

---

[1] In March 1928 a peasant was sentenced to three months' imprisonment for urging another man not to join the union "as it was nothing but a trick of the Fascist government on the labourers, especially the share-croppers, in favour of the landowners." (*Popolo d'Italia*, March 21, 1928.) In July 1934 a judge at Milan sentenced to four months' imprisonment a workman guilty of "having made insulting remarks" about an official of his union. In the same month, at Remazzo di Cento, province of Ferrara, a day-labourer was arrested for "having inveighed against" the secretary of his union (*Nuovo Avanti* of Paris, July 21, 1934). In Feb. 1935 a workman in Ferrara was sentenced to seven months' imprisonment for having insulted the secretary of his union (*Regime Fascista*, Feb. 19, 1935).

[2] Villari, in *Fascist Experiment*, p. 157, writes: "Associations invested with representative powers *may* impose a contribution on all persons thus represented." Had Signor Villari been really candid, he would have informed his readers that the organizations not only "may," but "have the right" to impose the contribution, that this right is exercised not only over the members but also the non-members, and that the members and non-members together form the body of "persons thus represented."

[3] In the *Daily Mail* of Feb. 7, 1927, Sir Leo Chiozza-Money stated that Fascist unions had a strong resemblance to British trade unions: "In England men are under

A circular of the Ministry of Corporations of May 1923 reminded the officials of all the organizations of the "absolute necessity" for "rigorously observing" their office hours "in order to avoid any discontent on the part of the members; the latter complain of the loss of time to which they are sometimes subjected when trying to obtain information or documents they need." (*Lavoro*, May 18, 1934.) In the pre-Fascist unions the officials needed no circular from a ministry to make them attend to their duties; the members of the unions saw to that by dismissing the officials if they found them unsatisfactory. The officials used to complain that the union members were too exacting, and there was even talk of the officials forming a union of their own to protect themselves against the exploitation of the unions. Today the situation is reversed. The officials are now independent of the members, who must be protected from the negligence of "their" officials by government circulars.

Meetings of the local and provincial organizations and conferences of the national federations and confederations are called only when the government deems them opportune. On November 18, 1927, the Ministry of Corporations published a circular letter informing all organizations that "public demonstrations are entirely unnecessary." Meetings held by the unions on their own premises were still legal, but it added:

> Such meetings may include only members of the associations concerned, and press representatives must not be present. The number of persons attending must be strictly limited according to the regulations. . . . The debates may be brought to the notice of the public only by succinct reports issued by the organizations concerned.[4]

Meetings and congresses are held chiefly for ceremonial purposes. A more or less important Fascist personage delivers an harangue exalting Mussolini and the regime; some secretary reads a report; occasionally there is the barest semblance of a discussion, but more usually not even that; and the acts of the secretary are approved by acclamation. Were anyone to be so bold as to offer criticism or even ask an awkward question, he might expect a visit next morning from a militiaman, to reduce

---

practical compulsion to join a trade union." Sir Leo saw no difference between practical compulsion which in England could be legally resisted, and legal compulsion which in Italy could not be practically resisted.

[4] *Industrial and Labour Information*, Dec. 12, 1927, p. 328.

him to "reason"; or he might be expelled from his union as "undesirable from the national standpoint."

In May 1928 the national secretary of the agricultural workers opened the congress of his organization by addressing the following remarks to Signor Rossoni, then president of all the national organizations of Fascist unions:

You will mark out this morning the line which we are to follow. We have but a single pride: that of regarding ourselves as interpreters of your will, for we know that your will is at the service of the Duce. We are here to listen to your commandments.

Signor Rossoni solemnly replied:

It is clear that the orders of the Duce must be respected. In the Fascist unions I allow no reservations in regard to the commandments of the Duce and of the Revolution. No reservations whatever!

In January 1932 the national congress of the industrial employers consisted of a presidential address, a speech by the Minister of Corporations, another by the secretary of the confederation and an "election" to fill the offices.[5] The national congress of the Confederation of Industrial Unions, which contains over two million members, met on April 6, 1933. The proceedings began with addresses of welcome by the president and by a representative of the Fascist Party; following which, one of the delegates declared that "any discussion would be superfluous"; another moved that the president of the confederation be confirmed in office by acclamation; another read the names of the national directorate, and requested the meeting to acclaim, so they promptly acclaimed; the under-secretary at the Ministry of Corporations delivered a sermon on Fascist syndicalism; and the congress adjourned.[6]

In the course of his sermon, the under-secretary pronounced among other amiabilities the following:

Your real syndical activity begins tomorrow. We must create the provincial unions not only on paper but in the reality of a living organism; we must make the local branches live. We must bring the workers into contact

---

[5] *Resto del Carlino,* Jan. 22, 1932.

[6] *Lavoro Fascisto,* Apr. 7, 1933. The British commerical attaché in Rome, Mr. Turner, in *Economic Conditions,* p. 158, states that non-members of the organizations "cannot participate in the deliberations of assemblies." The reader is given to believe by these words that there exist today in Italy assemblies in which the members of the organizations deliberate.

with their unions, have them discuss freely in the meetings their needs, the annual financial report, the activities of the leaders. Only in this way can the union become something alive and fruitful.

An employee "of a private enterprise in Florence" made the following comment on the under-secretary's speech in a Florentine weekly, *L'Universale*, on April 25, 1933:

That which is to begin tomorrow is something quite new. Never before have I been offered the opportunity of coming into contact, etc., discussing in the meetings, etc., expressing myself freely, etc. The invitation concerning contacts is very timely. It would be distinctly unpleasant to have these blessed unions turn out, as far as the majority of the members is concerned, to be nothing more than a sort of insurance company.

In the periodical *Problemi di Lavoro* for February 1933 a worker pointed out the fact that not even the "intelligent and competent" workers were permitted to "say many truths that ought to be made known," for the following reasons: "1, discussion meetings were not regularly held; 2, there always prevailed such an atmosphere of diffidence and fear that no one wished to expose himself to the inevitable results of being called an opponent of the regime with the usual undesirable personal consequences."

In an article in the review *Gerarchia*, June 1935, one reads: "The masses are still far from the unions, and scarcely are able fully to participate in the life of the unions. It is a case of a diffidence which perhaps [!] has remote origins, but which today, just for the operation of the party, ought [!] to be overcome." The *Lavoro Fascista*, July 10, 1935, stated that that article was "filled with understanding, complete, consonant with the moment, and therefore worthy of being taken into consideration." [7]

---

[7] To the assertion by a Socialist that "the workers have no say" in the Fascist unions, Sir Leo Chiozza-Money opposed the following invincible argument: "I can only beg him to go and investigate for himself." (*Forward*, August 9, 1930.) Goad and Currey, in *The Working of a Corporate State*, p. 96, have the audacity to write: "In the syndicate [legal organization] the individual producer, whether employer or workman, is brought into direct contact with his fellows, sharing their common interests and problems. . . . Each workman or employer is called upon to take his part in deciding and directing the policy of the syndicates [organizations]." Miss Haider, in *Do We Want Fascism?*, p. 20, comprehended perfectly that the workers "do not take an active and constructive interest in the affairs of their unions, but are apathetic at best, limiting their connection to the payment of dues and to submission to the collective contracts drawn up by the syndicates [unions]."

In associations of all kinds under the Fascist regime the administration rests entirely in the hands of the executive committees appointed from above, and the members have nothing to do with it. In the National Association of Retired Army Officers the members do not even have to take the trouble to seek admittance since they are already members *ex officio*. Nor may they resign unless they wish to be known as opponents of the regime, in which case they would lose their rank and return to the rank of private soldiers, as persons who have "engaged in activities contrary to the interests of the nation" (act of December 14, 1928).

When the Fascists speak of workers' organizations that decide to take part in a demonstration, send telegrams of homage and fealty to the Duce, conclude labour agreements, etc., we must always remember that this means that these acts are performed, not by the members of the organizations, but by the officials.

In January 1934, an official document had to admit that the local organizations, "the ones which should have lived in close and continuous contact with individuals, had gradually lost their importance and had slowly atrophied, while the higher organizations had continued to develop and gain in strength":

> The syndicate [local organization of employers or employees] was to have been the depository of the revolutionary spirit of Fascism, while the higher organizations were to have been organs of an administrative and bureaucratic nature. But gradually, as the lower organizations lost their vitality, and the confederations became powerful, Fascist syndicalism lost its revolutionary *élan*, and acquired a bureaucratic compactness.[8]

The author of these words would have been much embarrassed if he had been asked to state in just what period of their life the local organizations of employers or employees, created by the law of 1926, had possessed the slightest vitality and had been the depositories of a revolutionary spirit. From the very beginning the officials of the confederations were invested with full authority in the negotiation of labour agreements, which should have been the essential function of the local, provincial, and national organizations subject to the confederations. The lower organizations were without importance and atrophied from the moment of their birth. In reading that the confederations were gaining

---

[8] Memorandum accompanying the bill for the establishment of the corporations.

in strength, one must interpret these words to mean that the officials of the confederations were gaining unlimited power over the officials of the lower organizations. Aside from these questions and interpretations, the document contains an interesting official confession of the complete inefficiency of Fascist "syndicalism" in what should have been the living cells of the organization—the local associations of employers and unions of employees.

The Fascists claim that the dictatorship has bestowed a legal status upon the organizations of employers, employees, and professional classes. It has given them a place in the public law while in the pre-Fascist period they had merely a *de facto* existence. But the pre-Fascist organizations operated according to the will of their members. In the Fascist organizations the will of the members is suppressed. The members are passive and inert material. All action is the province of the officials, and these are accountable not to the members, but to the leaders of the party and to the governmental bureaucracy. "The organizations are no longer representative and militant organs of masters and workers but devised for the better disciplining of labour and capital." [9] Even those condemned to prison have a legal status in the public law. But who of us wishes to have such a legal status in public law? [10]

The negotiation of agreements concerning wages, hours, disciplinary sanctions, indemnities, etc., is carried out by the official organizations in each economic group, which means in the case of the employers' associations the representatives of the big interests, and in the case of the unions the appointed officials who run them.[11]

---

[9] Finer, *Mussolini's Italy*, p. 507.

[10] "The juridical person of the laborer is placed side by side with that of his employer as having equivalent weight and value. No such political equality was ever granted to the laborer under democratic or liberal regimes." This one reads in an article "The Fascist Working Man" contributed by Signor Paul Cremona to the *Christian Science Monitor*, weekly magazine section, Nov. 14, 1934.

[11] An English journalist wrote in the *Daily Express* on Jan. 26, 1927: "The object of Mussolini is the elimination of all strikes and the settlement of all industrial disputes by round table conferences between capital and labour." The gentleman of the press was careful not to mention that, in the "round table conferences," capital was represented by its own spokesmen, while labour was represented by officials in whose appointment the employees had no voice. Sir Leo Chiozza-Money, writing in the *Daily Mail*, Feb. 7, 1929, displayed even more astonishing candour: "It is impossible," he wrote, "to deny merit to a law which in effect makes Italy a national club, whose members are invited [sic] and enabled to use individual freedom [sic] in corporative activities. The truth is that the new law builds trade-unionism into a juridical system and looks with an equal eye on masters and men."

Agreements are never negotiated locally, but are drawn up between the representatives of the employers and the provincial secretary of the employees' unions. The local secretaries have nothing else to do but receive these agreements already concocted and inform the members thereof. If anyone in the union grumbles, the secretary turns him out, and so all those who remain in the union become satisfied and contented.

In the case of trades covering several provinces, agreements are made still farther away from the men immediately concerned, namely in Rome, where the representatives of the national employers' federation meet with the officials of the unions. In any case, no agreement, whether local, provincial, or national, becomes binding unless approved by the directorates of the relevant employers' and employees' confederations.[12] The agreements must then be approved by the provincial prefect or the Minister of Corporations, according to whether it concerns one or more provinces. After having been thus sanctified, the agreements are published in the *Bollettino degli annunci legali della Provincia* or in the *Gazzetta Ufficiale*. As soon as the agreement is published every employer and employee must conform to it, whether or not they belong to the official organizations (Articles 1, 5, 6, and 10 of the act of April 3, 1926). "One could not imagine," Monsieur Rosenstock-Franck has observed, "a more hierarchical system; in fact, the powers of the local unions, of

---

[12] A labour agreement was concluded in the province of Cremona during July 1928. The Ministry of Corporations sent out an official *communiqué* stating that the agreement must be regarded as nothing more than a proposal sent up to the superior authorities by the local organizations. In 1927, in his description of *Trade Organization in Italy*, p. 821, Signor Bottai explained that "this tendency towards centralization appears natural enough in the early stages of the establishment and functioning of the system. It is imperative that one of the most delicate attributes arising out of the function of a public body entrusted to the unions [employers' associations and employees' unions] shall not be left to the mercy of the masses who are liable to become unstable and irritable." In 1934, eight years after the system was established, the masses were still liable to become unstable and irritable, and consequently the agreements were still made beyond their control. M. Ulric Aillaud, in *The Growth of Corporations in Italy*, p. 663, puts the following question: "What part have the non-members of the associations in this collective arrangement? And since the collective regulations must be regarded as binding in one form or another on both members and non-members, how is it possible in the case of all, members and non-members alike, to speak of freedom of will, the essential requisite of a contract?" If M. Aillaud had really understood the method by which the workers' "representatives" are "elected" and to whom they are responsible for their acts, he would have made no distinction between members and non-members, and he would have come to the conclusion that the "contracts" emanate from the "freedom of will" of the officials rather than that of the members or non-members.

the provincial secretaries, and of the national federations are almost nil." [13]

In conclusion, and viewed in the most favourable light, in the Fascist legal organizations the rank and file have no greater authority than do the animals in a society for the prevention of cruelty to animals.

---

[13] *L'Economie Corporative*, p. 125. The weekly review *Cantiere*, in its issue of Oct. 13, 1934, wrote: "The worker ought not to be left in the dark as regards the preliminary discussions which take place between his representatives and those of the employers in the drawing up of wage agreements. . . . Ordinarily the union journals announce the terms of the settlement only in its final form." Signor Bottai, *Corporate State and N.R.A.*, p. 623, is bold enough to assert that there are "evident similarities" between the programmes of President Roosevelt and Premier Mussolini. "These similarities are to be found in the field of collective labor relations and in the institutions established for the conciliation of labor disputes." But in the United States "the actual elaboration of codes rules lies primarily in the hands of the employers" . . . "in Italy, on the contrary, labor relations are settled by negotiation between organizations of employers and workers, *both of which have equal rights and status.*"

IX

The Court of Labour

I F the representatives of the employers and the officials who run the unions of the employees are unable to reach a harmonious decision concerning the terms of new agreements, they may refer the question to an arbitrator.

In April 1927, a new agreement for bank employees was under discussion. The managements demanded from their clerks a working day of eight hours. The officials of the bank clerks' organization proposed seven and a half hours. Mussolini, called upon to act as arbitrator, decided in favour of eight hours:

The Head of the Government [runs the official *communiqué*] has decided that the normal working day in the banks shall be eight hours, with the definite intention that this longer day shall be regarded as the contribution of the bank clerks to the victorious battle for the economic independence of the country. He further explained that the bank clerks are not to consider themselves depreciated by the fact that their working day is of the same length as that of the workmen; no labour is less noble than another; there is only one kind of labour, which is equally noble in all its manifold forms: that which is honest, steady, disciplined, and productive.[1]

The bank clerks must have attained the consummation of bliss on learning that all kinds of work are equally noble, whatever the duration.[2]

Generally speaking, the office of arbitrator or of mediator is exercised by the Ministry of Corporations, that is, by the high permanent officials of the ministry. From 1927 to 1933, the ministry intervened as arbitrator or mediator in 498 labour agreements.[3]

If the sides do not agree on the choice of an arbitrator, the question is

---

[1] *Corriere della Sera*, April 14, 1927.

[2] Robertson, *Mussolini and the New Italy*, p. 135, asserted in 1930 that Mussolini had never yet failed to send both parties away perfectly satisfied with his decision.

[3] *Sindacato e Corporazione*, Feb. 1934, p. 298. See also above, p. 66, n. 12 and below, p. 171, n. 4. During the London Conference of 1933, the Fascist spokesmen asserted that "the state does not intervene *either directly or indirectly* in the negotiations" (*The State and Economic Life*, p. 265); "the conditions of work are *freely* established between the *representatives* of the two categories *without any intervention from governmental bodies*" (*Ibid.*, p. 378).

brought before the Labour Court.[4] The decision of this court is binding on both sides. Anyone who refuses to abide by the pronouncements of the court, even if only acting as a single individual, is liable to imprisonment for a maximum of one year.

The Minister of Justice, Signor Rocco, in a speech which he delivered at Perugia in August 1925, and which was certified by Mussolini as being "the clear formulation of the basic principles of the Fascist programme," justified the abolition of the right to strike and the intervention of the state as the supreme arbiter between capital and labour, by the following moral, legal, and political postulates:

Unlimited and unrestrained class self-defence, evinced by strikes and lockouts, by boycotts and sabotage, leads inevitably to anarchy. The Fascist doctrine, enacting justice among the classes in compliance with a fundamental necessity of modern life, does away with class self-defence, which, like individual self-defence in the days of barbarism, is a source of disorder and civil war. Having reduced the problem to these terms, only one solution is possible, the realization of justice among the classes by and through the state. Centuries ago the state, as the specific organ of justice, abolished personal self-defence in individual controversies and substituted for it state justice. The time has now come when class self-defence also must be replaced by state justice.[5]

And in the memorandum laying before Parliament the bill which became the act of April 3, 1926, he reiterated:

The state is no longer the state, i. e., is no longer sovereign, if it is not able to deal out justice in conflicts between social classes and categories, forbidding them to exercise private justice, just as this is forbidden to individuals and families.

---

[4] Sir Frank Fox, *Italy Today*, p. 168, discovered in 1926 that "there has been created for each industry a governing Syndic; ordinarily the Syndic, it is expected, will decide amicably; but in the case of stubborn disagreement between the employers' representatives and the workers' representatives [sic], the points at issue will be decided by courts of industrial arbitration." The governing syndic has never existed outside the fancy of Sir Frank. Mr. Alexander Robertson, in *Mussolini and the New Italy*, p. 135, displays even a wilder imagination than that of Sir Frank: "Instead of one-sided trade unions, this law of April 3, 1936, has created Industrial and Professional Syndicates, composed of employers and of workmen, who are under the State. Should differences arise at their meetings which they themselves cannot settle, Mussolini has provided for such cases a Magistracy of Labour, to which they can be carried; and should these courts fail to bring about an amicable settlement, then the case can be carried to Mussolini himself."

[5] *The Political Doctrine of Fascism*, pp. 391, 406.

But what is "the state"? The state itself is an abstraction. What is essential is to know *who* it is that "deals out justice" in the name of "the state."

In the Fascist Italian state we find that at the bottom, labour agreements are concocted by the representatives of the big employers and the officials who are appointed from above to run the workers' unions. As Deputy Giardina proclaimed in the Chamber, November 25, 1931, "the task of settling labour disputes is vested exclusively in the leaders of the organizations." At the top there is the Labour Court, composed of three judges and two experts in production and labour problems. The latter are appointed to sit *ad hoc*, by the chief justice of the province, from a panel drawn up by the Minister of Justice after consultation with the Minister of National Economy. To avoid the danger of a workman's ever being chosen as an expert, Article 54 of the regulations of July 1, 1926, enacts that experts must have a university degree, or its equivalent. Thus, not even in this last resort do the workers have any voice.[6] From the decision of such a court there is no appeal.[7]

Judges and experts must decide cases in accordance with equity, but at the same time are enjoined to bear in mind "the supreme necessity of insuring the continuity of production." This formula is explained by

---

[6] Pitigliani, *The Italian Corporative State*, pp. 76–9. One will look in vain for any details on this subject in Schneider's *Making the Fascist State*, pp. 184–9. Sir Leo Chiozza-Money, in the *Daily Mail*, Feb. 7, 1927, states that "a special appeal court, sitting with expert advisors, drawn from a panel of masters and men [sic], decide the issue." Mlle. Lion, in *The Pedigree of Fascism*, p. 232, thus describes the system: "It is simply wonderful. The delegates of the two syndicates [the employers' association and the workers' union] meet, and they discuss the point at issue. Failing agreement, the syndicates themselves meet and discuss the matter. If agreement is not possible, the delegates meet again, but in the presence of a special magistrate." Mrs. O. Rossetti Agresti, in the *Encyclopædia Britannica*, fourteenth edition, 1929, vol. IX, p. 104, asserts that the judges are "assisted by experts selected from panels drawn up by the respective syndical associations." Kemechey, in *Il Duce*, p. 226, goes even further: the "experts" are "appointed representatives of the employers and workmen." Major Barnes, in *Fascism*, p. 181, is no less bold: experts are "appointed by the disputing parties." Sir Charles Petrie, in *Mussolini*, p. 141, had it on good authority that the two experts are the "representatives of the employers and workmen . . . appointed by the parties to the dispute." Prof. Welk, in *Fascist Economic Policy*, p. 103, states that the two experts "are chosen by the President of the Court from a carefully selected list of eligible citizens."

[7] From the *Report on the Commercial, Industrial, and Economic Situation in Italy*, compiled by the British commercial attachés in Rome, Mr. Rawlins and Mr. Carpenter, and dated March 1927, p. 54, we learn that "in order to avoid conflicts between capital and labour, labour courts are to be established; against the decisions of these courts, 16 [!] Courts of Appeal, consisting of three magistrates, with two experts acting as assessors, are furnished."

the following words in the memorandum with which the government presented the bill to Parliament:

The community is interested in production being maintained at a cost which is not excessive, i. e., at prices which permit Italian goods to compete with foreign ones.

This necessity of withstanding foreign competition is the universal battle-cry of employers in every country when they wish to cut wages.[8]

Fully to understand the working of the system, one should remember that in Italy judges have no independence. They may be displaced at the will of the government and they may even be removed if they "set themselves in contrast with the general trend of policies of the government" (act of December 24, 1925). Mr. Finer has wholly understood the implications of such a fact:

A representative of the Government must be notified by the Court that a case is to be called, and is present during the proceedings. He puts the "public" point of view in the course of discussion. No judgement may be rendered until the representative of the Government has delivered his opinion as to what it should be. The serious problems are thrashed out between the Fascist officials heading the associations [organizations]; and in the case of enduring differences, the offices of the Ministry of Corporations, the Inspectors of Corporations, or the Prefect are invoked. Many Fascists . . . deplore these hurried attempts at peace with the local Fascist Party leader as the go-between. But why not? Business is business.[9]

---

[8] Mr. Goad, in his address before the Royal Institute of International Affairs, in Oct. 1933, said: "Here I should like to point out the superiority of the judge over the arbitrator, in that his decisions are law, and therefore must be obeyed by both parties, and secondly, in that his aim in judging between the working-man and the employer is not merely peace or compromise but equity. That is an important difference. He considers his judgment not only in relation to the two sides between whom he is arbitrating, but also in relation to the community in general, to the consumer, to the interest of production, and so on." Mr. Goad evidently believes that compromise and equity are at loggerheads and that an arbitrator is an ignoramus who tries to solve labour disputes by disregarding all the pertinent facts, whereas a judge takes full cognizance of them. In reality, the arbitrator endeavours to give to his compromise a basis of equity, taking into consideration all the facts of the case. And he, like a judge, can err. The only superiority of a Fascist judge over an arbitrator is that the decision of a Fascist judge is law: if anyone regards himself as unjustly treated and refuses to obey the court, he will be sent to prison to demonstrate that Fascist judges are infallible.

[9] Finer, *Mussolini's Italy*, p. 511.

Strikes are forbidden by law and punished by a rising scale of penalties, according to whether they are economic or sympathetic, and whether they take place in privately owned or in public enterprises, the maximum penalty being seven years' imprisonment for a strike aimed at bringing pressure to bear upon the public authorities. Lockouts are forbidden as well as strikes. This is supposed to be a proof that equality reigns between capital and labour. But since the workers cannot strike, the employers have no need of recourse to the lockout. If an employer declares that he can no longer maintain the existing volume of employment in his concern, the stoppage of work is then not a "lockout," but a "closing-down" induced by a "justified motive." [10]

The Turin daily paper *Stampa*, on July 2, 1926, gave news of a sentence passed against strikers under the act of April 3, 1926. About fourteen hundred workers, most of them women, had gone on strike at a jute factory in Carrosia, in the province of Genoa:

Since the day when the Fascists occupied the Chamber of Workers [headquarters of all the unions in the town] at Novi—said some of the women strikers—we have been isolated and leaderless. The employers seized the opportunity to reduce our wages by nearly forty per cent. Finding all attempts vain to induce the Fascist unions to intervene, we were forced to strike.

Some of the women, suspected of being leaders of the strike, were sentenced to six months' imprisonment.

During the second half of 1926 eight thousand people in Italy were found guilty of the crime of striking. Such newspapers as attempted to give information about these condemnations were silenced by the government. No wonder, therefore, that Sir Leo Chiozza-Money in the *Daily Mail*, February 7, 1927, stated: "There was no strike or lockout in Italy in 1926." [11]

---

[10] *Lavoro d'Italia*, Sept. 3, 1929, declares: "It is well known that the employers can reduce the number of employees or of working hours without closing their factories and producing a lockout." Finer, *Mussolini's Italy*, p. 505, affirms that: "When economic circumstances are pressing, the workshop may be closed, and the courts are satisfied, if the matter comes to them, with the plain economic explanation."

[11] According to official statistics there were between July 1, 1926, and Dec. 31, 1926, no more than 791 strikers (Istituto Centrale di Statistica: *Compendio Statistico, 1931*, p. 168). This number is most certainly false. The figure of eight thousand condemnations for the crime of striking in 1926 was given by Signor Rocco, then Minister of Justice, to Monsieur Rosenstock-Franck, *L'Economie Corporative*, p. 204.

The London *Observer*, September 11, 1927, published the following item:

The tribunal of Pisa has given an important decision. It has decided that the abandonment of work invariably constitutes an offence. When a conflict arises between the two parties, the only way open to them is to have recourse to the competent organs established by the law to settle labour disputes. The crime of striking, concludes the sentence, is punishable, whether it be perpetrated for political reasons or for the purpose of obtaining a betterment of treatment, and even if it is perpetrated in support of an undeniable right.

Not all of the judges, it must be admitted, accepted this theory. The *Corriere della Sera*, January 13, 1928, gave the following account:

The standing joint committee of agricultural employers and labourers in Vigevano had agreed that the latter should receive a daily wage of 15.20 lire. If the employer engaged hands in excess of the number allotted to his acreage under cultivation, he would pay them only 12.20 lire. The employers, claiming that a large proportion of their land was uncultivated, reduced the number of labourers paid at the higher and increased those at the lower rate. Seventeen labourers struck for one day in protest at the employers' failure to honour the accepted agreement.

The judge at Vigevano acquitted the strikers on the ground that the employers "by having recourse to deplorable subterfuges tried to evade the agreement and pay their labourers at a lower rate":

It was the employers who broke the agreement, not the workers. If the worker abstains from work because the employer does not honour his pledge, it is not the worker who ought to be punished, but the employer.

But the verdict of the judge of Vigevano was bitterly attacked in the following terms by the *Informazioni Fasciste*, the official bulletin of the Ministry of Corporations:

By the light of simple logic the fallacy and danger of this theory become clear. The leading characteristic of the Fascist labour law is to penalize self-defence in labour disputes and substitute judicial intervention by the state. Therefore to suppose that today the workers can take justice into their own hands by striking against employers, even if the latter act illegally, is to ignore that characteristic and return to the mentality and policy over-ridden by Fascism. The Fascist labour law penalizes strikes and lockouts in themselves, as weapons of social strife, not on account of their objectives. It would be dangerous to tell workers and employers that they may fight when the other side is guilty of a breach of contract. It would be re-opening the door to those disastrous labour struggles which have been finally banished from the life of the nation.[12]

The tribunals, however, up to the present, have not been unanimous in accepting this uncompromising point of view. Some of them have shown a certain indulgence in cases in which workers have abstained from work in order to protest against an employer who had violated the agreement already legally entered into.[13] But very few workers dare to strike even in these cases, because—in view of the fluctuating policy of the courts—the danger of imprisonment is always present.

In England, in January 1935, after two years of debates and negotiations, the larger railway companies and unions embracing four hundred thousand railwaymen came to an agreement. The strike is not to be resorted to until all other means of conciliation have been exhausted. There will be a Railway Staff National Council, consisting of eight representatives of the companies and eight of the unions. This council will consider questions of salaries, wages, hours of work, and other standard conditions. Moreover, there is to be a Railway Staff National Tribunal consisting of a chairman appointed by agreement between the companies and the unions, or failing this, by the Minister of Labour after consultation with both parties, and two members, one nominated by the companies and one by the unions:

Even so the decisions of the Tribunal [thus *The Economist* of January 26, 1935, comments on the agreement] are not to be specifically binding. It is hoped, however, that they will normally be accepted by both sides. The power still retained by each side to reject the findings of the Tribunal in the last resort may very likely prove not so much a loophole as a safety-valve.

The Stefani Agency, in giving out to the Italian press the news of the English agreement, omitted to mention certain essential facts: 1, that the unions of railwaymen, in the negotiations with the companies, had been represented by officials who had been elected by the membership of the unions and not appointed by the English government or by the

---

[12] *Tevere*, Feb. 17–8, 1928.

[13] Rosenstock-Franck, *L'Economie Corporative*, pp. 204–5. Cf. *Sindacato e Corporazione*, Sept. 1934, pp. 277 ff.

English Conservative Party; 2, that the representatives of the unions in the council and the tribunal are to be "elected" by the membership of the unions; and 3, that the Tribunal does not have power to pass a final judgment on the disputes submitted to it, *but the unions preserve the right to strike if dissatisfied with its findings.* The Italian newspapers proclaimed that the English agreement was "based on the principles of the Italian corporative system" and was a new victory of Mussolini's genius:

> The corporative idea is making progress in the world. The corporative spirit is pervading all peoples, one after the other; even those among whom the worship of so-called liberty has been carried so far—until today—as to sacrifice the interests of the nation to those of the individual. Now, with the example of Fascist Italy before their eyes, such aberrations are no longer possible. The piece of news published above is proof of this statement.[14]

The truth is that if one compares the system evolved in England with the object of making strikes as rare as possible with the system imposed by law in Italy upon employees of all trades forbidding them to have recourse to strikes under any circumstances, one understands the wide gulf which separates a country in which trade-union liberty is really respected and one in which it has been completely suppressed.

---

[14] *Resto del Carlino,* Jan. 25, 1935.

X

Individual Labour Controversies

IN the pre-Fascist era individual controversies between industrial employers and workers were settled without all these expenses and complications inseparable from civil suits, by boards of conciliators (*probiviri*) chosen in each province according to an act of 1893, and composed of representatives elected by the employers and by the workers of each trade. In 1922 this institution was extended to agriculture by means of the Provincial Conciliation Committees.[1] On February 26, 1928, a royal decree abolished these "outmoded" institutions. Individual controversies were to be settled amicably by the officials of the local organizations. Mr. Finer, in *Mussolini's Italy*, pp. 511–2, has clearly detected the weak point of this system:

The procedure is more complicated than the old. . . . Not every worker knows the law. It is true that he can get aid from . . . the trade union secretary. But this takes trouble, and makes trouble. He is obliged to explain the nature of his complaint to several people, to set in train a dispute which will be embarrassing to all parties, and to ask assistance of an official who is not elected by him as his trusted comrade to support his case. Therefore, though it is possible that the law would protect the man's rights if the dispute came before the courts, too many disputes do not. Before the courts the employer will be able to afford better legal assistance than the worker. Nor is there complete immunity from the fear of dismissal if a workman seeks his rights. There are dozens of ways in which employers can, and do, get their revenge.

The union officials also had to make the same remarks. In August 1929 one of them complained as follows:

Anyone who has no experience with such matters might think that the workers could always call upon the union. But, on the contrary, the headquarters of the unions are often too far away from the factory, in towns even more so than in the country, to permit the necessary contacts between the workers and the officials. Again, the workers do not always

---

[1] *Industrial and Labour Information*, March 24, 1922, p. 57.

live in the locality where the factory is situated, and those who have seen industrial centres know that a great part of the workers have to hurry to the station to catch the trains which take them to their homes at a considerable distance from their place of work.[2]

The worker, even if he is not a member of the union, must present his case to the officials of the union in his trade. It is easy to imagine in what state of mind he will present his case if he is not a member. The best thing for him to do is to join the union before going to the officials (see above pp. 31–2.

If the union officials do not succeed in settling the individual dispute, the worker may carry it to the ordinary courts. The procedure in these courts is slow and complicated.

Disputes, except in rare instances, are never definitively settled by the first adjudication. At least fourteen or fifteen months are required before a ruling is given, and in complicated cases the delay is even longer. Furthermore, it must be kept in mind that a considerable number of cases are appealed against, with the result that normally cases take two years without counting an eventual recourse to the Supreme Court.[3]

Even having obtained a favourable verdict, the worker still has a long way to go before he gets what is due to him:

The rules which are intended to insure the greatest promptness are never observed. It never happens that a judgment is entered within less than ten days after the hearing on the case. At the earliest, a month will elapse before the payment ordered by the court is made to the worker, who, if he is unemployed, may suffer the pangs of hunger. In bringing his suit, the worker is subject to numerous expenses, which may well total more than the sum involved, and the money for which in any case he does not possess. When he reads in the court's decision that all public officials are solemnly commanded to execute it, whereas he is powerless to do so, the whole affair becomes for him tinctured with irony.[4]

With the hope of remedying these deficiencies in some degree, the unions began in the spring of 1928 to name in each factory or factory

---

[2] *Resto del Carlino*, Aug. 26, 1929, p. 282.

[3] *Lavoro Fascista*, Dec. 2 and 8, 1932.

[4] *Resto del Carlino*, Jan. 13, 1933. Mr. Goad, in his address on *The Corporate State*, p. 787, states that "the new system is felt to be giving more power to the working man to obtain the redress of his grievances." Mr. Goad and Miss Currey, in *The Working of a Corporate State*, p. 33, inform us that "decisions must in all cases be given with as little delay as possible"; they "must," but *are* they?

department certain "factory delegates," who were charged with the duty of collecting all complaints from the workers and transmitting them to the secretary of the proper union. The *Lavoro Fascista* admitted that in a way this was a resurrection of the system abolished in October 1925, but went on to observe that this was inevitable if the unions were to be able not only to make agreements but see that these agreements were carried out by assisting the workers in their individual differences with the employers.

The unions are not in a position to give effective help to their members if they have no first-hand knowledge of the internal working of the factories, and if they do not possess the necessary powers of inquiry and defence. . . . The factory delegate is the keystone of the relations between the wage-earner and the union.[5]

Speaking before the provincial conference of Fascist trade-union leaders in Milan on June 30, 1929, Signor Begnotti, an organizer, asserted that workers' delegates in the factories "were emphatically desired by the workers." The conference moved that such delegates were necessary "in order to enable the workers' organizations to determine the scope of disputes, to negotiate with knowledge of the facts, and to fix piece rates with precision." [6]

A certain number of industrialists accepted these "representatives" in their factories. But their confederation declared itself unable to admit this new institution because it was contrary to the agreements of October 1925. The most intransigent began to discharge the "delegates" as well as those workers who were members of the local directorates and who took too seriously their function of demanding that agreements be lived up to. These "reprisal discharges" were typical examples of the "spirit of co-operation" animating the employers.[7]

Signor Fioretti, president of the Confederation of Industrial Unions, denounced these conditions in *Lavoro Fascista* on August 8, 1929, but tried to placate the industrialists by proposing that the "delegates" be called "correspondents" by way of emphasizing that their function was not to intervene between the workers and the management of the factories, but only to denounce those infringements that came to their

---

[5] *Industrial and Labour Information*, July 1, 1929, p. 29.
[6] *Idem*, July 29, 1929, p. 138.
[7] See below, page 170.

notice to the secretaries of the unions. They were intended to have "an informative, not conciliatory function"; they would furthermore have had the duty of carrying on "a healthy corporative propaganda" among the workers, of seeking to get them to join the unions, and of administering the mutual aid society of each factory. He nevertheless stated: "the unions have the right to know whether the labour agreements are carried out or not":

> This indeed is an elementary duty on their part if collective agreements are to have any real juridical content and if they are to be the expression of a corporate life. . . . The worker very often does not possess the capacity to discuss the dispute in which he is concerned; more often he feels himself intimidated before the employer. A representative of the workers possessing a certain authority in the union will have more capacity and more prestige in discussions with the employers.

"In any case," said Signor Fioretti in concluding his plea, "it matters nothing what may be the views of individuals, since the task of solving the problem is now entrusted to Mussolini. Needless to add, the decisions of the Duce will be accepted by the workers with perfect discipline and without any reservations, not even mental ones." [8] At this point Arnaldo Mussolini, the brother of the Duce, in an article appearing in the *Popolo d'Italia* on August 13, 1929, proclaimed: "The question of workers' delegates is of secondary importance; the most important problem is still that of producing the largest possible amount of wealth." On September 9, 1929 the Central Inter-Organization Committee, presided over by Mussolini himself, examined the proposal that the union officials should be authorized to name works delegates. On the motion of the general secretary of the Party and the Minister of Corporations the committee "rejected the proposal both in theory and in practice." It was, however, good enough to recognize the necessity for rendering the solutions of individual controversies more expeditious. This objective would have been attained if, in places far from the headquarters of the unions, the directorates of the employers' associations and of the employees' unions had appointed "committees of conciliation" entrusted with the task of settling individual disputes. But it was always understood that the workers chosen for these committees must not be considered as delegates of the workers: they were delegates of the directorates of the legal or-

---

[8] *Industrial and Labour Information*, Aug. 26, 1929, p. 283. See also *Corriere della Sera*, Aug. 6, 1929.

ganizations and they might not "intervene in disputes concerning undertakings in which they were interested or employed." [9] Thus the victory went to the employers, who had no intention of accepting any representation by workers in their plants. Signor Fioretti was thoroughly satisfied with this solution of the problem:

> There is no need to make a melodramatic episode of the disappearance of the delegates. No one has won and no one has lost, but we have a clear and explicit principle to follow, i. e., that we must secure complete observance of labour contracts and that we must always act in the spirit of Fascist loyalty.[10]

The "committees of conciliation" began to function in October. If the Fascist statistics are to be believed, these committees by the end of December 1929 had settled 54,775 cases, while 2089 cases were taken to the courts.[11] Of the 26,299 disputes that arose between employers and workers in agriculture in 1930, 15,744 were settled by the committees of conciliation and 4795 went to the courts, where the procedure remained as complicated and slow as before. Of these 4795 agricultural cases taken to the courts in 1930, only 1273 were settled during that year.[12]

Of the 7341 cases carried to the courts by the agricultural organizations during the first ten months of 1932, only about a third—2555—had been decided by January 1933.[13] In that month, taking all the organizations together, more than 25,000 cases brought before the judges in 1932 were still awaiting decision.[14]

---

[9] *Industrial and Labour Information*, Sept. 30, 1929, p. 450.

[10] *Ibid.*, p. 455. Wider information on this episode is to be found in Rosenstock-Franck, *L'Economie Corporative*, pp. 73, 102 ff.

[11] *Corriere della Sera*, Apr. 6, 1930.

[12] *Ibid.*, Sept. 27, 1931.

[13] *Sindacato e Corporazione*, Jan. 1933, pp. 47, 67, and Feb. 1933, p. 253. These are the official figures. What the truth may be, probably no one really knows. Mussolini, in an interview given to the correspondent of the London *Times*, Nov. 30, 1932, stated: "Since 1927, 18,633 disputes have been settled." If for the first ten months of 1932 the agricultural organizations alone had had 2555 of their cases decided by the judiciary, how is it possible that the judiciary had entered decisions in only 18,633 cases in five years for the whole mass of employers and employees? Speaking to the National Council of Corporations on Jan. 17, 1933, Signor Roberti stated that in 1932 the courts had settled 2818 cases for all the organizations (*Lavoro Fascista*, Jan. 18, 1933); this figure is in contrast with that of 2555 cases given for merely the first ten months of 1932 for the agricultural organizations alone. On the other hand, the Milanese review *L'Industria Lombarda* for Oct. 1933, stated that during the *three* years 1929–31 the courts had settled 65,304 cases, or four times the number alleged by Mussolini for five years.

[14] Rosenstock-Franck, *L'Economie Corporative*, p. 187 ff.

In a report regarding the work of the judiciary in settling disputes, the Minister of Justice stated in January 1934 that things were going "much better than one would suppose from the complaints repeatedly heard" and that "in general" the decisions of the courts were given with promptitude. But he had to admit that when it was necessary to examine witnesses, a month or two was required, and that when an appeal followed the first decision, another fifteen days were lost in some courts; in others a month or two was required, and in that at Milan, from forty-five to seventy-five days.[15] This is a far cry from the shameful democratic era, when the boards of conciliators came to decisions within a few minutes.

The Duce could not leave this scandal without a remedy. Therefore he solemnly declared on January 18, 1933, that "justice must be easy and rapid; he who asks justice must not be suffocated by too complicated a procedure, and justice must be rendered in as short a time as possible." Eleven days later the Minister of Justice requested the courts to settle the cases more rapidly.[16] But the courts were overwhelmed with an avalanche of disputes and could not perform miracles.[17] There were still, on Nov. 30, 1933, 9440 cases awaiting adjudication.[18] In August 1934 the minister again had to take cognizance of this matter: "In a great many courts the number of judges assigned to labour disputes was insufficient"; therefore the chief justices in the provinces were urged to assign a larger number of judges to this service "with the aim of speeding up the administration of justice." [19]

---

[15] *Sindacato e Corporazione,* Feb. 1934, pp. 307–8.

[16] *Ibid.,* Feb. 1933, p. 242.

[17] On March 3, 1933, the Minister of Justice stated in the Chamber of Deputies: "The number of individual disputes is great. On this head complaints have often been made concerning the length of the trials. This condition must not in all cases be attributed to the judges or to the lawyers, but in part to the mass of work, and in part to the special [?] difficulties encountered in some of the cases."

[18] *Sindacato e Corporazione,* Jan. 1934, p. 46. The President of the Supreme Court, in an article in the *Corriere della Sera,* March 17, 1934, stated that "a recent statistical work has shown how as a general rule the judges proceed with the desired speed and simplicity." The British commercial attaché in Rome, Mr. Turner, in *Economic Conditions in Italy:* July 1933, p. 173, asserts that unsettled disputes lead only "on rare occasions" to recourse to the judiciary. Commendatore Munro, in *Through Fascism to World Power,* p. 355, writes: "Any employer who tries to override the rights of an employee will *rapidly* discover that the Corporative State is not just a thing of paper."

[19] *Corriere della Sera,* Aug. 7, 1934.

XI

Professional Classes and Public Officials

THE act of April 3, 1926, provided also for the organization of the professional classes, men of letters, and artists. According to the terms of this act, there are in each province seventeen associations, corresponding to the following professions or categories of intellectual workers: solicitors and barristers; university graduates in economic and commercial studies; university graduates in the social sciences; accountants; engineers; architects; university graduates in natural and mathematical sciences; surveyors; artists; musicians; authors and writers; agricultural experts; physicians and surgeons; veterinary surgeons; chemists; midwives; journalists. The provincial associations for each profession form a national federation; and the seventeen national federations thus formed, combine in a national confederation.

Membership in these associations is, of course, not compulsory. But, in the words of the national secretary of the Federation of Physicians, "everyone can evince the minimum of sympathy towards the Fascist regime by enrolling in the association" [1]; and since one cannot practice any profession without being registered in its official register, it would require no slight amount of courage to refrain from evincing that "minimum of sympathy." A doctor cannot take a patient's pulse if the secretary of his legal association has obtained the cancellation of his name from the register because of his lack of "good moral and political behaviour."

However, not all who knock are permitted to enter the sacred precincts.

A decision of the Central Executive Board of the National Federation of the Press, March 12, 1927, divided journalists into four categories: 1, journalists already registered as members of the Fascist Party, who had given proof of their loyalty to the regime—they became *ipso facto* members of the organization; 2, journalists who did not possess the above-mentioned qualification, but were deemed to have given a satisfactory account of their previous political attitude—these might be ad-

---

[1] *La Federazione Medica*, Jan. 31, 1932, p. 90.

mitted as members; 3, journalists who had held positions of responsibility on newspapers of the opposition, or who had been guilty of offences against the Party, but who had made amends and submitted—they were denied membership, but their names were placed on a special list and they were allowed to pursue their profession, provided that they did not hold posts where they might wield political influence; 4, journalists guilty of opposition to the regime, and still unrepentant—these were denied all pardon and were completely excluded from the exercise of their profession.

On May 1, 1927, an official communiqué contained the following announcement:

> More than one hundred journalists, some of whom had great influence in Italian political life under the old regime, have been definitely excluded from the ranks of journalism. The Fascist organizations will allow none of them to resume in any way the exercise of the profession of journalism.[2]

In 1925, the Rome Press Association had 1700 members. Following the "purge" of 1927, its membership fell to 344; of these 77 were registered in special lists because "they had given proof of a faith as uncertain as the flame which is subject to every current of air."[3] There were 3330 journalists in Italy during 1924–5[4]; by December 30, 1927, their number had shrunk to 1664.[5]

The following document from Reggio-Emilia shows how the directors of the journalists' associations exercise jurisdiction over their members. Don Razzoli, a Catholic priest, had committed, among other indiscretions, the offence of writing an article in which he advised his readers to save money as a preparation for the hard winter that was approaching. The Fascist journalists at the head of the association discovered in this pious discourse on practical economics certain proofs that Don Razzoli had failed in his duty as a Fascist: he should have joined the patriotic chorus in repeating that Italy was happy and prosperous. Punishment was meted out to him in the following ruling of the committee of the local association:

> At its meeting of August 1, 1929, the committee on the tenure of the roster of journalists examined several articles in the weekly, the *Era Nuova*,

---

[2] London *Times*, May 2, 1927.
[3] Report by Signor Interlandi, chief editor of the *Tevere*, in Feb. 1927.
[4] *Annuario della Stampa Italiana*, 1925.
[5] *Corriere della Sera*, March 11, 1928.

of which Professor Don Gastone Razzoli is the responsible editor. The committee took cognizance of the pleas put forward by the defendant, but decided that they were insufficient to mitigate or extenuate his culpability. It therefore decided to strike off the name of Don Gastone Razzoli from the register.

Journalism, under the Fascist regime, has ceased to be a free profession. Journalists have become public officials controlled by the Fascist Party. Although newspapers are supposed to be the private property of their share-holders, editors succeed each other at the discretion of Mussolini, who transfers them from one paper to another as if they were public servants. The dictator announces the resignation of one newspaper editor and the appointment of his successor, before the unfortunate wretch is informed that he is superseded. The editors of the *Corriere della Sera* and the *Stampa* have been changed three times in this way.[6]

Under the old regime there was an association for barristers and another for solicitors in every province. These two organizations acted as guardians of the ethical standards of the legal profession. All lawyers, without distinction of party, could become members, and as such participate in the election of the boards of directors. After the law of April 3, 1926, had set up an association of Fascist lawyers in every province, the old associations were not disbanded but continued to exist and to include non-Fascist lawyers among their members. But a royal decree of May 6, 1926, enacted that all lawyers should take an oath that they would exercise their profession "in conformity with the superior interests of the nation," and granted to the board of directors of each new Fascist association the authority to propose to the directorate of the old non-political association of its province the cancellation from its roster of all "who had been engaged in public activities opposed to the interests

---

[6] Here is the way in which the system is described in Goad's *The Making of the Corporate State*, p. 64: "Journalists get special privileges when recognized as members of a genuine association which is careful as to the admission of new applicants." Sir Leo Chiozza-Money, in the Glasgow *Forward* of Aug. 9, 1930, held up to the admiration and envy of British journalists the fact that "no Italian journalist can be dismissed without six months' pay." Had he been less innocent about things Italian, Sir Leo would have known that before the war there already existed in Italy a collective agreement between the journalists and the managers of the papers, whereby the former were indemnified upon dismissal, not with six months' pay, but with one month's pay for every year of service. The journalists were entitled to this indemnity even if they resigned from the newspaper because of a change of its political attitude. This provision has no reason for existence today.

of the nation." This measure was supplemented by another decree, of August 26, 1926, enacting that the cancellation from the register could be motivated by "past acts, the moral consequences of which lasted into the present" (Article 26). The lawyer who had committed some anti-Fascist sin in the past, was consequently under a permanent threat of cancellation, because the directors of the Fascist association could always hold against him a past the effects of which lasted into the present. The same decree authorized the government to dissolve the directorates of the old associations and to entrust their administration to extraordinary commissioners, who were, naturally, zealous Fascists.[7]

In December 1926, the names of twenty-eight lawyers were struck off the register of the province of Rome "for having manifested aversion to the regime." [8] In June 1927, a questionnaire was sent to all lawyers in the province of Rome with a strict order to reply to all questions. The first read as follows: "Do you believe that Fascism is identical with the nation?" In the province of Alessandria, all who had been hostile to the regime up to that time were obliged to sign a declaration in which they disavowed their past and bound themselves to "co-operate to make Fascism the sacred religion of all Italians."

That year, the names of more than two thousand lawyers were struck off the lists. Signor Rocco, the Minister of Justice, in a speech to the Chamber on May 6, 1931, deplored the anti-Fascist attitude manifested by the lawyers before 1926, but declared with satisfaction that things had changed, that now "all Italian lawyers understood the spirit of Fascist legislation," and that the Fascist government "might count the lawyers among the most sincere supporters of the regime." But it is doubtful whether he believed the truth of his own statement, for until the autumn of 1933 the old non-political associations of lawyers continued to be governed by extraordinary commissioners. Finally, in November 1933, they were abolished, and the task of keeping the register and deciding upon membership or cancellations was put in the hands of the Fascist associations. A Supreme Council of the Bar, which, according to the decree of May 1926, was to have been elected by the lawyers of Italy, was never established. In its place there still functions an ex-

---

[7] F. L. Ferrari, "La Profession d'Avocat en Italie sous le Régime Fasciste," in the *Journal des Tribunaux*, Brussels, Apr. 28, 1928.
[8] *Manchester Guardian*, Dec. 24, 1926.

traordinary commission of fifteen members, appointed by the government, as usual, from among trustworthy Fascists.

The other professions are in more or less the same condition as those of the journalists and the lawyers. Here is a letter from an engineer, published in *Avanti*, September 3, 1926:

> The old National Association of Italian Engineer-Architects had about 10,000 members. About two years ago an association of Fascist engineers was formed. It did not gain a large membership. At the same time, Signor Belluzzo was elected president of the old association, his election being moved and seconded by a group of Fascist engineers. When elected, Signor Belluzzo declared the old National Association dissolved, and summoned each member to make an individual request for membership in the new Fascist association; and he enclosed the form of the request. Very few individuals signed it; but some local branches were induced to adhere in a body to the Fascist national association. Other local branches—those of Milan, Naples, etc.,—did not follow this course. The president of the Milan branch, which has 1500 members and is 400 years old, is now circulating a referendum to bring about the collective adherence of the branch to the Fascist association, warning members that in case of opposition, a royal commissioner will be sent to settle the matter. He has declared that non-voters will be reckoned as favourable to adherence to the Fascist association, which latter will take over the library, the funds, etc., of the old organization. In a few days we shall hear that the engineers of Milan are—to use the words of the president's circular—"enthusiastic supporters of the Fascist association."

Directorates, provincial and national, appointed by the procedure with which we are familiar,[9] manage the affairs of the associations, without rendering account to the members. Since the latter have no voice in the management of their associations, they naturally are indifferent to them. This lack of interest on the part of the lawyers was severely censured by Signor Rocco, Minister of Justice, in a speech to the Chamber on March 26, 1930:

---

[9] See, for instance, in the *Stampa*, May 15, 1934, the report of the annual meeting of the association of lawyers in the province of Turin. Signor Maiorino, who had until then administered the association as commissioner of the government, read a report on the activities of the organization. Then the secretary of the Fascist Party in the province "read out the list proposed by some of our comrades," containing the names of those who were to form the new directorate; the first name was that of Signor Maiorino; "the list was unanimously approved amid loud applause"; finally, the secretary of the Party delivered a speech "on the new dignity and the exalted functions which the lawyer enjoys in Mussolini's Italy."

Since I am accustomed to telling the truth, I must add that I am much dissatisfied with the lawyers' associations. In many cities, the association exists in name only; in some, it has no means of action; in others, it is not represented by the best and most prominent lawyers, who would keep up the prestige of the legal profession.

Public officials, whether national, provincial, or local, and the employees on the railways, in the postal and telegraph services, and generally in all those economic activities run by the government, the Provinces, or the municipalities, are forbidden to form unions. They may form associations only for purposes of mutual aid, education, amusement, and similar objects.[10]

These associations must be authorized by the government. The secretary general of the Fascist Party "fully represents" them, draws up their charters, appoints their national executive committees, and selects their provincial secretaries. The members of the local branches "elect" their secretaries and committees. But the reader understands that these "elections" are nothing more than acclamations given to candidates chosen by the Party leaders. The provincial secretary of the Party, or his delegate, attends the meeting at which an "election" is to take place and announces the names of the candidates; those present raise their hands, and the "election" is over. Only members of the Party may hold posts in the organization, and the provincial secretary of the Party may at any time dismiss a local secretary or committee.

The man who refuses to join the association of his group risks dismissal. Here is a circular from the secretary of the Fascist Association of Janitors of Public Buildings in Milan:

> I find that you have not yet joined our association. For the last time I summon you to join and to report to the undersigned at the City Hall before the fifteenth of this month. In case of default you will be considered an opponent of the Fascist regime and will be subjected to the measures already determined by our executive.[11]

The energies of the executive committees of these associations are

---

[10] These "authorized associations" are five in number: public officials; workers in the employ of state institutions; railwaymen; postal, telegraph, and telephone employees; educational staffs. The last mentioned is divided into five sections: elementary schools, secondary schools, university professors, instructors ("assistenti") in universities, librarians.

[11] *Avanti*, May 7, 1926.

mostly devoted to ensuring that their members participate in all demonstrations glorifying the Duce and the regime; sending to the Duce on every occasion, happy or otherwise, telegrams of submission, devotion, loyalty, love, enthusiasm, and the like; and promoting declarations of fealty and subscriptions for valuable gifts to be presented to all those Party dignitaries, high and low, whose favour the secretaries and committee members wish to curry in order to advance their own careers.

When, by a royal decree of May 7, 1927, the civil servants and officials of the local bodies lost a good share of the bonus they received to cover the high cost of living, the executive of the Public Servants' Association for the province of Milan voted the following declaration:

> The public servants, as the vanguards of the nation, accept in a lofty spirit and with conscious trustfulness the new sacrifice *which in no slight measure cuts into their already slender means of existence.* They feel certain that the new sacrifice imposed on them and on their families by higher necessities will help to conquer the resistance of the rapacious and callous groups of producers, industrialists, shopkeepers, and landlords, and induce them to adapt costs and prices to the increased purchasing power of the lira, the result of the efforts of the whole people under the unerring guidance of the Duce, in whose great heart, which beats for the greatness of Italy, every distress finds generous succour, *distress which for many families of public servants is only too truly and without hyperbole described as torment and anguish.*[12]

The words which we have put into italics represent the opinion of the membership; the others, that of the executive.

Here is a circular from the secretary of the Public Servants' Association of Milan:

> March 29, Year V (1927). From many quarters complaints reach me that some of our colleagues do not salute in the Roman fashion, and that some even make a display of their neglect to follow regulations on this point. Before denouncing individual cases to the authorities, I beg to remind all colleagues of their duty. Let me add that the salute should be made with a rapid and definite movement. Those who raise their arms in a languid manner, and only half-way, as though suffering from rheumatism, are requested to recover speedily from their infirmity, so that I shall not have to subject them to an energetic and salutary massage. By way of friendly warning I would remind those who make a point of not giving the salute in the Roman

---

[12] *Corriere della Sera*, May 8, 1927.

fashion, that there descend from above, not only rain, snow, and roast stuffed iarks, but also first-rate clouts on the head, warranted to restore memory, even in the most obstinate cases. Signed: F. Jachetti.

In October 1929 the secretary of the Party in the province of Bologna ordered all public officials and employees to pay ten lire each towards a statue of Mussolini to be erected on the athletic field at Bologna, the ten lire to be deducted from their salaries and paid over to the committee in charge. Someone pointed out to the prefect that the Party secretary did not possess the legal right to deduct from the salaries of public employees in this manner. The prefect admitted the justice of this observation, annulled the secretary's order and directed that all the employees should be invited to subscribe "freely" ten lire each for the monument. Naturally, they all hastened to subscribe "freely." And now all distinguished foreigners who go to Bologna are taken by the Fascists to admire this equestrian statue of Mussolini, erected by the "free" contributions of the citizens of Bologna as a token of their boundless affection for the Duce.

XII

The Corporations and the Charter of Labour

THE institutions which we have been describing up to this point are the "syndicalist" institutions, and not the "corporative" institutions of Fascism. The "syndicalist state" and the "corporative state" are not identical. The syndicalist state creates associations of employers and unions of employees, and endows them with authority to fix wages and other conditions of labour. The corporative state would go further. It would compel the employers' and employees' organizations to combine into higher units and would empower the latter to discuss and decide problems of production. These higher units are the corporations. They presuppose the existence of the legal organizations or syndicates of employers and employees. The syndicalist state, therefore, is a preliminary step towards the corporative state. But until the corporations have emerged, the syndicalist state is not yet a corporative state, because it confines itself to regulating the relations between capital and labour, and abstains from those other forms of intervention in economic life which are the distinctive marks of the corporative state.

The characteristic features of the corporative state were outlined in an article, "Crisi dello Stato e Sindacato," published by Signor Rocco in the review *Politica* of December 1920:

The workers' unions and the employers' associations should be unified, trade by trade, into one mixed syndicate. This syndicate should be organized in two, nay, rather in three, sections, because it would be advisable to give collective representation to the administrative personnel; i. e. to engineers, experts, and superintendents. The mixed syndicate should be managed by an executive council with a view to achieve the common aims of its members.

The "mixed syndicate," or "corporation," would also be empowered to take over the management of economic enterprises and "to act as a friendly arbiter or conciliator in disputes arising among its members." [1]

Only a vague reference to the "corporation" as Rocco had delineated

---

[1] Schneider, *Making the Fascist State*, p. 150; Rosenstock-Franck, *L'Economie Corporative*, p. 16 ff.

it in 1920 crept into the law of April 1926. This occurred in Article 3, which enacted that "central co-ordinating organs," with an upper hierarchy in common, *might* be created between the organizations of employers and employees. That law created the syndicalist state—syndicalist after the manner of Mussolini, and not after the manner of Georges Sorel—and not the corporative state.

The regulation of July 1, 1926 gave the name "corporations" to the "co-ordinating organs" which the law had mentioned, and assigned them the following tasks:

1. To conciliate differences which might arise between the organizations of employers and employees
2. To encourage and support attempts to improve the organizations production
3. To found labour exchanges wherever they were needed.
4. To regulate apprenticeship

But not even then was it made clear how the staffs of the "corporations" were to be composed and by whom they were to be appointed or elected. It was merely made known that they were to be "organs of public administration" and that "any clause in existing labour agreements which clashed with the rules established by the corporations, would be annulled." [2]

On July 2, 1926, the Ministry of Corporations was created. A Ministry of Labour in Italy had been set up in 1920. The Fascist government abolished it on April 27, 1923, and set it up again in 1926 under the new name. But this so-called Ministry of Corporations had no corporations either above it, or beside it, or below it.

At the end of 1926, Mussolini began to apply the term "corporative state" to that form of social organization which was destined to supersede the democratic state. But the exact nature of the corporations remained a mystery.

At last dawned April 21, A. D. 1927. On that day the Grand Council of Fascism, assembled in solemn session at Rome, promulgated the Charter of Labour, or the "Declaration of the Rights and Duties of the Producer," which, no doubt, will eventually relegate to oblivion the Declaration of the Rights of Man and of the Citizen promulgated by the French Revolution.

---

[2] G. Bottai, *Il Consiglio Nazionale delle Corporazioni*, pp. 5 ff. Schneider, *Making the Fascist State*, pp. 180–94.

The Charter of Labour [writes a Fascist "thinker"] contains Mussolini's economic philosophy, is the keystone of his political system, and gives the substance of the Mussolinian Revolution.[3]

The "corporations," and the "corporative organs" were mentioned in Articles 6, 10, 12, 23, and 25 of the epoch-making document:

The corporations are the unifying organs of the factors of production and represent the interests of the latter as a whole. In virtue of this joint representation, and since the interests of production are national interests, the corporations are recognized by law as organs of the state. As representative of the unified interests of production, the corporations may issue rules which are binding on capital and labour and rules which aim to co-ordinate production, on condition that they are empowered to do so by the legal organizations which they unite. In labour disputes there can be no recourse to the Labour Court until the corporative organ has exhausted its efforts for conciliation. Labour exchanges are controlled by the corporative organs of the state. The state, working through the corporative organs, will strive to co-ordinate and unify the insurance institutes. The corporative organs supervise the observance of the laws governing accident prevention and safety of labour.

Of what persons were the corporations and the corporative organs to be composed? The mystery on this point remained impenetrable. To make up for the obscurity, Article 1 of the document announced that "the Italian nation is an organism possessing a purpose, a life, and instruments of action superior to those of the individuals or groups of individuals composing it; the nation is a moral, political, and economic unity embodied in the Fascist state." Thus was settled for all time the knotty controversy which raged among philosophers and sociologists about the organic or non-organic nature of society; society, nation, and state became interchangeable terms.

Article 2 revealed that "labour was a social duty." St. Paul also, in his day, said that he who does not work should not eat. Unfortunately, his moral precept was not buttressed by any legal sanction. That is why it has given solace to many noble souls during the last nineteen hundred years, but has never forced a millionaire's son to put brawn or brain to work. Article 2 of the Charter has likewise not yet compelled any Roman princess to engage in harder occupations than bridge-playing or fox-hunting. Nor have the Italian unemployed been able to fulfil, as they would have been glad to do, the "social duty" of working. The

---

[3] Orano, *Mussolini da vicino*, p. 134.

Fascist principle that labour is a social duty remains up in the air—like angels and sparrows.

Article 3 set forth that "organization by trades and professions was free, but only the organizations recognized by the state and subject to state control were empowered legally to represent the whole category of employers and employees for which they had been formed, to protect the interests of the category in its relations with the state and other organizations, and to negotiate collective labour agreements binding upon all those belonging to the category." Thus, freedom of organization was granted in the first six words, but immediately thereafter the organizations to which freedom was granted, were divided into two classes: those to which the state, i. e. the Fascist Party, gave its own protection, investing them with a monopoly of those functions which made organizations worthwhile to employers and employees; and those which would be as useful to them economically as a Bible class or a dancing club. Moreover, one who was cognizant of existing Fascist legislation knew that employers, employees, and professional classes could not form any organization unless authorized to do so by the party in power; in other words, they were not free to organize at all, if by freedom to organize we mean what all persons of good sense and in good faith mean, namely, the right to form associations that are not controlled by the party in power.

A clause in Article 3 said: "Wages cannot be fixed by any general rule, but the task of negotiating and fixing them is entrusted to the interested parties." Here was something that approached a well-defined legal principle; that is, the prohibition of general rules. But in May and October 1927, in November 1930, and in the spring of 1934, general rules caused wages to be reduced (see below, pp. 189, 194, 204).

Article 4 declared that the "collective labour agreement gives concrete expression to the principle of solidarity by reconciling conflicting interests between employers and employees and subordinating them to the higher interests of production"; Article 5 explained that the "Labour Court intervenes in order to settle labour disputes"; Article 6 assigned to the legal organizations the task of "enforcing legal equality between employers and workers"; and Article 12 asserted that the action of the legal organizations and the pronouncements of the labour courts "gave assurance that wages would be in proportion to a normal standard of living, to the capacity to pay of the productive machinery, and to the output of labour." No sensible person can deny the interests of production, because a decline in a given branch of production has an adverse effect not only upon the employers and employees of that particular branch, but upon the consumers, or community at large, as well. Similarly, no sensible person will dispute the principle that wages should be determined with reference not merely to the workers' standard of living but also to the output of labour. But how can one know whether increased wages threaten the higher interests of production; whether a wage cut endangers the standard of decent living to which every human being is entitled; and whether the output of labour is such as to render increased wages possible or reduced wages inevitable? On these points the employer's answer will probably be quite different from the employee's. Who is to decide between them? Signor Bottai, in the *Corriere della Sera* of April 23, 1927, stated that "thanks to the Charter of Labour, there are no limits, either maximum *or minimum*, to the material and moral well-being of the individual."

Article 9 proclaimed that "the state intervenes in economic production only in cases where private initiative is lacking or where the political interests of the state are involved." The most fanatical believer in *laissez-faire* would not deny this proposition: he would simply take the cases one by one, and maintain that in each of them private initiative is sufficient, and that in none of them are the political interests of the state involved. And vice versa, a Communist would avail himself of the same proposition in order to place the entire economic life of the nation under government control, proving that private initiative is never sufficient and that the interests of the community always demand the abolition of private ownership. Fortunately for private ownership, Article 7 stated that Fascism "regards private initiative in the field of production as the most useful and efficient instrument for furthering the interests of the nation." Those who went too far in asking for state intervention would be faced with this provision.

The same article proclaimed that the manager of a private enterprise "is responsible to the state for his management of production," and what is more, that the employee "is an active partner in the economic enterprise." But these were simple moral principles analogous to the principle that "work is a social duty." The employee who really wanted to become "an active partner in the economic enterprise" would learn from the text immediately following in Article 7 that "the management of the enterprise belongs to the employer who shoulders the responsibility for it."

A series of articles stated that "the employee is entitled to a holiday falling on Sunday," that "after a year of uninterrupted service in an enterprise the employee is entitled to a vacation every year with wages," that the "employee is entitled, in case of discharge through no fault of his own, to compensation based on his years of service"; and that the Fascist state "intends to improve the laws on accident insurance, maternity insurance, and involuntary unemployment insurance, and to adopt insurance against industrial diseases and tuberculosis, general insurance against sickness, and special forms of insurance for young workers." In the second part of this book the reader will be informed about pre-Fascist social legislation. He will conclude, we are sure, that Fascism did not need to startle mankind with its "Declaration of the Rights and Duties of the Producer" in order to reach its achievements.

In conclusion, the Charter of Labour is merely a collection of abstract principles, equivocal propositions, laudable intentions, and meaningless words. Signor Ciccotti, speaking in the Senate on March 14, 1930, said:

> The Charter of Labour consists of thirty aphorisms, which I hope may be translated as soon as possible into acts, but which for the present are merely thirty aphorisms.

Monsieur Rosenstock-Franck, to whom we are indebted for the best study on the Charter, has called attention to the fact that the Charter of Labour was promulgated in April 1927; i. e., when the economic crisis caused by the revaluation of the lira was most acute, and on the eve of the "voluntary" wage reduction of May 1927 (see below, pp. 185–6). Mussolini, Monsieur Rosenstock-Franck argues, had to give Italian business men a compensation for their losses resulting from the revaluation of the currency. That compensation took the form of a ruthless reduction in wages. At the same time he had to give the workers some compensation for the cuts in their wages, and this recompense consisted of the aphorisms of the "Declaration of the Rights and Duties of the Producer." [4] In other words, he resorted to the magician's vanishing trick. He diverted their attention from hard economic realities by dangling before them the iridescent bauble of the Charter of Labour.

---

[4] *L'Economie Corporative,* pp. 65–77, 116–7, 399–400.

XIII

Looking in a Dark Room for a Black Cat Which Is Not There

O N June 1, 1927, Signor Bottai, at that time under-secretary at the Ministry of Corporations, declared in a speech to the Chamber of Deputies that "he believed that in the present state of theory and practice, no jurist was yet in a position to give an exact definition of the nature of the corporation." And in January 1928, he had to admit that "in the preceding year, the corporation had not yet emerged as an institution"; but "the conception underlying it had been fully illuminated, and this was more valuable than hasty experimentation would have been." [1]

In the volume, *Civiltà Fascista*, issued at the beginning of 1928 and containing contributions from all the luminaries of the Fascist intelligentsia, Professor Volpe announced that the promised land was not far off:

> The corporations are on the way. . . . The corporative state is on the horizon. At the present moment, all this is an ideal or a hope rather than a reality. But the government has been considering the enormous consequences that such a new economic order will have, particularly in the realm of Italian agriculture. Through the action of the legal organizations and the corporations, capital and labour will be placed upon a footing of greater equality in all fields, and an equal right to control the national economic system will be granted to all social classes. [2]

But Mussolini, in a speech of May 7, 1928, warned the impatient that "the syndical phase would not be of short duration."

In 1929, Miss Haider, went to Italy for the discovery of the "corporative" state. She had to admit that "at present the Italian state was still in the syndicate phase," i. e., in the phase in which there were only separate organizations for employers and employees without any higher co-ordinating organs. But she was so polite as to be convinced that "even if the corporations did not yet exist, the establishment of the Ministry of

---

[1] Bottai, *Il Consiglio Nazionale delle Corporazioni*, p. 8.
[2] *Civiltà Fascista*, p. 28.

Corporations was a gesture demonstrating the intention of Fascism to develop in that direction." [3]

At the end of 1929 "the corporative system had not yet gone beyond the syndical stage," as Signor Bottai admitted in a speech of January 21, 1932.[4] And Senator Ciccotti, in the Senate on March 14, 1930, pointing out that no corporation had yet been born, said: "The corporative system indeed is corporative as *lucus a non lucendo.*"

In a lecture delivered at Basle on October 12, 1927, Signor Bottai admitted that the corporative system was still "in germ" and "the corporations had not yet been set up," but announced that "their establishment was to take place in the near future":

> The corporative state will be brought to life with extreme care, attention, and delicacy, so as to avoid the danger that the state by its intervention might overstep the line beyond which the economic development of the country might suffer, and private initiative, instead of being co-ordinated and strengthened, might be harmed and depressed.

Wonderful, however, is the power of words, provided that they are continually repeated and, in addition, are devoid of a clearly defined content. Humanity lives on obscure myths more than on bread.

Major Barnes, in his book *The Universal Aspects of Fascism*, released at the end of 1927 with a preface by Mussolini that gave it an official stamp, spoke of the "new corporative organization" as if it already existed: the corporations "grouped together" the organizations of employers and employees and "co-ordinated the whole system" (pp. 209, 212); they were there, within reach, alive, and flourishing. A person desirous of more detailed information could have found it, still with the aid of Major Barnes, on p. 93 of the volume *A Survey of Fascism*, published in 1928:

> The associations of employers and associations of workers engaged in the same industry *are* grouped together to form a Corporation. Its duties *include* the supervision of its associations to the end that they answer the requirement of the law and fulfil their duties according to the law; the establishment and the keeping of statistics of the employed and the unemployed; the co-ordination, encouragement and subsidizing of the welfare work of the associations and the conciliation by means of their good offices, when charged with the task by the parties concerned, of any labour dispute.

---

[3] *Capital and Labor under Fascism*, pp. 96, 143, 145.
[4] *Industrial and Labour Information*, Feb. 8, 1932, p. 134.

In March 1928 an American philosopher, Professor Schneider of Columbia University, admitted that the Fascist corporations did not yet exist and that the confederations of employers and employees were "not Corporations at all, but the very antithesis of Corporations." Impelled, however, by an enthusiasm perhaps exaggerated, he applied himself to imagining what the corporative state would be like if the corporations did exist:

> I shall attempt to sketch the outlines of the Corporate State of Italy much as Plato sketched his perfect city, leaving aside the question of whether or not such a State is either actual or possible. After all we live in this world of imagination more than we realize. The Fascists must be understood not merely by what they *are* doing, but by what they *think* they are about to do.

Turning thus "to the imaginative and theoretical side of the question, where fancy runs free and no one can be accused of either truth or falsity," he announced that although "the actual and practical transformation of Italian economic organization was at present not very conspicuous . . . it was quite possible that when the dust and storm of political strife in Italy should have passed away, the most conspicuous permanent aspect of the revolution would turn out to be the transformation of Syndicalism into Corporationism." [5] In addition, Professor Schneider revealed in his book, *Making the Fascist State*, pp. 212–3, that "the establishment of the Corporate State" would create a kind of reconciliation between the Hegelian and Marxian philosophies:

> For, now that Fascism is taking this positive direction, many who formerly saw in it nothing but the devil incarnate are beginning to understand the mysterious ways of Providence. And it is possible that before long both Hegelian and Marxian philosophers will discover that syndicalism is the middle term by which Socialism and Fascism have been joined in higher dialectic unity. Already certain Socialists are revising their philosophy. . . . Perhaps, they are suggesting, Fascism is but Socialism's logical antithesis, which is soon to be resolved into the higher state in which both will be reconciled.

Another philosopher, Friedrich Paulsen, has written that the absurd has this advantage in common with truth: that it cannot be refuted.

Monsieur Alliaud, admirer of Fascist institutions and contributor to

---

[5] Schneider, *Italy Incorporated*, pp. 3, 11, 12.

Fascist reviews in Italy, devoted himself to a more positive task, in an article to which the complaisant International Labour Office in May 1928 afforded the hospitality of its *International Labour Review*. Yes, it was true, he admitted, that "no Corporation had so far been constituted," but the Corporation "existed virtually and in principle," and this was the important thing. Moreover, if the corporations themselves did not exist, there did already exist "corporative functions," and "pending the wide diffusion of a corporative consciousness," they were exercised, not by the Corporations yet unborn, but by other organs. For example, when labour agreements were negotiated by the officials of the organizations concerned, this was a "syndical" function; but when they were negotiated under the mediation of the secretary-general of the Party, this mediation was the "corporative" function. The labour court was not a corporation, but it fulfilled a corporative function. The Ministry of Corporations fulfilled a corporative function.

When there is introduced, as umpire between particular interests, a third element which is superior to the other elements and represents the national interest, it may be said that we are already on the "corporate" plane.

Italy was full of "corporative function" before she possessed a single corporation.[6] Having undertaken the mission of finding in a dark room a black cat that was not there, Monsieur Alliaud gave the name of cat to every object that was there.

Mr. McClure Smith furnished the following information to the readers of the *English Review* of July 1928, pp. 58–9:

The economic organization *does not end* with the vertically built up hierarchy which we have been considering. Outside of this *are* the great national guilds, which *are* built up horizontally by combining all the various associations, whether of employers, employees, or professional men, which *are* concerned with any given industry; they thus *serve* as a bond of union between the various classes which *are* separated for the purposes of the associations. These guilds *supervise* the general condition of the industry, its organizations, its technical advancement, and its internal peace. They act as arbitrators before the machinery of the labour courts *is* brought into action.

In that same year, Mr. Edward Corsi, while visiting Italy at the request of the Italian government and making a complete survey of the country, was deeply impressed by Italian corporations:

---

[6] Cf. Miceli, *Manuale di Norme Corporative*, p. 160.

What the Fascist syndicalists are trying to do is to create an economic order in Italy with corporations, or guilds, of employers and employees, which shall be self-governing with respect to production, but wholly subservient to the state politically. These guilds, *which now regulate wages, hours of employment, and conditions of labour,* will ultimately control production, as the Soviets control production in Russia. In other words Fascism is contemplating a Syndicalist state run by a powerful nationalist Government, in which capital, if it survives, will be assigned the role of a co-worker (New York *World*, Oct. 28, 1928).

It is not to be wondered at, therefore, if in the fourteenth (1929) edition of the *Encyclopædia Britannica*, vol. IX, pp. 105–6, Mrs. O. Rossetti Agresti stated that "the guild [corporation] feature of the system was developing under the direct control of the Ministry of Guilds":

National Guilds, affording equal representation to employers and employees, under a chairman appointed by the Minister, *are* formed for the several branches of productive and business activity. Their duties *are* to study the organization and development of the industries they represent with a view to securing greater co-ordination and simplification so as to reduce the production costs and intensify the output. The scientific organization of production is as much an interest of the workers as of the employers, and the guilds *afford* them an opportunity of expressing their views and recording their vote *on a footing of full equality.* They may be described as permanent deliberative and advisory bodies, on a representative [!] basis, in direct touch with the government, appointed for the study of all phenomena affecting the prosperity of an industry. The guilds also *act* as boards of conciliation in trade disputes before they are referred to the Labour Courts; they *organize* employment bureaus under the joint control of employers and workers, and *regulate* the condition of vocational training and apprenticeship.

In 1930 a Magyar Fascist, Herr Kemechey, in a book on which Signor Bottai collaborated (this fact deserves to be recorded) gave the following information concerning the still unborn corporations:

The co-operation of the different social classes *has found* its expression in the corporation. The corporations *are* higher bodies connecting the various factors of production. The different syndicates [legal organizations] of employers and workers *have to select equal numbers of representatives,* and these representatives *form* together the corporations at the head of which *is* a representative of the state itself. There *are* six great corporations, which correspond to the six chief groups of production and their twelve confederations.

The corporations *are* but at the very beginning of their development. *Their constitution has not yet been completely* worked out, but their aim has been defined.[7]

A new literary genre was thus invented by Fascist "thinkers"—the corporative fairy-tale.[8]

---

[7] Kemechey, *Il Duce,* pp. 13, 254–7.

[8] Since we have so many times cited the mis-statements of Signor Villari, we feel it our duty to recognize that on this point at least he happened, in 1929, to write the truth: "The Fascist programme provides for the formation of the corporations, six in number. As yet these bodies have not been constituted" (*Italy,* p. 227). The compilers of the July 1934 issue of *Fortune,* p. 57, admit that for a long time the corporative state has existed solely in the imagination; but urge the reader to take into account the fact that "the Italian does not share the Anglo-Saxon's firm distinction between the present and the future tense. In Italy, when a road is about to be built, you may be told that it has been built. No lies intended." Also the author of the report on *The Economic and Financial Position of Italy,* p. 4, thinks that Italians have the habit "illogical to the English mind, of passing law which refers, as if existing, to machinery which, though designed on paper, is in fact only to be set in motion later on." If these words referred solely to Italian Fascists and their non-Italian, including Anglo-Saxon, friends, they might be received without protest. But why attribute this wealth of imagination to Italians only and to all Italians?

The National Council of Corporations

Iₙ the early months of 1930 the corporations had been so magnified both in Italy and abroad that it had finally become imperative to give tangible proof of their existence.

By the act of March 20, 1930, therefore, the National Council of Corporations came into the world. On the eve of its inauguration it was hailed as the beginning of a new era of social peace and justice; [1] and in a speech delivered at its opening session Mussolini compared its role in the corporative state to that of the general staff in the army: "the thinking brain which prepares and co-ordinates."

The council is made up of ten ministers and under-secretaries, about forty high officials of the government, of the Party, and of the national associations controlled by the Party, ten "experts" chosen by the Minister of Corporations, and about a hundred members designated by the national directorates of the thirteen confederations according to Fascist procedure: i. e., the president chooses and announces the names and the directorate agrees.[2] Mussolini ratifies the nominations, presides over the council, is entitled to modify its composition, draws up and may at any moment change its docket. The councillors, like all public officials, must be members of the Party, and as such are subject to its military discipline. No document may be considered by the members of the council without preliminary authorization from the head of the government. Mussolini determines the method of voting, case by case. A committee appointed by Mussolini prepares the agenda for each meeting. The proceedings of the council are not reported to the press unless Mussolini so desires. If the advice of the council displeases him, he disregards it; if its discussions disturb him, he does not convoke it. These are not infringements of the law, for the law places the proceedings and the convocation of

---

[1] Article by the president of the Confederation of Commercial Unions, in the *Corriere della Sera*, Apr, 20, 1930.

[2] Professor Welk, in *Fascist Economic Policy*, p. 106, states that the council is "constituted not by a government bureaucracy, but by the *direct* representatives of all the major productive forces existing within the nation."

the council under the control of the head of the government.[3] Mussolini is merely exercising his constitutional powers.

Only the head of the government [affirms Signor Bottai] is able to see the national life as a whole. Only he can co-ordinate the forces of production, allot to individuals and groups their respective tasks, balance conflicting demands, and assure justice to all social classes. He alone can estimate all the possible effects that a given measure may have on production in general.[4]

In the preliminary discussions, that group of Fascists who awaited the corporative state with the same eagerness with which the Hebrews awaited the Messiah, asked that the council should be invested with legislative powers in economic matters. Article 12 of the law of March 20, 1930, seemed to grant their demands. It conceded to the council authority to "formulate rules governing the reciprocal relations of the various productive groups"; for example, between steel manufacturers and ship-owners, between silkworm growers and silk weavers, between beet-root producers and sugar dealers, etc. But after establishing this principle, it proceeded to annul it by decreeing that the council could not exercise this power unless the directorates of both employers and employees in the concerned trades authorized it to do so; in other words, it granted to the employers' directorates a right of liberum veto against any proposal which endangered private initiative. Moreover, the directorates concerned might not authorize the council to formulate such a rule unless they themselves had been authorized by the head of the government to grant such authorization!

The functions of the council were baptized "pre-legislative functions." Mussolini affirmed in the inaugural speech of April 21, 1930, that "in Article 12 was the complete corporation as the Fascist state understood it," and that, thanks to that article, the law "deserved to be called revolutionary." And, of course, everybody was satisfied.

The Council of Corporations included a Central Corporative Committee composed of those ministers and under-secretaries who were members of the council, of the secretary-general of the Party, and the presidents of the confederations. In the interval between the meetings of the general assembly, the committee exercised all the functions of the council—in other words, it merely made suggestions.

---

[3] Bottai, *Il Consiglio Nazionale delle Corporazioni*, pp. 346–62, 405–14; Rosenstock-Franck, pp. 303 ff.

[4] Bottai, *Il Consiglio Nazionale*, p. 42.

On January 27, 1931, the National Council of Corporations was divided into seven sections charged with the special problems of agriculture, industry, commerce, maritime transport, land transport, credit and insurance, and the professions. These sections were called "corporations" of agriculture, industry, commerce, etc. Naturally, their authority was not superior to that of the plenary council and central committee.

The activity of the Fascist Council of Corporations, its committee, and its sections, has consisted in the giving of advisory opinions on the subjects with which all labour councils are occupied, and on the minute bureaucratic questions which cannot fail to multiply under a regime in which all classes are obliged to organize according to rules laid down by the government, and in which the officials of the organizations cannot move a step without the previous authorization of the government.

There was a Labour Council in Italy from 1902 to 1923, which had only consultative powers and did not contain elected representatives of the classes concerned. In 1920, when the Ministry of Labour was set up, the government recognized the need of reforming the Labour Council, and a bill prepared in the autumn of that year provided that the council should be empowered to issue legislative rules regulating the economic and social life of the country and should consist of an equal number of representatives of the employers and of the employees, elected from each occupational group by proportional representation.[5] The Fascist government in 1923 abolished the pre-Fascist Council.

A comparative study of the Council of Corporations, the pre-Fascist Labour Council, and similar councils in other European countries during the post-war period reveals that the Fascist council is but an inefficient and insignificant bureaucratic machine. It is true that no country has a labour council invested with legislative powers. The labour councils give advisory opinions, they do not make laws; and their advisory opinions acquire the force of law only when they are accepted by parliament. But in democratic countries such consultative organs, when supported by influential social groups, may exercise moral pressure on the government, if only because their proposals and discussions are reported in the press. The Fascist Council of Corporations cannot even make its ideas known to the public against Mussolini's wishes.

When the advice of the "thinking brain" of the corporative state does

---

[5] I.L.O., *The Reform of the Supreme Council of Labour in Italy.* Labriola, *Le Due Politiche*, p. 313.

not suit the employers, this advice falls on deaf ears. On two occasions, in June 1932 and in January 1933, the "thinking brain" ruled that after a labour agreement had been cancelled, it was to remain in force until a new agreement had been concluded. Both pronouncements remained a dead letter (see below, pp. 218–9). On October 31, 1931, the "thinking brain" ruled that no cut in wages should take place unless it was justified by a decline in the productivity of the work, by the conditions of the market, and by the needs of the enterprise. A rule of this sort should have entitled the officials of the unions to receive in each case from the employers the indispensable information on which to base an enlightened decision. For this result, a "corporative" state was not necessary. A mere "syndicalist" state would have sufficed. But the employers were uncompromisingly opposed to any claim on the part of the union officials to investigate their private affairs. Signor Clavenzani, President of the Confederation of Industrial Unions, made a speech in the Chamber on May 23, 1933, in which he mournfully asked the government to remedy this injustice:

> It ought to be possible for us to ascertain all the elements, such as productivity, time, technical equipment, which enter into the determination of wages. In this way we should be able to avoid the danger of giving to him who does not need it, and of not giving to him who does. These entreaties express the keenest desire of all the labour leaders.

Some days later in the *Lavoro Fascista* of June 2, 1933, the same Signor Clavenzani made a similar complaint:

> The unions continue to receive requests for a lightening of the wage burden. But the employers do not make it possible for them to examine all the elements of time, productivity and technical equipment, a knowledge of which is necessary to an exact appraisal of the requests themselves. It is necessary that the union of the workers shall also be constantly in possession of all the elements of evaluation. This is desirable in order to avoid granting reductions to employers who could do without them, and withholding them from those who really need them.[6] Nobody took notice of this complaint and its author did not complain any longer.

---

[6] In a speech at Basle in Oct. 1927, Signor Bottai affirmed that "for the old disputes concerning wages between employers and employees were being substituted more complex questions, in which the pure and simple economic demand [he meant discussion of wages] was being succeeded by a broader and more complete investigation of the conditions of production, the methods used by the company, the productivity of labour, the possibilities of expansion and exportation, in short, all phases of the problem of

All the legislative measures with which the government has sought to face economic crises were decided upon by the political organs of the dictatorship: the Grand Council, the Council of Ministers, the National Directorate of the Party, and, in the last analysis, by Mussolini and his private advisers. Only once, in November 1931, was the council asked to express an opinion on a question of vital importance—the problem of exports and imports. The council discussed this subject with great solemnity. Naturally, there was a clash between the free trade group and the protectionist group. Mussolini ended the discussion by declaring himself to be in favour of the protectionist regime—on condition that it did not encourage idleness. *This discussion took place two months after a royal decree of September 24, 1931, had imposed a duty of 15 per cent ad valorem on all imported commodities.* The discussion, therefore, could not have had any practical importance whatsoever. It was merely one of Mussolini's little jests.[7] Not once in the course of its existence has the council ever found that the situation called for the proposing of a rule to regulate the relations of the different productive groups. Moreover, during 1934 and 1935 the council did not hold a single meeting. Thus the "thinking brain" of the regime stopped thinking.[8]

After the establishment of the National Council of Corporations, in 1930, the enthusiasm of the Fascist propaganda agents knew no bounds.

That the National Council of Corporations has had solely an advisory function has been so evident that even the strongly pro-Fascist Rome correspondent of the *New York Times*, on November 19, 1933, wrote as follows:

Hitherto the National Council of Corporations has had no legislative powers, its functions being advisory. Its transformation into the principal legislative body will represent a great step toward the realization of the corporate state, which has always been among the Fascists' aspirations.

---

production"; and that "to these inquiries and discussions both the associations of the employers and the unions of the employees were bringing their contribution, almost always amicable, although at the same time very much in earnest" (*Civiltà Fascista*, p. 389).

[7] Monsieur Rosenstock-Franck, pp. 312 ff., has made a systematic analysis of the work of the council and its sections.

[8] The Report of the Royal Institute of International Affairs, *The Economic and Financial Situation of Italy*, p. 8, affirms that the National Council of Corporations "meets periodically." Its author did not find from any Fascist source the information that in 1934 and 1935 the council had never met.

Miss Haider also, in *Do We Want Fascism?*, p. 27, has seen clearly that "such deliberations as the council undertook affected only minor issues; all major decisions in the Italian Fascist state are made by the Fascist Grand Council." The legal organizations are only "a machine for handing down and enforcing decisions made by the government." On this point at least, therefore, there should have been no possible difference of opinion.

Yet Major Barnes, in *Fascism*, p. 180, stated that the Council of Corporations acted "as a kind of social, technical, and economic parliament"; "this Central Council *has quasi-legislative powers* within the limits set by the legislative measures passed by parliament."

Sir Charles Petrie in *Mussolini*, p. 137, found those *quasi-legislative* powers not to his liking, and stated definitely that the "Corporative Council has legislative powers within the limits laid down by parliament."

Neither Major Barnes nor Sir Charles Petrie felt obliged to explain that the limits laid down by parliament consisted in the preliminary consent of all the interested parties and of the head of the government, together with the final sanction of the head of the government. That is, the legislative powers of the council did not exist.

Professor Welk, in *Fascist Economic Policy*, p. 106, writes that the National Council of Corporations "is empowered by law to issue direct rules for the regulation and co-ordination of the economic activities of the nation according to plans and programs which the Council may work out and approve."

Signor Biagi, the under-secretary at the Ministry of Corporations, was so bold as to declare, in a lecture delivered on July 12, 1933, in an international convention at Rome, that "the National Council of Corporations, *by reason of its legislative power* in the field of labour problems and of economic relationship, is clearly distinguished from all the economic councils in other countries, which are nothing but *purely consultative organs* attached to the public administrations *for whose service they are constituted.*" At the end of the lecture, Dr. Fenigstein, a Swiss professor, "cordially thanked Signor Biagi, in the name of all the foreign members of the congress, for the clearness with which he had illustrated the great achievements of the corporative idea accomplished by the Fascist regime" (*Corriere della Sera,* July 16, 1933).

In an article published in the *Tribuna* of September 23, 1933, Signor Maraviglia affirmed that the Council of Corporations "has a positively revolutionary importance," because "it does not have merely consulta-tive functions, but fulfils functions that are really of an administrative nature." In a later part of the article he forgot his previous statement, and complained that Article 12 of the law of 1930, by giving to the council no other authority than that of offering "mere suggestions," "encompasses the exercise of the regulatory power with such reserves as practically to nullify it."

XV

Towards Social Revolution

O N December 6, 1930, the government established a "Corporation of the Stage," entrusting it with the task of "studying the problems of the stage, of the films, and of related industries." This corporation differed from the seven sections of the National Council of Corporations in that its competence extended to only one of the many branches of Italian industry, while each section of the council covered a major division of the economic life of the nation: industry, agriculture, commerce, transport, etc. The corporative state, then, was to have corporations of category distinct from the sections of the council. The first in order of time, the corporation of the stage, was a purely consultative body, consisting of twenty-six members designated by the national directorates of the organizations of employers and employees engaged in the theatrical business, and of five high officials of the government.[1] After the establishment of this new organ, the legitimate stage in Italy as in other countries continued to decline on account of the rivalry of the cinema; the films produced in Italy were neither better nor worse than before; a trust composed of theatrical companies, which the corporation promoted, was so inefficient that within less than a year after its formation, it had to be dissolved; and the activity of the corporation eventually consisted in asking the government to subsidize various companies and in promoting the foundation of a labour exchange for stage and film actors.[2]

In the session of the Senate on May 31, 1931, Signor Ciccotti observed that "the nature of the corporations did not stand out very clearly." Signor Bottai majestically replied in the name of the government:

The hour of the corporation will strike when our social experiment has attained its meridian, and the national consciousness has become mature.[3]

---

[1] Bottai, *Il Consiglio Nazionale*, pp. 370 ff.

[2] Pitigliani, *The Italian Corporative State*, p. 111. *Sindacato e Corporazione*, July-Aug. 1933, p. 4. On Feb. 24, 1932, Bottai praised the "exemplary activity" of the Corporation of the Stage; "it has given the public an idea of what similar organs could accomplish in the way of concrete achievements."

[3] *Il Consiglio Nazionale*, p. 15.

But, as Miss Haider would say, the Corporation of the Stage, like the Ministry of Corporations, proved that Fascism was developing in the direction of the corporative state. Moreover, on June 18, 1931, the provincial economic councils were rechristened "provincial corporative councils" or "provincial corporations"; on December 28, 1931, the Inspectorate of Labour, which had been in existence since 1912, received the name of "Corporative Inspectorate"; and in January 1933 the *Bollettino del Lavoro e della Previdenza*, which had been published periodically for thirty years, changed its title to *Sindacato e Corporazione*. Do you wish to build a corporative state? Nothing is easier. Merely bestow the adjective "corporative" on the existing institutions of your state, and the corporative state is an accomplished fact.

On February 24, 1932, in a speech before the Chamber, Deputy Lusignoli observed sorrowfully:

We are still getting ready for the corporative state. The minister, indeed, has told us several times that we were rapidly nearing the corporative state. But we cannot say that we have quite reached it.

The minister in question, Signor Bottai, in the same session spoke at length of the resistance opposed by certain "categories of production" to a "harmonious corporative construction":

The resistance comes from certain groups which either retain the individualistic and monopolistic mentality, or else wish to remain quietly as they are. There are some shortsighted producers who for years have been practising an economic policy revolving upon exactly two hinges: lower wages and a protective tariff.

After being liberated by the act of April 3, 1926, from the "incubus of the strike," these producers "were claiming autonomy for themselves, *so that in many cases the class struggle had been succeeded by the struggle of the categories"*: "all this was the antithesis of the corporative spirit."

Another Fascist deputy, Signor Angelini, said in the Chamber on March 8, 1932:

Today a real corporation of agriculture does not exist; there is merely a sort of committee that meets two or three times a year to discuss various problems.

The tourists in Italy who turned from the art museums to the quest of the corporations were somewhat bewildered to learn that the National Council of Corporations had under it only one corporation, the Corporation of the Stage. A corporative state with only one corporation—and that of the stage in addition!—would soon become ridiculous.[4] The corporative magician once more had to intervene.

The first indication that a momentous event in the history of the human race was about to take place manifested itself on October 16, 1932, when Mussolini took up the problem of whether there was any hope that the world would ever emerge from the depression into which it had plunged in the autumn of 1929, following the American crash.

> Those who are seeking miraculous remedies for the depression are mistaken. Either the present depression is a periodical depression within the system, in which case it will be overcome, or it is a crisis of the system itself, in which case it represents a transition from one stage of civilization to another.

On May 16 the great coming event cast a second shadow before. Mussolini, speaking before the Central Corporative Committee (see above, p. 103) ruled that "corporations of category" were soon to be established and that they were to "promote the development of the different branches of production and bring them into harmony, with the aim of furthering the progress and discipline of production." [5]

Under-Secretary Biagi, in an article published in the review *Gerarchia* of May 1933, explained with the authority derived from his high office, that Fascism had finally reached the decisive point in its career:

> Until now the syndical phase was regarded as not yet closed, and it therefore seemed premature to initiate the corporative phase. But now that syndical institutions are functioning satisfactorily, the moment for a further advance has been reached. The next step is to complete and perfect our work,

---

[4] D. Hugh Dalton in the London Conference of 1933 said: "The conception of the corporative state and its theory, *concerning which I read a good deal,* led me to think there had been set up a network of corporative institutions. With regard to that I confess I came away, not disappointed exactly, but finding that *these things had not yet fully come to pass.* . . . I asked Signor Mussolini how far the network of corporative institutions *which he desired* had been established in Italian industry. He replied: 'We are proceeding with great prudence.' And he went on to add that, *excepting one particular and rather small case,* that of the theatrical profession, the corporative machinery was not yet completed" (*The States and Economic Life,* p. 222).

[5] The Italian text runs as follows: "armonizzare e sviluppare le categorie produttive ai fini del progresso e della disciplina della produzione."

by integrating the syndical with corporative organization. This is to be done by creating those co-ordinating organs provided for by the law of April 3, 1926, which represent perhaps the most original and daring feature of our system.

But what were these "corporations of category" to be? What persons were to form them? What were to be their powers?

On September 18, 1933, at a plenary meeting of the National Council of Corporations, the Duce announced that "the problem was now ripe":

In this phase of the Revolution we can take decisive steps. We need not shrink before bold measures. We must determine how many corporations of category there are to be, how they are to be formed, what they are to do. We must create institutions that will be not mere theoretical structures but strong and stable living organisms.

On October 7, 1933, a new cannon shot was fired, in an interview with a special correspondent of the *Écho de Paris:*

Do you know that I am preparing great things? I want to establish the corporative regime. I wish labour to be organized according to the interests of the consumers, producers, workmen, and technicians. The state will intervene only as a supreme arbiter and as a defender of the community. The corporation will be called upon to regulate *all* the problems of production. A policy of unregulated production is folly and generates catastrophe. We must get rid of the old ideas of liberal capitalism. I will create my corporations. Every branch of industry and each product of agriculture shall have its own corporation. My plan has already formed. I have accomplished the essential political reforms, and my hands are now free to modify the economic system. I intend to experiment as Roosevelt and Stalin are doing.[6]

The new era was really about to commence.

Undoubtedly [wrote a high official of the Fascist unions] the corporation has hitherto been merely the dream and the vague aspiration of a few theorists. Up to now the workers did not know what the corporation meant. But now that the Duce has said that he "wants to establish the corporative regime," the workers are coming to understand the meaning and potentialities of the corporation. At least, they have appreciated the Duce's thought sooner and more completely than anyone else.[7]

---

[6] In the text of the interview, as published by the Italian newspapers of Oct. 8, the last sentence was suppressed.

[7] Galbiati, *Le Corporazioni di Categoria*, pp. 7–8.

From that time on, the future corporations of category were no longer called corporations of category, but merely corporations. They, and not the National Council and its sections, were to be regarded as the true corporations, which had been under discussion for so many years.

On November 14, 1933, finally the hour struck for revealing whether the world economic depression was a crisis *in* or *of* the capitalist system:

The question was serious. It was a question which could not be answered immediately. In order to reply, it was necessary to reflect, to reflect at length, and to gather evidence. Today I reply: The crisis has penetrated so deeply *into* the system that it has become a crisis *of* the system. It is no longer a wound, it is an organic disease. Today we can affirm that the capitalistic method of production is out of date. So is the doctrine of *laissez-faire*, the theoretical basis of capitalism. . . . Today we are taking a new and decisive step in the path of revolution. *A revolution, in order to be great, must be a social revolution.*

This speech, according to the Italian press, "awakened an echo throughout the world," and "put the Duce in the international spotlight," because "it opened a new source of life to humanity."

Eleven years before, on November 8, 1921, Mussolini had denied the socialist doctrine that capitalism "as a system of production was nearing its end":

An economic system, being a creation of the ages, cannot be changed suddenly. It can be transformed only by a long and slow process.

On May 18, 1923 he had reiterated the same idea:

The aggregate of forces in industry, banking, agriculture, and transport, which are collectively designated as capitalism, does not seem to be on the verge of decline, as some socialist doctrinaires assert that it is.

On May 28, 1926, he had declared that capitalism still "had several centuries of existence to look forward to." To be sure, two years later, on May 7, 1928, he had prophesied that the twentieth century would see the birth of a new economic system, the corporative, "just as the past century had seen the birth of the capitalist system." But as the nature of the corporative system was still unknown, he had continued to be described as the man who had saved the world from Bolshevism.

The historic utterance of November 14, 1933, rent the veil concealing the future. Mussolini had "gone to the Left." The Hearst press printed the speech under the headline: "MUSSOLINI ABOLISHES THE CAPITALIST SYSTEM."

But, strange to relate, the capitalistic world was not electrified by the Duce's revolutionary manifesto. The Paris bourse and the London stock exchange did not collapse. Wall Street remained imperturbable. The partners of the Morgan bank lost neither appetite nor sleep.

The explanation of this extraordinary calm is not far to seek. Immediately after pronouncing the death sentence of capitalism, the Duce asked his audience an unexpected question: "What is capitalism?" He then quickly replied to his own question: "Do not confuse capitalism and bourgeoisie. The bourgeoisie is one thing, capitalism another." While giving a death blow to the economic abstraction, "capitalism," Mussolini granted a reprieve to the concrete social class, "the bourgeoisie." Hence there was no danger that the Fascist corporation would absorb the factories, the banks, the shipping companies, and the private ownership of the land.

The Duce then proceeded to give his audience a formal lecture on the history of capitalism. Ignoring the commercial capitalism which prevailed from the thirteenth to the eighteenth centuries, disregarding English industrialism of the eighteenth century, and confusing capitalism with industrialism, he made capitalism originate in 1830. Then he divided the history of capitalism into three periods:

1.   Dynamic or heroic capitalism, from 1830 to 1870, the golden age of private initiative and free competition. This period was dominated by the doctrines of economic individualism of the *laissez-faire* school, which said to the state:

You, the state, have a paramount duty. It is to keep your hands off economic matters. The less you interfere with economic problems, the better you will govern.

2.   Static capitalism, from 1870 to 1914. This was the period when unions, corporations, and trusts were formed. Capitalism became protectionist, and the era of free competition came to an end. *Laissez-faire* "received a death blow."

The law of supply and demand ceased to be a dogma, because the combinations and trusts made it possible to control the forces of supply and demand.

3. Decadent capitalism or supercapitalism. This came into existence during the World War and produced the Kruegers and the Insulls:

Capitalistic enterprises became inflated. Enterprises grew in size from millions to billions. . . . The situation was abnormal. At this moment capitalism gets into difficulties and throws itself into the arms of the state. State intervention begins, and the more it is exercised the more it is necessary. The state intervenes in every aspect of economic life. A surrender to this type of capitalism would lead to state capitalism, which is nothing but state socialism turned upside down. This is the crisis of the capitalist system.

Thus not capitalism but supercapitalism was coming to an end. Italy was fortunately immune from almost all the evils of supercapitalism, and it would be easy for her to return to dynamic and heroic capitalism:

Italy must remain a nation of diversified economic activities, with agriculture as the basis of her economic life, with a medium-sized but healthy industry, a non-speculative banking system, and a trade that places commodities in the hands of consumers quickly and efficiently.

The Italian bourgeoisie, therefore, could count upon Mussolini's protection as long as it remained heroic.

But how did heroic-dynamic capitalism degenerate first into static capitalism and then into supercapitalism? The fault, according to Mussolini, lay with economic individualism, which had removed all restraints from private enterprise. Most people believe that capitalism and economic individualism are inseparable. They are wrong. Mussolini informed his audience that dynamic-heroic capitalism and the bourgeoisie could be prevented from falling into the aberrations of static capitalism and supercapitalism if they were divorced from economic individualism and subjected to state supervision. The word "supervision" was used advisedly, instead of "control." Private enterprise would continue to "control" the production and distribution of wealth under the "supervision" of the state.

At this point the corporations descended from heaven to earth. Theirs would be the task of supervising the national economic machinery. "The corporative system is a disciplined and therefore supervised economy, because it is impossible to imagine a discipline that does not imply super-vision." But their number and composition still remained in darkness.

The "revolutionary bill" establishing the corporations was passed unanimously on January 13, 1934, amid the wildest enthusiasm by a Senate composed of wealthy bondholders, army chiefs, high civil serv-ants, large estate owners, big business men, former university professors, and successful professional men. Its passage was probably facilitated by the following statements in the Duce's speech asking the Senate's ap-proval of the bill:

The corporative economy respects the principle of private property. Private property completes the human personality. It is a right. But it is also a duty. We think that property ought to be regarded as a social function; we wish therefore to encourage, not passive property, but active property, which does not confine itself to enjoying wealth, but develops it and increases it. The corporative economy respects private initiative. The Charter of Labour ex-pressly states that only when private initiative is unintelligent, non-existent, or inefficient may the state intervene.

Every Senator was convinced, no doubt, that *his* property was active and intelligent property. If any Senator still harboured a doubt as to the advisability of the measure, the Duce reassured him with another promise:

We shall proceed with great caution and not try to rush things. We are sure of ourselves, because our revolution has a whole century before it.

A revolution which will take a century to materialize, can safely be applauded by septuagenarian army chiefs.

The Chamber also, unanimously and by acclamation, approved the social revolution on January 18, and on February 5 social revolution be-came the law of the land, thanks to the signature of that bold revolu-tionary, King Victor Emanuel III. But only at the end of June 1934 did it become known how many corporations there were to be and of whom they were to be composed.

XVI

Mussolini's Permanent Revolution

THE corporations are twenty-two in number: 1, cereals; 2, horticulture, flowers, and fruit; 3, vines, wine; 4, oil; 5, beets and sugar; 6, zoötechnics and fisheries; 7, wool; 8, textile products; 9, metallurgy and engineering; 10, chemicals; 11, clothing; 12, paper and printing; 13, building and public works; 14, water, gas, and electricity; 15, mining industries; 16, glass and ceramics; 17, sea and air; 18, internal communications; 19, stage; 20, tourist industry; 21, insurance and credit; and 22, professions and arts.

In each corporation are assembled the producers of raw material, the producers of the finished products, and both wholesale and retail merchants. For instance in the corporation of paper and printing will be manufacturers of paper, publishers, authors, booksellers, newspapermen, owners of printing presses, and manual workers in all these trades gathered together. In the corporation of building and public works will be the producers of lumber, brick, and cement, builders, masons, realtors, etc.

The councils of the first twenty corporations are composed of delegates of the national federations of employers and employees, together with experts and delegates of the Fascist Party. For instance, the council of the corporation of cereals consists of thirteen delegates of the employers, thirteen delegates of the employees, three experts in the matters connected with the cultivation of cereals and with the milling and commerce of cereals and flour, and three delegates of the Fascist Party. The councils of the last two corporations consist wholly of experts and delegates of the Fascist Party. The councillors of all corporations number together 622.

The president of all the corporations is Mussolini, and the vice-presidents are designated by Mussolini from among the delegates of the Fascist Party. The experts are appointed by Mussolini. The delegates of the Fascist Party are appointed by the secretary-general of the Fascist Party, who in his turn is appointed by Mussolini.

The delegates of the employers and employees are appointed by the presidents of the national federations, who—as we already know (see above, pp. 43–4)—are designated by the leaders of the Fascist Party and "acclaimed" by the provincial and national officials of each federation. The rank and file of the organizations will continue to be *taillable et corvéable à merci*.[1]

As if 622 persons were not sufficient to abolish supercapitalism and set the Fascist social revolution in motion, the corporations will also include the chiefs of those departments of the civil service which are interested in the questions to be dealt with by the corporations; and all the other experts whom Mussolini may deem it expedient to summon to each corporation in particular cases in order to avail himself of their specialized knowledge.

Each corporation, within the field of its competence, has the following tasks: 1, the giving of advice to the public administrations on subjects to be defined by decrees emanating from Mussolini; 2, the conciliation of labour disputes by means of committees, the members of which would be individually designated by Mussolini from among the members of the corporation itself; 3, the determination of wages, to become obligatory only after approval by the National Council and Mussolini, and 4, the "formulation of rules regarding economic relations and the discipline of production," rules which are also called "plans."

Point 1 has no revolutionary implications. All governments have advisory committees. According to points 2 and 3, the corporations have the right to help determine wages. No provision gives them the right to determine profits or dividends.[2] Thus the wage-cutting machine in the corporative state has received a new wheel. In Fascist Italy, one's house, one's land, one's car, one's brakes are one's property, but if one is a worker with no other property than the labour of one's hands, that labour is not one's property. A host of people—the officials appointed from above to control the unions, the Ministry of Labour, the judges of the Labour Court, the corporations—have the right to issue regulations about wages, hours of work, and the worker's duties towards the employer.

---

[1] Read Signor Bottai's *Corporate State and N.R.A.*, p. 622, and you will be informed that each corporation includes "representatives" of the workers and employers.

[2] Signor Bottai, *Corporate State and N.R.A.*, p. 620, asserts that Article 10 of the law of Feb. 5, 1934, empowers the corporation "to establish rates for economic services and consumption prices of those goods offered to the public under monopolistic conditions," and that Article 11 "describes the legal means for enforcing rates for monopolistic services and prices." This is a definite lie.

Everyone has the right to dispose of labour, except the labourer himself. A socialist state would nationalize capital on the ground that it is redeeming the worker from the slavery of wages. The Fascist state has nationalized labour and hires it out to private capital at the price that it, the state, deems expedient.

Point 4 requires more comment. We know (see above, p. 103) that Article 12 of the act of March 20, 1930 enabled the National Council or its sections to "establish rules concerning the reciprocal relations of the various categories of production" only when the directorates of the organizations concerned were unanimous in authorizing them to do so. The newly established corporations are empowered to formulate rules and plans without obtaining the preliminary consent of all the interested parties. It is sufficient that the proposal to formulate those rules and plans emanate from *only one* of the organizations concerned. But the clause still remains in force which forbids the corporations to discuss any measure unless they have been previously authorized to do so by Mussolini. Moreover, the rules and plans formulated by the corporation can become obligatory only when approved by the National Council and Mussolini. As a French jurist, M. Barthélemy, observed in the *Temps* of June 12, 1934:

> The corporation is never permitted to pass a majority decision. The power supposedly emanating from the corporation never goes beyond the consultative stage. What does the corporation do? It talks. Who acts? The government.

Finally, the corporations are subject to the same rules as the National Council, i. e., Mussolini fixes the time and subject-matter of their discussions, formulates their decisions, determines their method of voting, and decides whether their discussions and decisions are to be kept secret or to be communicated to the press.

> The Fascist corporation [writes a Belgian jurist who has earnestly studied Italian institutions] is Mussolini. If Napoleon were living again today, he would hasten to imitate Mussolini, or rather, he would take back from his disciple that which the latter had borrowed from him.[3]

---

[3] Prélot, *Le Corporativisme Italien*, pp. 470, 490. It would be useless labour to seek in the study of Signor Bottai, *Corporate State and N.R.A.*, the least information as to the powers which Mussolini exerts upon the corporations.

In short, the Fascist social revolution will be carried out by 268 representatives of the capitalist class, 268 officials appointed from above to control the employees' class, 66 Fascists, and an indeterminate number of experts and high civil servants. These will be divided into 22 advisory councils, the corporations, above which will function another advisory council, the National Council; and both the lower councils and the higher council will be equipped with "pre-legislative" powers, that is, they will be able to do nothing without Mussolini's consent.

The mountain laboured and brought forth a mouse.

On March 4, 1934, one month after the king had affixed his signature to the bill establishing the corporations, the government gave the country a foretaste of the authority to be enjoyed by the interested social groups in disciplining production through the corporations. It conferred legal personality upon an Italian Cotton Institute, which had previously existed as a *de facto* association of manufacturers, and authorized this institute to deal with all problems connected with the production and sale of cotton fabrics. What did this leave for the textile corporation to do in matters affecting the cotton industry? In announcing this measure, the *Lavoro Fascista* pretended not to understand that it made the whole corporative system ridiculous, and expressed confidence that the workers "would undoubtedly be called upon to form part of the cotton institute." On May 7, however, the Italian newspapers, with the exception of the *Lavoro Fascista*, gave out that the managing council of the Cotton Institute would consist of twelve manufacturers and a single "representative" of the workers' unions, the latter to be designated by the President of the National Federation of Textile Unions. Thus, the delegates of the unions form almost a third of the textile corporation, which has nothing to do; but where there is real work to be done, as in the Cotton Institute, the unions will have only one nominal delegate against twelve authentic representatives of the manufacturers' interests.

A royal decree of July 12, 1934, enacted that the possession of a minimum capital should be required of all existing insurance companies —four million lire for life-insurance companies, two millions for fire-insurance companies, and one million for all others; companies failing to meet these requirements must be dissolved before June 30, 1936. This decree sentenced to an unexpected death many small companies which spent very little for overhead, and whose members, generally small holders, were perfectly satisfied. All the business of these little companies will, of course, be inherited by the big insurance companies.

The Federation of Co-operative Insurance Societies of Alba (Piedmont), composed of two hundred companies doomed to dissolution, published in the thirty-ninth issue of the review *Lavoro Co-operativo* for 1934 a protest reading as follows:

The co-operative insurance societies guarantee economy to the citizen who insures with them, because every year he pays only about half of the premium on the policy. All the offices in our co-operative societies are filled without charge; the secretaries receive salaries ranging from 100 to 500 lire a year, while the general expenses are reduced to an absolute minimum. . . . Now let us turn to the big companies. The Assicurazioni Generali Venezia in 1931 paid out 999,244.75 lire in salaries to its directors. The Riunione Adriatica di Sicurtà paid 599,912 lire; the Fondiaria paid a little under 459,962 lire. This fact too should be noted: the directors of one society often hold similar offices in another company: they live at ease, while peasants foot the bill. Before the issue of the royal decree of July 12, 1934, the agents of the big companies prowled about our countryside, throwing discredit upon the organizations which our tenacity and honest toil have built up during the last thirty years, and proclaiming to the four winds of heaven that, if the peasants wished to insure themselves, they had to pass under the yoke of the private companies.

We have here an odious monopoly created by the government in the interests of the big capitalistic companies through the arbitrary extermination of the little societies. Clearly, the *laissez-faire* of the small enterprises is disappearing, in order to intensify the *laissez-faire* of the large enterprises.

It is noteworthy that this decree-law was promulgated just a few days after the issue of the regulations founding the prospective corporations. Before issuing this decree, the government did not ask the advice of the National Council of Corporations or its sections, nor did it deem it necessary to wait until the corporations began to function and to remit to them the consideration of this subject. It simply suppressed the little co-operative societies and consigned the small holders, bound hand and foot, into the clutches of the big companies.

The summer and part of the autumn of 1934 were spent in getting ready for the Fascist social revolution—that is, in selecting the persons who were to form the twenty-two corporations. On October 6, as the epoch-making event was drawing near, the Duce expounded the programme of the revolution in a speech to the Milanese workers, which, according to the *Corriere della Sera*, was directed to all the peoples of the world and which, according to the *Stampa*, "would be echoed everywhere":

You are at this moment the principal participators in an event which the political history of tomorrow will call the Address to the Milanese Workers. Around you at this moment are millions and millions of Italians, and beyond the seas and the mountains many other people are listening. Five years ago [1929], on these very days, the columns of a temple which seemed to defy the ages [Wall Street] suddenly collapsed. It was the end of the period which may be called the period of liberal and capitalistic economy. We are now living in a period of transition from one phase of civilization to another. No longer can economics place the emphasis exclusively upon individual profit, it must have regard for the collective interest. In the face of this obvious and irrevocable decline, the solution imposed by logic and by the intrinsic needs of the situation is the corporative solution—the production which disciplines itself through the will of the producers. When I say producers I do not mean merely the industrialists and employers; I mean the workers too. Fascism ordains that all individuals shall be truly equal in respect to their labour and before the nation. The difference between individuals is merely that of the degree and extent of their responsibilities. The economic objective of the regime is the realization of a higher quality of social justice among the Italian people. This promise will be kept in full. But what is the meaning of this higher quality of social justice? It means that the worker's *job will be secure, his wages constant, his home comfortable*. It means the possibility of continual development and improvement. This is not all. It means that the workers, the labourers, are to penetrate more and more deeply into a knowledge and control of the productive process. If the last century was the century of the power of capital, the twentieth century is that of the power and glory of labour. I tell you that modern science is destined to solve the problem of the distribution of wealth to the end that we shall no longer behold the illogical, paradoxical, and cruel fact of want in the midst of plenty.

The most vulgar demagogue in the most degenerate democracy has never regaled an audience of workers with such a display of resounding promises.

A few days later, on October 15, the Confederation of Industrial Employers assembled in Rome for its national conference. The government commissioner, Signor Pirelli, one of the richest Italian industrialists, in his inaugural address failed to mention social justice, job security, constant wages, comfortable homes, and the distribution of wealth. State intervention in the regulation of production, he explained, was not a Fascist novelty, because it had existed even "in the liberal period." The industrialists were "deeply sensible of the recognition which Fascism had given to individual initiative and private property." Since this "indispensable motive force of civic progress and collective well-being" had been safeguarded against all attacks, the employers had no reason to repel "the regulatory, harmonizing, protective, and co-ordinating intervention of the state," rather, "they were intensely aware of its necessity":

> I do not need to call your attention to the importance which we employers attach to the recognition of individual initiative and private property—two aspects of the same phenomenon. This principle of Fascist economic doctrine is engraved on the tablets of the political and economic legislation of the regime. Individual doctrinal deviations cannot even scratch it—the office of the representatives of the Fascist Party in the corporations, the powers of the National Council, *and above all the powers reserved to the head of the government* constitute the surest guarantee that the dominance of egotism in the various categories will be avoided.

When Signor Pirelli's address was finished, Mussolini took the floor, praised the Italian industrialists who "had nothing to fear from a comparison with those of other nations"—his eloquence ordinarily consists of flattering his audience—and took good care not to breathe a word concerning the Fascist social revolution. A few days later he entrusted to Count Volpi, one of the wealthiest capitalists in Italy, the task of carrying out the social revolution in his capacity as president of the Confederation of Industrial Employers.

At last, on November 9, the press published the names of the members of the corporations. As was natural, among the representatives of the employers were found almost all the most important Italian capitalists. Among the persons who were supposed to represent the employees there were 127 lawyers, professors, doctors, engineers, accountants, etc. Of men who really came from the rank and file of manual labour there were scarcely twenty.

The names proposed by the presidents of the federations had remained shrouded in secrecy until Mussolini had ratified them. Like all secret transactions, they gave rise to all kinds of guesses and rumours. In Italy it was whispered about that the national directorate of the Fascist Party had paid no attention to the primary nominations and had compiled at its own discretion the list that had been submitted for Mussolini's ratification.

Among the persons supposed to "represent" the professional classes were two women. Immediately, the Rome correspondents of the foreign papers heralded this event as the proof that Mussolini had abolished all political barriers between men and women, and that at last Italy too was calling her women to a share in the government of the country.

The speech with which Mussolini inaugurated the corporations on November 10, is easy to imagine: "This assembly is perhaps the most important in the history of Italy"; it is a "revolutionary assembly"; "to-day, on November 10 of the Year XIII, the great machine is starting to move." A single point in the speech was unexpected. The Duce exhorted his audience not to expect "a miracle" from the new corporations.

On December 9, 1934, the members of the twenty-two corporations had the satisfaction of being informed through an official *communiqué* that the Central Corporative Committee had been reorganized. Henceforward it would be composed of the following persons: ministers and under-secretaries of state, whom Mussolini appoints and dismisses at his discretion; the vice-presidents of the twenty-two corporations, chosen by Mussolini from among the members of the corporations who are designated by the secretary-general of the Fascist Party, himself an appointee of Mussolini; three other high dignitaries of the Fascist Party, chosen by Mussolini; and the nine presidents of the confederations, likewise appointed by Mussolini. The committee, therefore, will consist of about forty members, among whom the employees are supposed to be "represented" by the presidents of their four confederations, although these personages are neither elected by the employees nor accountable to them.

On January 7, 1935, the first of the twenty-two newly created corporations, that of zoötechnics and fisheries, began operations. The first problems which engaged its attention were the measures to be taken to prevent the different types of Italian cheese from being confused with one another, methods of disciplining the production and commerce of milk and increasing its consumption, and other matters no less pregnant with social-revolutionary implications. The textile corporation came next. It considered the means of relieving the silk industry, which had been in difficulties for many years. The pro-Fascist Rome correspondent of the *New York Times*, January 27, 1935, gave the following account of the debates:

> The agriculturists suggested that the government guarantee a minimum price for cocoons. The industrialists proposed that the bounty the government at present pays on silk yarns should be increased. Other proposals were that a heavy tax should be placed on the production of rayon, the proceeds to be used to subsidize the silk industry, and that silk should be mixed with wool in the manufacture of underwear. All these proposals were rejected. The suggestions that the government guarantee a minimum price for cocoons or increase the bounty on silk yarns were deemed too burdensome for the Treasury. The proposal to lessen the burden by taxing rayons was unacceptable because it would have damaged one of the most flourishing Italian industries. Nor was it deemed feasible to mix silk with wool in underwear because of the resulting increased cost in the finished product. Silk is still considerably more expensive than wool, even at its present extremely low prices. The corporation therefore limited itself to counseling the interested parties to achieve a closer co-ordination of their efforts.

Since the corporation of silk was unable to help them out, the silk industrialists took matters in their own hands. In April 1935 they gathered in Milan and in Rome to examine ways and means of promoting the exportation of their products. The *Lavoro Fascista* May 9, 1935, asked how it happened that the employers had set themselves to act on their own account instead of bringing the problem before their corporation. The industrialists did not deign to reply.

The last corporation which held its meeting before the manuscript of this book was released, was the corporation for oil, which concluded its labours on July 10, 1935, by discussing ways and means for extending in Italy the cultivation of castor oil.

One of the most ardent admirers of Mussolini and of the Fascist regime, Monsieur Kerillis, acknowledged on July 21, 1935, in the *Écho de Paris* that the corporations were merely "a façade behind which there was not much of anything": "half at least of the 22 corporations had never been convoked." On none of the economic and financial provisions which were made in connection with the Ethiopian war, was ever any corporation asked to give its advice. Everything went on as though no corporation ever had been set up in Italy. Thus the Fascist social revolution was being carried out.

Undoubtedly by this time the reader is aware of the scope and real import of the Fascist social revolution. Therefore, he will find it natural that in Spain also there is "a powerful movement to replace the Spanish Republic with something akin to Italy's corporative state." The Duke of Alba, "a scion of one of Spain's most distinguished lines," has declared himself in favour of this programme. "High monarchist circles say the movement has the approval of former King Alfonso." "Also expected to sign is General José Sanjuro, leader of the monarchist revolt of 1933" (*New York Times*, December 6, 1934). In Austria also a similar situation exists. After Dr. Dollfuss had stamped down the Socialist organizations, he introduced the new corporative constitution "designed to ensure stability and justice for all classes," as Chancellor Schuschnigg explained in an interview with the *Morning Post* of February 27, 1935. Mussolini's social revolution is spreading all over the world. Like Trotsky's it is "permanent." But unlike Trotsky's, it does not frighten anyone.

In his *Talks with Mussolini*, Herr Ludwig asked the Duce why it was that the Fascists, after so many years of rule, were still talking of a permanent revolution: "It reminds me of Trotsky's theory." Mussolini replied:

We need to speak of permanent revolution, because the phrase exerts a mystical influence upon the masses. It is stimulating, too, for persons of higher intelligence. When we talk of permanent revolution, we imply that the times are exceptional, and we give the man in the street a feeling that he is participating in an extraordinary movement.[4]

---

[4] *Talks with Mussolini*, p. 103.

XVII

The Great Humbug

SINCE the corporations were inaugurated on November 10, 1934, it is obvious that they cannot possibly have existed before that date. Prior to that date there existed only the "syndicalist" institutions created in 1926, a National Council of Corporations created in 1930 and divided into sections in 1931, and a Corporation of the Stage, created in 1931. It is true that the "syndicalist" institutions were destined to lead up to the corporations and formed their indispensable groundwork, but it is also evident that there can be no corporative state until there are corporations. The corporations are the *sine qua non* of the corporative state. The term "corporative" could be applied to the Fascist state before 1935 only by courtesy, in recognition of the fact that before 1935 there actually existed the syndicalist institutions which made the corporative state possible.

On September 15, 1934, Signor Panunzio, a high personage of the regime and a professor in the Law School of the University of Rome, wrote in the *Critica Fascista:*

> The truth is that from the day when the corporations were first mentioned in Italy down to the present no one has ever conceived of them as flesh-and-blood institutions. Only the corporations instituted by the latest law stand out clearly as to nature and function. If the corporations had ever really existed, it would not have been necessary literally to drag them into life in 1934. The truth is that even today they exist only as an aspiration.

But in 1931, Major Barnes, on pages 176-9 of his book *Fascism*, stated that the organizations of employers and employees in each industry, by means of "elected representatives," formed a corporation, which was "so to speak, the board of directors" for that particular industry all over the nation. Each board had local decentralized organizations; and directly or by means of these local organizations harmonized the interests of employers and employees, supervised the labour exchanges for its own industry, collected statistics of all kinds, founded technical schools, appointed commissions of inquiry with a view to diminishing the cost of production and rationalizing the industry. Major Barnes filled two whole pages with these and similar statements, representing as already existing in 1931 those corporations which were still non-existent in the spring of 1934, and attributing to them a multitude of functions which were at that time exercised by the Ministry of Corporations or which were entrusted to no one and therefore carried out by no one (for example, the appointment of commissions of inquiry with a view to diminishing the cost of production).

In the same year, while Major Barnes was constructing the corporations with the aid of his imagination, Pope Pius XI still cherished some hopes of softening Pharaoh's heart and inducing him to permit the existence of Catholic working-men's organizations. He therefore pretended, in his encyclical "Quadriginta Annos," to believe that the corporations already existed, that they were "made up of the representatives of workers and employers," and that "they directed and co-ordinated the work of the organizations in all matters of common interest." He approved of these corporations on the whole, although he expressed the tentative criticism that "the organization had an excessively bureaucratic and political character" and "could be employed for political purposes instead of hastening the advent of a better social order." He hoped that the criticism would prove to be unfounded, but he was soon disillusioned. In June 1931 he was compelled to publish the encyclical "Non Abbiamo Bisogno," in which he finally recognized the existence of Fascist totalitarianism and deplored the fact that registration in the Party or its subsidiary organizations was "for many people a condition of their careers, their bread, and their lives." In the following September, however, the Holy Father again made peace with Mussolini, and it seems that thenceforward the dangers of Fascist totalitarianism ceased to disturb him.

In 1932, Professor Volpe became convinced that four years before he had erred in affirming that the corporations then were scarcely "in the process of birth" (see above, p. 96). Therefore, in the second edition of his *Storia del Movimento Fascista*, published as a pendant to Mussolini's *Dottrina del Fascismo*, p. 120, he gave the following information:

The corporations were created on the basis of the Charter of Labour. Each corporation united the local and national organizations of the three classes of producers—employers, technicians, and employees—with the aim of conciliating disputes between the organizations, co-ordinating enterprises tending to increase production, etc. The last of these functions was no longer directed to the distribution of wealth but to its creation—an objective to be attained not by socialization, but by better co-ordination of private activities. The creation of the corporations was accompanied by that of the National Council of Corporations.[1]

Singing the praises and benefits of the corporative state in the *Harvard Business Review* of April 1932, Mr. Clough ascribed to it even the agreement on the war debts which took place in December 1925 before the enactment of the law of April 3, 1926, that created the syndicalist state and may be regarded as the first dawn of the corporative state. It is evident that, in Mr. Clough's mind, the corporative state and Fascist dictatorship were one and the same thing, and that consequently the corporative state came into existence in October 1922, when Mussolini seized the government. Everything depends upon an understanding of the meaning of words.

In the volume *The Italian Corporative State*, published in 1933, Signor Pitigliani admitted that "the corporative organization only began to manifest its independence in 1930," with the emergence of the National Council of Corporations (p. 101), that "only a single corporation, viz. that of the stage, had so far been established in Italy," that "the other existing corporations were simply sections of the National Council," that "the establishment of other independent corporations to deal with the problem of particular categories was at present under consideration," and that "it was impossible to judge, in the light of any practical results, how that system was actually working in the corporative field properly so-called" (p. 110). But he dedicated forty-three beautiful pages to describing the "corporative organization," through which the state "wishes to act as an umpire who, in every decision and in all circumstances, takes into account the interests of the nation conceived as an indivisible whole" (p. 91). The person who reads in his book that the corporations "*are* the distinctive feature of the new political and economic order in Italy"

---

[1] Galbiati, *Le Corporazioni di Categoria*, pp. 17 and 19, expressed amazement that the corporations, which were not yet in existence in the autumn of 1933, were represented by Professor Volpe existing in 1927: "In the early days of 1933, when Professor Volpe heard that, by the will of the Duce, the Central Corporative Committee had decided to proceed to the establishment of the corporations of category, he must have been greatly surprised. How could Professor Volpe, an Italian historian and writer living in Italy, have represented as created and existing in 1927 corporations which even now do not exist in Italy? So many things are understood and may be understood under the name 'corporation'!"

(p. ix) gets an impression comparable to that which would be produced by seeing a man riding an invisible horse.

At the beginning of 1933, another "expert," the Transylvanian-British Dr. Paul Einzig, entered the lists to reveal to the world *The Economic Foundations of Fascism.* Dr. Einzig knew absolutely nothing about Italian economic life, and throughout the entire one hundred and fifty-six pages of his book he gave not one piece of concrete information about imports, exports, manufactures, agriculture, wages, cost of living, taxes, or any other phase of Italian economics, although he acknowledged that "it is upon its economic side that Fascism stands or falls: the success of the Fascist system can only be measured in terms of its economic advantages" (p. 12). But concerning the miracles which the yet non-existent corporations were performing in Italy he was perfectly informed:

> The corporate state is a new type of constitutional system in which the employers and employed, grouped into mixed national corporations, *play a predominant part* in the government of the country. It is a new kind of democracy as contrasted with the parliamentary democratic system (p. 25). Within the framework of the system a feeling of solidarity between the apparently conflicting interests of various groups *has developed* (p. 30). In Fascist Italy cartels and trusts are not encouraged. In as much as they are tolerated, they *are placed* under the supervision of corporations so as to fit their activities into the general working of the system. (p. 35). *The employers have had to cede a larger percentage of their profits to their workmen* (p. 60). The Italian government exerts a strong influence on banking *through the intermediary of the corporations.* The decision of the corporation of banks and insurance companies is in practice an act of legislation which is compulsory on every bank (p. 86). Government intervention is increasingly assuming the form of regulatory action by the corporations themselves. It seems that producers, like every other section of the community in Italy, find it increasingly less unpleasant to obey. There is not greater happiness in the world than to want to do what we have to do in any case (pp. 45–6).

The miracles which the non-existent corporations were performing in 1932 were nothing in comparison with those which they would accomplish in the future. Dr. Einzig was convinced that only a planned economy could save the world from ruin, on condition, of course, that this planning should be done "under the guidance of the right people in the right way" (p. 123). In Italy "scientific planning" had not yet been deliberately adopted; but there was in the working of the corporate system a "subconscious planning" (p. 33); and the logical conclusion of the corporate state would be the establishment of a planned economic system (p. 27). To what heights would the corporate state not rise when it passed from subconscious to scientific planning?

In the *Giornale degli Economisti*, April 1933, p. 288, a contributor marvelled that the "creation of the corporative state was attributed to Rossoni, without Bottai's name ever being mentioned." In its issue of May 1933, p. 382, the review published a *communiqué* from the head of Mussolini's press bureau, which "begged to call attention to the fact that the corporative order took its inception from the political thought and the will of the Duce earlier than from Rossoni and Bottai."

The writer who excels all others in this regard is, as usual, Mr. Goad. In 1932, he was of the opinion that the corporative system had reached completion and perfection with the setting up of the National Council of Corporations and its sections. These were the corporations that people were talking so much about:

The confederations were grouped together in pairs, workmen and employers, into national corporations and summoned to discuss all the outstanding problems affecting each department of the productive national life. These corporations send delegates to a supreme National Council of Corporations which represents the entire productive forces of the nation.

The activities of the corporations were remarkable:

If the profits of an industry increase as a result of a new tax, the corporation, consisting both of employers and workers, would reconsider the division and after measures had been taken to consolidate reserves, improve machinery, lower prices, and increase production, would distribute bonuses to the workers, especially in the form of the allotment of shares, thus making them actually what they are effectually, share-holders in a business in which they have already invested their individual skill and training. Workers and employers should equally share in the benefits of prosperity, from whatever source it comes.

But this was nothing. The corporations established and supervised many provincial and municipal bodies which were almost more miraculous than the corporations themselves:

Their chief purpose is not only to harmonize all possible interests of work-men and employers, but also to form bases of co-operation between factory and factory, between manufacturer and transporter, manufacturer and dis-tributor and so forth. They help the struggling but essentially healthy firm to obtain credit from the banks, when such help is necessary and expedient; they discourage speculation and unhealthy ventures; they assist research and give prizes for new inventions and good work; they regulate the rates of in-terest and market-prices, as well as wages, in a spirit of patriotism, goodwill and helpfulness. They consist of representatives both of workmen and em-ployers, who thus come in constant contact with each other in the common work of extending as well as conciliating their common interests.[2]

Among the institutions which looked out for the happiness of the Italian people under the supervision of the corporations, Mr. Goad did not omit to mention the "Guild of the Stage." But a single guild did not satisfy him. He therefore summoned half a dozen other guilds to keep it company, among them a National Guild of Tourism, an organization which "considered the interests of the silk industry," and a Guild of Milk. The Corporation of Tourism, together with all the other corpora-tions, came into existence only in the spring of 1934, that is, eighteen months after Mr. Goad's book had been published. The silk organization was created on December 30, 1929, when the sections of the council were still non-existent, to defend the Italian silk industry from foreign competition, particularly that of the Japanese. It was composed ex-clusively of manufacturers and bankers, and the workers' unions had no real share in it. The workers participated in the affairs of the trust only in so far as the unemployment fund contributed to the formation of its capital and made up for eventual losses, while eventual profits remained in the treasury of the association.[3] As for the milk guild, it consisted of an agreement on the price of milk, which was concluded in December 1931 by the milk-producers of the countryside around Rome—the "Ro-man campagna"—and the milk-sellers in the city. The former demanded that the merchants should be compelled to purchase their milk in pref-erence to that coming from the Lombard cows, while the merchants found that the milk of the cows in which flowed the blood of the ancient Romans, was much more expensive than the milk from Lombardy. The delegates of the legal organizations of the two groups met in the office

---

[2] *The Making of the Corporate State*, pp. 83, 91.
[3] Perroud, *L'Economie Corporative et Système Capitaliste*, p. 1433.

of a high official of the Ministry of Corporations, without any intervention on the part of the day-labourers who fed and milked the cows or of the Roman citizens who drank the milk; and they agreed that the milk merchants must give the preference to the milk of the noble-born Roman cows, and that consequently the population of Rome would have to pay a higher price for its milk. The corporations or sections of the Council for Commerce and Agriculture gave opinions favorable to this agreement, and did nothing else.[4]

When assisted in his labours by Miss Currey, Mr. Goad reached the following conclusion:

The Corporate State is "government for the people," for never before have the working classes been cared for as they are under the present regime. It is "government by the people," for under the Corporate State they have a control of their own destinies, economic, social, and political, by the method of electing representatives, not for their general popularity in geographical constituencies, but for their tried knowledge and experience in their particular trade or industry. It is "government of the whole people," since the state and nation are identified without the intervention of political parties or the artificial division of classes.[5]

According to Signor Bottai, a corporation is a "liaison between the organs at the top of the structure":

As far as 1926 corporations were established. . . . But it was only in 1930 that the reorganization of the National Council of Corporations definitely oriented the whole syndical movement towards its new and corporate phase. The transition is still taking place.[6]

It will be interesting to see what heights of enthusiasm Mr. Goad, Miss Currey and Signor Bottai will attain when the corporations have really begun to function. But whatever secrets the future may hold, of one fact we may be sure: the corporations which were glorified from 1927 to 1935, were the greatest humbug of the twentieth century.

The author of the report on *The Economic and Financial Position of Italy*, pp. 6–7, published in the spring of 1935 by the Royal Institute of International Affairs, has derived, probably from the books of Major

---

[4] Rosenstock-Franck, pp. 297–8, 325. Bottai, *Il Cons. Naz. delle Corp.*, pp. 337, 387 ff.

[5] *The Working of a Corporate State*, p. 110.

[6] *Corporate State and N.R.A.*, p. 616, 618.

Barnes and of Mr. Goad, the information that before 1930 there existed in Italy some corporations, to which he gives the name of "old corporations," in which the confederations of employers and employees met "to discuss their particular branch of economic industry, the government using the discussion as a basis of future policy." These "old corporations" never existed, unless one wishes to give the name of "corporations" to those meetings in which the officials of the organizations, in the presence of some high officials of the Ministry of Corporations, met to negotiate labour agreements—that is, to cut wages.

From the "Homo Œconomicus" to the "Homo Corporativus"

A n enormous literature has accumulated on the corporations, the corporative state, the corporative law, the corporative philosophy, the corporative revolution, the future of the corporative idea. A new economics has grown up in Italy, the country which during the past half century gave to the old economics the names of Pareto, Pantaleoni, De Viti de Marco, and Einaudi. An improvised army of economists has applied itself to the construction of the new science, "attracted a little by the novelty of this subject and a little by the desire to simulate a competence that might serve as a passport to the realization of practical ideals," [1] i. e., towards a university chair. [2] The new science is called "Corporative Doctrine."

The old doctrine of economic individualism developed in a society that made the state an instrument for achieving the well-being of the individual. It was based on the postulate of the "homo œconomicus," or "economic man," that is, of the individual whose aim in life was the realization of his material interests. The new corporative economic doctrine has grown up in a society in which the individual is an instrument for achieving the greatness and power of the state, and it therefore takes as its basis a new postulate, the "homo corporativus," or "corporative man."

The homo œconomicus—Mussolini announced in the *Popolo d'Italia* of May 31, 1935—is dying. He was the representative of that equivocal frame of mind on which the economic liberalism of the last fifty [!] years was based. He has now received his coup de grâce from the corporative state of Fascism.

The corporative man is free to pursue his own interests, but his interests are not purely selfish, because he is guided by the "corporative conscience"; "he conducts himself according to the dictates of the Charter of Labour, and unlike the 'homo œconomicus' is endowed with a

---

[1] Lama, *L'Economia Corporativa*, 1931, quoted by Perroud, *Economie Corporative et Système Capitaliste*, p. 1410.
[2] Einaudi, in *Riforma Sociale*, 1933, vol. XLIV, p. 646.

feeling for the higher interests of the national collectivity." [3] If we are endowed with a "corporative conscience," we feel that "in every act of our lives as Italians, Italy is present; that every one of our acts is conditioned by the interests of the fatherland." [4] The corporative man acts freely, but his freedom is inspired and guided by the general interest. Where his corporative conscience falls short, the laws of the corporative state intervene to keep him in the straight path.[5]

Having established this postulate, the Fascist "thinkers" ask how the corporative man will act in respect to particular problems of individual and collective life, and, passing from deduction to induction, they logically construct the new corporative society. The corporative society respects private property and entrusts the management of production and the responsibility for business enterprises to individual initiative. But it intends that individual initiative shall not abuse its liberty and that private property shall serve, not the egoism of the proprietor, but the well-being of the community and the power of the state. The capitalistic system has individual profit as its motive force. The motive force in the corporative system is the public interest. The juridical structure of capitalism engenders antagonism between classes. That of corporationism creates co-operation. The motives behind the economic act, the legal environment in which the economic act takes place, and the effects of the economic act are transformed.

The Fascist system, as far as production is concerned, aims at retaining individual initiative without allowing it to lead to excesses. The beneficial effects of free competition are retained, and if a manufacturer succeeds in improving his methods, there is nothing to prevent him from enjoying the benefit of his success. The government will, however, always be ready to intervene in cases of cut-throat competition. The Fascist system of produc-

---

[3] Fasiani, "Contributo alla Teoria dell'Uomo Corporativo," in *Studi Sassaresi*, Jan. 15, 1933.

[4] Serpieri, *Problemi della terra nell'Economia Corporativa*, p. 62. Signor Serpieri is one of the few Fascists who have made a careful study of Pareto's sociology and have thoroughly assimilated its principles: from Pareto he learned that "in actual fact, with or without universal suffrage, it is always an oligarchy that governs, a minority, a ruling class, an élite; it acquires power and maintains itself partly by force, partly by consent, in varying proportions. Consent is always facilitated by the use of cunning" (*La Bonifica Agraria in Italia*, pp. 51–2). Are we to believe that his "corporative conscience" is but one of the tricks aimed at facilitating consent by the use of cunning?

[5] The inventor of these buffooneries was Signor Arias, Professor of Economics at the University of Florence. See his volume, *Economia Nazionale Corporativa*, published in 1929.

tion is thus based upon a curious mixture of individualism and state intervention.[6]

In so far as it respects private property and individual initiative, the new science rejects the errors of communism. In so far as it subordinates private property and individual initiative to the prosperity of the community, it repudiates individualism. But it inherits all the truths contained in both systems and fuses them in a higher synthesis. "Corporationism is conquering socialism and it is conquering liberalism: it is creating a new synthesis."[7] "Corporationism," writes Signor Spirito, à la Hegel, "is absolute liberalism and absolute socialism."[8]

The outmoded doctrine of economic individualism affirmed that a community made up of "economic men" would enjoy a maximum of prosperity because it would be composed of individuals each of whom would realize the maximum of prosperity for himself. Similarly, the communist doctrine, setting out from the postulate of a "Bolshevist man," logically constructs a society that functions with a clock-like precision. And the Christians too founded their City of God on the postulate of the "Christian man." To make a hypothetical man the initial postulate of a logical construction, and to deduce a system of theorems from that initial postulate, is just as permissible for economists of any school as similar methods are for mathematicians.

But it is one thing to construct a logical system, another to construct a concrete social system, in which real, not hypothetical, men must live and work. The Fascist "thinkers" are right in maintaining that the economic man of the individualistic doctrine does not exist in real life, because the real man is motivated not only by the economic impulse but by many other impulses also: egoism and altruism, personal likes and dislikes, vanity, the spirit of sacrifice, family solidarity, religious feeling, national sentiment, etc. But the corporative man does not exist in real life, any more than the economic man, the Bolshevist man, or the Christian man.

Economists of the old school make no pretence at constructing a new social system. They take the existing social system and try to explain its economic phenomena, recognizing that men's acts sometimes coincide with and sometimes diverge from those which the economic man would

---

[6] Einzig, *Economic Foundations*, p. 45.
[7] Memorandum introducing the bill on corporations to the Senate, Jan. 1934.
[8] *Nuovi Studi di Diritto, Economia e Politica*, II, 1932, Fascicle VI, pp. 285–98.

logically perform. The postulate of the economic man is not capable of explaining all of life or even all of economic life. But the economic man, although an abstraction, is less remote from reality than are the corporative man, the Bolshevist man, and the Christian man. Consequently, in explaining existing economic phenomena, the old school does not need to insert in its hypotheses so many variable coefficients as would be required to explain the phenomena of real economic life if the other hypothetical men were used. Nay more, the economic phenomena of the Christian middle ages, of Bolshevist Russia, of Fascist Italy, and of Nazi Germany are much more easily explicable by the postulate of the economic man than by the other postulates.

But what the Fascists aspire to do—and in this respect they are at one with the Communists—is not to explain the functioning of the old economic machine with the aid of an hypothesis. They aim at constructing a new machine with the aid, not of an hypothesis, but of a certainty. The corporative man is already born, he exists, works, suppresses everybody who refuses to allow himself to be imbued with the new mentality, educates the rising generations, is sure of the future. From this certainty as to the future to the description of the future as a present reality it is but a brief step:

The supreme achievement of Fascism has been to mobilize the spiritual forces of the vast majority of Italians in a campaign of national co-operation and self-sacrifice against the forces of greed, of speculation, of selfish individualism, against cut-throat competition and ruthless exploitation of the weaker, that is to say, the poorer classes.[9]

In Italy Fascism has succeeded, to a remarkable extent, in undermining the cult of selfishness. The corporate spirit has become nation-wide, thanks to the development of a new conception of the public character of the function of everybody engaged in the production and distribution of goods. According to this conception, every employer and employee is a civil servant in the broadest sense of the term. At the same time, they are also part of the legislative and administrative organization of the country. This dual capacity confers upon them certain rights and duties which are unknown in a parliamentary democratic system. Above all, it creates in their minds a feeling that they form a part of the state and that their interests are identical with those of the state.[10]

---

[9] Goad, *The Making of the Corporative State*, p. 13. Cf. Goad and Currey, *The Working of a Corporate State*, p. 13 ff.
[10] Einzig, *Economic Foundations*, pp. 9, 31.

In the corporation are mingled the producers of raw material, the consumers of the finished product, and both wholesale and retail merchants. The jurisdiction of the corporation will embrace both employers and employees in each branch of production and of commerce. This means that the corporation will have to "discipline" at one and the same time the director of the Fiat Motors firm, the 25,000 workers employed in the Fiat factories, the keeper of a little repair shop, the unemployed labourer, the hardware merchant, and innumerable others. Who will harmonize the interests of such diverse groups and individuals?

In the review, *Riforma Sociale*, March–April 1934, p. 134, a letter was published from an anonymous contributor, who revealed himself to be especially anxious concerning the following problem:

How shall we organize corporations which are composed of those workers, employers, agricultural labourers, and managers, *who do not yet exist?* Hitherto society has progressed, not through the efforts of men who have followed some established industry and placed on the market some commodity that was already known, but through the efforts of those who have proved the possibility of destroying existing businesses by using new systems of production and organization or by creating new industries for new or unknown commodities. What will be the lot of the inventor, of the innovator, in an economic world organized in corporations? Such a man does not belong to any corporation and, if his activities are successful, he may subvert, perhaps ruin, some of the existing corporations. Will not the innovator find himself faced with a bronze wall of vested interests, which derive added strength from the legalization of their organization? What organization, moreover, will represent the point of view of the consumer? Will there not be a danger that the corporation, inevitably emanating from the productive classes, workers and traders, will be inclined to shift the centre of gravity of the economic world, which has hitherto hinged upon the needs of the consumer, to the interests of the producer? Will it not, little by little, try to discipline, regulate, and control in its own interests the will of the consumer? It makes me shiver to hear and read many of the complaints of my colleagues, who are distressed because the consumer is incapable of picking out the best article, is plagued by a hundred superstitions, and prefers the article with this or that trademark or label, domestic or foreign. Give but a taste of power to these men who are comfortably esconced in their economic nooks, and there will be no escaping from them. Does it not seem as if we should soon see all branches of human industry at the point where barristers, solicitors, and druggists have already arrived, and where doctors, accountants, graduates of schools of business administration, engineers, geometricians, etc., would like to arrive—that is, the proclamation of closed ranks and the exclusion of all newcomers from the field?

The author of the letter ended with the statement that nevertheless "he was not worried because he knew that the system was in the hands of Signor Mussolini, a man gifted with extraordinary intuition, etc., etc." All psalms in Fascist Italy terminate in praise of Mussolini. "But [continued the writer] it is natural that I should wish to be convinced that the corporative system is capable of functioning by its own merits as well as by those of its head."

The editor of the review, Senator Einaudi, commenting on this letter, explained that if the Fascist corporation was to be useful to the country, it must not interfere with the mobility of men and capital or prevent the rise of new enterprises. It must not result in the "limitation of new plants" but in "the continual creation of new plants and the simultaneous elimination of old and superfluous plants":

What this organ or group of organs may be, or what the regulatory mechanism may be, I do not know. I only know that the corporative system will live *because and if* it creates organs and mechanisms capable, not of "limiting" but of "selecting" firms, employers, workers; not of excluding and reducing, but of receiving and increasing the number of producers and products (pp. 146–7).

Men like Einaudi are subject to such doubts because they are children of the past. If they were endowed with "corporative faith" they would repeat with Dr. Einzig:

In the corporate State it is not possible for the producer of a raw material to sacrifice the interests of the users of raw material in order to satisfy the wage demand of their employees nor is it possible for the manufacturers of finished goods to buy industrial peace at the cost of consumers.[11]

Mussolini solemnly announces that "in the corporative state labour is no longer the object of the economic system, but its subject, because it is labour which forms and accumulates capital."[12] In the corporative state "the direction of production is not imposed from above, by an organ or a body external to the productive activity; it is imposed by the

---

[11] Einzig, *Economic Foundations*, p. 33.
[12] Mussolini's speech, March 19, 1934.

categories themselves, for the categories express themselves through the corporations; the corporation is the instrument through which production organically disciplines itself." [13] "For the first time in modern economic history the workers are taking an active part in directing economic life." [14] "In antiquity labour was predominantly the task of the slave, who was legally neither a person nor a thing; in the legal philosophy of liberalism labour was an economic commodity not to be distinguished from other commodities; in the Fascist philosophy labour is something above and beyond this conception: it is a manifestation of the human personality, the realization of an ethical and cultural principle." [15]

Do you wish a picture of the Italian workman, not as he will be when the corporation has transformed him from an object into a subject, but as the corporation, which did not yet exist, had already transformed him? Mr. Odon Por in the review *New Britain*, January 17, 1934, has painted his portrait for you:

> Corporate action is a great spiritual function. It gives a new spiritual status to the producer, lends a new significance to his work. His point of view changes, his work assumes a value, becomes a public function. With everything he does or makes not only the immediate value and the immediate indispensable interests are considered, but there arises spontaneously the question whether it is done in the public interest or not. The individual becomes permeated with public responsibilities. The corporate conscience, dynamic and constructive, drives him ahead; he seeks to affirm himself in social tasks, beyond the narrow limits of his daily work, though his daily work itself may be regarded in the light of a social task. The true corporate action is born and is developing from a spiritual need: it is an action in which the individual's profit-motive is one of the minor factors and often a handicap. The corporate attitude and spirit is that of the future man.

Do you wish to understand the tragic error of liberalism? Signor Bottai will explain it to you. The liberal state "granted political rights to the working classes without granting them equality before the civil law." [16]

---

[13] Memorandum introducing the bill to the Senate. The last words in the Italian text are: "La Corporazione fu definita lo strumento dell' autodisciplina organica della produzione."

[14] Statement of Signor Cianetti, Italian delegate, at the session of the International Labour Office on June 15, 1934.

[15] Address by Signor Longhi, Attorney-General of the Supreme Court, in *Corriere della Sera*, Oct. 30, 1934.

[16] In Sillani (ed.), *What is Fascism and Why?*, p. 31.

It was obviously to put an end to that tragic error that the Fascist dictatorship abolished political rights in Italy and so placed them on the same plane as civil rights. If you thought this, you were mistaken. Signor Biagi, the Under-Secretary of Corporations, speaking to the International Labour Office at Geneva on June 24, 1933, stated that "the equality of right between capital and labour is not only an affirmation of high moral, social, and political value, but it is being constantly applied under the Fascist regime. Italy is the first country in the world to have a corporative and syndical system placing capital and labour on a footing of equality." [17]

In the corporation the representatives of the employers and those of the employees will voice their immediate needs, but they will be corporative men. The experts and the high state officials, likewise corporative men, will look at things from the point of view of technique, which transcends the immediate needs of the two particular groups. The delegates of the Fascist Party, also corporative men, will watch the affairs of the corporation from still another point of view, taking as their criterion the interest of the nation. And Mussolini, the corporative man *par excellence*, will take the most elevated view of all, and will correct—Mussolini the infallible, Mussolini "the state"—the eventual deviations which weakness of the flesh may produce in lesser corporative men. "National necessity," "higher interests of the country," "higher aims of production"— Italy today is full of these and similar sublime expressions. Who defines, in individual cases, those necessities, those interests, those aims? The "state." Who is the "state"? Mussolini.

If one does not seek realities behind the veil of words, one will swallow all this verbiage, and repeat that "Fascism guarantees to labour a social equality with capital by the system of class equalization in the corporative state." [18] But if one is accustomed to take a realistic view of things and succeeds in penetrating behind the smoke-screen with which propaganda conceals the concrete features of the system, one cannot help reaching the conclusion that the Fascist corporations may be compared to the mechanism conceived by the imagination of Heine, which was similar to a man and capable of doing a man's work to perfection, but to which its creator had not been able to give a soul. They are a mechanism without a soul.

---

[17] *Corriere della Sera*, June 25, 1933.
[18] Sokolsky, *Recognizing the Company Union*, p. 298.

The Fascist "thinkers" teach that "for Fascism the social problem is a question of production and not of distribution of wealth"; that "one must overcome the criteria of distributive justice"; that "destiny is rarely just in the distribution of goods among men"; that "the wealth of the few in whose hands capital is concentrated is also the wealth of the proletariat"; and that "the Kingdom of Love must be established in spirit as well as in matter: that is the great teaching of Fascism." [19] It may be said that these doctrines are the best that the human spirit has thus far been able to find to solve the problem of poverty. But to pretend that they can lead, indeed that they have led in Italy to a social revolution is to take a little too much advantage of human imbecility.

Mussolini has solved the problem of the relations between capital and labour by the same methods which Marinetti used to create a new art, a new literature, and a new cuisine. Marinetti invented the word "futurism," organized a diabolical outcry around that word, and finally succeeded in making people believe in the existence of futurism. Mussolini took over a nebulous term "corporation," organized around that war-cry an uproar still more diabolical than the example given by Marinetti, and succeeded in convincing many people that the salvation of the world lay in the corporation. All the categories of the traditional economic system remain intact: profit, interest, and wages. But profit becomes the corporative salary of the employer; interest becomes the corporative salary of the capitalist; wages become the corporative profit and interest of the worker. The worker is no longer a worker, but has become "a civil servant in the broadest sense of the term." Don Quixote attacked windmills as if they were real monsters; Mussolini deals with real monsters as if they were windmills.

---

[19] Elwin, *Fascism at Work*, pp. 194–5.

Part Two

THE ACHIEVEMENTS

I

Italian "Bolshevism" in
1919 and 1920

To prove that in the Fascist organizations and corporations the lower classes have no other right than that of paying annual dues, is not to prove that the Fascist system is actually harmful to labour. In an animal welfare society the animals do not elect the officials nor do they participate in the meetings at which the society's affairs are discussed. Therefore, as far as the animals are concerned, the society is not democratic. Yet no one can harbour any doubts as to the goodwill of the society's officials and the efficacy of their work for animal welfare. The fact that the officials of the Fascist unions are not "elected" from below but are "appointed" from above and that the members have no voice in the conduct of their organizations, does not give one the right to draw the conclusion that the workers' interests are sacrificed to those of the employers.

The Fascists maintain that their political system ought to be judged, not with reference to abstract democratic prepossessions, but with reference to the concrete social results which that system produces. If the Fascist regime has bestowed upon the Italian people a degree of prosperity and well-being superior to that which the pre-Fascist regime was able to assure them, then the Fascist regime requires no other justification. Political regimes, whether democratic or Fascist, are not ends in themselves but means to a higher end: the welfare of the people. What conditions obtained among the Italian labouring classes before the Fascist organizations superseded the Socialist and Christian-Democratic organizations? What have been the achievements of the Fascist system? The tree is judged by its fruits.

One cannot take up this problem without being overwhelmed by harrowing descriptions of the conditions prevailing in Italy under the free pre-Fascist regime before Mussolini had set out to rescue the country from chaos, disorder, and poverty. For example, in April 1927, Dr. Nicholas Murray Butler, president of Columbia University, described in the following terms the abyss out of which Mussolini had pulled Italy:

> Six million Italians were one day without water to drink or with which to cleanse themselves. The railways had broken down, the postal service was wrecked, the roads were in disrepair; brigandage, anarchy, and crime were rampant everywhere.[1]

Bernard Shaw, in the *Manchester Guardian* of October 28, 1927, asserted that before October 1922 Italy was not provided with "her daily material needs"; "the first job of any government is to carry on, and to make its citizens carry on, liberty or no liberty: nature allows no chance, and stands no nonsense; it is a case of work or starve"; Mussolini arrived; the putrefying corpse of liberty was then trampled down; and the Italian people began to work and ceased to starve.

No harm will be done if we do not take Bernard Shaw seriously; quite the contrary! But must we not genuflect in reverence before the utterances of such a dignitary as the president of Columbia University?

Yet Dr. Butler's assertions do not stand the test of a careful scrutiny.

1. "Bankruptcy." During the five years preceding the World War the annual average number of bankruptcies was 6029; in 1919 and 1920 there were 593 and 798 bankruptcies respectively: these were the two "Bolshevik years" par excellence! In 1921 and 1922 the number rose to 1896 and 3858 respectively. In 1927—the year in which President Butler eulogized the Fascist dictatorship—there were 11,418 bankruptcies![2] Still less can one speak of governmental bankruptcy. The extraordinary claims arising from the liquidation of the war were duly met. In January 1920 a national loan was floated that brought in 18 billion lire,[3] or about $1,300,000,000 at the rate of exchange then prevailing. The first instance of governmental bankruptcy in the financial history of Italy occurred in November 1926, when the Fascist government, unable to pay 27 billion in short-term bonds (*buoni del tesoro*), obliged their holders to accept consols instead of cash.[4]

2. "Six million Italians were one day without water to drink or with which to cleanse themselves." Probably Dr. Butler had been told by

---

[1] Butler, *Looking Forward*, p. 191.
[2] *Annuario Statistico Italiano:* 1933, p. 460.
[3] De Stefani, *Documenti:* May 1933, p. 367.
[4] Mortara, *Prospettive Economiche:* 1927, pp. 346–7; *idem: 1928*, p. 465.

someone—heaven knows by whom—that during the winter of 1921–22 there were acute difficulties in the electrical industries of northern Italy as a result of an exceptional summer drought, which had exhausted the reserves of water power. His informant had neglected to tell him that the government had met this crisis by importing electricity from Switzerland.[5] Drawing upon his own fancy, Dr. Butler invented the fairy-tale of the six million Italians who were one day unable to cleanse themselves.

3. "The railways had broken down." The roadbeds and the rolling stock had been put to a severe test during the war when the necessary repairs and replacements could not be made. The government had even been obliged to tear up certain stretches of lines in order to utilize the steel rails for military purposes. By 1918 the *matériel* had been reduced to a disastrous state.[6] Furthermore, the import of coal was frequently interrupted during 1919 and 1920 by the strikes of the English miners, transport workers, dockers, and seamen; the Italian railway service suffered especially from this.[7] The indiscipline of the Italian railwaymen increased the disorder, which was especially severe during 1920. But it is untrue to say that "the railways had broken down." As soon as the war was over, the railroad administration took up the question of placing new orders for equipment with Italian firms, and a programme covering the needs of the railways for five years—it would now be called a "five-year plan"—was set in motion.[8] By the end of 1922 the rolling stock had been considerably augmented and in large part renewed.[9] That is why the trains from then onwards could "run on time." In 1913–4, the Italian railways had carried 42 million tons of freight and 93 million passengers. By 1917–8, the last year of the war, there had been a drop to 33.5 million tons and 65 million passengers. In 1922 the railways carried 41 million tons and 91 million passengers.[10]

4. "The postal service was wrecked." The postal service shows the following statistics:

---

[5] Bachi, *L'Italia Economica nel 1921*, pp. 221, 305.

[6] *Commerce Reports*, May 27, 1919; Feb. 13, Apr. 27, 1920; March 20, 1921; May, 1, 1922.

[7] *Ibid.*, May 27; Sept. 1, 6, 16; Oct. 19, 28; Dec. 19, 29, 1919; Apr. 27, 1920; March 2, 7, 1921.

[8] *Ibid.*, May 27, 1919.

[9] Mortara, *Prospettive Economiche: 1923*, p. 330.

[10] *Ibid.*, 1923, pp. 338–9. *Annuario Statistico: 1930*, p. 586.

Years	Letters
1918– 9	2,371,000,000
1919–20	2,126,000,000
1920– 1	1,808,000,000
1921– 2	1,809,000,000 [11]

The fall in 1919–21 was to due demobilization: the men, no longer being under arms, had no need to exchange letters with their families. In January 1921, the postal rates were raised, and this caused another fall in the volume of mail. In 1926–7, when Dr. Butler made his statement, the number of letters was 2,005,000,000,[12] or less than in 1919–20, when "the postal service was wrecked."

5. "The roads were in disrepair." The following figures give the number of motor cars registered in Italy:

Year	Private Cars	Public Vehicles	Commercial Vehicles
1918	5,592	1,235	5,547
1919	21,759	2,124	10,613
1920	28,604	2,862	17,410
1921	31,161	2,977	22,422
1922	75,842	8,934	? [13]

The growing number of motor cars increased the wear and tear on the roads, but the government, being obliged to meet the extraordinary expenses dependent on the war, was unable to expand road appropriations in proportion to the needs. In 1927 the state of the Italian roads was not better than in 1922. It was not until 1928 that the Fascist government began, with adequate means and a coherent programme, to face this problem, which could no longer be deferred.[14]

6. "Brigandage and crime were rampant." Brigandage was even before the war nothing but a memory, nor was there any sign of it in Italy during the after-war years. There were at that time outlaws and fugitives from justice, just as there are in the United States today without anyone's speaking of "brigandage." As regards "crime," it must be admitted that in Italy crimes of violence have always been more than

---

[11] De Stefani, *Documenti*, 1923, p. 417.
[12] *Annuario Statistico Italiano:* 1930, p. 308.
[13] *Ibid.*, 1919–21, p. 377; *idem:* pp. 273–4. The figure for 1922 is unknown.
[14] *Il Bilancio dello Stato*, p. 402.

they should be in a civilized country. In 1914 there were 3411 homicides and 109,740 injured in criminal assaults. During the war crimes of violence diminished, and in 1918 the figures were 1983 and 58,148 respectively: the bloodthirsty had been enrolled in the army, along with the pacifically inclined, and had excellent opportunities for venting their instincts and talents on the national enemy. After the war was over, not only the bloodthirsty returned home, but also the peaceable, many of whom had become bloodthirsty. Hence the homicides rose to 3100 in 1919 and to 5034 in 1920, while the number of injured rose to 75,334 in 1919 and to 92,792 in 1920. In the same way the homicides committed in France, which in 1913 had been 591 and in 1918, 398, rose to 781 in 1921;[15] and in Germany the number of homicides which had been 120 in 1913, and 92 in 1918, rose to 283 in 1921.[16] During the two years of civil war in Italy, 1921 and 1922, crimes of violence increased still more:

Year	Homicides	Persons injured in criminal assaults
1921	5,735	101,710
1922	6,278	108,208

In 1923, after the civil war had been ended by the Fascist conquest of power, homicides began to diminish, until in 1926 they had dropped to 3445, the level of 1914. But the number of persons injured in criminal assaults rose to 117,295 in 1926.[17]

7. "Anarchy." If by anarchy is meant every strike, every fight in the street, every loud noise, it is undeniable that during 1919 and 1920 Italy was in a state of anarchy; the Italians are a noisy people: they cannot do anything without making a great noise, and they often make a great noise without doing anything. And if by anarchy we mean the civil war of 1921 and 1922, then likewise during those two years Italy was in a state of anarchy. But if instead, by "anarchy" we mean the disruption of political machinery or the disorganization of economic production—then there never was a moment of anarchy in Italy from 1919 to 1922.

Anyone who wishes can consult the dispatches sent from Italy to Washington during those years by the American commercial attachés and printed in *Commerce Reports*. In these reports there is not the slight-

---

[15] *Annuaire Statistique de la France:* 1926, p. 40.
[16] *Kriminalstatistik des Deutschen Reiches:* 1913, pp. 294–5; *idem:* 1918, pp. 20–1; *idem:* 1921, pp. 8–9.
[17] *Annuario Statistico Italiano:* 1911, p. 85; *idem:* 1916, p. 118; *idem:* 1929, p. 126.

est indication of any state of anarchy, chaos, bankruptcy, or the like. "Many American firms are extending their business connexions in Italy" (October 16, 1919). The Italians who had emigrated to America were so little frightened by "Bolshevism," that they were returning to Italy with their pockets full of money: "the wealth brought back by these people forms at present a large source of income in southern Italy" (August 14 and October 10, 1919). Nor were tourists being scared away by anarchy: "the volume of tourist traffic is now steadily increasing, and the big hotels report a fair amount of business" (October 22, 1920). The Italians were even indulging in the luxury of organizing an international art exposition at Venice (April 15, 1920). "Textile industries have reached a point where they are able not only to supply the ordinary needs of Italy, but to produce a surplus for export" (August 22, 1919). "The year 1919 was an extremely prosperous one . . . a period of unusual activity which has since continued" (July 22, 1920).

The Italian people have given tangible evidence of their faith in the ultimate ability of their Government to support the financial burden it has been called upon to assume as a direct result of the war. The increase of over 35 per cent in the deposits in the Italian savings banks from December 1918 to October 1919 . . . demonstrates very clearly that the Italian people are ready to confide their savings to the Government. Another indication of the same attitude is given by the prices of the securities comprising the consolidated 5 per cent loan issued in 1917 at 86.50 lire. These securities have been consistently selling above the price of issue, and at the present time are quoted at 87 lire, in spite of the fact that the campaign for the new 5 per cent loan is being carried on with the utmost vigour. In 1866, after the wars of Italian independence, the 5 per cent bonds issued at that time fell to about 41 (February 20, 1920).

Almost without exception Italian industries have been and are extremely active; whenever possible electric power has been utilized; the use of fuel oil is steadily increasing; an exceptional demand for agricultural implements exists; automobile manufacturers are swamped with orders; the increase in the demand for manufactured silk products has been very marked, so much so that silk manufacturers are declining to accept any new orders for delivery before 1921; this may be accounted for by the greater purchasing power which has been acquired by certain classes of the population who are spending their increased earnings freely on articles of personal adornment; exports of silk textiles have practically ceased; moreover, silk textiles are being imported from Switzerland and are selling freely in spite of high prices; during the past six months the Italian banks report a volume of business considerably greater than in their period of greatest activity during the war; both the savings deposits and the deposits on current accounts have increased rapidly; the security market has been active, and prices have been well sustained (April 27, 1920).

According to the figures published by the Ministry of the Treasury, ordinary deposits increased from 1,491,170,560 lire on June 30, 1914 to 3,567,426,189 lire on June 30, 1919, and savings deposits from 6,000,-548,747 lire to 13,586,086,947 lire. The money deposited in the banks would not have been so utilized if the depositors had had debts on which they were obliged to pay interest, for necessarily such interest would be greater than that received on their bank deposits. The pawnshops are practically bare. . . . For several years there have been very few business failures in Italy and none of importance (July 30, 1920).

The amount of net investments in banking enterprise is [during the first six months of 1920] far greater than that in any of the other industries and reaches a figure never even approached by any other up to now. The investments in textile industries have in the first six months of 1920 reached a figure almost ten times greater than that for the corresponding period of 1919 (February 10, 1921).[18]

Who has not heard it repeated again and again that Mussolini found in October 1922 a deficit of 15 billion lire in the budget and that he reduced it to 3 billions during the same fiscal year? These figures are correct, but they should be supplemented with the information that the huge deficits during the fiscal years 1918-9 to 1921-2 were due to the extraordinary expenses dependent on the war. In May 1923, Signor De Stefani, Minister of Finance in Mussolini's cabinet from October 1922 to July 1925, pointed out this fact in the following words:

---

[18] From 1919 to 1921 the United States had among her commercial attachés in Italy a certain Mr. A. P. Dennis, who sent to Washington many reports that were published in the *Commerce Reports*. In none of these reports was Italy described as a country plunged in economic chaos and misery. The same Mr. A. P. Dennis, in Aug. 1929, described the condition of Italy from 1919 to 1922 in the following terms: "One's general impression of the black years of 1919, 1920, and 1921 was slackness—endless, tantalizing, heartbreaking slackness. Tens of thousands of soldiers still in uniform turned their hands to no useful account. Five husky laborers were employed by the state railways to do the work of two men. The country swarmed with beggars. Chaos, disorder, poverty reigned supreme. Lack of coal, lack of bread, worst of all lack of discipline. . . . Every man exercised not only the God-given liberty to talk but the license to act. One strike after another disheartened and demoralized the business enterprises of the country" (*World's Work*, Aug. 1929). Was Mr. Dennis carrying on propaganda in the period from 1919 to 1921 or in 1929?

The budget deficits of the last few years do not result solely from the discrepancy between current revenue and current expenditure, but from the fact that the deficits are swelled by many exceptional items dependent on the war. These, instead of being acknowledged in the budgets of their own years, weighed down the balance sheet of succeeding years. If the revenue and expenditure of 1921 are purged of all these items, the normal budget closes with a considerably smaller deficit. Also for 1922, the normal deficit is diminished to no small extent if the war claims are deducted.[19]

Signor De Stefani did not give definite figures, but if we search them out in the official documents where they are buried,[20] we come to the following results:

	Deficits	*Exceptional Expenditure Dependent on the War*
1918– 9	23,345,000,000	25,683,000,000
1919–20	11,494,000,000	12,424,000,000
1920– 1	20,955,000,000	22,339,000,000
1921– 2	17,169,000,000	18,264,000,000
1922– 3	3,260,000,000	4,837,000,000

This table shows that the deficits resulted from the exceptional war expenditures. The heaviest strain was felt in the four years immediately after the war.[21] When in 1923 the strain relaxed, the deficit likewise fell. In December 1921, Professor Mortara predicted that the deficit in the budget would probably disappear by 1924.[22]

The zone along the Austrian frontier, where the military operations had taken place between 1915 and 1918, was completely in ruins in 1919: 163,000 private dwellings, 346 town halls, 255 hospitals, 1156 schools, over a thousand churches, 122 cemeteries had either been destroyed or badly damaged; 80 drainage and irrigation works with an area of 120,000 hectares had been devastated; 349 kilometers of railway and 1158 kilometres of roads had been wrecked; 450,000 head of livestock had disappeared. During the years 1919 and 1922, everything—private houses,

---

[19] *Documenti*, May 1923, pp. 169–71.

[20] Rèpaci, *La Finanza Italiana*, p. 68.

[21] Mr. McGuire, in *Italy's International Economic Position*, p. 85, ignored the existence of the extraordinary war expenditures and was thus able to praise the financial efficiency of the Fascist regime for having caused the disappearance of the enormous deficit inherited from predecessors.

[22] *Prospettive Economiche: 1922*, p. 20. Cf. Salvemini, *Twelve Years of Fascist Finance*, p. 481.

churches, hospitals, schools, drainage, wells, public fountains, aqueducts, canals, embankments, bridges, railways, roads—all these had been rebuilt or repaired; the lost livestock had been entirely replaced. In order to effectuate these works of reconstruction the treasury was called upon to spend 8 billion lire.[23]

The so-called "Italian Bolshevism" of the post-war years referred to a disturbed social situation, not to an actual overthrowing of the capitalist social and political structure. Everybody spoke of social revolution, but neither a social nor even a political revolution took place.

Undoubtedly it would be absurd to assert that Italy enjoyed prosperity and happiness. She was a patient recovering from a terrible illness, the war. She passed through a severe crisis. But this was a crisis of readjustment and not of disorganization.

One of the features of this crisis was the epidemic of strikes, especially intense and troublesome in 1920. All countries were then suffering from this disease. In France the railwaymen and the postal employees did not even wait for the end of the war before striking,[24] whereas in Italy the railway and postal employees waited until 1920 to strike. A high French official, when conversing with Count Sforza, to whom we owe this information, revealed that in 1919 in the Department of the Doubs (Franche Comté) alone, there were fifty strikes in six months with 35,000 strikers; every mention of the war in public speeches was greeted by loud boos; anyone who wore war decorations was regarded with scorn. When President Poincaré made an official visit to Besançon, it was necessary to resort to the stratagem of having him announced as travelling on one train—which was assailed with stones and rifle shots en route—while in reality he was on another. In Italy demobilization gave occasion to none of those seditious movements which broke out in the British Army soon after the armistice,[25] nor was there ever, as there was in England in September 1919, a general railway strike, which paralysed the economic life of the country for nine days.[26] In Belgium during 1919 and 1920 there were so many strikes that the *Revue du Travail*, an official publication of the government, had to devote twenty-one columns of the index in its volume for 1920 to the enumeration of the

---

[23] Porri, *L' Evoluzion Economica*, pp. 88 ff., 249 ff., Serpieri, *La Guerra e le Classi Rurali*, pp. 235–9.

[24] Berget et Allard, *Les Secrets de la Censure*, p. 379.

[25] *Encyclopædia Britannica*, Suppl. 1926, VIII, p. 548.

[26] Webb, *History of Trade Unionism*, pp. 538–40.

strikes of the two preceding years. In the United States there were 2665 strikes with 4,160,000 strikers during 1919.[27] A police strike, such as occurred in Boston, never took place in Italy.

But Italy is the only country whose government has organized a spectacular world-wide propaganda campaign to prove that its people was so backward as to be incapable of self-government and that to educate it there was necessary the Fascist bludgeon and castor oil. Italy is the only country in the world whose government has striven intensively to erect the false glory of a single man on the unmerited discredit of an entire people.

---

[27] *Encyclopædia Britannica,* Suppl. 1926, p. 661.

II

Wages and the Cost of Living
under Italian "Bolshevism"

THE following table, drawn from official sources,[1] gives the index numbers of industrial wages and of retail prices in 1913, on the eve of the World War, and in 1921, the year in which Mussolini took upon himself the task of rescuing Italy from "Bolshevism," chaos, misery, anarchy, and all the other evils by which she was afflicted:

	Retail Prices	Industrial Wages
1913	100	100
1920	452	424.70
1921	501	557.74

Statistics of this sort are to be taken with several grains of salt:[2] the average between a man who suffers from a surfeit and another who is dying of hunger, is a man who has had a good dinner. But the increase in the real wages of the Italian workers during the years 1919–20 was a fact well known in those years. One of the accusations made against the workers' organizations by the "anti-Bolshevists" at that time was that they had caused wages to rise "beyond the point to which the prices of those goods which composed the items of the worker's budget had been raised": "the peasants and workers had never enjoyed such well-being and comfort as during these years."[3] During 1920 unemployment was insignificant.[4] This fact is to be explained by the following circumstances:

1. 1920 was a year of monetary inflation and hence of great industrial activity.[5]

---

[1] *Conto Riassuntivo del Tesoro*, July 31, 1926, pp. 27, 68.
[2] Cf. Giusti, *Methods of Recording Retail Prices*.
[3] Pantaleoni, *Bolscevismo Italiano*, pp. xiv, xvii.
[4] Maclean, *Labor, Wages, and Unemployment in Italy*, p. 13. Banca Commerciale Italiana, *Movimento Economico dell'Italia: 1922–5*, p. 9.
[5] *Commerce Reports*, Jan. 30, Feb. 13, Apr. 13, 17, 27, July 21, 1920; Jan. 19, Feb. 10, March 25, July 7, 1921; *Industrial and Labour Information*, Feb. 9, 1923, p. 18.

2. Six hundred and fifty thousand men of working age had died in the war; 460,000 had been disabled; and a million people, of whom a fourth were men of working age, had died in epidemics. In all there had been a loss of about a million and a half workers between 1915 and 1919.[6]

3. No sooner had the regulations prohibiting emigration been revoked in June 1919, than the Italian workers and peasants began to emigrate again; in 1920 there were 400,000 emigrants as against 200,000 repatriated.[7]

4. By a decree of November 17, 1918, the government had set aside 3,300,000,000 lire for public works in order to avoid unemployment during the transition period between the state of war and peace.[8]

The well-being of the Italian working classes in 1919 and 1920 is not to be attributed to high wages: in 1921 wages had a purchasing power scarcely ten per cent higher than those of 1913. But every member of each working-class family—man, woman, or boy—was gainfully employed. The great strikes of 1920 were made possible by the scarcity of labour, while the inflation was raising the cost of living and driving the workers to demand higher wages.

In 1921 the depression which the other countries had begun to feel in the spring of 1920 became evident in Italy.[9] The policy of monetary deflation initiated by the government in January 1921 only aggravated it.[10] Throughout 1921 unemployment increased and was intense during the first months of 1922.[11] But as the year 1922 progressed, the symptoms

[6] *The Effects of the War on the Population of Italy*, p. 2. Mortara, *La Salute Pubblica in Italia durante e dopo la Guerra*, pp. 107, 563.

[7] Mortara, *Prospettive Economiche: 1922*, p. 382. The figures for emigration and repatriation must be regarded as rough approximations. There were extensive clandestine currents which elude official statistics.

[8] International Labour Office, *L'Action gouvernementale dans la lutte contre le chômage en Italie*, p. 22.

[9] "The crisis was evident in the world markets during the second half of 1920, and now warns us of difficult times and severe economic stress ahead. It made itself felt during last spring [1920] in Japan, whence it spreads step by step over the entire world. The immediate future promises great economic hardship."—Bachi, *L'Italia Economica nel 1919*, pp. xii, 193, 224; *idem* for 1921, pp. 221, 305.

[10] *Commerce Reports*, Feb. 3, June 9, Aug. 19, Nov. 14, Dec. 29, 1921; Jan. 9, 16, March 13, Apr. 10, 1922; *Industrial and Labour Information*, Feb. 9, 1923, p. 16; MacLean, *Labor, Wages and Unemployment in Italy*, p. 2.

[11] Signor Villari, *The Economics of Fascism*, p. 105, states that "in 1919–22 unemployment averaged between 500,000 and 600,000." This is not so. Not until Feb. 1922 did the official statistics give the unemployed figure as high as 602,000. In 1919 the unemployed statistics had not yet been organized; in 1920 the figures oscillated between 88,000 and 107,000; in 1921 between 250,000 and 512,000 (*Annuario Statistico Italiano: 1919–21*, p. 400).

of recovery became more and more evident.[12] In the meantime wages began to go down. The movements of retail prices and industrial wages in 1921 and 1922 were as follows:

	Retail Prices	*Industrial Wages*
1921	501	557.74
1922	527	503.57

The reductions in wages during 1922 were admitted without question by all experts.[13]

Coming to the agricultural workers, we have no official statistics giving the ups and downs of their wages for the whole of Italy. From a study on the province of Milan we gather that agricultural wages went down from the index number 100 for a working day of seven and one-half hours in 1920–1 to the index numbers of from 75 to 71.12 for an eight-hour day in 1921–2.[14]

A study of the other provinces of Italy would doubtless lead to analogous results. Take, for example a farm in the province of Bologna, comparing a year's earnings under the Socialist agreement of 1920 with those under the agreement stipulated by the Fascists in 1922. The farm-worker's family was composed of five able-bodied persons, three men and two women:

	1920	*1922*
Men	12,087.93 lire	9,967.44 lire
Women	5,331.20 "	4,429.60 "
Total	17,419.13 "	14,397.04 "

[12] *Commerce Reports*, June 12, Oct. 2, 9, 30; Nov. 2, 6, 13, 1922; *Industrial and Labour Information*, Feb. 9, 1923, p. 18. Bachi, *L'Italia Economica nel 1921*, p. 7. Mortara, *Prospettive Economiche:* 1923, pp. xvi ff; *idem:* 1924, pp. xi, xiii. Einaudi in *Encyclopædia Britannica*, Suppl. 1926, p. 573. Perroud, *Contributions*, p. 62. Mitzakis, *Les Grands Problèmes*, p. 95. McGuire, in *Italy's International Economic Position*, p. 15, admits that by 1922 Italy had already passed the post-war crisis; yet he goes on to asseverate that Italy "must surely have been engulfed in economic chaos if no change had come." He who wishes to speculate on how things might have been had they been different, can always maintain that they would have taken place exactly as he likes to imagine.

[13] Mortara, *Prospettive Economiche:* 1925, p. 422. In regard to the wage-cuts undergone by the Milanese workers in 1922 we have the data collected by Ernesto Rossi, *I Salari degli Operai Milanesi*. Signor Rossi was condemned in 1931 to twenty years imprisonment for his anti-Fascist activities; but no one has ever disputed the results of this and of other studies by him on the economic and financial history of Italy during the post-war years.

[14] Rossi, *I Salari degli Operai Milanesi*, p. 562 ff.

While the farm-worker's family had its share thus reduced by 3,022.09 lire a year, the owner had his profit increased by 3,232.05 lire.[15]

In the province of Cremona the Socialist pact of 1920 assured each agricultural day-labourer an annual income of 5254 lire, while the Fascist pact of 1922 reduced this to 4900 lire.[16]

A great deal was said in March 1921 about a certain agricultural agreement whereby the Fascists of the province of Ferrara promised to transform the farm hands into small independent proprietors, thanks to the generosity of the landowners imbued with the Fascist spirit. The details of this agreement were as follows: the former proprietor was to cede the land to the cultivator for a price to be paid in annual instalments over a long term of years; but the contract was to be considered fulfilled and title conveyed only when the cultivator had paid the last instalment; by missing a single payment, the contract would automatically be invalidated and the old proprietor would resume absolute possession of the property, retaining also those instalments already paid; the cultivator was to put his harvested crops in the storehouses of the owner, who would take charge of their sale, subtracting his own claims before handing over what was left to the cultivator; the former proprietor retained the right to supervise the activities of the cultivator and to interfere when he considered them harmful to the land. Signor Missiroli, a journalist at present one of Mussolini's faithful followers, in August 1921 commented as follows on this agreement:

The agreement is final as far as the rights and guarantees of the vendor are concerned, but in a state of flux as regards the obligations of the buyer. The latter may not dispose of the land freely, unless he has completed the final payment. Reciprocal treatment is absent. Not only is the use and even the cultivation of the land subject to the surveillance of the vendor, but the agreement contains an absolutely fatal clause which provides that the passing of a single payment annuls the entire agreement. It goes so far as to stipulate that any loss, even if caused by *force majeure* [e. g., floods, earthquakes, cyclones, etc.], is to be charged to the buyer who, however, cannot allege *force majeure* in case he misses one of his payments.[17]

---

[15] *Mondo*, Aug. 1926. The *Mondo* was an anti-Fascist paper, but its figures were not challenged.

[16] Avarna di Gualtieri, *op. cit.*, pp. 118–20. Villari, *The Awakening of Italy*, p. 233, reproduces an article from the *Popolo d'Italia* which is most enthusiastic over the Cremona agreement, but he gives no intimation as to its actual effect upon the workers.

[17] Missiroli, *Il Fascismo e la Crisi Italiana*, pp. 40–1.

A Fascist of syndicalist origin, Signor Lanzillo, wrote in 1922:

The description given by Missiroli of the local conditions with which he is acquainted [in Emilia] scarcely differ from those obtaining in Apulia, Umbria, Tuscany, and the province of Parma. Idealism is here nothing but a cloak for the contraband of an agrarian class organization which has for its object the defeat of the peasants' organizations and aims at preventing the enforcement and renewal of the agricultural agreements.[18]

In the province of Ferrara the Socialist pact of 1920 had assured the day-labourers a wage which fluctuated from 1.50 to 2.30 lire an hour according to the season; under the Fascist agreement of 1922 the hourly wage ranged from 0.85 to 1.05 lire.[19]

It would, however, be unfair to attribute the fall in industrial and agricultural wages exclusively to the Fascists. As we have already mentioned, during the second half of 1921 and the first half of 1922 Italy was labouring under a somewhat acute economic depression. In a period of depression wages cannot fail to be pared down more or less drastically whatever the political conditions. The Fascists did not create the depression; but by dissolving the Socialist and Christian-Democratic unions and creating in their stead new unions which did nothing to protect the workers, they certainly aggravated that downward trend in wages which the depression had already rendered inevitable.

---

[18] Lanzillo, *Le Rivoluzioni del Dopo Guerra*, pp. 225–6.
[19] Avarna di Gualtieri, *loc. cit.*

III

Italian Labour from 1923 to 1925

THE years from 1923 to 1925 were a period of prosperity for the whole world, and Italy participated in it. Furthermore, in Italy during 1925 a new wave of monetary inflation gave an artificial stimulus to economic activity.

But the real wages of Italian labour continued to decrease, as the following table shows:

	Retail prices	*Wages*
1913	100.00	100.00
1922	527	539.53
1923	518	503.57
1924	538	505.95
1925	605	566.37
1926 (first half)	633	594.05 [1]

This decrease in real wages in Italy during a period of economic expansion can be explained in only one way: the Socialist and Christian-Democratic unions had collapsed, and the Fascist unions did not make any serious attempt to protect Italian labour against the omnipotence of the employers.

In 1925, Professor Gini, a one-hundred-per-cent Fascist, wrote as follows:

The food ration, which during the war had substantially declined for the civil population, had been increasing during the post-war period, having again reached in 1922 the pre-war level and even having slightly exceeded

---

[1] *Conto Riassuntivo del Tesoro*, July 31, 1926, pp. 27, 68. Sir Ernest Benn, in the *Star* of Apr. 7, 1926, asserted that in Italy "prices were always falling a little." Mortara, *Prospettive Economiche: 1927*, p. 442, gives a different set of index figures. But this difference in statistical methods does not in the least affect the results obtained. After 1927 Mortara found it advisable not to concern himself with certain dangerous subjects and therefore ceased to include a chapter on labour in his *Prospettive*. Nay more, in the *Prospettive* for 1929 (p. 454), 1930 (p. 517), and 1931 (p. 459) the index numbers which had been given in the issues for 1927 (p. 442) and 1928 (p. 442) disappeared, and in their places appeared other series, according to which wages had increased rather than fallen in 1923. *La trahison des clercs!*

it; but after that year it declined, and for 1924 it appears to be notably less than before the war. . . . The indices of food consumption prove that the Italian people, who even before the war were not abundantly nourished from the physiological standpoint, have been compelled to reduce still further their consumption of food, and in the last two years have been in a situation constantly less favourable.[2]

An inquiry made into the wages of the workers in Milan from 1921 to the first half of 1926 [3] enables us to trace year by year the movement of nominal and real wages for workers in the following categories: printing and bookbinding trades, building trades, carpentering, engineering, and the chemical industries. In all these categories conditions grew worse during the years 1923, 1924, and 1925. In the first half of 1926, the Fascist unions, under pressure of the ever-increasing cost of living, obtained some improvements, which, however, in hardly a single instance brought real wages up to the level of 1921 and 1922.

A French writer to whom no one could possibly attribute an anti-Fascist bias, writes:

Thanks to the authority of the new regime, wage reductions were effected without great difficulty until 1924 . . . Unfortunately, the retail price levels rose again beginning with the second half of 1924. The reductions in wages had been considerable, since in three years the general index had dropped around seventy points. Taking advantage of the mortal blow struck at the regime by the assassination of Matteotti, the unions demanded and obtained an increase in wages. But on the whole, these were insufficient; wages remained in general below those of 1923 and of 1913. . . . With the year 1925 we notice an alteration in the policy of the government, which thenceforth paid more attention to the betterment of the workers' lot in order to compensate, *at least in part*, the increased cost of living. . . . Thus we see the general index of wages augmented by 100 points, passing from 487 to 584. *During this same time, it is true, the cost of living underwent a still more notable increase*, which carried the general average to 657 for December 1926, as against 536 for the second half of 1925. Real wages hence were still kept at an insufficient level. Yet Fascist industry enjoyed its two years of greatest prosperity.[4]

---

[2] In McGuire, *Italy's International Economic Position*, pp. 514–5.

[3] Rossi, *Salari degli Operai Milanesi dal 1921 al 1° Semestre 1926*, p. 552.

[4] Mitzakis, *Les Grands Problèmes Italiens*, pp. 99–101. Concerning the difficult conditions of the Italian working class in 1926, see another French writer, likewise anything but hostile to Fascist "syndicalism," yet intelligent and honest, L. Naudeau, *L'Italie Fasciste et l'Autre Danger*, p. 154 ff.

Thus, "the betterment of the workers' lot" to which the Fascist government is supposed to have applied itself in 1925 and 1926 consisted in raising the cost of living faster than money wages, thereby reducing real wages, while Fascist industry "enjoyed its two years of greatest prosperity."

As regards the workers in agriculture, a high official in the agricultural unions declared in 1931 that the average agricultural wage in Italy had gone up from 13.41 lire a day in 1922 to 14.34 lire a day in 1926.[5] In the province of Bologna, according to the calculations of the Fascist authorities, the agricultural wage remained constant at 19.80 lire a day from 1922 to 1926.[6] Even if these data are blindly accepted, all that is necessary is to compare them with the cost of living, which, as a result of inflation, climbed from the index number 498 in 1922 to the index number 653 in 1925, and it will be immediately apparent how marked a deterioration manifested itself in the real wages of this section of the Italian people.

But reasons are not lacking to make us suspect the trustworthiness of information concerning wages that is derived from Fascist sources. Let us compare some labour agreements concluded by the Socialist unions prior to 1922 with those made by the Fascist unions in 1924, 1925, and 1926.

Province of Cremona [7]

	1921–2	*1924*
Head stable-boys	3560 lire per annum plus 4.5 quintals of cheese and 4 quintals of maize	3100 lire per annum plus 4 quintals of cheese, 3 quintals of maize, and a share in the production of milk which may reach a value of 500 lire
Cattlemen	3960 lire per annum plus cheese and maize in the same amounts as head stable-boys	3100 lire per annum plus cheese, maize, and a share in milk production in the same amounts as the head stable-boys
Day-labourers	2.20 lire per hour for	2 lire per hour for men

---

[5] *Corriere della Sera*, Sept. 27, 1931.
[6] *Resto del Carlino*, Dec. 1, 1931.
[7] International Labour Office, *Conferences*, Seventh Session, 1925, vol. II, Third part, appendices and index; pp. 616–7.

	1921–2	*1924*
	men and 1 lira per hour for women	and 0.80 lire per hour for women
Potters	2.35 lire per hour plus a cost-of-living allowance of 6 lire per day	2.15 lire per hour
Woodworkers	From 3.17 to 2.23 lire per hour	From 2.50 to 1.50 lire per hour
Masons	25.65 lire per day	23.20 lire per day

PROVINCE OF PADUA [8]

	1920–1	*1925–6*
Day-labourers		
Men	1.40 lire per hour	1.35 lire per hour
Women	0.80 " " "	0.75 " " "
Labourers on yearly contract	700 lire per annum, plus wages in kind as follows: maize, 10 quintals per annum; wheat, 4 quintals per annum; wine, 200 litres per annum	600 lire per annum, plus wages in kind as follows: maize, 8 quintals per annum; wheat, 2 quintals per annum; wine, 200 litres per annum

PROVINCE OF FOGGIA [9]

(Daily Wages for Harvesting During the Hottest Months, for Ten Hours' Work)

	1920	*1926*
Worker of first category	25　lire	20　lire
"　" second　"	23　"	20　"

---

[8] *Avanti*, Feb. 26 and March 19, 1926. A parish priest living in the province of Padua wrote in the *Corriere Veneto* of Sept. 24, 1926: "The agricultural wage earners receive 1.35 lire per hour. If they dare ask for more, they run the risk of being turned out of the miserable hovels which, as a rule, are provided for them. This rate of payment is quite inadequate for the needs of a family, given the high prices of the bare necessities of life; all the more so, as the labourer works an entire day only in summer and in autumn, being often unemployed in winter and spring. Let us hope that next year more humane conditions will be established."

[9] *Ibid.*, Aug. 24, 1926. The *Avanti*, a Socialist organ, never had its statements challenged. In the *Westminster Gazette* of Aug. 4, 1926, Signor Villari wrote: "I can state from recent personal investigation in the province of Grosseto, *which is typical*

	1920	*1926*
Worker of third category	19¼ lire	17½ lire
" " fourth "	18 "	16 "
Women and boys	12 "	6.60 "

The above-mentioned author of the inquiry on wages in the province of Milan reached the following conclusions:

The condition of the peasant became worse in 1921–2 [after Fascist pressure began to make itself felt] and continued to grow worse until 1925. With the agreement of 1925–6 their condition improved, without, however, reaching the level of 1920–1, or even that of the two subsequent years. This depression seemed to make itself felt also in other Italian provinces. In the July 1926 number of the *Indici del Movimento Economico Italiano* of Padua University, a chart is given of the wages of workers in the province of Ferrara, which shows that the wage curve is practically stationary, in sharp contrast to the upward curve of prices and living costs.

Confronted with these facts, one may perhaps maintain that the economic structure of Italy could not bear the weight of the wages which were being paid to the Italian workers in 1920 and 1921, and that, therefore, a regime of lower wages was indispensable if a breakdown of the economic system was to be avoided. One may perhaps also maintain that the destruction of democratic institutions was necessary to compel the workers to give up the conditions secured by them in the years of so-called "Bolshevism," and content themselves with a lower standard of living. What no one can in good faith affirm is that the well-being of the working classes improved after the advent of the dictatorship. Yet in 1926 Signor Villari gave an alluring description of the growing prosperity enjoyed by the Italian people thanks to the Fascist regime:

No one who comes to Italy today after an absence of a few years can fail to be struck by the improved appearance of the people and by their manner of living. One need only visit the country districts of Italy and the working-class quarters of the towns, notice the clothes and shoes worn by the common

---

of many other areas, that agricultural day labourers, who were paid two lire a day before the War, now receive 18 lire, i. e., nine times more, whereas the cost of living has increased only six or seven times." Signor Villari's "personal investigation" as regards "many other areas" is confirmed by no reliable source. His comparison, based on his own, and for us unverifiable, personal investigation in the province of Grosseto, should have been, not with the pre-war years, but with 1920 and 1921.

people, see the food they buy, the toys which they give to their children, the manner in which they furnish and keep their houses, and compare these conditions with those obtaining *before the war* to realize the immense material improvement.[10]

Signor Villari unwisely did not confine himself to general statements about toys and shoes but descended to concrete statistics in order to prove that "immense material improvement" had been effected. According to him, from 1913 to 1925 the consumption of sugar had increased from 5 to 8 kilograms per capita per annum, and that of coffee from 800 grams to 1300; while every Italian had spent 9 gold lire on tobacco before the war, he now spent 16 gold lire in the Fascist era; the consumption of table oil had increased from 19 to 29 kilograms per capita per annum; etc. Anyone consulting the available official statistics would have discovered the following data: [11]

	1913	*1918*	*1922*	*1925*
Population:	35,238,000	36,563,000	38,800,000	40,130,000
Coffee:				
Annual consumption in quintals	283,565	516,374	472,603	422,125
Average per capita in kilograms	0.80	1.40	1.21	1.05
Sugar:				
Annual consumption in quintals	1,754,876	1,242,212	2,856,562	2,879,377
Average per capita in kilograms	4.69	3.39	7.37	7.17

If he had not ignored the figures for 1918 and 1919, Signor Villari would have found that the increase in coffee consumption took place

[10] *The Fascist Experiment*, p. 131. In his addresses before the 1931 Institute of Politics at Williams College, Signor Villari reiterated that "in the years 1922–7 when business was doing well after the stagnation and disastrous anarchy of the previous years, the regime promoted an increase of wages" (*The Economics of Fascism* p. 108).

[11] *Annuario Statistico: 1917–8*, pp. 223–4; *Idem: 1919–21*, pp. 263–4; *Idem: 1922–5*, pp. 199–200. The population figures are those given in the *Annuario* for 1922–3, pp. 13 and 388.

during the war and was entirely due to the soldiers at the front; [12] in 1919 coffee consumption began to fall, and continued to fall after the advent of Fascism. As regards sugar, the increase took place during those post-war years described by Fascist propaganda as years of economic breakdown and destitution.

In 1922 the per capita expenditure on tobacco was 60.80 paper lire, or 16 gold lire at the then prevailing rate of exchange—which was also the figure for 1925. However, if Signor Villari had taken account of the quantity of tobacco smoked rather than the amount of money spent for it, and further, if he had not ignored the figures for 1918 and 1922, he would have arrived at the following annual averages expressed in grams: 1913, 558; 1918, 584; 1922, 722; 1925, 697. The increase in tobacco consumption, like that for sugar, had taken place during the years immediately following the war. We read in the U. S. *Commerce Reports*, April 3, 1920:

> The consumption of tobacco in Italy is increasing rapidly; in fact, the figures for the last three months of 1919 are about double those for the same period of 1914. The production of cigarettes has been unable to keep pace with the demand, and at times cigarettes are almost unobtainable.

In tobacco, coffee, and sugar consumption the advent of Fascism was followed by regression and not advance. Professor Gini, as faithful a Fascist as Signor Villari, wrote in 1925:

> The last years reveal, as compared with 1921–2, not an increase, but actually a decrease in consumption of coffee. The index number of the average consumption per capita was 138 for 1921–2 and has gradually descended to 133 in 1924–5.[13]

According to the official statistics the consumption of table oil averaged 4.04 kilograms during the quinquennium 1910–4; it averaged a little less than 5 litres (approximately 4.5 kilograms) for the quadrennium 1921–4; and it went down to 2.5 kilograms in 1925 as a result of the very bad crop of the preceding year.[14]

Nothing would be gained by pursuing Signor Villari's figures any

---

[12] Serpieri, *La Guerra e le Classi Rurali Italiane*, pp. 47, 148.

[13] In McGuire, *Italy's International Economic Position*, p. 516.

[14] *Compendio Statistico: 1931*, p. 190. *Annuario Statistico: 1930*, p. 269. Mortara, *Prospettive Economiche: 1926*, p. 83. It must be remembered that these statistics, like most agricultural statistics, are by no means reliable.

farther.[15] It is rather useful to point out the trick by means of which Signor Villari manufactured Fascist successes: he systematically ignored the figures of the last pre-Fascist years 1919–22, compared the pre-war figures with those of the Fascist years, and gave the Fascist regime the credit for all improvements that had taken place between 1914 and 1925, concealing the fact that most of those improvements had occurred during the years 1919–22. This same trick constantly is being employed by all the propaganda agents of Fascism. For instance the Central Institute of Statistics, in the *Compendio Statistico 1934*, pp. 153, 160, wishing to show that the standard of living of the Italian people had been improved under Fascism, calculated how many calories the average Italian had had at his disposal not in 1922, the last pre-Fascist year, but in 1910–4, and how many he had under Fascism, and found that under Fascism the average Italian swallowed more calories than in 1913. Dr. Marraro of the Casa Italiana of Columbia University gave the results of those inquiries in *Current History*, May 1935, pp. 158–9. If the Institute and Dr. Marraro had gone back not to 1910–4, but to 1860–70, they would have been able to attribute to Mussolini an even greater progress. The game of statistics is an entertaining one. By displacing the terms of his comparisons a statistician can prove everything he chooses.

---

[15] The figures given by Signor Villari for meat consumption are disproved by Gini, *The Present Economic Status of Italy*, p. 515.

IV

The "Army of Believers"

IN 1926, as a result of the law of April 3 and the regulations of July 1, the "army of believers," that is, the officials of the Fascist unions, were invested with the exclusive right of representing the employees in negotiating labour agreements with the employers.

It would be absurd to think that among these men no one is to be found who is sincerely desirous of serving the interests of his fellow workers. If for no other reason than personal prestige, they must make an effort to obtain victories in their tilts with the employers. On September 6, 1933, the Minister of Corporations and the general secretary of the Party had to publish a circular forbidding employers to discharge union officials as reprisals. Whenever the Ministry of Corporations found that a workman had been discharged as a reprisal, the employer "who resorted to such an expedient" would be compelled to re-engage the worker, paying him back wages in full for the time between his discharge and his re-engagement. Such reprisals also engaged the attention of the Central Corporative Committee in June 1931.[1] This goes to show that cases of union officials who do not care to earn the good graces of the employers are not exceptional. But desire and success are not the same thing.

During 1928 Miss Haider was struck by the incapacity of many of the officials whom she met.[2] Having lived in Italy for a year, assembling data for her inquiry, she was in a position to present a much more exhaustive report than certain other "experts" who describe Italian life after having spent a week or two in an expensive hotel in Rome as guests of the Italian government. In 1933, M. Rosenstock-Franck's impressions after his investigation in Italy were not dissimilar from Miss Haider's.[3]

In view of the inexperience of many officials during the first years of Fascist syndicalism, many labour agreements were drawn up in Rome

---

[1] *Resto del Carlino*, Sept. 17, 1933.
[2] *Capital and Labor under Fascism*, pp. 221–2.
[3] *L'Economie Corporative*, pp. 107–9, 168.

by high officials in the Ministry of Corporations.[4] Again in 1933 the ministry had to take part in the drawing up of no less than 102 agreements, of which 28 "were entirely formulated at the ministry."[5]

On June 30, 1929, a governmental Commissioner sent to establish order in the unions of the city and province of Milan, declared publicly:

> When I was appointed to take charge of the trade organizations in Milan, there was no administrative or hierarchical discipline whatever, and no serious thought was devoted to the trade-union movement. The leaders spent their time in political campaigns, and the masses were disorganized. Salaried industrial employees, with few exceptions, had no collective contracts. The discontent among the workers was fully justified.[6]

If this was the situation in the most important industrial city in Italy, which had been committed to the care of Mussolini's closest intimates, and in which lived his brother, what must have been the disorder in the rest of the country!

The legal texts state that "there can be appointed or elected to organization offices only those who belong to the category or *in some wise are the expression of it*" ("che comunque ne siano l'espressione"). As Deputy Lusignoli observed in the Chamber on March 8, 1933, "according to this formula, *any one* can be the expression *in some wise* of the category." Most of the Fascist officials are so-called intellectuals, i. e., persons edu-

---

[4] Bottai in his speech of March 3, 1929, declared: "At the Ministry of Corporations, where hundreds upon hundreds of collective agreements have passed through our hands, we have frequently noted this phenomenon: that while the employers come to the discussions well equipped with data, with a precise knowledge of the figures, and with projects well supported by statistics, the other party sometimes [!] turns up with statements suspended in mid-air." In his speech of Sept. 26, 1930, he said: "There was a time when a great majority of the collective agreements were concluded here in the ministry, because the unions [the union officials] had not yet acquired the necessary experience, and the organizations asked the ministry to intervene. We undertook the thankless task of elaborating a large number of collective agreements. Then I begged the presidents of the confederations to spare the ministry this labour, which after all properly belonged to the confederations." In his speech of June 3, 1927, at Geneva, Signor Rossoni stated: "It is not true that we make labour agreements behind the backs of the workers. There are orders signed by myself that no negotiation can be entered upon without the participation of the workers. The democratic principle is not violated in our country. Perhaps it is applied in a different way. Mussolini himself said recently that the Fascist regime is in essence nothing but a great democracy."

[5] *Sindacato e Corporazione*, Jan. 1934, p. 70. Mr. Jones, in *Is Fascism the Answer?*, p. 146, asserts that "the greatest freedom is allowed in collective bargaining between employers and workmen: *there is no paternalism or government interference.*"

[6] *Industrial and Labour Information*, July 29, 1929, p. 137.

cated beyond their intelligence. There are organizers who pass with perfect tranquillity from the secretaryship of an employees' association to that of an employers' organization, like those lawyers who are equally ready to argue the pro and the con of any case. In August 1930 the *Lavoro Fascista* deplored the fact that "certain organizers have suddenly passed over to the other side, surprising and disorienting the workers."[7] In the fall of 1932 the butchers had as the secretary of their national federation an architect, the tanners had an M.D., and the metal workers a bankrupt storekeeper.[8] Signor Klinger, who in 1930 was government commissioner for the Confederation of Unions in Industry, is today the manager of a company which operates air lines.

On April 27, 1934, in a meeting of the high officials of the Confederation of Commercial Employers, "the Commissioner [see above, p. 20] made it clear that henceforth statistical tables showing the fluctuations of wages should be compiled and kept up to date. Moreover, a schedule should be drawn up of labour agreements and wages agreed upon." Thus, in April 1934, after Fascist syndicalism had been functioning for eight years, there was still at least one confederation which had not yet perceived the necessity of compiling wage statistics or of keeping a systematic record of the agreements which the confederation itself had concluded or sanctioned.

On August 30, 1934, the London *Daily Telegraph*, which, until the British-Italian entente broke down because of the Ethiopian affair, might have been regarded as a semi-official organ in Britain of the Italian Fascist government, announced that Mussolini had had a meeting with some former Socialists who were at present abstaining from politics, and had urged them to join the Fascist Party on the ground that the unions needed capable leaders in whom he, Mussolini, could have confidence, and who at the same time enjoyed the confidence of the workers. The

---

[7] Quoted by Rosenstock-Franck, *L'Economie Corporative*, p. 97.

[8] Information obtained personally by the author. The French journalist, M. Francq, discovered in 1933 among the union officials "professors, lawyers, doctors" and even "some workers, especially in the local organizations" where the officials are, as we have seen, without any real authority. This fact he justified by two considerations: 1, "during the revolutionary period which is not yet over" it is natural that "all the syndical apparatus" should be controlled by the Fascist party" (he did not mention the number of decades that must elapse before the revolutionary period will be over); 2, "the management of the confederations requires general knowledge which the worker in the ranks seldom possesses." "Anyway," he added, "all the officials are elected" (*Vu*, Aug. 9, 1933, p. 1186).

Stefani Agency denied that this meeting had ever taken place. But the *Regime Fascista* of Cremona had already published the information in Italy without its being contradicted. Anyhow, one fact is sure: namely, that the pro-Fascist author of the report to the pro-Fascist English paper was convinced that as late as the twelfth year of the Fascist era the Fascist unions still needed capable leaders in whom Mussolini and the workers could have confidence.

In order to turn out union officials capable of "representing" the workers, a school was created in 1928 at Genoa. There are now in existence six of these schools, which in 1932–3 had 514 students.[9] The Fascists naturally hail the results of these schools as nothing short of splendid. Mlle. Lion wrote two years before the opening of the first of these schools:

These secretaries [of the unions] must hold a diploma testifying to their technical and economic knowledge of the problems they may have to treat. The fact that they must belong to the trade they represent and actually exercise it sweeps away all professional secretaries of the trade unions, who living out of their leadership of the workmen are ready to do anything to retain their posts.[10]

Deputy Rotigliano in a speech before the Chamber on May 14, 1930 requested that the union secretaries should be really elected by the workers on the grounds that in this way the representation of the workers' interests would be confided to persons better qualified to treat such questions:

I should like the workers' representatives to be, as they were in the past, workers themselves. It is not necessary, in order to be excellent organizers and union leaders, to have taken an advanced course in corporative studies. It is much better to have lived the life of the factory, to understand the needs of the working class through having belonged to that class, to see at a glance what effects on the worker's income will be caused by the fixing of piece-rates, by the formation of a working team and by the distribution of the hours of labour. The best officials, those who enjoyed the greatest prestige, were, even in the past, those who rose from the ranks, who were sometimes self-made men of a truly remarkable character [Interruptions, noises]. I do not understand why this view should arouse protest.

---

[9] *Sindacato e Corporazione,* Jan. 1934, p. 81.
[10] *The Pedigree of Fascism,* p. 232.

Signor Rotigliano is a former nationalist whose professional and political activities have always been on behalf of the heavy industries. His speech gives us an interesting glimpse into the attitude of the industrialists. From 1921 to 1926 these gentlemen subsidized the Fascist storm troops to demolish the Socialist and Christian-Democratic unions and to create tame ones in their stead; and they found it perfectly natural for the union officials to be placed under the control of the government and the Fascist Party. But being now assured that they can always dictate the law, the industrialists prefer to deal with experienced persons rather than with amateurish chatterboxes who do nothing but waste precious time. On the other hand, someone might be tempted to remark that if the officials were also employees, it would be easy by threatening them with dismissal to keep them from taking too seriously their duty of representing their comrades, and that this is the reason of Signor Rotigliano's hostility to the present Fascist officials.

Let us, therefore, seek the opinion of a union official. In the record of the sitting of the Chamber of Deputies of April 30, 1931, we find the following words of Signor Ciardi:

In my opinion collaboration between the employers' associations and the employees' unions is effected more easily by the organizers who come from the ranks of the workers than by those whose education is purely scholastic. The former, by their acquaintance with technical problems, assist the attainment of equitable and rational settlements, while the latter, on the contrary, contribute chicane. . . . If it has been possible for the dockers to direct the port unions with honesty and competency, I do not see why it should be impossible for the other workers to govern their own unions.

Signor Ciardi hails from the old revolutionary syndicalism. Thus, a man who is not only a representative of the heavy industries but also a former revolutionary syndicalist, shows himself sceptical about the results of the new schools.

The opinion of Signor Rotigliano and Signor Ciardi is shared, as regards agricultural unions, by Senator Einaudi, an economist of the old liberal school. In the review *Riforma Sociale* of November-December 1934, p. 642, he wrote:

Organizers, local secretaries, regional delegates, and heads of provincial federations should be wisely chosen. I have an idea on this subject which I now advance. In the rural districts a great step forward would be taken, if in the choice of these officials a disqualification was attached to the holding of a doctor's or bachelor's degree or of a certificate from a law school, a higher institute of economics, a school of accounting, or a school of corporative studies. The sole academic diplomas which should be valued in this connexion are those of the practical schools of agriculture.

It is worthy of note that the technical competence of the officials representing the employers has never been the object of criticism or discussion. Undoubtedly, they know their business perfectly.

It would be worthwhile to know how much the "army of believers" costs the Italian people. The act of 1926 did not oblige the legal organizations to give a public account of their income and expenditures. This financial secrecy was so absurd that the act of June 17, 1929, compelled the organizations to present to parliament summaries of their budgets; but these summaries were so devoid of particulars that matters in reality remained as before. In fact, in the autumn of 1933 the government had to recognize that the act of 1929 "has not fulfilled its purpose: it has been several times remarked that these reports to parliament are neither complete nor useful"; and a royal decree of October 12, 1933, subjected the organizations to "a system of publicity," which "does not infringe upon the autonomy of the organizations themselves." The balance sheet of each provincial organization is to be left for eight days at the provincial headquarters of the organization, and the members can take cognizance of it and lay their remarks and complaints before the officials. The decree does not state what will happen to the member who has ejaculated his remarks and complaints. When the eight days are up, the balance sheet is sent to the national confederation on which the provincial organizations depends, and there "the system of publicity" ends. Apparently the word "autonomy" has altered its meaning in the "new era." The autonomy of the organizations no longer means that their members have the right freely to elect and dismiss the officials and that the officials may govern their organizations without governmental interference as long as they enjoy the confidence of the membership. Fascist "autonomy" means that the officials have the right to handle the funds of their organizations without having to render an account to their members.

On March 15, 1929, Signor Bottai declared that in 1927, when many organizations were still in a formative stage, the dues assessed on members and non-members had amounted to 150,870,000 lire. He did not give the figure for the supplementary dues (assessed on members only), but confined himself to the statement that they had varied from a maximum of 21,000,000 lire for the aggregate of the employees' unions to 1,976,000 lire for the Confederation of Banking Employers.[11] Miss Haider, studying Fascist "syndicalism" on the spot during 1927 and 1928, succeeded in finding out that the two kinds of dues together had in 1927 equalled 181,758,000 lire,[12] of which the supplementary dues represented approximately 31,000,000 lire. Speaking to the Chamber on May 6, 1931, Signor Bottai asserted that the supplementary dues had amounted to fifty million lire for the fiscal year 1928–9, but he admitted that it was "difficult to verify" these figures. In the Senate on April 3, 1933, he stated that during the fiscal year 1932–3 the dues assessed on members and non-members alike had yielded 275,000,000, but he persisted in his silence as to the supplementary dues.[13]

In 1934 the income fell to 232 millions,[14] probably as a result of the crisis which compelled many employers to suspend business and of the unemployment which was reducing the number of workers able to keep up their contributions. In September, therefore, the idea of in-

---

[11] *Industrial and Labour Information,* Apr. 2, 1928, p. 15.

[12] *Capital and Labour under Fascism,* pp. 164–6.

[13] According to information supplied to Signor Pitigliani by the Ministry of Corporations, the income of the official organizations amounted to 281,000,000 lire in 1930, 278,000,000 in 1931, and 282,000,000 in 1932 (*The Italian Corporative State,* pp. 254–5). The supplementary dues are obviously not included in these figures. Mr. Clough in the *Harvard Business Review,* Apr. 1932, p. 303, states that the annual cost of the system amounts "approximately to 68,207,000 lire," and comments that "this is very little when one compares it with the loss caused by strikes and lockouts: from 1916 the average number of days lost annually on account of strikes in industry alone amounted to 7,600,000; at the present average daily wage of 16.50 lire this would amount to the formidable total of 125,856,000 lire, or twice the running cost of the new system." There are two errors in this calculation: 1, the sum 68,000,000 represents only that part of the income of the legal organizations which is taken over each year by the government and which keeps the Ministry of Corporations going—in the estimates for the fiscal year 1933–4 this figure has been reduced to 58,700,000; and 2, when comparing the Fascist with the pre-Fascist system, the employers must be kept separate from the employees. In the case of the employees we must find the algebraic sum of the following: *a,* the amounts they formerly paid their Socialist or Christian-Democratic unions; *b,* those lost on account of strikes, and *c,* those they gained when wages were raised after successful strikes. This sum must then be compared with the amounts they now pay to the Fascist unions and those which they lose through the wage reductions forced upon them. In the case of the employers we must put on one side of the scales the sums that they were formerly accustomed to pay their organizations, those they lost owing to strikes, and those lost when the workers won higher wages from them; and on the other side we must place the sums they now pay the Fascist organizations and those that they save through lower wages and the absence of strikes.

[14] *Lavoro Fascista,* Sept. 7, 1934.

creasing the amount of the compulsory contribution began to dawn here and there among the officials of the unions. In its issue of September 19, the *Lavoro Fascista* even published a letter from a worker who demanded this increase of his own accord and who affirmed that the workers would "be more than willing to pay their contributions to their unions, *regardless of how heavy they might be*," and that "new sacrifices would not create discontent, but would be received with the most joyful sense of responsibility." A fortunate country, Italy!

Addressing the Chamber on May 15, 1930, Deputy Paoloni complained that the supplementary dues were too high, and that the fee paid on joining the union was likewise excessive:

> It is unfortunate that we know the amount of the general dues but not that of the supplementary ones. The total would probably be a handsome figure. But the elements of such a calculation have not been laid before Parliament. We have been given an account of the general dues but not of the supplementary. There lies the difference. The figures presented for our inspection offer no specific bases for evaluating the cost of the system.[15]

In short, no one seems to know just what amount in dues is paid into coffers of the legal organizations.[16]

It is even less possible to discover the number of officials who make up the "army of believers." Miss Haider learned that in March 1927 the employers' organizations had 10,000 paid officials, and that those of the employees had 8000. However, by February 1928 this latter figure had risen to 10,000.[17] In an interview with the *Corriere della Sera* April 14,

---

[15] Camera dei Deputati, *Discussioni*, May 15, 1930, p. 2689. This part of the speech was almost wholly omitted in the press reports.

[16] According to the *Lavoro Fascista* of Jan. 24, 1934, working-class organization is more costly in France than in Italy: in fact, the French workers pay their unions an annual contribution that varies from 0.43 to 0.67 per cent of their wages, while the Italians pay only from 0.30 to 0.34 per cent. As a matter of fact, the Italian figures are too low, because the workers inscribed in the Fascist unions have not only to pay for the annual membership card but an infinity of "voluntary" contributions: plaque to give the Duce, gift for the secretary of the party, subscriptions for this, that, and the other. Furthermore, the comparison between France and Italy cannot stand for two reasons: 1, in France the contributions are paid by only a part of the workers, since they are not obliged to join the unions as in Italy—hence the comparison should be made not between the dues paid by each union member in France and Italy, but between the sums paid by the totality of union members in the two countries; 2, in France a considerable part of the amounts paid by the workers to the unions is used to help the workers when they strike in defense of their wages, while in Italy strikes are forbidden and hence there is no need for building up a fighting fund.

[17] *Capital and Labor under Fascism*, p. 166.

1930 Signor Bottai stated that the organizations had one official for every 200 members. Since in 1930 the organizations had 4,780,000 members, it follows that there were 23,900 officials. If we assume that the same proportions have been preserved in the supervening years, we have it that in 1933 there were 29,000 officials as against 5,780,000 members.

On November 3, 1927, the *Corriere della Sera* shed considerable light on this side of Fascist "syndicalism":

Some anxiety must be felt lest the worst bureaucratic traditions of Italian life be perpetuated in the Fascist unions: such as the human but imprudent custom of finding places for masses of unemployed in useless offices, political and personal favouritism, and the tendency to suppose that the importance of an organization is in direct proportion to the number of its employees. If Fascist organizations served solely, or largely, to create posts, to give employment to clerks and stenographers, to pay salaries, frequently anything but small, to chiefs, directors, and secretaries, the new system would run the risk of failure. A grave danger arises if we compare the treatment of the civil servants with that of the union officials, and especially some of them. It is neither prudent nor just that our modest public servants (modest even in the highest ranks) should be made discontented by seeing what happens in the Fascist unions where there are higher salaries, higher bonuses, and easier advancement. The official balance-sheets of the workers' organizations are not yet available, but there is a general feeling that the ranks of their officials are not only overcrowded but are rewarded with a liberality that contrasts with the sober tradition of the service.

In 1928 Professor Volpe discreetly pointed out the fact that there were those who "regarded the ponderous corporative machine with its numerous and well-paid bureaucracy, with its fiscal system superimposed upon that of the state, as an unknown quantity." [18] In 1929 even Signor Villari had to admit that "it is alleged that some of the secretaries and other officials are too highly paid as compared with the regular civil servants" and that "a more serious drawback is that these officials should become too numerous." But on the first point he consoled himself with the thought that "the rate of pay in Italy is so small that even if these men are better paid than other officials the harm is not very great"; and as for the more serious drawback, he was encouraged by the fact that "the Ministry of Corporations is looking into the matter and a limit will

---

[18] *Civiltà Fascista*, p. 31.

probably be put to the number of appointments made." [19] A year later the ministry was still "looking into the matter," but with such scant results that on May 15, 1930, Deputy Paoloni felt obliged to express the hope that the minister would see to it that "expenditures are kept as low as possible" . . . "avoiding a plethora of functionaries and employees, and salaries disproportionate (as regards merit and seniority) to those of the civil service."

In the spring of 1931 it was an official body, the parliamentary committee charged with examining the estimates for the fiscal year 1931–2, which gave vent to the discontent circulating underground:

It is the generally accepted opinion that this personnel is too numerous and too highly paid. The ministry considered a remedy which would have made possible the revision of those particular individual positions which appeared least in consonance with the present economic situation. But after mature reflection, even a remedy of this sort was felt not to be practicable. . . . The committee has not at its disposal all the facts necessary for a proper judgment.[20]

The deputies who were officials in the organizations, protested. The supervision of the organizations, they held, belonged to the Ministry of Corporations and not to parliament. If the committee did not possess the necessary facts, it should have procured them, and not make insinuations. "It is well worth while to put up with certain annoyances in order to preserve that spirit of initiative which can exist only where there is a reasonable autonomy in the choice of men and *in the distribution of means.*" The committee, they intimated, would have done better to direct its scrutiny towards the amount of subsidies with which the government aided debt-ridden industrialists. In evaluating the effectiveness and the cost of the official organizations "with objective criteria," it should be borne in mind that these organizations were "the basic formations of the Party and the regime with functions and aims entrusted to them by the revolution"; and that therefore "they had needs and budgets proportionate to the returns which they would give." The committee was merely repeating "polemics, in large part oral" and "anonymous, irresponsible, and frequently not disinterested vociferations

---

[19] *Italy*, p. 288.
[20] *Relazione della Giunta Generale del Bilancio sulla Stato di Previsione per il Ministero delle Corporazioni 1931–2*, p. 15.

against a labour performed with faith and passion and carried out in noble and dignified poverty." [21]

Signor Bottai, speaking in the Chamber on May 30, 1929, remarked that the officials of the organizations were not entitled to pensions, as were the civil servants, and that it was hence natural that they should receive higher salaries. But on May 6, 1931, forgetting what he had said two years before, he asserted, "for the great majority of organizers the salaries not only are not equal, but lower than those of the civil servants." Such a patent contradiction was certainly not calculated to reduce the critics to silence. In 1932 and 1933 new complaints about the lack of clarity in the budget of the Ministry of Corporations and about the high salaries were voiced in the Chamber and Senate. [22]

These muffled protests appear to have originated among the civil servants. In the summer of 1932 it transpired at a civil trial that an official, and not one of the highest, in a workers' confederation was receiving after only two years of service a salary of 3000 lire a month, plus an annual bonus of 3000, [23] making a total annual salary of 39,000 lire. [24] The highest officials in the organizations draw between salary, indemnities, bonuses, etc., incomes of hundreds of thousands. The maximum salary to which a civil servant can aspire after forty years of service is 48,000 lire. Only the president of the Supreme Court and the highest officers in the armed forces receive 74,000 lire.

Speaking before a national conference of the officials in the legal unions on May 7, 1928, Mussolini proclaimed "with full knowledge of the facts" that "the leaders of Italian trade unions are, almost without exception, worthy of their mission and of their responsibilities," and added that "it is necessary to take measures against all the calumniators, against all the ranters, against all the defeatists, who from a single episode try to extract a universal rule, and by means of one incident attempt to slander an entire movement." The calumniators, ranters, and defeatists must have been rather numerous if the Duce felt called upon in a solemn

---

[21] Camera dei Deputati, *Discussioni*, May 1, 1931, p. 4451; May 6, 1931, p. 4523–4; May 7, 1931, p. 4557.

[22] *Ibid.*, Feb. 24, 1932, p. 5780. *Informations Corporatives*, 1932, p. 877. Senate, speech by Tofani, April 1, 1933. Rosenstock-Franck, *L'Economie Corporative*, pp. 52, 111–2.

[23] *I Problemi del Lavoro*, Aug. 1, 1932, p. 23.

[24] The "Group of Students of the Corporate State in Italy" in their letter to the *New Statesman*, May 26, 1934, asserted that "the syndical officials are unpaid voluntary workers."

address to treat them with such vehemence. Everybody in Italy, beginning with the Fascists, will tell you *sotto voce* that the depredations of the ones higher up are never published, much less punished. From time to time one of them disappears from circulation; no one knows why, but everyone guesses. Now and then a quarrel breaks out between two high personages, and one accuses the other in more or less veiled language of being a black sheep. For example, in the Chamber on May 20, 1930, Deputy Rotigliano violently attacked one of the highest dignitaries in the Fascist unions, the president of the National Confederation of Commercial Employees, describing him as an individual who "without having originated either among the workers or among the adepts of the new law, had *usurped* his position as leader in the union just as he had *usurped* the editorship of a daily paper: both being jobs highly remunerated with money coming from the sweated toil of the real workers."

Occasionally a document falls into the hands of the anti-Fascist exiles in Paris and is published in one of their organs. *La Libertà*, a weekly paper, published on December 1, 1932, a secret report presented in 1930 to the Minister of Corporations by Deputy Begnotti covering the acts of Deputy Magrini, his predecessor in the office of president of the Seamen's Confederation. It is revealed in this document that between March and December 1927 Magrini pocketed as salary, travelling expenses, etc., the sum of 163,998 lire, which in 1928 rose to 369,928 lire, and for 1929 and the first two months of 1930 amounted to 532,178 lire. Among the other high officials in the organization, Signor Leale in the same period made off with 305,160 lire, Signor Tanzini with 334,296 lire, and Signor Agazzi with 194,459 lire. Leale and Tanzini were also deputies in parliament. The accounts of the organization were in disorder and had been faked. Magrini borrowed 685,427 lire from the Banca di Credito Marinaro, a co-operative bank created by the seamen before their organization had been "conquered" by the Fascists. Signor Magrini in his capacity as president of the confederation, was president of the bank. Another 500,000 lire had been loaned by the bank to Magrini's friends. The manager of this bank received a salary of 5000 lire a month for attending his office two hours a day.

Addressing the Chamber on May 16, 1930, Deputy Caprino said: "In the field of organizers there are both good and bad, honest and dishonest; but purification is on the march." The problem was to establish the proportion between the two categories and to determine at what speed purification was marching.

Naturally, a sweeping judgment on this question can never be made. There is no way of comparing Fascist with pre-Fascist morality, since we lack documents regarding what happened behind the scenes, both in pre-Fascist and in Fascist organizations.

Union officials who have been bought up by the employers have always existed everywhere, and it would be strange indeed if their like had disappeared in Fascist Italy. Every expectation would be that in a regime where the workers can neither elect nor dismiss their union officials, nor publicly discuss their acts, corruption would be more widespread than in those countries where working-class organization is free and where the organizers are responsible to the mass.

This alone can be affirmed with certainty: that in the old Socialist and Christian-Democratic unions no organizer ever lived a life of luxury, and none ever left wealth to his family; that those of them who had to leave Italy after the Fascist "conquest" now live abroad under very difficult circumstances, which means that they did not save any money when they were in power; and that on the contrary many of the high officials of the Fascist unions today live a life of wasteful extravagance. For instance, Rossoni lives in one of the luxurious palaces on the Via Veneto in Rome; before he moved into this princely establishment anyone who wished to see him had to go and seek him at the Excelsior, one of the most expensive hotels in Rome. The lad has made good.

Naturally, the propaganda agents of Fascism are always ready to swear that the officials of the Fascist unions are the finest conceivable as regards competence and honesty. They are all imbued with a "corporative conscience."

V

Fascist "Syndicalism" from 1926 to 1929

THE Fascists, and those "scholars" who lap up all the information originated by the Fascists, assert that it is to "Fascist syndicalism" that is due the introduction into Italy of the collective labour agreement as a means of regulating the labour market.[1] The truth of the matter is that the use of labour agreements had been introduced into every field of production in Italy by the Socialist organizations long before the Fascist "conquest." In the agricultural areas of northern Italy there existed collective agreements even before the war,[2] which were extended after the war to all parts of Italy. As for the industrial workers, let it suffice to mention the collective agreement concluded in October 1920 by the National Federation of Metal Workers, fixing the conditions of labour for around 500,000 workers.[3] Analogous agreements existed in the textile trades and for the printers, journalists, etc.[4] It was, then, hardly necessary to impose on the working classes of Italy the military discipline of a bureaucratic and centralized organization to convince

---

[1] For example: Professor Schneider, *Making the Fascist State*, p. 177, states that "the recognition of collective contracts" was a result of the Vidoni Palace Pact in Oct. 1925 (see above p. 16) and it "marked the beginning of the breakdown of individualism."

[2] Signor Biagi, under-secretary at the Ministry of Corporations, wrote in the *Corriere della Sera* on July 25, 1933: "Before the war there were in existence numerous collective agreements regulating agricultural labour. Already by the end of the nineteenth century the union organization of the agricultural workers had reached a notable efficiency; above all, this was true in the Po Valley, where, due to the special requirements of their calling, the so-called 'braccianti' (day-labourers who depend upon their 'arms' for a livelihood) had come to have their work regulated by agreements of a collective character."

[3] The text of this agreement may be read in *Studies and Reports*, published by the International Labour Office, Series A, Number 11, Nov. 5, 1920, p. 10 ff.

[4] Further details concerning these pre-Fascist collective agreements in industry and agriculture may be found in *Collective Agreements in Italy*, by Signor Gino Olivetti, secretary of the General Confederation of Italian Industry. See also *Industrial and Labour Information*, Jan. 27, 1922, p. 67; Aug. 4, 1922, p. 247; Aug. 25, 1922, p. 23; Sept. 22, 1922, p. 25; Sept. 29, 1922, p. 26; Nov. 3, 1922, p. 281. The complete texts of several of the 1920 agreements were published in the *Bollettino del Lavoro e della Previdenza Sociale*, Sept.–Nov. 1920, pp. 364–415, and December 1920, pp. 559–67.

them of the advantages obtainable through the adoption of collective labour agreements.

This much is true: all economic groups have been compelled by the act of April 3, 1926, to organize and to pay salaries to union officials who draw up collective agreements.[5] As a result, the number of collective agreements has increased enormously. According to an official announcement published in the press on March 31, 1933, there had been concluded up to the end of December 1932, 566 national agreements and 10,026 local ones.[6] This figure is given as a proof of the spirit of "cooperation" with which both the employing and the employed classes are imbued under Fascist "syndicalism." The significant question, however, is not whether the number of agreements increases or decreases, but whether the new agreements raise or lower wages.[7]

Scarcely three months had elapsed since the enactment of the law of April 3, 1926, when on June 30, 1926, Mussolini granted the employers authority to increase the working day from eight to nine hours:

The additional hour [he declared in an interview with the *Daily Mail* on July 2, 1926] will have to be worked without increase in wages only in those industries, such as textiles, which bear the brunt of foreign competition. In the prosperous industries I anticipate that the additional payment for the extra hour will be fixed by negotiations between the organizations representing capital and labour.[8]

All the union secretaries sent him telegrams declaring that the workers counted themselves fortunate in being allowed to make this joyful sacri-

---

[5] A single trade still remains within the domain of *laissez-faire*, without unions, without collective agreements, without secretaries, and without annual dues—that of the prostitutes. These pay directly to the government a tax on brothels, introduced in 1928, which varies from 5000 to 20,000 lire a year, according to the population of the town.

[6] According to information from Signor Biagi, under-secretary at the Ministry of Corporations, published in the *Corriere della Sera*, Feb. 14, 1934, up through 1933 there had been made 486 national and 6258 local agreements. Fascist statistics are always somewhat erratic!

[7] Mr. Clough, in the *Harvard Business Review* of Apr. 1932, p. 304, contends that the large number of agreements is "an indication that considerable progress has been made in effecting satisfactory working agreements between the two classes." It would be, then, not the contents, but the number of agreements, which ought to serve as an index of the value of the agreements themselves. Similarly, one hundred strokes of the lash would no doubt be preferable to one, whether for him who gives them or for him who receives them.

[8] *Industrial and Labour Information*, July 5, 1926, p. 2; July 19, 1926, p. 104; Aug. 23, 1926, p. 276.

fice for their country. Three peasants, who at Oria in the province of Lecce circulated a leaflet against the nine-hour day, were condemned to terms of imprisonment ranging from four years and six months to five years and seven months.[9]

One month later, in August 1926, Mussolini threw himself into the "battle" to revaluate the lira. In December 1920 the lira had fallen to 28.5 to the dollar; it had been cautiously and slowly revaluated under the last pre-Fascist ministries to an average of 20.15 to the dollar by the first half of 1922. But there was a set-back during the summer of 1922, mainly due to the bad harvest of that year. On attaining power in October, Mussolini found the lira at 23.9. He raised its value to 21.8 in 1923; but devalorized it anew to 22.9 in 1924, to 25 in 1925, to 25.4 in the first half of 1926, to 30.5 by August 1926. Only at this juncture did he become aware of the necessity for saving the lira from ruin. He abruptly restricted the money in circulation, authorized private industries to contract new loans in the American market, thus revalorized the lira precipitously to 17.2 by June 1927, and finally stabilized it at 19.10 to the dollar in December 1927. This violent revalorization produced an acute crisis in all domains of Italy's economic life. In a speech on November 9, 1927, Mussolini plainly admitted:

There has been a crisis and it has been a grave one. It was bound to come because of the monetary policy for which the regime accepts full responsibility. What stage has the crisis reached? I am convinced that the peak is already past.

The peak was far from past. In another speech on June 22, 1928, Mussolini reiterated: "I believe that the end is in sight"; and on December 9, 1928, he gave the following assurance: "We are out of the dangerous waters; we are in full convalescence." [10] As a matter of fact, during 1929

---

[9] *Corriere della Sera*, July 28 and 29, 1927. One of the agents of the "propaganda" in America wrote: "It is scarcely surprising that *the workers themselves* should have suggested the experiment of adopting the nine-hour day with eight hours' pay, wherever this added hour might be advantageous in agriculture or in industry. And it is important to note that the additional ninth hour was *voluntarily offered by the workers themselves* as their contribution toward helping the nation solve its difficulties. Labor in Italy does not clamor senselessly for increased wages, but strives to help reduce living costs": (J. P. Roe, "Mussolini's Fourth Year" in the review *Il Carroccio*, New York, Jan. 1927).

[10] This crisis naturally remained unknown to the agents of the "propaganda." Reference may be made to the Apr. 1929 and Sept.–Oct. 1932 issues of the collection *Italy Today* (London, Henderson) for an exposé of the deceptions by which Signor Villari endeavoured to demonstrate that there had been no crisis from 1927 to 1929.

there were indications that readjustment of business to the stabilized lira value was taking place and that the hardships of the two preceding years were decreasing. But in October 1929 came the Wall Street crash.

What line of action was followed by Mussolini's syndicalism during the years 1927–9?

During March and April 1927 the press carried on a campaign to prove that in consequence of the policy, initiated in August 1926, of revaluating the lira, the cost of living must go down, and that the Fascist state would make it go down. On May 2, 1927, the officials of the peasants' unions in the province of Brescia held a meeting, attended by Signor Augusto Turati, general secretary of the Fascist Party. Signor Turati gave a discursive address leading up to the conclusion that the revaluation of the lira had not produced the expected fall in retail prices because "employers of agricultural labour had not yet been able to lower wages": "it is evident that sacrifices must be demanded all around." After he had taken his leave amid ovations, a resolution was read by the secretary of the provincial peasants' union to the effect that the peasants of Brescia, full of enthusiasm and discipline, "perceiving in the words of Signor Turati the pure spirit which must animate all Italians from the highest to the lowest, entrusted him with the task of determining how great a cut should be made in their wages." The resolution, needless to say, was adopted without a dissenting vote. Whereupon Signor Turati wired the Duce that the Fascist peasants of the province of Brescia accepted a cut of ten per cent in their wages.[11]

Shortly afterwards, the unions in the province of Pavia—i. e., their secretaries—resolved to accept, not in their own salaries, but in the wages of the peasants, a cut "equal to that of the province of Brescia." [12] The next day, a meeting of "representatives of the Fascist unions" in the province of Bologna adopted a resolution to reduce by ten per cent all the wages in the province.[13] On May 11 the executive of the Seamen's Union of Genoa, "sure of voicing the sentiments of the Genoese seamen," announced that "of their own accord they renounced five per cent of the bonus for the cost of living," or five million lire annually of their aggregate wages.[14] On May 24 the national directorates of the em-

---

[11] *Corriere della Sera*, May 3, 1927.
[12] *Ibid.*, May 8, 1927.
[13] *Popolo d' Italia*, May 10, 1927.
[14] *Corriere della Sera*, May 12, 1927.

ployers' and employees' textile organizations decided to reduce wages ten per cent.[15] All over Italy a virtuous contest went on among the secretaries of the unions to see who could be the first to cut other people's wages.[16]

In the "old era" people thought that the cost of living was going down if the price of food, clothes, and rent went down while wages either remained stationary or fell less than prices. In 1927 the old economic ideas were "revolutionized": henceforth it was wages that were the first to be reduced, while a drop in the cost of living was hopefully awaited. That the latter must drop was certain, for had not the Duce so decreed? This farce was excellently summed up in a statement by Signor De Stefani, a prominent Fascist, which appeared in the *Corriere della Sera* on June 25, 1927:

> The wage-earner in his simple mind reasons: if the cost of living goes down five per cent and my wages go down ten per cent, who benefits by that difference? From January to August 1926 the cost of living rose in Milan from 146 to 150, yet during that period nobody thought of raising my wages.

In order that the farce be not too obvious it was necessary that something should be done to make people believe that prices would go down. House rents had been governed by legal restrictions during and after the war until the end of 1922. The restrictions began to be removed in 1923 and were intended to cease altogether by June 1930. The consequence was that rents rose enormously: whereupon Mussolini was lauded to the skies, not only by the landlords, but by the Italian and foreign press, because, by consenting to a rise in rents, he had made possible the construction of new houses. Yet the discontent was widespread among the public officials as well as among the workers. Having cut wages and salaries on the promise that a decrease in the cost of living would follow, Mussolini on June 14, 1927, decreed that rents could not exceed four times the pre-war rate.[17] This time the same newspapers glorified Mussolini for having had pity on the poor by reducing their rents, while the landlords consoled themselves with the thought that the 1927 rents were still considerably higher than those of 1922. According

---

[15] *Industrial and Labour Information*, June 27, 1927, p. 510.
[16] *Ibid.*, June 6, 1927, p. 395.
[17] *Ibid.*, Sept. 12, 1927, p. 341.

to this decree lower courts (*pretori*) were to settle disputes between landlords and tenants concerning the rents. In the one city of Milan during a month and a half, thirty thousand tenants resorted to these lower courts.[18]

At the same time the government authorized the municipalities to fix the prices of the principal articles of consumption. To make the "battle" more effective, the Party instituted in each province an "inter-organization committee" consisting of the secretaries of the provincial employers' associations and employees' unions, and presided over by the provincial secretary of the Party; a "Central Inter-Organization Committee," presided over by the general secretary of the Party was created in Rome. These committees were to break the backs of the refractory prices and oblige them to go down.

Rents to some extent obeyed, but retail prices continued to go their own way.[19]

In the meantime the employers came to the conclusion that the "spontaneous" wage reductions of May 1927 were not sufficient. In a speech of July 9, 1927, Signor Benni, president of the confederation of employers in industry, said:

As for the workmen's wages, they have certainly not been reduced in a manner equivalent to the revaluation of the lira. They could not be so re-

---

[18] *Corriere della Sera*, July 31, 1927.

[19] Rosenstock-Franck, *L'Économie Corporative*, p. 359. An admirer of the Fascist regime, Monsieur Aillaud, wrote in the *International Labour Review* for May 1928, pp. 664–5: "This last measure as usual did not produce the effect desired. This action is still in progress. It is not easy to ascertain how far the results up to the present can be regarded as a consequence of it." Those who lived in Italy were unaware of any result and hence felt no need to argue as to whether that result was the consequence of the activities of the committees created in 1927. The *Lavoro d' Italia*, official organ of the Fascist unions, on July 7, 1927, reviewing the prices prevalent in the city of Genoa, asserted that there had been no real diminution, but rather an increase: "On the whole, after three months of struggle [?], after the spilling of so many rivers of ink, after so many tons of protests and after so many other tons of promises, nothing has been accomplished, and if things go on as they are, nothing ever will be." Signor Bottai admitted in 1928 that "the equalization of wages, costs, and prices under the policy of revaluating the national currency has not yet been complete and perfect" (*Civiltà Fascista*, p. 387). In the autumn of 1930, when a new offensive was launched against the recalcitrant prices, the *Régime Fascista* wrote on Nov. 25, 1930: "Let us hope that the lowering in the cost of living does not turn out, as it has in the past, to be a flame which is no sooner lighted than it burns out." Cf. Mitzakis, *Les Grands Problèmes Italiens*, p. 101: "In general, the new sacrifices asked were obtained, even when the lowered wages were not justified by a corresponding drop in the cost of living, the retail prices of many commodities remaining rebellious against every measure to lower them."

duced because the reduction in the cost of living was comparatively small and therefore it was not possible for the moment to demand greater sacrifices from the workmen.[20]

The moment for the greater sacrifices arrived on October 3, 1927 when the National Directorate of the Fascist Party issued the following statement:

The Party Directorate assembled under the chairmanship of His Excellency Benito Mussolini, head of the government and Duce of Fascism. The general secretary of the Party informed the meeting that the employers wished to bring before it the necessity of a wage cut to adjust the cost of production to the increased value of the lira. A discussion took place after which the Duce ordained that the demands of the employers should be considered, province by province, following the instructions issued by the Ministry of Corporations and the general secretary of the Party. The reduction must not be less than ten per cent or more than twenty per cent of the existing wages, because in the former case it would not be commensurate with the required adjustment, and in the latter it would exceed the present fall in the cost of living.

At this point a doubt arose: should this reduction be added to the preceding one of May 1927, which had amounted to an average of ten per cent? The National Directorate of the Fascist Party solved the problem in the following manner on October 6, 1927:

The new cut, when added to the preceding one, shall not exceed a total of twenty per cent, e. g., if there has already been a reduction of ten per cent, the new reduction must not exceed another ten per cent.

But next day another official *communiqué* from the directorate announced that the case must also be considered in which "owing to the special conditions of certain industries, it becomes necessary to exceed twenty per cent." The local organizations were left to carry out the cuts "in conformity with instructions to be issued by the Ministry of Corporations and the general secretary of the Fascist Party." [21]

After these ruthless bleedings of 1927 and 1928, Mussolini solemnly

---

[20] *Popolo d' Italia,* July 9, 1927.
[21] *Corriere della Sera,* Oct. 8, 1927. Cf. *Industrial and Labour Information,* Oct. 31, 1927, pp. 143–5. The secretary-general of the Party, speaking at Trieste on June 30, 1929, exhorted "our comrades" the employers, not to forget that "a year and a half previously Fascism ordered a reduction of one tenth in wages, and then another tenth."

ordered on August 1, 1928, that no further reductions should take place.[22] But wages continued to fall in complete disregard of the orders of the Duce. From 1928 to 1929 the wages of the seamen dropped twenty-four per cent in Genoa and thirty per cent in the other ports.[23] According to Mortara, during 1928 and 1929 a characteristic worthy of note was the contrast between the increase in the cost of living and the decrease in wages.[24]

NOTE

Professor Schneider received from his Fascist friends the information that in 1927 the Fascist organizations "had dictated the limits beyond which wages could not be reduced." [25] Thus, a measure which had reduced wages by twenty per cent was transformed into a measure aimed at preventing wages from being reduced beyond a limit which remained mysterious. Moreover, he made the following discovery:

In general, by his collective contracts, Rossoni has been able to gain concessions for labour, which, though small, are steady and of practical financial value to the workers. Labour has never [!] had much bargaining power in Italy. . . . In general there can be no doubt that within the last year [1927], since Rossoni has made his power felt, Italian workers have been less at the mercy of their employers than they were during the early days of Fascism, and it is probable that they are protected more than they would have been by independent organizations. . . . It is no longer possible to accuse Fascism of being an out-and-out bourgeois reaction.[26]

In a letter to the London *Daily News*, June 18, 1928, Signor Villari communicated the following interesting information concerning the cuts which had taken place during 1927:

With regard to wages, there have been cuts amounting to between ten and twenty per cent. These cuts have been agreed to *after free discussion between employers and workers.*

In the summer of 1931, in his address at the Institute of Politics of Wil-

---

[22] *Corriere della Sera*, Aug. 4, 1928, and *Industrial and Labour Information*, Aug. 20, 1928, p. 195. Signor Villari, addressing an English Summer School in 1928, affirmed that "there has been a temporary reduction in wages, but this is now ceasing." (*Sutton Coalfield News*, Aug. 11, 1928).

[23] Chamber of Deputies, *Discussions*, Apr. 3, 1930, p. 2161.

[24] *Prospettive Economiche: 1930*, p. 518.

[25] *Italy Incorporated*, p. 12.

[26] *Making the Fascist State*, pp. 209–10.

liams College, he stated that the regime had promoted an increase in wages in 1927.[27]

Robertson, in *Mussolini and the New Italy*, p. 138, wrote:

In 1926 the lira had fallen very low. . . . But in 1927 the value of the lira increased, indeed its purchasing power was nearly doubled [!]. Mussolini, therefore, appealed to all the merchants and shopkeepers, and to all house proprietors and house agents to lower their prices from ten to twenty per cent. The same reduction was recommended [!] to be made in the salaries of all civil servants. But what is more remarkable still, *the syndicates* [unions] *of workmen voluntarily and spontaneously* voted to accept a reduction of from five to twenty per cent in their wages. This fact alone shows that a true spirit of comradeship, a true democratic brotherhood has been created.

In 1930 Mr. G. K. Chesterton explained to the people of Great Britain what Mussolini, if he had ruled Great Britain, would have done in order to prevent the owners of the coal mines from reducing the wages of their employees:

By every analogy from his own theory and practice, what Mussolini would very probably have said in the British Coal Strike is this: "You, coal owners, will continue to pay the coal miners the full wages which they demand; and if you do not, I will take it from you. If you say your business would be ruined, you must take the risk or leave it to us and the future. We will do nothing for you out of the government funds. We will help you to do justice. But we will not suffer you to oppress the hireling in his wages and to add to the chaos of unemployment. See to it, therefore, that every man jack among the miners receives the full payment which you say you cannot pay, when he turns up at the pay-desk on Saturday, and if you do not do it, Corpo di Baccho [sic], you will get what is coming to you." That is what Mussolini would probably have said to our Conservatives and Coal-Owners. It is because Mussolini does talk thus firmly to employers that there is no labour opposition to him worth talking about in the new Fascist state.[28]

This fable had two bases: 1, Mussolini's specious circular of August 1928 (see above, p. 190); and 2, a complete ignorance of Italian affairs.

Goad and Currey, *The Working of a Corporate State*, p. 17, give the following account:

---

[27] *Economics of Fascism*, p. 108.
[28] *The Resurrection of Rome*, pp. 215 and 235.

When the currency was forced up to the level of 92 lire to the gold pound, the cost of living for the working classes was correspondingly reduced. This was facilitated by the action of the National Confederation of Commerce, which saw that retail prices followed closely the fall of wholesale prices, by controlling the profits of the middlemen. Wages, salaries, and rents were made to follow the cost of living, and the loss and gain were distributed to all classes of the nation. Reduction of salaries and wages were voluntarily accepted by the syndicates [unions], *while the number of men employed was increased.*

As we shall see in one of the following chapters, the official Fascist statistics themselves admit that the number of the unemployed steadily increased during 1927 and the following years.

VI

Fascist "Syndicalism" from 1929 to 1933

As a result of the Wall Street crash things took a turn for the worse all over the world and in Italy also. "Just as we were almost in sight of land, the American crisis of October 24, 1929, drove us back into the high seas." [1] In a speech on October 1, 1930, Mussolini recognized that the situation had become "considerably worse all over the world, and hence in Italy"; and he added:

The question that comes spontaneously from the mind to the lips is: At what point are we? How long will it last? If unforeseen and irreparable events, such as war, do not take place, if the phases of the phenomenon are not disturbed by extraneous forces, we are already leaving the night behind us and are marching towards the dawn. In these very days the crisis has reached its lowest ebb. The alternative is now simple: either the end or recovery. But since humanity cannot perish, it is recovery that will come. We

---

[1] Speech of Mussolini on Dec. 18, 1930. Signor Villari wrote in the *Boston Evening Transcript* on Feb. 20, 1930: "To talk of the economic stagnation in which Italy is drifting, is childish. One has but to consult the statistics of all kinds, Italian and foreign, beginning with the reports of the British embassy at Rome, and above all to keep one's eyes open, to see how the people live, what they eat, how they dress, what amusements they indulge in, to realize the immense improvement effected within the last few years. . . . Exports are increasing and imports decreasing, as the latest statistics prove." In Feb. 1930 the most recent available report of the British commercial attachés in Rome on *The Economic Situation in Italy* was dated Apr. 1929. In it, pages 8 to 10, one reads the following passages: "The year 1927 was one of crisis for almost all industries. These are, at the present time, still depressed, although signs of improvement are visible. . . . The present tension and stringent conditions must be expected to continue for some time. . . . Trade statistics for 1928 do not appear quite so satisfactory as those for 1927. Whilst imports have increased by some eight per cent over 1927, exports have decreased by some seven per cent." The Italian ambassador to the United States, Signor De Martino, declared in Oct. 1930: "Present-day Italy is as happy and flourishing as is possible considering the world economic depression" (*Il Grido della Stirpe*, Oct. 18, 1930). In the same month, on Oct. 28, 1930, Signor Farinacci, secretary-general of the Fascist Party in 1925 and 1926, wrote in the *Regime Fascista*: "The Italian people today are by no means lying on a bed of roses. They are tormented by an economic crisis the gravity of which it would be ridiculous to deny or even attenuate. It dominates all industry, commerce, and agriculture. Even the most favourably situated provinces find themselves faced by economic difficulties that are neither light to bear nor easy to solve. No one, however affected by an incurable frenzy or abject servility, can deny the reality of things as they are, or, with the aid of artificial rhetoric, make them appear other than they are."

must not, however, at this point be too precipitate: this cycle of recovery will not be shorter than three years.

That ancient astrologer who promised the king of Egypt to teach a goat how to talk was more prudent than Mussolini, for he asked not three, but ten years, thinking that within that period either he, the goat, or the king would be dead.

At any rate, the crisis had not yet touched bottom by October 1930. On January 21, 1932, the president of the Confederation of Industrial Employers reported: "The year 1931 was marked by an intensification of the economic depression." [2] And the parliamentary committee on the estimate for the fiscal year 1932–3 stated in April 1932:

> It is necessary to face the hard reality—that for Italy too the crisis has become more serious, more widespread and more cruel. The situation is much worse than we faced twelve months ago. It is estimated that the national income of the United States fell 33 per cent. We assume that in Italy the total national income was reduced in the same proportion.[3]

This economic whirlwind struck Italy just as she was beginning to recover from the storm of the revaluation of the lira. The catastrophe that overtook the rest of the world in 1929 was in Italy superimposed on a "private" crisis, provoked by the revaluation of the lira, for which the Italian people had Mussolini alone to thank. As Mr. Field stated in the *New Republic* of May 16, 1934, "the crisis in Italy had lasted eight years, as against four in other countries."

A remedy for the fresh disaster was easy to find—a new reduction in wages. In November 1930, therefore, the employers' and employees' confederations gave new proof of "class co-operation" by agreeing on wage reductions of from eight per cent to ten per cent in industry and from fifteen to twenty per cent in agriculture.[4] The "instructions" sent out by

---

[2] *Industrial and Labour Information*, Feb. 8, 1932, p. 132.

[3] *Relazione della Giunta Generale del Bilancio*, Apr. 29, 1932, p. 37.

[4] The documents concerning this new "battle" will be found in *Industrial and Labour Information*, Nov. 15, 1930, p. 404; Dec. 8, 1930, p. 397; and Dec. 29, 1930, p. 461. The British commercial attaché in Rome, in his report on the *Economic Conditions in Italy; June 1931*, p. 16, mentioned only a "movement in favour of the reduction of *certain* agricultural wages by *8 per cent.*" In the report of Sept. 1932, p. 14, this misstatement took the following form: "Wages, after being nearly constant in terms of lire *from 1925 till the autumn of 1930*, were, *in general, reduced by 8%* in Dec. of that year." If the attachés of foreign embassies tamper with such ease with the facts in official documents intended for publication, it is no wonder that the correspondents of foreign newspapers do even worse.

the Agricultural Employers' Confederation to its local offices and published in the *Lavoro* of Genoa on December 6, 1930, pointed out that "in some cases even this maximum of twenty per cent could be exceeded." The new wages were to be given only to those workers whose efficiency was one hundred per cent; the workers' efficiency and the corresponding scale of wages was "to be determined, case by case, by the employer." Furthermore, the reductions "need not be calculated mathematically," meaning that in reality there was no limit.

Speaking in the Senate on December 18, 1930, Mussolini announced that the wages of the agricultural workers had been or would be cut by from ten per cent to twenty-five per cent "and even more . . . on the condition no worker gets less than eight lire a day." [5] As a matter of fact, this is what one reads in the *Lavoro Agricolo Fascista* of March 8, 1931:

Agricultural wages, especially during the winter, are not very high; indeed, they are particularly [sic] low. . . . The highest figure is that for the province of Genoa in January, and the simple reason is to be sought in the continuous, assiduous, and special work in floriculture. Alongside the specialists engaged in such work, we have the humble day-labourer [*bracciante*] at Rovigo, receiving on the average 7.20 lire. In the zone where *braccianti* are employed in Piedmont, the figure is in the vicinity of 8 lire. In Lombardy wages for this class of labour go from a minimum of 7.20 at Bergamo to 10.40 in zones where the *braccianti* are employed in large numbers; while in other provinces the figures are slightly higher. Emilia goes from a little more than 8 to 13 and 14 lire per day; the Marches, around 9 lire; the Abruzzi and Molise, from 7 to 10 lire; Campania, around 8 lire; Apulia, from 7.50 to 9 lire; Sicily, from 7.50 to 9, 10, and even 11.90 lire; and finally Sardinia, around 9.50 lire per day.

There were in 1931 in the province of Rovigo families of six persons, of whom three were wage earners, whose joint earnings for a whole year's labour were 2289 lire, and there were others even more unfortunate who earned as little as 1.266 lire: [6] this means that in the first case each of the six members of the family barely existed on 1.05 lire (5 cents) per day, or in the latter case, on 0.62 lire (3.2 cents) per day.

In the province of Mantua, in 1931, the day-labourer, "working on an

---

[5] The Italian lira consists of 100 centesimi; in 1930, before the dollar went off gold, the lira was worth about 5 cents; it is now worth around 8.9 cents.
[6] *Lavoro Fascista,* Dec. 14, 1931.

average not more than 160 days a year, received 1456 lire a year; his rent alone amounted to 700 lire on an average" (*Lavoro Agricolo Fascista*, January 25 and March 8, 1931)—that is, scarcely 756 lire were left for all the other expenses of the family.

The labour agreements concerning the agricultural day-labourers in the province of Foggia, southeastern Italy, as published in the *Lavoro Fascista* on February 10, 1931, divided the province into seven zones, in each of which the workers were again divided into four categories: 1, men from 18 to 60; 2, youths from 16 to 18 and men from 60 to 65; 3, women from 17 to 50 and boys from 14 to 16; 4, girls from 15 to 17 and women over 50. In all there were 28 categories, each with its own wage rate. The highest wage was assigned to the first zone, in which category 1 made 10.80 lire for an eight-hour day, category 2 earned 8.64 lire, category 3 earned 5.92 lire, and category 4, 4.58 lire a day. The lowest wages were given in the seventh zone, in which category 1 earned 8.40 lire; category 2, 6.72 lire; category 3, 4.56 lire; and category 4, 3.36 lire. On an average these workers lost from twenty per cent to sixty per cent of their wages, an incredible fact were it not printed by the official daily paper of the Fascist unions. In Campania the girls were earning 4 lire a day in January 1931.[7] The commandments of Mussolini are respected only when at the workers' expense.[8]

It would, of course, have been iniquitous to reduce wages and salaries without at the same time reducing the cost of living. Therefore, Mussolini forthwith fought two more "battles." The landlords, who, in spite of the orders given them in 1927, had been raising rents, were again ordered to cut them by ten per cent; retail prices were again ordered to go down. But in July 1934 the Supreme Court ruled that no landlord was

---

[7] *Giornale dell'Agricoltura della Domenica*, Mar. 8, 1931.

[8] While making a trip through Italy in 1928 upon the invitation of the Italian Government, Mr. Edward Corsi found that the peasants were "the main beneficiaries of Fascist rule" (New York *World*, Nov. 4, 1928). Signor Villari, *Italy*, p. 289, stated: "The Fascist syndical system tends to equalize wages between the various parts of Italy: whereas in the North a very considerable improvement has already been attained and wages are comparatively high, in the South more primitive conditions prevail and the workers are still, to a large extent, sweated on inadequate wages. Fascism set itself to raise the conditions of the South so that they should at all events approach those of the more progressive North." Two years later (*The Economics of Fascism*, p. 104) he assured the Institute of Politics at Williams College: "The conditions of labour in the more backward and poorer parts of Italy are tending to attain the standards of the more advanced parts." For these, as for many of his other assertions, he would have found it impossible to adduce any proof.

obliged to cut down rents as a result of the order given by Mussolini in 1930! [9] Such cuts were purely optional. The only cuts that were not optional were the wage cuts.

In all fairness, however, one must admit that after the second half of 1930 a certain reduction in the cost of living took place in Italy. But this fact was merely in accord with a world-wide trend, which included even those unfortunate countries that had not yet made up their minds to enjoy the blessings of Fascist "syndicalism." [10] The decline was due to the world depression and not to Mussolini's "battle."

Not a year had elapsed since the cuts of the autumn of 1930, when on October 30, 1931, the Central Corporative Committee under the presidency of Mussolini announced that "in the industrial field a further *general* wage cut was neither possible nor useful"; but "*in certain special circumstances* reductions might be allowed"; as regards agricultural wages, "they too had been adapted to present conditions and could not be further reduced, except *in some provinces* where a revision was advisable"; anyhow, wage reductions must be fixed by agreement between the employers' and workers' organizations, and must be a just compromise between the interests of the two parties.

Several Italian newspapers, for instance the *Corriere Padano* of October 31, reported this deliberation of the Central Corporative Committee under the heading "No Further Reduction In Wages," and even the London *Times* of November 2, 1931, presented the news under the headline "Further Reductions Discouraged." The correspondent of the *New York Times*, on November 1 reported that "Italy had authorized new cuts in wages" but added that "the unions had gained more power" since "the cuts must be the result of agreements among the legal organizations, and thus labor unions would treat with those employers who proposed wage reductions"—as if this had never existed in Italy and were an innovation of October 31, 1931.

From then on, wages were cut, not by means of general measures advertised in the press, but as a result of local negotiations, affecting now one group of workers, now another, now in this province, now in that.

On January 21, 1932 the president of the industrialists' confederation made the following statement:

---

[9] *Lavoro*, July 29, 1934.

[10] International Labour Office, *Year Book: 1932*, pp. 407–9; Rosenstock-Franck, p. 360 ff.

After the general reduction in wages in November 1930, further reductions have been successively agreed upon by the organizations representing the groups of industries most seriously affected. The position of other groups is under consideration with the same end in view (*Industrial and Labour Information*, February 1932, p. 133).

In the March 26, 1932, issue of the *Corriere della Sera*, Signor Biagi, at that time one of the high officials in the industrial unions, made the following confession:

We were forced by a system of mechanical wage reductions to put healthy and sick concerns on the same plane, bringing the workers' wages into line, not with the condition of the better concerns, but with that of the poorer ones, in order to permit the latter to keep alive and to avoid aggravating the situation.

"The farmers," wrote a union official in the *Lavoro Fascista* on July 31, 1932, "have installed the policy of 40 per cent; that is, every time we present ourselves at a wage discussion, they ask for a cut of at least 40 per cent."

On March 7, 1933, a high official in the Fascist unions, Signor de Marsanich, declared in the Chamber of Deputies:

During the last four years in some thousands of labour agreements set up in all sections of production, wages have been systematically reduced by considerable percentages. Class co-operation must not be understood as the sacrifice of one class for the benefit of the other.

In the *Lavoro Fascista* for May 20, 1933, a contributor remarked that "in order to justify the excessive adroitness of one side [that of the employers], the inability to resist on the other [that of the union officials], and perhaps the common hypocrisy," it had become customary to "change the names of things, thereby clothing harsh reality with a cloak of euphemistic words":

To reduce wages today is "to make a harmonious correction" [*fare un ritocco armonico*]; to deprive a poor creature of three or four lire is "to smooth down the peaks" [*smussare le vette*]; to slice repeatedly into the pay for piece work is "to file down the schedules lightly" [*leggermente limare le tariffe*]. To all these Petrarchian expressions we prefer, for example, that one worthy of Dante, which sums up all the others and judges them—"give no quarter to wages."

This poor devil must indeed have lost all his patience, to have taken the risk of being interned on some penal island for speaking with such slight respect of the vigilance exercised by Fascist syndicalism in defence of the Italian working classes.

Every time that a general or local wage cut was put through, the workers had the pleasure of reading in the official announcements the formula that the parties had "given proof during the negotiations of the most laudable spirit of class co-operation." [11] "Nothing is more desirable," Prince Metternich was wont to say, "than co-operation between a man and his mount, provided that one be the man and not the mount." In Fascist class co-operation the employer is the man and the worker is the mount.

---

[11] Here is an example worthy of Doctor Pangloss. It was dished up for the English public in the London *Times* on Feb. 29, 1932: "A further instance of the collaboration policy in the industrial field which is being carried out in Italy, is the special agreement reached at the Fiat Works in Turin. A reduction of ten per cent in wages and salaries, which had been decided upon some time ago and then postponed, will be enforced from tomorrow" (quoted by Strachey in *The Coming Struggle for Power*, p. 266).

VII

"The Capitalistic Method of Production
Is Out-of-Date"

NOTWITHSTANDING the aggravation of the world depression since October 1930, humanity had not yet caved in when Mussolini made his speech of November 14, 1933. Consequently, he could announce that "the capitalistic method of production had become out-of-date" (see above, p. 113).

Capitalistic production having become out-of-date, a new deal was called for. The Italian new deal was the "corporative system."

These institutions that we have created [Mussolini stated in that epoch-making speech] must be felt and heeded by the masses as the instruments by which they may improve their standard of living. It is necessary that, *at a certain time*, the worker, the tiller of the soil, be able to say to himself and to his family: "If today I am really better off, I owe it to the institutions created by the Fascist Revolution." We must wish the Italian workers to feel that we are creating those institutions which *at a certain time* will give positive, concrete, practical, and tangible results.

These positive, concrete, practical, and tangible results were not long in manifesting themselves. On December 9, the Under-Secretary of Corporations, Signor Biagi, made a "report on the present wage situation in all branches of national production" to the Central Corporative Committee in the presence of Mussolini. The brief official summary of this "ample and lucid report" communicated to the Italian press was a veritable masterpice of obscurity. But after reading and rereading it attentively, one could discover that the speaker at the end of his report pointed with pride to "two very recent cases in which the industrial employers' and employees' Confederations, in view of the higher needs of national production, had agreed to important wage *equalizations*." One of the cases was the labour agreement in the woollen industry of Biella; and the other was that in which "pay for piece work had been reduced in the shipyards of the Adriatic."

The agreement concerning the woollen industry in the district of

Biella had been arrived at in Rome on November 30, 1933, after three years of bickering. "The Fascist Party and the Ministry of Corporations had a direct hand in it" (*Lavoro Fascista*, November 25, 1933). Its text had been published in the *Lavoro Fascista* of December 1, 1933. As a result of cuts which had taken place since 1927, the wages of 30,000 workers had already been degraded below their level in 1927 to the extent of forty per cent for the men, from forty to fifty per cent for the women, and from forty-five to fifty-five per cent for the apprentices. The new agreement (i. e., that of November 30, 1933) had made it possible for the employers to impose still further reductions. For example, the women engaged in "finishing" had been divided into twenty-nine classifications, with wages ranging from 5.25 to 12.30 lire a day; since the differences between the various classifications were imperceptible, it was easy for the employers to shift the women from the higher-paid to the lower-paid categories.[1] As regards the shipyards of the Adriatic, on December 3, 1933, wages in those shipyards had been cut by 6.5 per cent.[2]

In the light of these examples it was easy to understand the significance of the conclusion of Signor Biagi's report:

> The activity of the ministry must continue along the path already marked out by the Duce and trod in the spirit of Fascist *obedience*, keeping in mind, on one hand, the exigencies of the domestic market, and on the other, the necessity of strengthening and maintaining the volume of exports.

The Duce, summarizing the discussion, observed: "The Under-

---

[1] The *Resto del Carlino*, Nov. 30, 1933, announced that reductions had been made, but added: "These reductions are so small as to justify that atmosphere of mutual understanding which everyone hopes will issue from the new wage agreement." The review *Problemi del Lavoro*, in its issue of Jan. 1934, made the following comment: "The woollen industry is still the most fortunate of Italian industries, because it is still working at full capacity, and its unemployed do not exceed the normal number; nevertheless the representatives of the workers have had to accept another five per cent cut in the wages of a section of their workers. The employers seek the point of least resistance. If the pressure from the workers were to be relaxed, or if the unions were to change their function, the workers would not be long in descending to the level of existence of the Japanese workers." If the former Socialists who edit this review had been willing and able to be outspoken, they would have written that no pressure from the workers was possible, that the function of the Fascist unions was precisely that of making such pressure impossible, and that hence the Italian workers were rapidly descending to the level of the Japanese workers.

[2] This news was given by *Il Nuovo Avanti*, an anti-Fascist newspaper published in Paris, in its issue of June 9, 1934.

Secretary of State has placed in their true light the most important problems concerning the wage policy which the regime is following at the present time," and concluded by affirming that the Central Corporative Committee would entirely agree to such a line of action.[3]

A few days later, the newspapers published the following *communiqué*:

In almost every province the associations of employers in agriculture gave notice of their withdrawal from labour agreements. They aimed at obtaining cuts in the wages. The situation was particularly difficult in the provinces of northern Italy, where agriculture had to face greater hardships. It was more than natural that the workers' wages should feel the effects of this state of affairs. But since the wage level had already in the past suffered reductions which made new changes inadvisable, the unions did not feel bound to concede further curtailments *in general,* declaring that only *for a few provinces* could an eventual change in wages be taken into consideration.

The newspapers went on to relate that the old contracts had been renewed without changes in thirty-three provinces; "new labour pacts" had been concluded in twelve; the contracts of twenty-three provinces were in course of discussion; the negotiations were especially difficult in four provinces for which the employers asked reductions of from ten to twenty per cent.[4] Since the provinces of Italy are ninety-two in number, and the *communiqué* accounted for only seventy-two, the fate of the other twenty provinces remained veiled in mystery.

The official organ of the Ministry of Corporations, *Sindacato e Corporazione*, January 1934, p. 71, explained that every time the ministry had intervened during the year in the drawing up of agreements, it had "had as its aim the highest interest of the economic structure of the Nation," and had sought to "equalize, as far as possible, the remuneration of the workers in every sector with the increased value of the lira, and with the diminished cost of commodities and services": a circumlocution instead of saying frankly that wages had been cut.

On April 14, 1934, Mussolini discovered that the purchasing power of the lira in terms of wholesale prices, after having been in 1930 one-fourth of what it was before the war, had by 1934 risen to one-third of its pre-

---

[3] The Italian newspapers of Dec. 10, 1933.
[4] *Resto del Carlino,* Dec. 27, 1933.

war capacity. At the same time he discovered that the cost of living did not correspond to the purchasing power of the lira.[5] The landlords too, therefore, received notice to reduce rents anywhere between twelve to fifteen per cent. Moreover, all the newspapers were again flooded, as in 1927 and in 1930, with columns of information about the precipitous decline in prices that would take place throughout Italy as a result of Mussolini's magnetic powers.

The correspondent of one of the most pro-Fascist papers published in England, the *Daily Telegraph*, May 1, 1934, commented on the new "battle" in the following words:

It is interesting to watch this experiment in unorthodox economics from close quarters. Will Mussolini succeed? And will internal prices respond to his command? Every Italian is asking these questions. The Italian housewife, who brings family budgeting to a fine art, is faced with a difficult problem. Food prices are higher than in England, and certain items, such as sugar, which is fourteen pence a pound, butter, and coffee, are almost prohibitive for people earning these salaries. Are people grumbling about the cuts? Of course they are. But a little murmuring does no harm, and when the cost of living is forced down it will subside. But here Mussolini faces a more formidable task than applying the axe to employees and landlords. He must so adjust internal prices that national health and content is ensured. In many cities the authorities are going back to the old system of *calmiere*, or fixed price-lists, which were introduced during the war and twice revived, but were allowed to lapse when lower purchasing power and general depression caused prices to fall. Within the past few days these lists have been a good deal in evidence. But the shopkeepers are as resourceful as were the landlords. They exclude the better cuts of meat, fresher fruit and vegetables, the good butter, the pure olive oil from the fixed price. They tell the consumers, "Oh, that is in the luxury class, and not included in the *calmiere*." In some cities the civil authorities have closed the shops of hardened offenders for periods varying from two days to a week. But will this stop the abuse? The shopkeeper argues that wholesale prices have not dropped since the decree came into force; that middlemen take all the profits; that the 15 per cent reduction in rents does not cover taxes and overhead charges; that he is saddled with bad debts; that, in short, he must close down unless he is able to buy cheaper than he does now.

---

[5] Rents had gone up thirty per cent between 1927 and 1933 (official *communiqué* of May 8, 1934, in *Lavoro*, May 9, 1934). Mr. Dennis wrote in 1929: "Let a tenement-house owner put up rents if he dares!" (*How Il Duce Works His Plan*, p. 44.)

If our memory is correct it is Æsop who relates the story of the monkey that was appointed arbiter between two dogs in regard to the division of a piece of cheese into two equal parts. The monkey began by cutting the cheese in two. But the two parts were not perfectly equal. The monkey then bit off a piece from the larger portion and swallowed the titbit. But this made the other part larger. The monkey then bit off a morsel from this part and swallowed it too. And thus seeking, without ever succeeding, to make the two halves exactly equal, the monkey ate the whole cheese. Mussolini follows the same method in "equalizing" wages with the cost of living. His endeavour to equalize the cost of living with wages and then wages with the cost of living bids fair to end with the total abolition of wages.

In fact, on April 26 the commissioners of the employers' and the employees' industrial confederations agreed that wages which had not been reduced since 1930 were to be cut seven per cent; while those workers who had already had wage cuts would lose enough more to make the total equal to a seven per cent reduction. On April 27, a meeting was held by the high officials of the commercial employees' confederation, in which "the problem of wages and salary reductions among the commercial employees was taken up"; that is, these officials decided that they too would accept a seven per cent cut, not in their own salaries, but in the wages and salaries of their flock. The cuts were not announced in the press, but were made known by private circulars issued by the commissioners of the confederations to the presidents of the federations and gradually communicated by the latter to the subordinate officials.

This did not mean that the cuts should in no instance exceed seven per cent. The secretary of the unions in the paper industry in the province of Milan accepted "with a praiseworthy spirit of understanding" cuts of ten per cent in the men's wages and of fourteen per cent in those of the women (*Corriere della Sera,* May 9, 1934). The *Lavoro* of July 8, 1934, announced that the wages of the seamen had been cut by from eight to twelve per cent and those of the personnel of the Società Italiana Radio Marittima (Italian Maritime Radio Company) by fourteen per cent.

The press of July 19, 1934 gave the following semi-official *communiqué:*

There is no need to point out the importance of industrial wages from the point of view of international trade competition—a principle that is especially true for Italy. We are therefore glad to state that during the early months of 1934 industrial wages continued to manifest that tendency to decrease which is their constant characteristic, and which is accelerated by the measures taken by the government in the interests [sic!] of the working classes.

In short, there was a new general wage-massacre, proceeding case by case, without the publicity which accompanied the general cuts of 1927 and 1930, but resembling those which took place after general wage cuts were "discouraged" in October 1931.

While this new "battle" was going on, Mussolini, in an address of April 21, 1934, released some good news:

It is certain that our indomitable courage will enable us to conquer these difficult times. Once they are conquered, the Italian people will have a right to a life that is not one of hardship and privation.

But a month later, on May 26, he was no longer so optimistic concerning the future that awaited humanity now that the capitalistic system had become out-of-date:

At what point have we arrived? Is this crisis dying down, is it becoming more complicated, or is it growing more acute? There are ups and downs. Things vary from month to month. A conclusion that may be accepted, however, is this: that we reached the bottom some time ago. We shall go no further down. Perhaps it would be difficult to do so. The future holds only two courses. We may either continue to lie on the bottom for a long time or we may gradually begin to live again. We must rid our minds, however, of the idea that what we have called days of prosperity may return. We are probably moving towards a period of humanity reposing on a lower standard of life. We must not be alarmed by this prospect. Such a humanity may be very strong and capable of asceticism and heroism such as we perhaps have no conception of.

These words raised a wave of wild enthusiasm in the official organ of all the unions:

The different social classes are blending—and Fascism has mightily contributed to this fusion—and the new social order *is establishing itself on a lower level,* but on a more universal one. . . . The Italian people is called upon to face a rude and decisive test, and will face it with the courage of those who are entirely conscious that sacrifices are necessary for the purpose of advancing to positions more secure (*Lavoro Fascista,* May 27, 1934).

All understood that fresh cuts in wages were on the way.

In a speech delivered ten years earlier, on October 25, 1924, Mussolini had made the following announcement:

If they leave us alone for five or ten years, at the end of that time Italy will be unrecognizable, she will have changed her appearance because she will be rich, tranquil, prosperous, powerful.

In 1934, when the ten years were about up, he offered to the Italian people a future of heroism and asceticism. It looks as if from now on, in the new Fascist terminology, wage cuts will be termed heroism and starvation be characterized as asceticism.[6]

---

[6] In the *Lavoro* for June 18, 1935, an expert in economics, Signor Soldi, was pleased that Italian agriculture presented definite symptoms of improvement although the costs of the goods acquired by the farmers had increased more than those of the goods produced by them. The improvement, according to him, was due to two facts: 1, by this time all the landowners and farmers who were oppressed by debts had been expropriated at very low prices by monied capitalists, and 2, "wages had undergone a decided contraction."

VIII

"Experimenta in Anima Vili"

T HE Labour Court also proved to be a convenient instrument for the paring-down of wages. Nor could it have been otherwise.

When a dispute arises as to whether a certain industry is able to pay the higher wages demanded by the workers, or whether the workers must accept a lower wage, the problem becomes insoluble for anyone unacquainted with the jealously guarded secrets of the more important concerns in the industry involved. These secrets are known only to the company managers and will not be revealed to the judges and the experts of the Labour Court, especially in those instances where they might support the workers' cause. Nor are these secrets known to the workers. Yet by observing from day to day whether the output of the factory increases or decreases, and whether the company hires new hands or discharges old ones, the workers can form a rough idea as to whether there is a probability of obtaining higher wages, or whether they should be content with the existing wage scale, or an even lower one. If, thinking that the probabilities are in their favour, they demand an improvement in wages and this is refused, they go on strike; and if they have calculated correctly, the strike will succeed. If the strike is unsuccessful, the workers, choosing between the company's going out of business and defeat, will accept the latter. The strike is without doubt a calamity for both employer and employees; in the case of industries involving large masses of workers, the strike may be injurious to the whole community. It is therefore desirable that the right to strike should be hemmed in with restrictions aimed at minimizing the influence of demagogues in labour disputes; it would be advisable to oblige the workers to try every possible means of amicable settlement before having recourse to the strike; the workers should be made to decide the question of the strike by secret ballot and not in a tumultuous assembly; and participators in strikes begun without regard for the procedure ordained by law, should be punished. As a last resort, however, the strike is the only means whereby the workers can test the truth of the employers' assertions concerning the state of their business. To withdraw completely the right to strike and to entrust the duty of determining the financial conditions and possibilities of business enterprises to judges, against whose decisions there is no appeal, is to put a rifle into the hands of a blind man.[1]

A French journalist, M. Ludovic Naudeau, to whom we are indebted for one of the few honest and intelligent inquiries into Fascist Italy, wrote in 1927 that by creating the Labour Court Fascism intended to "transform the state into a good and impartial *père de famille*," who in labour disputes "would be the last resort for the decision as to who was right and who must give way":

If he is satisfied that a certain concern is making only meagre profits, he will discourage entirely the demands of the workers; whereas prosperous employers will be impelled towards generosity. . . . This system would be ideal if Italy had at her disposal a certain number of saints. For saints, and intelligent saints, would be needed to decide those disputes in which either side refused to give way. But to expect that any arbiters, any officials, in short, any ordinary human beings, could be saints—is that not flying from the Marxist Utopia, which we are supposed to be destroying, to a still more distant Utopia? Is it not to be foreseen that in more than one instance the proletarian class will tend to suspect certain occult influences of having opposed what it considers the right? I should like to ask what recourse it would have against a decision which it considered thoroughly unjust. And furthermore, will the owners be satisfied in every case to have their transactions studied by inquisitors? What would become of their "trade secrets"? [2]

The weaker position of the union officials as compared with that of the employers' representatives before the court was described in the following fashion by the *Lavoro Fascista*, in May 1929:

On one side sits the representative of the employers' associations armed with economic data, charts, and figures, and supported by the willing testimony of the managers who belong to their association; on the other side is the representative of the workers' union, who is forbidden admission to the sacred precincts of the factory, and who has no other resource than to ground his case on the necessarily incomplete affirmations of the persons concerned. The contrast is obvious.[3]

---

[1] Rosenstock-Franck, *L'Economie Corporative*, pp. 59–61, 120, 169 ff., has made a thorough analysis of this point.

[2] *L'Italie Fasciste et l'Autre Danger*, pp. 246–8.

[3] *Industrial and Labour Information*, July 1, 1929, p. 29.

Certain Fascist publicists have been obliged to recognize the existence of this difficulty. Professor Arias in his exposition of the *Trade Union Reform*, p. 354, wrote:

> Doubts, which may perhaps have some foundation, have been raised regarding the judge's competence in matters which are essentially technical and economic. Apart, however, from the intervention of experts, it is safe to assume the prompt formation of a bench of judges who will be specialists in labour matters, and willing and able in the examination of these questions to harmonize the economic and the legal criteria; and who will possess a profounder knowledge both of economic theory and economic reality than the present judges have sometimes displayed. We also look forward to a time when special schools for labour judges will be established in our universities.

Even Signor Villari is compelled to admit that "the Italian judiciary is still somewhat hidebound by the traditions of the jurisprudence of the past; it will require some time before it becomes thoroughly steeped in the new doctrines which lie behind the syndical organization"; but he is certain that "in time a new legal *forma mentis* will no doubt arise in harmony with the new spirit in the relations between capital and labour." [4] Pending the creation of Professor Arias's new law schools and Signor Villari's new legal *forma mentis*, the judges reared in the traditions of the old jurisprudence are performing their *experimenta in anima vili.*

These *experimenta*, i. e., the cases in which the judges and experts of the Labour Court have been called upon to fix the terms of new labour agreements, were thirty-two in number at the end of 1934. In twenty of these thirty-four cases the Court succeeded in obtaining a peaceful conciliation, thus avoiding the obligation of issuing its pronouncement. In the other fourteen cases the Court had to take this extreme step.[5] According to the Fascists, this number, really very small, proves that the regime has been able to create between employers and employees an atmosphere

---

[4] *Italy*, p. 282. Mr. Goad, *The Making of the Corporate State*, pp. 80–1, has not the slightest doubt as to the judges' infallibility: "They are experienced in the administration of industrial and commercial codes and are assisted in each case by experts *who are appointed jointly by the contending parties.*" In order to confirm his enthusiasm he invents that "concealment or exaggeration or misleading interpretation of figures is severely dealt with."

[5] *Sindacato e Corporazione*, Jan. 1934, pp. 57, 62.

so serene and so favourable to mutual trust that recourse to the Labour Court rarely becomes necessary. But there is another explanation: the officials of the unions are so accommodating at the expense of the workers in negotiating the new labour agreements that the intervention of the Labour Court is very seldom required. This explanation rests upon the fact that, no sooner are the agreements concluded, with or without the intervention of the Labour Court, than serenity and mutual trust vanish, and lawsuits concerning their interpretation and application to individual cases multiply in spectacular fashion, as we shall see in the next chapter. In any case, which class has so far had reason to be satisfied with the pronouncements of the Labour Court, the employers or the employees?

The Fascist Government, which deluges the world with a flood of literature glorifying every aspect of Fascist syndicalism, has never thought of collecting in one volume all the documents relating to the cases dealt with by the Labour Court. The student therefore is obliged to search laboriously through the daily press for the relevant information, which he often fails to find at all or else finds in insufficient quantity. This task however, has been performed by M. Rosenstock-Franck,[6] and the conclusion to which his investigation has led him is that the workers always emerge from the Labour Court with their bones more or less broken.

In order that our readers may be able to form a personal opinion concerning the procedure hitherto followed by the Labour Court in obtaining this brilliant result, we shall place before their eyes some of the more characteristic and interesting cases.

In June 1927, the president of the Seamen's Confederation, Signor Magrini (see above, p. 181), agreed to reduce their high-cost-of-living allowances by from twenty-five to sixty lire a month, according to the category. Further negotiations were postponed until the following December. When negotiations were resumed, the shipowners asked that the pay of sailors on passenger ships be reduced from 575 to 468 lire a month, and that of sailors on cargo vessels from 585 to 468 lire a month. Thus the wages of both categories would have been equalized at the lowest level: democratic equality is commendable . . . in wages. Signor Magrini offered to scale the wages of sailors on passenger ships down to

---

[6] *L'Economie Corporative*, pp. 186, 192 ff.

560 and 535 lire, and those on cargo ships to 550 and 525 lire, according to whether the sailors were married or single. Since an agreement could not be reached, it was necessary to take the dispute to the Labour Court. While awaiting the court's ruling, the employers reduced wages to the level offered by Signor Magrini. The court then ruled that wages for the sailors on cargo ships should remain at Magrini's level, and that those of sailors on passenger ships should be reduced to the same level.[7] The president of the Confederation issued the following proclamation:

> Sailors, the Labour Court has done you justice. Long live the Regime! Long live the Duce! And now, sailors, to work, for the prosperity of the Italian merchant marine! Keep your spirits up! [8]

In the province of Rovigo, in December 1930, the wages of agricultural workers had been reduced fourteen per cent, and in consequence, in the winter of 1931, the daily wage of many workers had been 7.20 lire, notwithstanding the order given by Mussolini that no labourer should be paid less than 8 lire. In July 1931, the employers demanded that the wages in kind of the 40,000 labourers of their province should be reduced sixteen per cent, that money wages should be reduced twenty-five per cent, and that a diminution should take place in the number of labourers, proportionate to the acreage of each farm to whom each employer was obliged to give work during the year. The officials of the unions refused all these demands, with the following observations: wages had already been reduced fourteen per cent in November 1930; wages in kind had already undergone a marked depreciation and for this reason the workers would suffer a further loss if the quantity was diminished too; a reduction in the working-days compulsory for each acre of land would increase unemployment and decrease production. The Labour Court of Venice forbade the employers to reduce wages in kind, ordered them not to reduce the number of labourers to whom they were obliged to give work, and accepted the principle that wages should cover the bare necessities of life, but it recognized that they were higher than the cost of those necessities,[9] and reduced them by from 7.2 to 17.8 per cent.

---

[7] *Corriere della Sera*, Jan. 12 and 29, 1928. *Industrial and Labour Information*, Sept. 5, 1927, p. 314; Feb. 6, 1928, p. 204.

[8] Haider, *Capital and Labour under Fascism*, p. 206.

[9] According to Signor Ferrari, *How the Corporative State Works*, p. 9, "all employers must guarantee to their workers a minimum wage *above* the actual cost of living."

The official journal of the unions commented on this triumph in the following words:

> We proudly greet the Venetian decision as a confirmation of our faith, which has never wavered, in the social justice of the regime. For the first time a judicial decision solemnly tells Italian labourers that their bread is secure, since wages covering the necessities of life are to be paid in any case, regardless of the economic effect upon the management.[10]

Who knows to what heights enthusiasm might have climbed, if the Labour Court, instead of cutting wages, had abolished them entirely!

In July 1933 came the turn of the 30,000 workers employed in the silk industry. The wages of these workers from 1927 to 1932 had dropped by forty-two per cent (*Lavoro Fascista*, January 19, 1932). In January 1932 the manufacturers asked that some categories should give up from 12 to 30 per cent of their wages. The union officials consented to an 8 per cent cut (*Lavoro Fascista*, March 2, 1932). Thus wages were reduced fifty per cent in comparison with what they had been in 1926 (*Lavoro Fascista*, July 8, 1933). In 1933 the employers asked for further reductions which in some classifications amounted to thirty-three per cent. The union officials offered a reduction of ten per cent. The Ministry of Corporations proposed by way of compromise that the workers accept a cut of twelve per cent. The union officials again refused, and the case was carried to the Labour Court. The case was argued on July 6, 7, 8, and 11. The union officials maintained that the condition of the industry did not warrant reduction. According to *L'Industria Lombarda* of January 7, 1933, the silk industry had distributed 25,000,000 lire in dividends in 1932 as compared with 4,200,000 lire in 1931. (Why, then, had the union officials consented to a reduction of ten per cent?) They asked the Court to inquire into the facts of the case. They complained:

> They are always asking for wage differentials between one city and another, and between industry and industry. This situation is then called upon to justify the necessity for lowering the higher wages. But as soon as these are shaved down, the same old problem of establishing proper differentials arises. The Italian industrialists would like to reduce the wages of the labour to zero.

---

[10] *Lavoro Fascista*, Nov. 10, Dec. 14, 1931; Jan. 10, 1932. *L'Operaio Italiano*, Feb. 6, 1932.

The Court pronounced that an inquiry was unnecessary, thus showing that "trade secrets" are not in the least menaced, and ruled that one group of the workers should have their wages cut by ten and one-half per cent instead of thirty-three per cent; that another group should have their wages cut eleven per cent instead of thirty and one-half per cent; another group, eleven and seven-tenths per cent instead of thirty-nine and seven-tenths per cent; still another, twelve and two-tenths instead of thirty-seven per cent; while for certain small categories it permitted only a two per cent reduction. In consequence, the pay of girls from sixteen to twenty was forty-five centesimi an hour, or 3.60 lire for an eight-hour day. The highest wage was 1.48 lire an hour, or 11.84 lire a day.

After reading the Court's decision, the presiding judge expressed his great pleasure at the dignity, the correctness, and the competence of both parties; and voiced the hope that the prosperity of the silk industry would soon be such that more generous compensation could be vouchsafed the disciplined workers.[11]

The official organ of the unions, *Il Lavoro Fascista*, July 12, 1933, declared: "The court has completely fulfilled the expectations of the workers." The court, in fact, "reduced wages even less than had been suggested by the representatives of the workers" in the direct negotiations.

There does not exist to this date a single case in which the Labour Court has increased workers' wages. As a rule, when the Labour Court has had occasion to issue a pronouncement, the same farcical tactics have been employed. The employers asked for a big reduction in wages; the union officials countered with a refusal or more often an offer of a smaller reduction; the Labour Court either confirmed the concessions of the union officials or compromised on a figure somewhere between those of the employers and those of the officials. As a result, the union officials proclaimed that the employers had been defeated, and sang the praises of the Labour Court.

Among the cases in which the court succeeded in conciliating the parties, thus avoiding the discomfort of deciding the question on its own authority, the one which occurred in the province of Cremona in 1931 deserves to be recorded.

The agricultural workers of this province had already lost, between

---

[11] *Resto del Carlino*, July 12, 1933.

1927 and 1931, from twenty per cent to thirty-five per cent of their wages. This meant that the earnings of the regular worker had dropped from 3000 lire to 2050 lire a year, while the pay of the occasional worker went down from two lire an hour to 1.60–1.70 lire an hour. In 1932 the employers demanded a further reduction of twenty per cent. The union officials refused, and the case was taken before the Labour Court in Brescia. After three days of public and private argument, and before the court had officially announced its decision, the union officials accepted the reduction requested by the employers: namely, that the aggregate annual wages of the workers continuously employed should be reduced from 2050 to 1640 lire, and the wages of the seasonal worker reduced from 1.60–1.70 to 1.30–1.40 lire an hour. After this there remained nothing for the court to do but to telegraph Mussolini:

> The principle of collaboration, of class solidarity, of devotion to the paramount interests of the nation, proclaimed by Fascism, has found its realization.[12]

In an interview published in the *Paris-Soir* of February 8, 1928, Mussolini described in the following terms the merits of his system:

> The other democracies are being devoured by a terrible malady: incomprehension. On one hand, capital, imprisoned in its crenellated tower, and labour on the other hand, organized and armed by the dual strength of Socialism and Syndicalism, covering the plain and always ready to deliver an assault on the dominating tower. Between the two, beneath a ridiculously fragile tent, is the bourgeois state in the process of endless deliberations, receiving blows from each side in the midst of the tumult, and not even able to play the role of the disinterested arbiter. Whereas I make everyone come down into the plain and I proclaim, with my armed militia at my right and my judges at my left, that from now on capital and labour will have equal rights and equal duties, and will be brothers in the Fascist family.

To become enthusiastic about this brotherhood of capital and labour, one need fulfil only one condition—one must believe that the Labour Court has kept an even balance between capital and labour in Italy. Let the reader decide for himself if the facts warrant such a belief.

---

[12] *Resto del Carlino*, Apr. 1, 1932. *Corriere della Sera*, June 1, 1932. The author of the report on *The Economic and Financial Situation of Italy*, p. 12, published in the spring of 1935 by the Royal Institute of International Affairs, affirms that "the decision [of the Court] usually favours the workers"; but on page 40 one reads: "One has only to consult the Labour Court verdicts to realize that there were during these years heavy cuts in some [!] categories."

IX

"Scraps of Paper"

For many people fear is the beginning of wisdom. It is easy to guess what may happen in a country in which the workers do not have the right to strike, even to enforce respect for labour agreements, and do not have at their disposal a rapid and gratuitous procedure for the settlement of individual disputes.

Up to January 31, 1928, a thousand cases of breach of contract on the part of employers had been reported to the provincial prefects, and 1876 cases had been reported to union officials, of which 1542 had been settled.[1]

After the abolition of the *probiviri* (see above, p. 76) the number of breaches of contract multiplied. In October 1929 the workers in the sulphur mines of Riesi and Sommatino, Sicily, instead of receiving 14.60 lire a day as provided in the labour agreement, were receiving but 12.70.[2] In 1930 the officials of the Confederation of Agricultural Unions alone had to deal with 26,299 individual disputes, and in the first seven months of 1931, with 24,660 cases. A high official in the confederation commented on this figure in the following words: "It is to be foreseen that with the diffusion of the corporative conscience the number of such disputes will rapidly decrease." [3]

Two years later this prediction was still far from being fulfilled. The corporative conscience is slow in coming into being.

The number of unfulfilled labour agreements [stated the *Lavoro Fascista* on January 6, 1932] is there to prove that the employers continue obstinately to refuse to renovate their mentality in conformity with the historical period in which we are living.

A high official in the industrial unions, Signor Clavenzani, in February 1932 stated that in the chemical industries the workers were getting only fourteen lire a day instead of the 16.45 lire promised in the agree-

---

[1] Figures given by Signor Bottai in his speech to the Chamber of Deputies on March 15, 1928.
[2] *Lavoro Fascista*, Nov. 2, 1929.
[3] *Corriere della Sera*, Sept. 27, 1931.

ment: "Of these reductions which take place contrary to the will of the organizations, there may be found examples in every category of industry." He also complained that the union officials were not even allowed to examine the passbooks in which the employers kept the accounts of the wages paid their employees, in order to ascertain whether or not they were actually being paid the wages provided in the official agreements; he was obliged to invoke a regulation of March 13, 1904 (nothing less than eighteen years prior to the Fascist era) whereby such a right was granted the secretaries of unions.[4]

In the same month of February 1932 a high official in the industrial unions of Milan, Signor Capoferri, revealed the following facts:

In 1926 the average pay of a skilled metal worker in the province of Milan was four lire an hour; as a result of the reductions of 1927–8 and 1930 the average should have dropped to 3.16 lire, whereas the actual average in 1932 was 2.76 lire, or thirteen per cent lower than the wage stipulated in the agreement. In the cotton industry the average daily earnings of a weaver had fallen forty per cent instead of thirty per cent as provided in the agreements.[5]

In the *Lavoro*, June 25, 1933, we read the following circular by the secretary of the Fascist Party in the province of Genoa:

There can be no reduction in wages except as the result of an appropriate agreement between the legal associations. Nevertheless, for some time certain companies, alleging impelling necessity or unforeseen circumstances, take it upon themselves to alter the collective labour agreement by reducing wages. This must absolutely cease.

The *Lavoro Fascista*, on March 14, 1934, complained that for several years the rice-growers had been exacting an excessive amount of labour from the gangs of women who worked as rice-weeders:

Every day the women are obliged to work one hour more than is provided in the agreement; and they also have to work on holidays without obtaining the higher wage stipulated in the agreement.

In the *Lavoro Fascista*, February 15, 1935, we read the following lamentation:

---

[4] *Lavoro Fascista*, Feb. 19, 1932. Same complaints in *Lavoro Fascista*, Aug. 19, 1933.
[5] *Ibid.*, Feb. 12, 1932.

The seamen, who were formerly in the vanguard of the movement aimed at protecting the worker, have passed into the rearguard. Day after day, the seaman has to be on duty for four-hour periods alternating with pseudo rest-periods, also of four hours. In other words, he works twelve hours a day and has three so-called rest-periods totalling twelve hours. This regime prevails even in the North Atlantic when the weather is bad and the temperature at twenty degrees below zero. These are the results obtained by the seamen's union, and they certainly give the lie to all the fine words we hear about class co-operation. The reality is that the shipowners are just what they used to be twenty years ago.

If we were to lay before our readers all the cases which we have culled from Italian newspapers, the length of this chapter would be quadrupled. We shall confine ourselves to quoting two general statements emanating from sources of indisputable authority:

1. Signor Scotti, an industrial employer, who at the same time was a deputy, explained to the Chamber on March 7, 1933, that the cause of so many disputes was to be found in the fact that the wages provided in the labour agreements were too high: "It is necessary that the minimum wage be low enough to avoid the inevitable and unfortunately widespread violations such as, for instance, has occurred in regard to the agreement recently entered into by the cotton industry." The remedy against violations of labour agreements is, then, at hand: increase the dose of "class co-operation" by continuing to reduce wages.

2. On June 1, 1934, the *Lavoro Fascista* uttered the following sentence: "An employer who pays his employees the wages due them and scrupulously performs all his legal obligations towards them—we have never encountered such a man in our experience."

According to the report of the Minister of Justice of January 1934, 145,289 cases had been brought before the ordinary courts between February 1928 and November 30, 1933.[6] In the province of Siracusa the unions, with a membership of 18,000, in 1933 had to take up 1878 disputes involving 5530 workers, or nearly one-third of the total number enrolled.[7]

---

[6] *Sindacato e Corporazione*, Jan. 1934, p. 45.

[7] *Lavoro Fascista*, Nov. 7, 1933. Signor Pitigliani, in his book on *The Italian Corporative State*, pp. 68–75, refrained from presenting any information on the extent of this phenomenon. Signor Villari, in his address at the Williams College Institute of Politics in the summer of 1932, made the following statement: "A few attempts at evasion of the labour contracts have been made by employers, but they are not numerous" (*Economics of Fascism*, p. 109).

To the cases that are dealt with by the union officials or are brought before the courts should be added those in which the workers silently accept terms less favourable than those contained in the agreements because they are afraid of losing their jobs.[8] In a period of economic depression and of widespread unemployment, the worker does not dare to argue with his employer. Disputes arise, as a rule, after the worker has been discharged; then, no longer having anything to fear, he appears before the officials of his union and reports his case.

From the *Lavoro Fascista* of April 16, 1935, we learn that in November 1933 when a national agreement was stipulated in Rome for the workmen in the pastry-shops, the organizations of each province were entrusted with the task of adapting general principles to local conditions. But there were provinces, for instance that of Varese, in which the officials of the unions had not concerned themselves with the accomplishment of this task. As a consequence, the only thing the workers knew about their rights and duties, was that it was not permitted them to strike.

The employers, after having withdrawn from a labour agreement, often prolong the negotiations for a new agreement, and while the parleys are in progress, reduce wages, since there is no agreement in force forbidding reductions. The workers cannot strike and the union officials have no agreement on which to take a stand. The employers then demand that the reduced wages shall be written into the new agreement.

These manœuvres conflict with a regulation passed on July 19, 1929, by the Central Inter-Organization Committee under the presidency of Mussolini, enacting that "the collective labour agreement shall remain in force, even after its expiry, up to the time of its replacement by a new agreement." [9] But the sword of Fascist "syndicalism" is sharp only when it strikes a worker. On January 28, 1932, Mussolini solemnly announced, "it will be necessary to accelerate the procedure in cases where there is undue delay in reaching agreements." [10] In June 1932 and January 1933 the question came up again before the National Council of Corporations, as if it had not already been settled by the regulation of 1929. Finally on September 16, 1933, the Council of Ministers decided to introduce into parliament a bill designed "to eliminate uncertainty during the

---

[8] This fact is admitted in an article in the *Lavoro Fascista*, Jan. 30, 1935.
[9] *Industrial and Labour Information*, Aug. 26, 1929, p. 280.
[10] *Ibid.*, March 9, 1931, p. 284.

period between the expiry of an agreement and the formulation of the new conditions of work." The reader who takes Fascist "syndicalism" seriously cannot but be surprised that such uncertainty was not eliminated by simply declaring that the old agreement shall remain in force until the new one is made. The wonder of the reader will, however, vanish when he is informed that the act of January 25, 1934, while stipulating that the old agreement shall remain in force until the new one is concluded, thereby seeming to confirm the 1929 regulations, also provides that either one of the two organizations may ask the Labour Court to set up a provisional *modus vivendi* to be enforced until the establishment of the definitive regime. In other words, the Labour Court, pending negotiations, will be able to reduce wages all the more easily since the reductions are only "provisional"; after which, the "provisional" reductions will be more readily embodied in the final agreement.

A new decree, of May 21, 1934, was hailed as the conclusive remedy against this evil. It made it mandatory for the officials of the unions to try a compromise before resorting to judicial procedure. But it also has proved ineffective. "The duration of disputes has been in no way curtailed, instead it has been prolonged" (*Lavoro*, March 29, 1935). When the officials of the organizations try to settle the dispute before it is taken before the court, "the employers answer neither the first nor the second summons" (*Lavoro Fascista*, March 9 and 14, 1935). "Statistics show that the number of disputes taken before the court has gone up, while the number of disputes settled by conciliation before hand has decreased"; (*Lavoro Fascista*, March 14, 1935).

In June 1935 the Ministry of Corporations announced that 62,000 disputes had been settled by the officials during the last four months of the preceding year and the first two months of the current year (*Sindacato e Corporazione*, June 1935, p. 1495). How many disputes were settled in such a way as to meet the rights of the workers? It is rumoured in Italy that as a rule the union officials reach a compromise by inducing the workers to give up a share of their due wage. Since it is their duty to arrive at some compromise, they "compromise" by helping the employers cut wages.

The *Lavoro* of June 12, 1934 gave the news of a "controversy" between a firm in Sampierdarena and its employees. The concern wished to reduce the aggregate wages of its one hundred employees by eighty thousand lire a year, or the enormous sum of eight hundred lire a year for each employee (three lire for each working day). The union officials kindly offered forty thousand lire. "While discussions were in progress, there occurred a new fact: the discharge of about two-thirds of the employees because of reduced labour needs and their engagement later at wages considerably lower than the previous ones." The union officials, "holding that the new wages were too low," objected. The "controversy" was submitted to the arbitration of the Ministry of Corporations, which obliged the firm to raise its wages by eight per cent, three per cent, or two and five-tenths per cent, according to the category. This is a new procedure, probably destined to have a future: the employer reduces wages, let us say, twenty per cent; the union officials protest; the Ministry of Corporations intervenes and compels the employer to raise wages by two and five-tenths per cent, three per cent, or eight per cent. And the press recounts how the pay was raised in the second stage without mentioning anything about the cuts of the first stage.

The reader will note that our information relating to the infringement of labour agreements in Italy comes exclusively from Fascist newspapers. Thus experts in Fascistology as easy to satisfy as Sir Leo Chiozza-Money is, will feel entitled to maintain that in Italy there is freedom of the press.[11] The truth is that such lamentations are drowned in an ocean of panegyrics on Mussolini and the regime, making it necessary to wade through dozens of newspapers in order to track down some document betraying the real situation. Some feeble laments permitted from time to time do not demonstrate that the Italian citizen is granted freedom of the press. They merely are an example of that freedom of speech and freedom of the press that are permitted in Russia also under the name of "self-criticism." A modest amount of criticism against inconveniences occasioned by the routine functioning of the machine, without going deeply into the fundamental principles that make the machine function, is not in the least incompatible with the most despotic regime. The newspaper *Lavoro Fascista*, which as a rule indulges in this sort of harmless "self-criticism," is aimed at a clientele of working-men; it would lose its public if it failed to give vent to certain grievances. However, the other newspapers only infrequently reproduce the complaints of the *Lavoro Fascista*. These complaints thus scarcely stir a ripple; they disturb neither the employers of labour nor the lead-

---

[11] *New Statesman*, Oct. 5, 1935, p. 445.

ers of the party in power—while the number of labour agreements that remain dead letters increases without let or hindrance.

While the worker is threatened with imprisonment if he strikes, even in order to enforce a contract which the employer legally has accepted, no one sends the employer to prison when he treats an agreement as a scrap of paper. The new penal code, Article 509, threatens anyone violating a labour agreement with a maximum fine of 5000 lire. But as Signor Roberti, a Fascist "jurist," writes in the *Lavoro Fascista*, October 26, 1933, "the use of such a powerful weapon is exceedingly rare":

Reports of trials for the crime in question are very uncommon in judicial annals, but not because of lack of material. The organizers, profoundly animated by the spirit of collaboration and the necessity of cordiality between employer and employed, prefer amicable settlements.

The cases which come before the judges sometimes give rise to sentences which seem designed to encourage employers to regard the labour agreements as mere "scraps of paper." Here are two typical cases:

1.   A firm of Foggia was prosecuted because it had made part of its employees work for nine hours instead of eight without paying them any overtime. The judge absolved the firm, because it had violated, not the "collective" contract, but solely the "individual" contracts made with those workers who received no overtime (*Diritto del Lavoro*, 1934, II, p. 488). As long as an employer pays some workers according to the terms of the "collective" contract, apparently he is not held responsible for the violation of all the other "individual" contracts.

2.   An employer at Palermo was prosecuted for having violated a collective contract to the detriment of twenty-seven workers. The judge decided that, although the employer was responsible for the violation of the contract, his twenty-seven employees were his accomplices because they had consented to work on the illegal conditions offered them by their employer and that therefore they also ought to be punished. (*Diritto del Lavoro*, 1934, II, p. 471). The fine was commuted to imprisonment in the case of those unable to pay. If, therefore, a worker, impelled by hunger, accepts wages lower than those allowed by the officials of his union, he must go to prison. Thus a union official who had an employer condemned for the violation of a contract would by so doing send the members of his union to jail. How many union officials will carry their

zeal for justice as far as this, if the doctrine of the Palermo judge becomes generally accepted?

Employers who try to circumvent the provisions of labour agreements by cheating their employees out of the stipulated wage have always existed in all countries, just as have workers who try to cheat their employers out of some of the labour due them. The most perfect labour agreements and codes in the world are dead letters where there are no vigorous labour organizations guided by officials who can and will see that those agreements and codes are enforced. But in no country has class co-operation been so much talked about as in Fascist Italy. In no other country has the government ever boasted so greatly of having introduced a regime of justice into the relations between capital and labour. And no government has ever had such a multitude of persons ready to believe and to repeat parrot-wise that its ruler has finally discovered the method for assuring justice between capital and labour and that that country is a paradise of class co-operation.[12]

---

[12] Mr. A. P. Dennis, in *World's Work*, Aug. 1929, p. 48, announced that "the government is alert to enforce penalties against social injustice; defenseless, inarticulate people are protected at every turn against exploitation."

X

Industrial and Agricultural Wages

THE official statistics give a by no means adequate picture of the drop that has taken place in the standard of living of the Italian people, although Italy at the present time is flooded with statistics of money wages and cost of living, which profess to show the movement of real wages.[1]

Prior to 1927 the index figures for industrial wages were drawn up by the National Insurance Board, which collected data on daily wages from all parts of Italy, and on the basis of those data paid workmen's accident compensation. In March 1928 this task was taken over by the Industrialists' Confederation, with the result that for 1927, the year of the "spontaneous" reductions of 20%, the statistics remained and still are perfectly silent, blank. And when the index numbers reappeared in 1928, they indicated that wages had fallen no more than from 584 to 545 between the second half of 1926 and the first half of 1928,[2] or in other words, not by 20%, but by a mere 7%.

For the two years between the first half of 1928 and the second half of 1930, the official statistics admit that wages went down from the index number 545 to 532; that is, the workers lost in those three years only 2.5% of their wages. For 1931 they admit that in consequence of the cuts ordered in November 1930 wages went down from the index number 532 to 501; that is, the workers lost scarcely 5.5%. And for 1932 they admit a loss of 2.5%.[3] The falsity is apparent at first glance in the figures

---

[1] For an idea of the magnitude of this flood of statistics, see *International Wages Comparison*, pp. 75 ff. Cf. Rosenstock-Franck, *L'Economie Corporative*, pp. 155 ff.

[2] Mortara, *Prospettive Economiche: 1929*, p. 454. *International Wages Comparison*, pp. 207, 211. From other less brazenly falsified statistics it would appear that the workers of Rome between 1926 and 1928 lost 28.6% of their wages, while those of Brescia lost 18.9% in 1927 and 1928 (*ibid.*, p. 207). Mussolini, speaking in the Senate on May 26, 1934, cited the statistics of the International Labour Office on Italian wages and pointed out that those statistics were certainly accurate because the I.L.O. "had no interest in making out a favourable case for Fascist Italy," as if he did not know that the statistics of the I.L.O. were taken from the Italian official sources. Signor Pitigliani, *The Italian Corporative State*, p. 258, begins his history of Italian wages in Dec. 1928 and admits they went down from the index number 101.6 in Dec. 1928 to 86.5 in Dec. 1932.

[3] Mortara, *Prospettive: 1932*, p. 566; *idem*, *1933*, p. 590.

for 1931, in which a cut of 5.5% is admitted, while the cuts decided upon in November 1930 were for most groups 8% and for many of them higher.[4] The cuts of 1932 were certainly not lower than 5% or 6%, a figure given by the union officials to the British commercial attaché.[5]

According to another less mendacious official estimate, the industrial workers lost 15.30% of their wages between June 1929 and October 1933.[6]

In the *Corriere della Sera* of March 26, 1932, Signor Biagi, then a high official in the Confederation of Unions in industry, stated that "between June 1927 and December 1928 wages had fallen by about 20%; a further drop of approximately 10% had taken place in 1929,[7] and in November 1930 there had been a general downward movement, in some cases not exceeding 18%, but in particular instances involving as much as 25%; many other adjustments had been made in 1931." Adding the cuts of the following years and the cuts which have been effected by the employers despite the labour agreement, we reach the conclusion that from 1926 to 1934 the industrial workers on an average lost at least from 40 to 50% of their wages.[8]

The bank clerks from January 1, 1927, to December 31, 1931, lost

---

[4] In the port of Genoa the dockers, according to their category, lost from 5% to 16% of their wages (*Lavoro*, June 26, 1931). The seamen's wages, reduced by 10% in Dec. 1930, underwent a further paring down (by what percentage we are not informed) in July 1931, when—in the words of the President of their Confederation— they "gave further evidence of the spirit of co-operation prevailing among them" (*Industrial and Labour Information*, Dec. 7, 1931, p. 352). In the province of Como wages in the silk industry were cut by from 8% to 12% (*Corriere della Sera*, Dec. 1, 1931).

[5] Turner, *Economic Conditions*, p. 174. In Feb. 1932 the 25,000 workers of the Fiat Company lost 10% (*Corriere della Sera*, Feb. 27, 1932). In March the workers in the cement factories at Casal Monferrato lost from 5% to 7% of their wages (*Stampa*, March 28, 1932). In July the wages of the workers in the Turin clothing industry were reduced by from 5% to 12.1% (*Stampa*, Sept. 3, 1932).

[6] *Sindacato e Corporazione*, Feb. 1934, p. 453.

[7] Mr. A. P. Dennis, formerly American commercial attaché in Rome, while revisiting Italy in 1929, discovered that "Italian workmen are employed at higher wages than obtained before the war": *How Il Duce Works His Plan*, p. 49.

[8] The textile operatives in Biella (Piedmont) in Feb. 1928 were receiving a wage 24% lower than that of 1924 (*Gazzetta del Popolo*, Feb. 27, 1928). In Dec. 1933 their wages were from 40% to 55% lower than in 1927 (see above, p. 201). In the province of Milan the women weavers received in 1931 a wage 31% lower than that of 1927 (*Lavoro Fascista*, Jan. 12, 1932). Wages in the silk industry dropped by 50% from 1926 to 1933, and in 1933 were subjected to a further cut of from 10.5% to 12.2%. Examples could be multiplied. During the London Conference of 1933 the Italian delegate, Signor Righetti, stated that in industrial wages "the maximum reduction of 18% was reached in 1928" and that "the average diminution finally amounted to 24 or 25%" (*The State and Economic Life*, p. 267).

from 36% to 37% of their salaries, some of them losing as much as 40%.[9] The clerks of the Banca Popolare of Milan between 1926 and 1931 lost 47% of their salaries.[10] On January 28, 1932, the officials of their confederation consented to the suspension of their biennial raise in salary, to a cut of from 3% to 5%, and to the reduction of dismissal indemnities. They had scarcely finished digesting these reductions when in January 1933 they again experienced the delights of class co-operation. Along with all the clerks in other private corporations they had the pleasant surprise of being informed that beginning with January 1, 1933, the government was going to be so generous as to reduce the income tax on their salaries from 13% to 8%; but the employers who until that time had paid the tax for their employees, were henceforth, under the penalty of heavy fines, obliged to deduct the taxes from their employees' salaries, giving them as compensation an increase in salary that should correspond to 40%, 50% or 60% of the tax that the employers thus saved. In short, the state treasury lost one-third of its income tax, the employers saved from 4.8% to 7.2% on their salary disbursements, while the employees lost from 3.2% to 4.8% of their salaries. Of all the people in the world Mussolini alone is capable of inventing such an ingenious farce!

For agricultural labourers Signor Cognetti de Martiis, Reader in Rural Legislation at the University of Parma, wrote in the *Lavoro Fascista*, November 18, 1931:

The curve of nominal agricultural wages went upward immediately after the war, followed by alternations between rising and falling until 1926, after which came a pronounced downward tendency from 1927 to the present.

A report by a high official of the Confederation of Agricultural Unions in 1931 stated that the average wage of the agricultural workers throughout Italy had declined from 14.3 lire a day in 1926 to 10.44 lire a day in 1931; i. e., the workers' loss had been 27%. But these figures are certainly false. In 1927 alone wages were cut 20%, and at the end of 1930 and the beginning of 1931 many wages were further reduced 25% and even more. The report admitted that wages dropped 34% in Lombardy and 38% in Emilia, and that in Milan, Pavia, and Cremona,

---

[9] *Lavoro Fascista*, Jan. 21, 1932.
[10] *L'Industria Lombarda*, Feb. 20, 1933.

the richest provinces in Lombardy, the loss amounted to 45% and even 50%.[11] If the cuts in the richest sections of Italy reached 45% and even 50%, the poorer sections in southern Italy would have had to lose not more than 10%, in order to raise the general average to 28%. In actual fact, the cuts in southern Italy were no less ruthless than in the north.

Let us give some examples of cuts in agricultural wages as a result of the reductions of November 1930:

1. The workers engaged in land reclamation lost from 8% to 25% of their wages—*Resto del Carlino*, January 2, 1931.
2. Province of Foggia, cut of from 20% to 60%—*Lavoro Fascista*, February 10, 1931.
3. Province of Cremona, 27% cut—*Lavoro Agricolo Fascista*, March 8, 1931.
4. Province of Milan, 25% cut—*Lavoro Agricolo Fascista*, March 8, 1931.
5. Province of Bologna, 25% cut—*Resto del Carlino*, December 1, 1931; *La Provincia di Bologna*, p. 1524.
6. Province of Mantua, from 1926 to 1931, the workers lost 42.2% of their earnings—*Lavoro Agricolo Fascista*, March 23, 1931.
7. Provinces of Milan, Novara, and Vercelli, several categories of workers from 1926 to 1931 lost 50% of their wages—*Lavoro Fascista*, April 12, 1931.
8. Province of Rovigo, the worker lost 20% in 1927, 14% in 1930, and from 7.2% to 17.8% in 1931 (see above, p. 211).
9. Province of Pavia: between 1926 and 1931 the worker lost 50% of his wages—*Lavoro Agricolo Fascista*, June 17, 1931.[12]

The following examples will suffice for the period since 1931:

1. Province of Piacenza, 14% cut—*Lavoro Agricolo Fascista*, January 31, 1932.
2. Province of Forli, 12% cut—*Corriere della Sera*, April 8, 1932.
3. Province of Cremona, the worker lost from 20% to 35% of his wages from 1927 to 1931, and suffered a further reduction of 20% in 1932 (see above, p. 214).

---

[11] *Industrial and Labour Information*, Nov. 19, 1931, p. 99.

[12] The pay was to be 11.60 lire in case the worker had to "stand in water and mud," and might even reach 15.20 lire if the work consisted in "cutting grass while standing in water up to the waist." The women between 16 and 65 years of age were to receive 5 lire for an 8-hour day; and when they had to work in the water to plant rice, the figure rose to 5.80.

4. In the southern section of the province of Milan, the worker from 1927 to 1933 lost about 63% of his earnings—*Lavoro Agricolo d'Italia,* November 27, 1927; *Lavoro Agricolo Fascista,* January 25, 1931; May 15 and November 15, 1932; *Bollettino di Sericoltura,* June 20, 1933.

5. In several provinces of Sicily the agricultural day-labourers from 1928 to 1934 lost more than 50% of their wages—*Lavoro Fascista,* October 26, 1934. Add the 20% cut of 1927, and the total loss will exceed 70%.

6. Province of Ferrara: the daily wage, which had amounted to 19.71 lire in 1928, had been reduced to less than 9 lire by 1934; for certain kinds of work the pay was 6.60 lire a day—*Corriere Padano,* November 19, 1934.

A characteristic case is that of the 180,000 rice-weeders, who are almost all women.

On March 16, 1927, the representatives of the rice-growers and the officials of the National Federation of Agricultural Unions made the wage agreements for the coming season. The daily wage of the workers who left their own province to work in the rice fields was reduced from 21 to 19.50 lire. The pay of the local workers was likewise cut. The rice-weeding lasts from 30 to 40 days and is work of the most exhausting sort. After the work had been going on for a fortnight, the employers declared that they could no longer pay the wages agreed to, because meanwhile the price of rice had fallen 25%. They asked for a 20% cut in wages. If the price of rice had risen instead of falling, would they have thought of raising the labourers' wages? The union officials generously offered, in response to the employers, to reduce the daily wage of the imported workers from 19.50 to 18.90 lire, and that of the local workers from 18.90 to 18.30 lire. The employers thought this not enough. The dispute was referred to the Labour Court. In its decision of July 14, 1927, the court admitted that the employers had the right to demand a revision of the wage agreement in view of the fall in prices, but not to "let the consequences of the new state of things fall only on the labourers"; it allowed the 60 centesimi cut offered by the union officials, and made the workers give back to the employers what they had already received in excess.[13] On September 18, 1927, during the Congress of

---

[13] *Corriere della Sera,* July 20, 1927; *Industrial and Labour Information,* July 25, 1927, p. 109 and Aug. 1, 1927, p. 149. The London *Times* for July 16, 1927, reported the decision as follows: "The Magistracy of Labour yesterday refused the

Agricultural Labourers (i. e., of the officials of the unions) in the province of Milan, the provincial secretary of the Fascist unions presented Signor Rossoni, president of all the national confederations of Fascist unions, in the name of the women who had worked in the rice fields, with a "bronze statue representing Faith, in remembrance of the first decision of the Labour Court, at which Signor Rossoni had upheld the cause of the workers." [14]

The workers.were subjected to a further reduction of 7.5% in 1928.[15] This cut was decided upon by the Under-Secretary of State, Signor Bottai.[16] During 1929, the price of rice went up 20% and the growers generously offered the workers an increase of 1.5%, which the officials of the unions accepted with gratitude.[17]

In 1930 a new fall in prices led the officials of the unions to accept two new reductions in pay amounting to 17.5%.[18]

In 1931 the employers asked a cut of 35%, which would have reduced wages to 8 lire a day. The President of the Confederation of Agricultural Labourers, following the custom, hastened to offer a reduction of 20%. Since harvest time arrived without a settlement's having been reached, the workers "went to work not even knowing what their wages were to be." [19] The Labour Court compromised as usual, by

---

appeal of the Federation of Agriculturists for a decrease in the wages of the labourers employed in the rice fields greater than the decrease of 60 centesimi which had been agreed to by the Federation of Fascist Syndicates [unions]. The court ordered the employers to pay the arrears of wages which had been reduced by them pending the hearing of the case." This last sentence is the direct opposite of the truth. No wonder that such a scrupulous correspondent was decorated in 1931 by Mussolini with the insignia of "Commendatore" along with four other leading foreign correspondents in Rome.

[14] *Corriere della Sera*, Sept. 19, 1927.

[15] In *Industrial and Labour Information*, Dec. 21–31, 1928, p. 385, is the statement that for 1928 "in the sphere of agriculture, special mention should be made of the agreement for the weeding of the rice fields"; but there is no mention that this agreement had meant a reduction of 7.5% in wages for the workers.

[16] Rosenstock-Franck, p. 184.

[17] The newspapers devoted much space to this agreement without alluding to the smallness of the increase in wages. See *Industrial and Labour Information*, July 22, 1929, p. 116.

[18] These figures came to light during the arguments before the Labour Court in June 1931: *Stampa*, June 11, 1931. Concerning the reductions of 1930 the Stefani Agency announced only that "after long discussion under the presidency of the Minister of Corporations, the parties have made those changes in the wage scale necessitated by the recent price variations; in this contingency the employers and the workers [sic] have again given proof of their understanding of present economic necessities and of moral discipline" (*Corriere della Sera*, Apr. 27, 1930).

[19] *Corriere della Sera*, June 18, 1931.

allowing a reduction of 24%; [20] and in publishing its pronouncement, felt obliged to make the following remarks:

In conclusion, the court cannot do less than to hold up to public admiration the behaviour of the two Confederations and their representatives in the present serious economic dispute involving more than 200,000 workers. Both labourers and agricultural employers agreed that in the highest national interest production should not suffer from the dispute. Wherefore the labourers, not with class hatred in their hearts but singing patriotic hymns, returned to work, performing their tasks at the appointed time, although uncertain as to the actual wage which they would finally receive. Both parties felt complete confidence in the decision given by the Labour Court.[21]

History does not tell us whether the women who worked in the rice fields received with patriotic hymns the news of the 24% cut in wages.

On May 14 and 31, 1933, the newspapers announced the terms of the agreement for 1933, whereby the wage of workers imported from outside the province was lowered from 10.64 to 9.50 lire and that of the local workers from an average of 10 lire to one of 8.80 lire a day.[22] After the workers had thus lost from 11 to 12% of their wages, the Fascists organized a great demonstration in honour of the regime. The general secretary of the Party was present at the celebration, and a rice-weeder recited a speech thanking him for the interest that he was taking in the rice industry: "it was a sinister comedy." [23]

In March 1934 the contract for the following summer was drawn up. The *Lavoro Fascista* of March announced that the contract of the preceding year had been renewed without change. This was a lie. The wages of girls of fourteen to fifteen years of age was reduced from 9.50 to 8.28 lire a day.

The table on the following page indicates the "fluctuations" in the wage scale for the 180,000 rice weeders.

According to the *Lavoro Fascista*, October 26, 1934, the agricultural day-labourers in several provinces of Sicily from 1928 to 1934 lost more than 50% of their wages. According to the *Corriere Padano*, November 19, 1934, the daily wage of agricultural day-labourers in the province of Ferrara had fallen from 19.71 lire in 1928 to less than 9 lire by 1934.

---

[20] *Stampa*, June 19, 1931.
[21] *Sindacato e Corporazione*, Jan. 1934, p. 61.
[22] *Industrial and Labour Information*, June 12, 1933, p. 347, Aug. 21, 1933, p. 285.
[23] Rosenstock-Franck, *L'Economie Corporative*, p. 150.

DAILY WAGE IN LIRE

	Imported rice-weeders	Local rice-weeders in the districts of:			
		Alessandria & Vercelli	Novara & Mortara	Milan & Pavia	Crema & Lodi
Agreement 1926	21.00	21.80	21.00	20.26	19.50
Agreement 1927	19.50	18.90	18.50	17.50	16.50
Court Decision 1927	18.90	18.30	17.90	16.90	16.50
Agreement 1928	17.45	17.40	17.00	16.10	15.70
Agreement 1929	16.65	17.55	17.15	16.25	15.85
First Agreement 1930	16.20	14.55	14.25	13.50	13.15
Second Agreement 1930	14.00	14.55	14.25	13.50	13.15
Court Decision 1931	10.64	11.08	10.83	10.30	10.00
Agreement 1933	9.50	9.75	9.55	9.10	8.80
Agreement 1934 for girls only	8.28	8.53	8.33	7.88	7.58

Total reduction 1926–33
   in per cent:
   for women   54.77%   55.28%   54.53% 55.45% 54.88%
   for girls   60.95%   60.87%   60.33% 60.11% 61.12%

Add in both cases the 20% cut of 1927, and the total loss will exceed 70%.

In 1934 also, at the end of the season, on June 25, a celebration was held, during which, according to the press, the secretary of the Party addressed 40,000 women "to an accompaniment of indescribable enthusiasm." In July 1934 the newspapers announced that the health of the women weeders, who had spent forty days in the heat of the sun, their bodies bent over to gather the rice, "had improved since their coming to the rice fields"; many women, on returning home, had written letters "saying that they looked back with longing on the days which they had spent in the fields" (*Resto del Carlino*, July 22, 1934). However an official *communiqué* of February 26, 1935, contains the news that in the negotiations for the labour agreement of the coming season it had been decided that "each woman should be assigned a cot of her own." "This measure puts an end to the custom of sleeping on straw on the ground, which was so serious a menace from the point of view of health as well as of morality." It is clear that the improvement in the health of the women who in 1934 had slept on straw on the ground, must be attributed to that moral and hygienic mode of sleeping.

On the whole we may safely assert that from 1926 to 1934 the agricultural labourers lost from 50 to 70% of their earnings.[24]

Undoubtedly, in a period of depression wages cannot but fall, under any species of government, be it dictatorial or free. After the present crisis has passed then shall we ascertain whether and to what extent the union officials will be able not only to ask, but actually to obtain, higher wages.[25]

While waiting for the future to reveal itself, there are some cases that deserve to be put on record.

1. The *Lavoro Fascista* of March 2, 1932, admitted that in the silk industry production was constantly increasing and that therefore "further sacrifices" on the part of the workers were not "strictly indispensable," but went on to say:

These reductions were granted in view of the inevitable repercussions which England's going off the gold standard will have on the principal world market for silk, namely London, and in order to insure to Italian producers the means for maintaining their present position in the face of any eventuality.

In other words, if the industries are in a bad way, the union officials consent to wage cuts; if they are in good shape, the officials again accept wage cuts in order to avoid the possibility of an industrial crisis.

---

[24] According to the International Labour Office's *Year Book:* 1932, p. 405, the average wage of the agricultural labourers dropped from 100 in 1928 to 86 in Dec. 1932. If the compiler had taken as his basis the year 1926, he would not have been able to conceal the 20% reduction in 1927. In the memorandum laid by Signor Serpieri and Professor Mortara before the London Conference of 1933 one reads that agricultural wages "have sunk by some 20%" (*The State and Economic Life*, p. 381). *La trahison des clercs!*

[25] Rossoni, March 30, 1928: "The Italian workers have accepted in a most courageous manner the sacrifices demanded of them for the protection of industry. Much more has been asked of them than of the employers. It remains to be seen whether the employers will come forward and voluntarily offer a 10 to 20% increase in wages when industry is in a more favourable position. When the general economic situation improves, it will be necessary for the unions to resume their forward march." Mussolini, Apr. 29, 1929, to the workers of Milan: "If we have asked of you *some small sacrifice*, you have accepted it with perfect discipline. . . . But by accepting these renunciations you have placed yourselves in a better position to obtain improvement when conditions warrant it."

2. In 1932 the price of rice went up. As the previous wage cuts had been justified by the fall in prices, the rise of the latter in 1932 should have caused wages to rise. In spite of this favourable circumstance, wages were not raised: witness the following announcement in the official daily of the unions, *Lavoro Fascista*, on April 10, 1932:

The agricultural unions, [that is, the officials who run them] having taken into consideration the interests of production, do not believe it advisable to take advantage of the improvement of the market, and therefore consent that wages remain in 1932 at the level for 1931.

3. The *Lavoro Fascista* of April 13, 1932, complained that "industries which insisted on heavy wage cuts have made big profits in 1931 and have announced to their stockholders that dividends of 10, 12, and even 15% would be distributed":

A typical case is that of the Snia Viscosa. The 30 million kilograms of artificial silk produced in 1930 have become 34.6 million in 1931; while exports have gone from 19 to 21 million kilograms. Whereas the wage level was reduced in 1931, the profits have remained unchanged: 12 lire on every hundred lire invested. The same may be said for the Châtillon, which has set aside 22 million lire in profits for plant development. And the same can be said of other great industrial groups, as for example the Montecatini. In the case of these large companies there is only one side that suffers want— the workers, while the shareholders continue to receive interest more than handsome on their capital invested. Either the wage reductions were requested and justified on the basis of a false representation of the companies' situation, or else the wage cuts had as their sole object the protection of the high dividends.

These being the two horns of the dilemma, the union officials should have asked for a rescinding of the wage cuts from those firms which, contrary to the general tendency during the depression, were still making handsome profits. But none of them ever made a move in this direction.

4. The *Regime Fascista*, October 14, 1934, reported from a financial review the news that in the current year the Fiat Works had done enough business to be able to pay a dividend, without being obliged, as in the two previous years, to draw upon the reserves accumulated for this purpose before 1931. No paper ever reported that the union officials

had demanded that Fiat should raise the wages of its employees. At the end of September Fiat cut its workers' wages from 2.20 to 1.95 lire an hour.

5. Speaking in Milan on January 27, 1935, the president of the Confederation of Agricultural Unions instructed his subordinate officials that in renewing the agreements with the employers "they were not to grant reductions in wages, since increased wholesale prices in agricultural products had already had an immediate impact on the retail prices of commodities in general use." Thus, as wholesale and retail prices advance, the officials of the Fascist unions must pursue the policy, not of increasing wages, but only of preventing their decrease.

A high official of the Ministry of Corporations wrote in 1928: "The Italian system solves the question of minimum wages in the simplest of manners: it denies its existence" (quoted by Elwin, *Fascism at Work*, p. 207). By such a method any problem can be solved without any difficulty. But Mussolini has announced that "the capitalistic method of production is out of date."

XI

The Cost of Living

To be sure, the movement of money wages alone is insufficient to give us an idea of the changes for better or for worse in the standard of living of the people. If the cost of living falls more rapidly than monetary wages, real wages are increased, and to a lower money wage corresponds a higher standard of living.

What was the movement of the cost of living in Italy from 1926 to 1934?

The index numbers of the cost of living were compiled until the end of 1926 by the municipal governments of the more important cities in Italy, and they were used in the negotiations between employers and employees as a basis for determining wages. In 1921 the industrialists began to contest these figures because, they said, they had no means of verifying their accuracy.[1] On February 20, 1927, a royal decree entrusted the duty of compiling index figures on the cost of living to the *Istituto Centrale di Statistica*,[2] which was put under the immediate control of Mussolini. From then on no wage cuts took place which were not declared to be justified by a decrease in the cost of living. For instance, from January 1927 to December of the same year, the cost of living declined from 655 to 531, a fall of 19 per cent, which almost made up for the drop of 20 per cent in wages that took place at the same time, though no one in Italy had noticed any such fall. An important woollen manufacturer, Signor Targetti, declared in 1930 that from 1926 onwards wages had been reduced only 15 per cent, while the cost of living had declined 20 per cent;[3] and the president of the Confederation of Employers in Industry, speaking on January 22, 1932, at the national congress of the confederation, after having admitted that "the workers had contributed their wage reductions to the economic battle," added: "Wages are still higher than they were in 1927, in view of the drop in the cost of living." Obviously official statistics must not con-

---

[1] Galletti, *Sull'apprezzamento del carovita*, p. 7.
[2] *Industrial and Labour Information*, Apr. 25, 1927, p. 156.
[3] *L'adeguamento dei salari*, p. 437.

tradict such authoritative personages. For this reason, in Mortara's *Prospettive: 1932*, p. 566, we find a series of index numbers, according to which the index for industrial wages dropped from 600 to 501 between the first half of 1927 and the second half of 1931, meaning that the workers had lost only 17 per cent of their money wage—as if they had not lost 20 per cent in 1927 and 8 per cent in 1930. During the same period the index number for the cost of living was alleged to have dropped from 639 to 477, or 24 per cent. This would have made it appear that real wages had increased slightly. But Mortara himself wrote:

As for wages, we have some doubts as to the reliability of the figures given, and we are of the opinion that the actual reduction has been greater than the modest one represented by the figures.

According to other and more fantastic statistics, the cost of living dropped between 1926 and the second half of 1933 from the index number 516.7 to 350.4, a decrease of almost 32 per cent, whereas the wage index dropped between 1927 and 1933 from 93.78 to 74.70, or only 18 per cent.[4] Another set of figures, which the International Labour Office has swallowed without question, as is its habit and duty, would have us believe that from July 1928 to March 1933 wages dropped from 100 to 87.8, while the cost of living dropped more rapidly from 100 to 82.7. In the spring of 1934 Signor Villari [5] and the "Group of Students of the Corporate State in Italy" [6] made use of these figures to show that in the last years there had been a slight improvement in the conditions of the Italian working classes, whereas the workers in all the other countries had had to suffer great hardships. Signor Villari and the "Group of Students" pointed out that they were not giving "Fascist figures" but figures that bore the seal of the International Labour Office and of the League of Nations. They hoped that their readers would be unaware that the International Labour Office and the League of Nations merely dish up in the international market Fascist figures concocted in Italy, without submitting them to independent criticism.

In Italy the statistics of the cost of living, like those of wages, are

---

[4] *Sindacato e Corporazione*, Jan. 1934, pp. 225–6.
[5] Letter to the *Daily Telegraph*, May 29, 1934.
[6] *New Statesman*, May 26, 1934.

taken seriously only by Mussolini. In 1928, when the Central Institute of Statistics gave out the information that living costs in Biella were cheaper than in any other city in Italy, a correspondent from that city wrote in the *Gazzetta del Popolo*, February 27, 1928: "Let foreigners come and live with us, and they will soon find out if this is true." In the number of November 26, 1931, the *Corriere della Sera* taught that the decline in retail prices of which the statistics spoke was to be regarded as "theoretical," and explained how the average price of meat was established:

The statisticians first find out the prices prevailing for a given kind of meat in a given number of shops and markets in different districts; and then they take their average. Every one understands that it is enough for only one of the shops included in the survey to cut its prices for this to influence the final average. Add to this the fact that the formation of that average is considerably affected by the necessarily low prices of certain kinds of meat so poor that their consumption cannot be very widespread.

There are in Rome, Milan, and some of the other larger cities stores called "la Provvida" or "Liverani shops," which obtained their initial capital and fixtures from the government or the industrialists. Furthermore, the industrialists procure the merchandise directly from the producers, thus avoiding the middlemen. Consequently, it is possible for these institutions to sell their wares at prices lower than those prevailing in the open market. However, only a very small percentage of the population can take advantage of these shops, and even of those few who have the privilege only that minority who are able to pay cash can avail themselves of the opportunity. During the first half of 1931, only 3.9 per cent of the total amount of foodstuffs sold to the people of Milan was purchased from these institutions (*Corriere della Sera*, March 2, 1932). When figures for retail price averages are to be concocted, undue weight is given to the prices of these privileged institutions, with the result that the official averages are lower than the prices which daily experience teaches every housewife to be the real ones. The methods by which the statistics of the cost of living are cooked up are so arbitrary that even Fascist "experts" shrink from them (*Rivista Italiana di Statistica, Economia, e Finanza*, 1932, pp. 108 ff).

Signor De Stefani, a former Fascist Minister of Finance, wrote as follows in the *Corriere della Sera* of March 16, 1934, in regard to the official statistics of prices published monthly by the Central Institute of Statistics:

One might go to the market with a copy of the monthly statistics under one's arm and check up on the prices of the shopkeeper or of the carrot-seller and milk-vender. One would certainly return home spiritually perturbed. The shopkeeper would have nothing to do with the official prices. The official prices are average prices. The actual prices, of course, must frequently be higher. . . . Let the consumer not be vanquished when he discovers that the cost of living indices are not in agreement with the cost of living. . . . What happens is that they add the weight of an elephant and the weight of a flea in order to make their average.

Signor De Stefani might have added that statistics were invented in Italy in the Fourteenth Century, if we are to believe Franco Sacchetti, an Italian story-teller of that time. Bernabò Visconti, the capricious and cruel tyrant of Milan, insisted that a certain abbot, in lieu of a fine, should solve several extravagant problems, and among others should tell him the distance between the earth and the sky, and how much water the sea contained. The abbot did not know what to answer, but his miller appeared before the tyrant in his stead, and stated that according to his measurements the distance between the sky and the earth was 36,854,-072½ miles and twenty-two feet and the sea contained 25,982,000,000 fathoms, seven barrels, twelve decanters, and two tumblers of water, though it was more difficult to take measurements of the sea as "it was a thing that always moves and into which fresh water always flows." "How do you know that?" "Have it measured, sir, and if it be not so, command me to be hanged by the neck, or have me quartered." Bernabò judged the answer to be quite intelligent and decided that the miller should become an abbot and the abbot a miller.

Yet some reliable information about the cost of living is not lacking.

In an article published in the *Lavoro*, May 2, 1934, Senator Ricci accepts as exact the statistics concerning the cost of living in Genoa, which show that in January 1934 216.33 lire sufficed to buy goods that in June 1927 would have cost 287.14 lire. This would mean that living costs had declined 24.65 per cent. In the same paper on May 4, 1934, a reader stated that Senator Ricci had not taken account of the increase in taxes: since January 1933 private employees have paid their own income taxes, previously paid by their employers (see above, p. 225); furthermore, the income tax paid to the municipality had been raised: "One would not be far wrong if one estimated the increase in the tax burden on the salary at 10 per cent"; [7] therefore setting the decrease in the cost of living between 1927 and 1934 at 25 per cent was, at least for the private employees, unduly optimistic. Since in the same period wages were reduced by about 50 per cent, we must conclude that the Italian industrial workers lost 25 per cent of their real wages in those years. And if we remember the fact that real wages had already diminished 10 per cent between 1922 and 1926, we arrive at the result that in 1934 the Italian industrial workers were able to purchase with their wages less than two-thirds the goods that they could buy before the "march on Rome." Even the director of the International Labour Office, in his *Report* of 1933, p. 44, estimated that the purchasing power of the wage-earning population had shrunk by 19 per cent in Italy between 1929 and 1932. If we add the losses incurred before 1929 and after 1932, we easily overstep the figure of 33 per cent.[8]

---

[7] This affirmation is not exaggerated. Even the Fascist experts admit that taxation has on an average risen from 20% of income in 1926 to 29% in 1933 (Dean, *Italy in the World Crisis*, p. 309). The weight upon the lower classes must have been greater than 9%, because indirect taxes were augmented in preference to direct ones. Mr. Finer, in *Mussolini's Italy*, p. 532, has remarked that direct taxation rose from 28.5 per cent in 1913-4 to 38.59 per cent in 1921-2, but by 1931-2 under Fascist rule it was brought down to 28.41%. Since the yield of taxes on transfer of wealth, (21.61% of the whole governmental revenue) safely can be divided half and half between direct and indirect taxation, one reaches the conclusion that in Italy indirect taxation represents 60% and direct taxation 40% of the whole governmental revenue, "very nearly the reverse of the English system." During these last five years things have grown worse.

[8] In 1931 Mr. Mitzakis, *Les Grands Problèmes Italiens*, p. 104, after stating that "new wage cuts had not been effected for almost three years"—an affirmation not only false but contradicted by the same author on page 103—recognized that "the material conditions granted the proletariat remained on the whole insufficient in view of the relatively high cost of living." Signor Villari, in the *Economist*, July 25, 1931, declared: "If wages have inevitably declined, so have prices." And in the issue for Oct. 24, 1931, he insisted: "Altogether in the period from 1926 to 1927 the reduction in paper wages amounted to about 25 per cent, and this is just about the extent of the fall in prices." Signor Villari was apparently aware neither of the general cut of Dec. 1930 nor of the local cuts effected since 1927. Mr. Clough, in the *Harvard Business Review*, April 1932, p. 303, averred that "wages have been lowered" as well as the cost of living, but he refrained from any investigation which might have uncovered information displeasing to the Fascists. Mr. Goad, *The Corporate State*, p. 788, declared in Oct. 1933: "Wages have gone down, but it is on the average only by 15 [!] per cent. *There is no question* that the real wage of the Italian workmen is far higher than it has been in the past." Mr. Jones, *Is Fascism the Answer?*, pp. 61 and 162, informs us that "while the wages are not high, as considered on this side of the water, the purchasing power of the money is great, so that in reality the wages

During the second half of 1934, in spite of the new "battle" against the high cost of living, everyone in Italy noticed a general rise in retail prices. The Milanese paper, *La Sera*, was obliged to admit in November that "there was some alarm among the public on account of a tendency towards a rise in the price of necessities, while salaries and wages had been cut and were still stationary." Of course the newspaper advised its readers "not to exaggerate" the dangers of the situation, but it had to admit that the prices of milk, butter, and related products were on the rise; that an "excessive and systematic" increase in the price of meat had been noticeable for several months; and that eggs had reached a prohibitive price.[9]

How could the price of butter fall, when in May the government imposed a tax of two lire a kilogram on margarine in order to keep up the price of butter? Beginning with May 1, 1934, the customs duty on imported livestock was raised from 360 to 600 lire a head. According to the figures published by the financial journal *Il Sole* of Milan, Oct. 10, 1934, the meat consumed by the Italian people would cost 1.5 billion lire, but taxes on it reach the total of 700 million lire, that is, 45 per cent of the price of the product. How could the price of meat drop? Sugar costs in Italy 6.30 lire a kilogram (about thirty cents a pound), of which four lire go to the government in the form of taxes, and 1.65 go to the owners of the factories as a result of the protective tariff. Thus, for a pound of sugar which one could buy in a foreign country for eight or nine cents, one must pay thirty cents in Italy. How could the price of sugar drop?

Speaking in the Chamber on March 28, 1935, the Fascist deputy, Signor Sertoli, complained that "by 1934 wages had become much lower than those of 1914," while the cost of living was rapidly going up. The *Lavoro Fascista* of July 3, 1935, stated that in thirty-four out of thirty-seven provinces, for which it had been possible to gather reliable information, the real wages of day-labourers were lower than those in 1914; the same condition obtained for bricklayers in twenty-

---

are relatively good; in Italy the aim is to increase the purchasing power of the consumer by keeping down the cost of his necessities; higher standards of labour are sought." During the London Conference of 1933 the Italian delegate, Signor Righetti, had the audacity to assert that "taking account of the average consuming capacity of the workers, we notice an average increase of about 20 per cent"; and that the Fascist regime "has allowed salaries to be placed once more on the level to which prices had fallen" (*The State and Economic Life*, p. 382).

[9] Quoted by the *Nuovo Avanti* of Paris, Nov. 17, 1934.

seven out of twenty-nine provinces investigated, "this without taking into account the more or less prolonged periods of unemployment."

The pro-Fascist Rome correspondent of the *New York Times*, April 28, 1935, announced that an increase in internal retail prices had taken place, but found it difficult to say with certainty what the increase amounted to, as if he could not have obtained information on this point from any housewife he cared to consult. Anyhow he admitted that "some people said the increase was as high as 15 or 20 per cent." [10] In the *Commerce Reports*, Nov. 2, 1935, one reads:

On certain grades of meat, food-stuffs, butter, etc., increases of from 30 to 40 per cent have occurred, while such necessities as coal, soap, gasoline, and textiles have advanced sharply in cost. Wheat prices soared recently to 135 lire per quintal for hard wheat and 115 lire for soft, as compared with the guaranteed price of 90 lire.

To balance this increase in the cost of living, Mussolini did not ordain a corresponding increase in wages. But the Party announced a new "battle" against the rise in retail prices. Every time one of these battles is launched, the consumer only too well knows that words are not deeds. The battle remains on paper and prices soar.

---

[10] According to official Italian statistics, there had occurred in the index number of commodity prices an increase from 42.7 in the first week of January to 44.8 in the last week of March (*New York Times*, Apr. 8, 1935). The phenomenon must have been much more marked than the official statistics admit. According to Sir Leo Chiozza-Money (*New Statesman*, Oct. 5, 1935, p. 445) nominal wages went down from 100.00 in 1926 to 75.75 in the first half of 1935, while the cost of living went down from 100.00 to 64.83; therefore the real wage went up from 100.00 to 116.84, i. e. the worker gained 16.84% in real wage. Sir Leo stated that his figures were "accurate and official" and that "Italian statistics are compiled by one of the most famous statisticians in the world." As a matter of fact, from a letter from Italy to the London *Economist*, July 27, 1935, p. 179, one learns that in the first half of 1935 "the cost of living rose some 12 per cent without any increase in money income or money wages." In the province of Genoa in the month of June 1935 alone the increase in retail prices oscillated between 7 and 20% (*Lavoro*, June 18, 1935). Even the *Compendio Statistico 1934*, p. 163, was obliged to admit that if one gave the value of 100 to the real wages of 1913–4, the latter had risen by 1919 to 168 and had gone down by 1933 to 143. It is clear that the statistics of Sir Leo must have been invented by the "most famous statistician in the world." Results analogous to ours have been reached by Elwin, *Fascism at Work*, pp. 209–13.

XII

Italian Unemployment Statistics

THE movement of wages and the cost of living do not suffice to give an idea of the deterioration which has taken place in the condition of the Italian working classes. Unemployment also must be taken into account.

The Italian unemployed fall into two categories: those who draw unemployment benefit and those who do not.

In respect of the unemployed who draw benefit, the figures given by the Board of Social Insurance ("Cassa Nazionale per le Assicurazioni Sociali") are reliable, since the board must render account on its balance sheet of the sums it pays out. But the figures of doles paid after January 1924 cannot be compared with those of the preceding years, because on December 30, 1923, a royal decree excluded from the benefit all agricultural labourers, artisans, homeworkers, and domestic servants, categories which, up to that date, had enjoyed rights similar to those of the employees in industry and commerce.

Moreover, the small owners who cultivate their ground, the farmers, and the white-collar men are not taken into consideration in the statistics of the unemployed. Again, to be eligible for benefit, an employee must have paid in at least forty-eight weekly contributions during the two years preceding the loss of employment and must have been unemployed for at least one week. In addition, trades subject to seasonal unemployment are not eligible for benefit during the period when seasonal unemployment is likely to occur; for example, bricklayers receive no relief between December 16 and January 31. To the above must be added the young men who reach working age without finding work, and those who return from their military service; the former have not yet started to pay contributions, while the latter ceased paying them during military service; hence neither group is eligible for the benefit.[1]

---

[1] Senator Ricci, in the Senate, on Jan. 15, 1934: "There is one category of the unemployed, whose lot is particularly distressing to us—the young men, especially the young men who have completed the term of their military service, who find in unemployment the most bitter disappointment of their hopes . . . These unemployed young men are not legally entitled to an unemployment benefit."

Again, the benefit is granted for a maximum period of ninety days (except in instances where during the preceding two years the recipient has paid in seventy-two contributions, in which cases the benefit is extended for another thirty days); as a consequence, the unemployed disappear from the lists just when their need grows greater. And lastly, the unemployment relief is so small (from 1.25 to 3.75 lire per day), and the red tape before obtaining it so burdensome, that "many unemployed, rather than submit to the formalities and waste precious time that might be used in looking for work, prefer not to draw the benefit toward which they have paid their contributions for many years." [2] As a consequence, the unemployed who receive assistance are a minority; in February 1932 only 214,000 workers received unemployment relief, whereas the total number of unemployed tabulated in the official statistics amounted to 1,147,000.[3] During the first three months of 1934 the number of subsidized unemployed amounted to scarcely 18 per cent of the total number of registered unemployed.[4] Hence, to gain a correct idea of the trend of unemployment, one also needs the figures of the unemployed who receive no benefit. What sources give these figures?

In Italy between 1920 and 1922 there were two sources of information:

1.   The monthly returns communicated to the Board of Social Insurance in Rome by the municipal authorities. In every municipal office sat a clerk, who, once a month, filled in on a form the figure that seemed to him most probable, and this figure was sent to the board. What means had a mere clerk of knowing the number of unemployed in industry, commerce, agriculture, and among the small independent artisans, even in a small town, when there was no regular, general system of unemployment benefits, such as existed in England? In these conditions, the only thing a wise clerk could do was to fill in on the form some plausible figures, and then pass on to the next job. It should further be noticed that it was to the interest of municipalities to send up to the government a high figure of unemployed, as a sure means of getting the government to carry out public works within the municipal area, at govern-

---

[2] Article of Signor de Marsanich, Fascist Deputy and President of the Confederation of Commercial Unions, in the *Lavoro Fascista*, Oct. 30, 1931.

[3] *Bollettino Mensile di Statistica*, Sept. 1933, p. 872.

[4] *Ibid.*, Apr. 23, 1934, p. 384. Mr. Clough, in the *Harvard Business Review* for April 1932, p. 305, asserts that *all* unemployed receive unemployment benefit.

ment expense. Hence, unemployment figures were always judiciously exaggerated.

2. The labour exchanges, set up in many municipalities by decrees of January 5 and December 10, 1919, were entrusted with the duty of distributing aid to unemployed at the government's expense. The officials sought only to satisfy the greatest possible number of their friends, with the government's money. Moreover, they exaggerated the number of unemployed for the same reasons as did the municipalities; in order to induce the government to carry out as many public works as possible. Where there were no labour exchanges, as was the case especially in southern Italian towns, the only source of information was the returns fabricated by the municipal clerks.

The statistics of unemployment for the years 1920–2 were always the result of a combination of systems 1 and 2.[5]

After June 30, 1922, the labour exchanges were no longer authorized to give aid. The workers had thus less reason to register. Then came the royal decree of December 30, 1923, eliminating the appropriations for the labour exchanges from the national budget. Their upkeep was taken over by the municipalities, which sooner or later abolished practically all of them. As the labour exchanges disappeared, the unemployment figures went down.

After this reform, unemployment statistics were furnished only by the clerks in the manner described above. But the attitude of these functionaries was no longer what it had previously been. Before 1922, they had exaggerated the number of unemployed in order to persuade the government to undertake a large number of public works in their municipalities. Now, Mussolini intended that Italy should be prosperous and contented; and hence there was to be no more unemployment. The municipal clerks saw which way the wind was blowing and dutifully adopted new criteria in filling out the monthly schedules for the Board of Social Insurance at Rome.

In 1924, one of the ablest Italian economists, Signor Porri, issued the warning that it would be better not to be too complacent about the lowness of the official unemployment figures, as these were "incom-

---

[5] Rossi, *Cosa valgono le statistiche della disoccupazione in Italia*, pp. 484 ff. At the end of 1922, Mortara, *Prospettive Economiche: 1923*, p. 423, wrote: "Owing to the inadequacy of the unemployment statistics, the figures given in official documents must not be used as an exact measure of unemployment, but only as a rough indication of it."

plete." [6] In 1926, an expert in labour questions, Signor Galletti, showed that the local officials entrusted with "estimating" employment made use of different methods in the different regions of Italy, and in certain districts arrived at preposterous figures, whose total erred on the side of optimism. In no sense did they represent the actual facts; at best they furnished little more than a rough indication from which to guess whether there was a rise or a fall in a given period. [7] In the same year, 1926, another student of economic conditions, Signor Ernesto Rossi, arrived at the conclusion that these figures, "for the reputation of our statistics, ought no longer to be published in official documents." [8]

Beginning with 1929, there was a new source of information concerning unemployment, for the government re-established the labour exchanges which it had suppressed in December 1923. But of the 7000 cities and towns in Italy, at most 2000 possess a labour exchange, [9] and of these the majority are in the more important industrial and agricultural centres of northern Italy. For the remaining 5000, inhabited mainly by an agricultural population and including practically all the towns in southern and the majority of those in central Italy, it is still the municipal clerks who continue to fill out the monthly returns.

Even in the figures collected by the labour exchanges there are two sources of error, the first resulting in overstatement, and the second in understatement:

1. Many workers enter themselves as unemployed simultaneously in the registers of several trades, hoping in this way to increase their chances of getting a job; thus the same individual is counted as unemployed several times over. Many, again, fail to report to the labour exchange that they have found work.

---

[6] *Riforma Sociale,* Nov.-Dec. 1924, p. 466.
[7] *La disoccupazione in Italia e quello che se ne sa,* pp. 563 ff.
[8] *Riforma Sociale,* Sept.-Oct. 1926, p. 484.
[9] At the beginning of 1930 there were 1400 (*Corriere della Sera,* Feb. 2, 1930). In the three succeeding years they probably increased, but not by a large number, owing to the financial stringency. According to official information published in the review, *Sindacato e Corporazione,* Jan. 1934, p. 141, the expenditure on labour exchanges during the fiscal year 1933–4 amounted to 17,502,389 lire. Since it would be impossible to keep any exchange going without spending at least 8000 lire a year (salary for an official, rent, lighting, stationery, etc.), it is safe to conclude that the number of labour exchanges cannot exceed 2000. At a meeting of officials of the agricultural unions, held in Sept. 1934, one of the speakers maintained that the number of labour exchanges should be doubled, "because many workers and peasants had to travel twenty-five or thirty miles in order to register at the nearest labour exchange; naturally they preferred to stay at home" (*Lavoro Fascista,* Sept. 7, 1934).

2. The workers know that if they do not show the badge of a Fascist union they will be looked upon with suspicion by the officials of the labour exchange, and therefore do not take the trouble to register unless they intend to join a union.[10]

In the *Riforma Sociale* for March-April 1933, p. 253, Signor Rinoni stated that "there is no sure method in existence for ascertaining the amount of unemployment in towns." This assertion applies with still greater force to the rural districts. There are in Italy no less than one million small freeholders who cannot live on their little bit of land, but during a part of the year must work in neighbouring factories or as hired hands for other landowners. When these people cannot find work outside their own strip of land, they are still not registered as unemployed because they are "landowners," and as such are classed with millionaires enjoying their leisure.

As if all this were not enough, the figures when sent to Rome are systematically falsified.

We have given proofs in support of this statement in the review *Social Research*, August 1934, pp. 349–54. Instead of repeating those facts, we shall give two more proofs from among those which may be drawn from other sources:

1. In 1932, in the province of Reggio-Emilia, according to a report of the provincial secretary of the agricultural unions, each of the 12,000 day-labourers could obtain, on an average, only ninety days' work. In this class of workers, therefore, the number of unemployed must have been about 9000, although the figures for individual months may have varied from this general average. Nevertheless, the official statistics for that year oscillated between a minimum of 905 for the month of May and a maximum of 2402 for November.

2. In the province of Forlì, according to the *Lavoro Fascista*, October 23, 1934, the unemployed agricultural day-labourers amounted to

---

[10] In a circular of Feb. 1930, the Minister of Corporations spoke of having noted that "on the part of many working people there exist perplexities and fears which prevent them from registering on the rolls of unemployed kept by the labour exchanges"; these perplexities, he continued, "arise from the belief that registration on the list of unemployed workers might lead to an obligation to join a union." Therefore, the minister "invites the superintendents of the labour exchanges to exercise persuasion and dissipate this misunderstanding, explaining that the labour exchanges are intended for all unemployed workers whether union members or not. This of course does not mean that workers should not be urged in *every possible way* to become members."

18,185 on July 31, 1934, and to 19,641 on July 31, 1934. To the contrary, the statistics "doctored" in Rome stated that there were 959 unemployed agricultural labourers on July 31, 1933, and 4633 on July 31, 1934.[11]

Anyone who takes Italian unemployment figures seriously betrays his ignorance of the methods by which they are concocted. Mr. Hugh Quigley, Chief Statistical Officer of the Central Electricity Board in Great Britain, to whom we owe a most penetrating study on Italian economic conditions under Fascist rule, is of the opinion that Italian unemployment figures "are not complete and do not apply to the entire body of labour." He estimates that at the end of January 1934 the number of unemployed was between 1,800,000 and 2,000,000, and not 1,158,418, as official statistics made out.[12]

One must not assume from this that Italian unemployment statistics are useless. Quite the contrary, *they reveal that part of the situation which the Fascist dictatorship fails to conceal.* Even if we do not know the exact extent of unemployment, we may be sure that it is not less than that given in the official statistics.

Anyhow one should never compare Italian figures with those of other countries and conclude, as admirers of Fascism do, that "when compared with the many millions of unemployed in Germany, Great Britain, the United States, and other countries, even if the differences of population are taken into account, the Italian percentage compares very favourably with that of the countries mentioned."[13] In a still half-agricultural country, like Italy, the conditions are not the same as in highly indus-

---

[11] *Sindacato e Corporazione*, Sept. 1933, p. 390; Sept. 1934, p. 410.

[12] "Fascism Fails Italy" in *Current History*, June 1934, p. 261. Signor Villari asserts that "Italian statistics are known to be at least as accurate as those of any other country" (*Economist*, Oct. 24, 1931). The Minister of Corporations, Signor Bottai, speaking in the Chamber, Feb. 24, 1932, said: "It is to be observed that we expect an absolute scrupulousness in reporting unemployment without any recourse to trickery or camouflage." Also Mr. Knickerbocker tells us that "questioning not only of official sources, but of a series of disinterested neutral observers with long experience here [in Italy] elicited nothing to indicate that the figures are not authentic" (quoted by Jones, *Is Fascism the Answer?*, p. 193). Mr. Knickerbocker certainly owed to these same "disinterested neutral observers with long experience," the consoling information that by the summer of 1932 "Italy had passed its financial crisis" (*ibid.*, p. 186).

[13] This is an argument to which Fascist and pro-Fascist writers methodically resort in their propaganda. See, for instance, letters from Signor Villari in the *Boston Evening Transcript*, Feb. 20, 1930, in the London *Economist*, July 25, 1931, in the London *Daily Telegraph*, May 29, 1934, and in the New York *Nation*, Feb. 21, 1934; the letter from Sir Leo Chiozza-Money in *Forward*, Glasgow, Aug. 2, 1930; articles by Mr. Knickerbocker in the *Boston Evening Transcript*, Sept. 24, 1932; Mr. Cortesi

trialized countries, like England, Germany, or the United States. Let us compare Italy and England. Both in England and in Italy agricultural workers are excluded from unemployment benefit; but while in England these form less than one-tenth of the working people, in Italy they form about fifty per cent. The consequence is that when the English statistics show, for example, 2,085,000 unemployed in December 1934, we must remember that these are drawn from a total of 12,500,000 workers in industry and commerce; i. e., they represent 16.6% of the total. But when we find the Italian statistics giving 961,000 unemployed for December 1934, we must be careful to differentiate between the 211,000 unemployed in agriculture and the 750,000 unemployed in industry and commerce; and we must further remember that these 750,000 unemployed in industry and commerce are drawn from a total of no more than 3,500,000 workers.[14] We therefore must conclude that in Italian industry and commerce, even according to the statistics concocted at Rome, 21% of the total number of workers were unemployed in December 1934.

---

in the *New York Times*, Oct. 30, 1932; and Mr. Jones, *Is Fascism the Answer?*, pp. 193–223; and Dr. Marraro, *The Fascist Record*, p. 161.

[14] *Annuario Statistico Italiano: 1933*, p. 184.

XIII

Mussolini's "Battle" Against Unemployment Up to 1930

UNEMPLOYMENT is the enemy against whom Mussolini has fought his most heroic "battles," and over whom he has won his most resounding victories. *Arma virumque cano.*

As we have already seen (above p. 157), unemployment was insignificant in 1920, increased in 1921, and was intense in the first months of 1922 due to the depression which Italy, like all other countries, was then passing through. But during the rest of 1922 there were everywhere symptoms of recovery; these continued after Mussolini seized power, and became accentuated in 1925. At the same time France needed to import Italian labour to fill the gaps created by the World War, to rebuild the devastated areas, and to replace German labour in Alsace-Lorraine. According to Italian official statistics, emigrants totalled 400,000 annually in 1923 and 1924,[1] and 300,000 in 1925, while there were 115,000 repatriates in 1923, 168,000 in 1924, and 180,000 in 1925. Thus in those three years the *net* emigration removed 600,000 workers from the Italian labour market. Finally, Mussolini embarked on a grandiose programme of public works designed to impress Italians and foreigners with the idea that something great was going on. Public works have always been the preferred field of action of dictatorships, and Italy is no exception to this rule. Most of these undertakings were made possible, neither by direct payment out of current revenue nor by public loans, but by promising to pay contractors and other creditors in instalments extending over a period of ten years or more and in some cases fifty years. Annuities due for this reason leaped from about 2.7 billion lire in 1922 to 6.5 billion lire on March 29, 1924, and stood at 26.2 billion lire by the end of 1928. The

---

[1] Following his usual habit of assuming, when it suits his purpose, the credit for all that happens or does not happen, Mussolini declared in the Senate on Dec. 11, 1924: "We have succeeded in increasing the figure of our emigrants from a figure which in 1921 and 1922 had fallen below 300,000 to 400,000 in 1923, and to 260,000 in the first eight months of the current year."

dictatorship thus created a large hidden debt, leaving the future to take care of itself: *"après moi le déluge."* [2]

Influenced by the preceding factors, unemployment became quite rare in northern Italy during 1925 and 1926. It was, however, not so rare in southern Italy. During the last five pre-war years America had absorbed on the average 400,000 Italian emigrants every year, while the countries of Central Europe and the Mediterranean had taken around 170,000. The south Italians went largely to America and the north Italians principally to central Europe. After the war the usual currents of migration were disrupted, especially after the latter part of 1924, when American and Canadian anti-immigration laws came into effect. These laws hit the south Italian worker most severely, since the north Italian workers continued to be welcome in France, Belgium and Luxemburg.[3] The result was that in 1925 and 1926 conditions in southern Italy began to grow distressing. But the Fascist statistics gave no information concerning the unemployment situation in southern Italy, although everyone in Italy was aware of it.[4] And Mussolini was credited with the miracle of "conquering unemployment." [5]

In order to magnify the dimensions of this miracle, the propagandists recounted that before the war the average number of emigrants from Italy had been 670,000 per annum, that it had dropped to 400,000 in 1924 and to 300,000 in 1925, while at the same time unemployment figures had fallen from over 600,000 in January 1922 to 100,000 in 1925. Mussolini had thus "conquered unemployment" in spite of having to provide a livelihood for the millions of Italians who were unable to emigrate.[6] A more truthful statement would have taken account not only of those who left Italy, but also of those who returned to it, and would have

---

[2] Salvemini, *Twelve Years of Fascist Finance*, p. 479.

[3] L. Einaudi, *Italy: Economic and Financial History*, in the 1926 supplement to the *Encyclopaedia Britannica*, pp. 572–3.

[4] Mortara, *Prospettive Economiche: 1926*, pp. 464–5: "The regions which furnished the larger migratory currents to central Europe have found new outlets in western Europe; those regions which sent their emigrants overseas feel in greater degree the consequences of the closing of the North American outlet. The contraction of emigration is the cause of the gravest distress in the South, also because the natural increase in population since the war has been greater there than in other parts of Italy, while industrial development has been small and agricultural progress slow and spotty."

[5] Sir Ernest Benn, in the *Star* of Apr. 8, 1926, wrote: "The results achieved include the disappearance of unemployment, increased prosperity, and tranquillity and happiness brought to millions who have not known these things for a generation."

[6] Villari, *Fascist Experiment*, p. 153–4; *Economics of Fascism*, p. 105.

revealed that, before the war, ninety per cent of the emigrants to European countries returned to Italy, while fifty-five per cent returned from overseas, and that, therefore, the *net* emigration figure, instead of being 670,000 per annum, was, roughly, between 160,000 and 200,000.[7]

The propagandists further swelled Mussolini's "victory" by comparing the winter figures for the pre-Fascist period with the summer figures for the Fascist period, concealing the fact that in Italy unemployment is always at its greatest in winter and at its minimum in summer.[8] Only a person well acquainted with Italian economic life could detect these frauds.

In the meantime Mussolini discovered that the population of Italy was not enough to construct an empire, and that emigration was depriving him of too much potential cannon fodder. The first measures to restrict emigration were taken in 1925; in that year French farmers in the south began to experience difficulties in obtaining Italian workers.[9] In 1926 and 1927 the restrictions became more rigid. Beginning with the first of September 1927 the government left emigration open only to intellectuals, business men, and professional men of sound Fascist faith who could become Fascist propaganda agents in foreign countries. Manual labourers had to promise to return within three years and could not take their families with them. Those who were already abroad could rejoin their families only by returning to Italy for them, thereby exposing themselves to the risk of not being allowed to leave again; a fiancé could send for his fiancée and a husband for his wife, but not vice versa; and a father could send for his sons only in case they were still minors, and consequently incapable of working, bearing arms, and procreating sons.[10] Anyone who was caught trying to leave the country was subject to imprisonment if not already shot dead by the frontier guards. A close watch was maintained, especially along the French frontier. As a consequence, annual emigration to France fell from 201,000 in 1924 to 51,000 by 1929; and the net emigration, which in the quinquennium 1920–4 had withdrawn a million men from the Italian labour market,

---

[7] Foerster, *Italian Emigration of our Times*, pp. 23, 28, 38.

[8] This deception was continually adopted by Signor Villari. See for example: *Manchester Guardian*, March 25, 1926; *New Statesman*, April 10, 1926; *Westminster Gazette*, July 3, 1926; *Economist*, July 25, 1931.

[9] Manco, *Les étrangers dans les campagnes françaises*, p. 107.

[10] See the laudatory comments on this law made by Deputy Torre in the report on the budget of the Ministry of Foreign Affairs for 1928–9.

fell during the quinquennium 1925–9 to a bare 350,000. Between six and seven hundred thousand workers accumulated in the country as in a huge prison.

The measures for preventing emigration and the economic crisis resultant upon the revaluation of the lira (see above, pp. 185, 194) could not but produce an enormous increase in unemployment beginning with the autumn of 1926. The statistics of the unemployed in industry and commerce in receipt of unemployment benefits—figures which could not be falsified—showed that between 1926 and 1928 the number had quadrupled,[11] while the total of unemployment—which the Fascist authorities were free to compute as they liked—gave the winter maximum as rising from 156,000 in 1926 to only 259,000 in 1927 and to 439,000 in 1928. Meanwhile, the propaganda machine continued undauntedly to repeat during 1928 that Mussolini had conquered unemployment.[12]

On September 18, 1928, Mussolini decided that unemployment could not be combated by falsified statistics alone, and announced that the government would spent 238,000,000 lire on extraordinary public works to give work to 20,000 men. Another bomb followed shortly afterwards: the Act of December 24, 1928, which appropriated 4,300,000,000 lire for land reclamation to be spread over fourteen years.

Now that the government was giving employment to the entire Italian people on public works or land reclamation, the peasants no longer had

---

[11] *Annuario Statistico Italiano: 1929*, p. 327.

[12] "The Italian Government has conquered unemployment not by granting millions in doles and outdoor relief but by making it possible for Italian industrialists to give employment to the worker" (*Daily Mail*, Jan. 25, 1928). "Mussolini has performed a very notable feat in solving a problem with which our British statesmen have been fumbling for nine years without satisfactory results. In a country which is over-populated, and has few manufactures, Mussolini has abolished unemployment" (A. S. Toms in *The Monthly Record* of South Place Ethical Society of London, Jan. 1928, p. 7). "Business is thriving everywhere; the towns are humming hives of industry; there are no throngs of 'out of works,' pitifully depending on the dole, as in our country; those who can work have plenty of opportunity for doing so" (Rev. C. J. Street in *The Inquirer, a Journal of Free Religious Fellowship, and Organ of Unitarian Christianity*, London, Feb. 25, 1928). In Aug. 1928 Signor Villari had the audacity to state that "unemployment was on the decrease: *the maximum* figure was 439,000 in June last year; in June this year it was 270,000 (*Sutton Coalfield News*, Aug. 11, 1928). In June 1927 the statistics had given the unemployed as 214,000 and not as 439,000. That was the figure given by the statistics for Jan. 1928. Even if he had attributed, as he should have, this figure to Jan. 1928 instead of to "June last year," Signor Villari would still have had no right to affirm that the seasonal decrease from Jan. to June 1928 was a proof of permanent improvement. In Mussolini's *Pseudo-autobiography*, p. 277, the hero boasted in 1928 that he had assured "continuity of employment" to the Italian working class.

any need to leave the country for the city in search of work. A royal decree of December 24, 1928, therefore authorized the police to expel from the cities and send back to their native parishes all who had no visible means of support. A circular of February 1930 from the Minister of Corporations instructed the labour exchanges "to take *a firm attitude of persuasion* in order to keep agricultural workers other than those indispensable for the needs of production from pouring into the cities"; moreover the labour exchanges were expected "to promote the return to the farm of all workers who had formerly been agricultural labourers and who are now unemployed." (*Stampa*, February 26, 1930.) The *Popolo d'Italia* of July 25, 1930, reported that the provincial secretary of the Fascist Party had taken up with the Podestà mayor the question of the unemployed pouring into Milan:

> The Podestà will see to it that, by an appropriate method of supervision, the repatriation of emigrants who have not found work and lodging takes place within a fortnight. Effective work in this direction will be performed by the labour exchanges, to which precise instructions have been given.

Whoever leaves the country for the city in search of work must report to the police, who will give him a permit to remain only if he can show that he already has obtained employment. During the first six months of 1931, 323 newcomers were turned back from Milan.[13] The *Corriere della Sera* of July 11, 1933, published the news that during April, May, and June 1933 "2129 unemployed persons, among them 245 heads of families, were repatriated." On coming back to their native villages, these poor people did not find a farmer father to relieve their hunger. There were among them, it is true, persons who had left the country for the city in quest of adventure, but most of them had gone to the cities because the country could not give them a living. In many cases they had left their native villages ten, twenty, or thirty years before.[14] Without discrimination, all were sent back to starve without hope, far from the cities. These measures were described by Mussolini as the "reduction of urban overcrowding" or "back-to-the-land."

As a consequence, many workers in industrial centres kept away from the labour exchanges for fear that the police would send them back to their native parishes in the country as having no means of support. As

---

[13] *Corriere della Sera*, Aug. 18, 1931.

[14] Silone, describing with rare artistic power in his novel *Fontamara* the life of an Italian village under Fascist rule, gives an idea of this phase of Fascist economic policy.

the British commercial attaché in Rome wrote in 1933: "The *statistical situation is somewhat improved by the policy of repatriating destitute unemployed workers not natives of urban centres to their place of origin, where a certain proportion are doubtless [!] absorbed in agricultural or domestic [!] pursuits, and relinquish at least temporarily their standing and enumeration as unemployed industrial hands.*" [15] Were these words intended to be taken seriously, or were they a veiled satire on the heroism with which Mussolini combated unemployment—in statistics?

From the end of 1928 onwards the foreign admirers of Mussolini split into three classes: 1, those who, having already become accustomed to repeating that "Mussolini has conquered unemployment," continued to recite the same formula,[16] reinforcing it every so often with falsified statistics—that is, with statistics which were falsifications of statistics already falsified by the government; [17] 2, those who were waiting for the autumn of 1929, namely, for the American crash, in order to recognize that in Italy there existed considerable unemployment, the responsibility for which, however, belonged entirely to that crash; [18] and 3, those who glorified Mussolini because he, for the first time in Italy, had contrived

---

[15] Turner, *Economic Conditions*, p. 171.

[16] "Unemployment continues to be a major concern especially in Germany and England. In fact it is practically non-existent in France and Italy" (Dr. Julius Klein, Director of the Bureau of Foreign and Domestic Commerce of the U. S. Department of Commerce, in the *New York Times*, Apr. 29, 1929). "Unemployment in this country has been reduced to less than one per cent. . . . Italian workmen are more continuously employed and at higher wages than obtained before the war" (A. P. Dennis, formerly commercial attaché at the American Embassy in Rome, in *World's Work*, Aug. 1929, p. 48).

[17] The American commercial attaché in Rome, in *Commerce Reports* for Jan. 14, 1929, p. 72, asserted that "unemployment registers totalled 223,000 towards the close of the year 1928"; the truth was that the official statistics gave 282,000 unemployed in Oct. 1928, 321,000 in Nov., and 360,000 in Dec. (*Annuario Statistico: 1929*, p. 325). In a letter to the London *Spectator*, Aug. 31, 1929, a correspondent with the pseudonym "Vita Nuova" stated that: "Unemployment used to average from 500,000 to 600,000, but today is 200,000." The average of from 500,000 to 600,000 was an invention and 200,000 was not the average but the summer minimum for 1929. In regard to the reports of the American commercial attachés in Rome, it may be remarked that until the summer of 1928 they constituted a sure and abundant source of precious information. From Aug. to Dec. 1928, Italy was unreported. In Dec. 1928 the reports were resumed, but their tone was completely altered; they had ceased to give impartial information, becoming mere translations or summaries of the data furnished by the Fascist government.

[18] Marriott, *The Makers of Modern Italy*, p. 204: "There is no dole, yet unemployment, until the advent of the world-blizzard, did not exist." See also the letters of Signor Villari in the *Economist*, July 25 and Oct. 24, 1931, reproduced in *Italy Today*, Sept.-Oct. 1932.

the method of combating unemployment with public works, instead of throwing away the money of the tax-payer on "doles." [19]

Mussolini himself, in a radio address broadcast to the inhabitants of the United States on January 1, 1931, made the following statement:

I am against the dole. I prefer public works that increase the material efficiency of the country. The dole accustoms the worker to his state of unemployment.

The truth was that the dole exists in Italy as in England. The number of days for which in Italy unemployment benefit was paid rose from 18,-700,000 in 1929 to 48,200,000 by 1931.[20] Mussolini deserves credit for something quite other than having abolished the dole. The act of October 19, 1919, introducing compulsory unemployment insurance into Italy, created an unemployment fund composed of the contributions of the employers, the employees, and the government, the latter binding itself to furnish 50,000,000 lire per annum. This governmental contribution was abolished in December 1922 by the Fascists, recently ensconced in power. Since that time only the employers and employees have paid into the fund.[21] Not only this, but in 1928, the government, finding itself short of money, commenced borrowing from the unemployment fund. Between 1920 and the end of 1929, the employers and employees together contributed 1,087,486,000 lire to the fund; the benefits paid out to the unemployed totalled 413,549,000 lire; the costs of administration amounted to the respectable sum of 68,836,000 lire, i. e., sixteen per cent of the amount paid out.[22] The remaining half billion was used by the National Fund for Social Insurance to make loans to the state treasury.[23]

---

[19] The London *Daily News*, Sept. 20, 1928: "It is impossible not to respect the energy with which he [Mussolini] is facing the apparently insoluble problem of finding work for Italians at home. He has realized, in fact, the national opportunity which masses of unemployed labour afford." The London *Spectator*, for Aug. 16, 1930: "In Italy, now the home of authoritarianism, larger and larger schemes are proposed for setting the unemployed to work under authority." *The New York Times*, Aug. 26, 1931: "Italy puts up $45,000,000 for work, not dole; winter programme will give jobs to 100,000 men."

[20] *Annuario Statistico Italiano: 1933*, p. 194.

[21] *Industrial and Labour Information*, Dec. 22, 1922, p. 605; March 10, 1924, p. 309; March 24, 1924, p. 412.

[22] *Lavoro*, Apr. 17, 1930; *Industrial and Labour Information*, May 14, 1928, p. 260; Dec. 8, 1930, p. 395.

[23] *Rivista Bancaria*, Nov. 1933, p. 928. According to the *Conto del Tesoro* of June 30, 1934, the government by that date owed 1214 million lire to the institutions which administer insurance funds (Istituti di Previdenza).

As if this were not enough, a royal decree of December 30, 1929, obliged the fund to finance a silk cartel under the following terms: if the cartel lost money, the loss was to be met out of the unemployment fund; if it made profits, seven per cent of them were to go to the fund and the rest to the cartel.

In short, while in other countries the governments annually contribute large sums to the unemployment funds,[24] in Italy the government utilizes the capital of that institution for its own advantage, and even puts it at the disposal of private capitalists. Concerning this "most beautiful deceit"—as Machiavelli would have called it—of using the money of the unemployed to stop up the gaps in the state budget and subsidize depressed industries, the propaganda agents preserve a most conscientious silence. Nay more, in an announcement on October 21, 1929, the government went so far as to boast of having reduced payments to the unemployed from 141,056,000 lire in 1922 to 65,344,000 lire in 1929:

This budget is extremely eloquent: it proves, if there be any need of it, the very notable diminution in unemployment wrought by the Fascist regime, and likewise demonstrates the impulse given national production by the government.[25]

Anyone who reads the publications of the Italian Government today will do well to bear in mind what Pococurante, the noble Venetian in Voltaire's *Candide*, stated about eighteenth-century Italy: "Throughout our Italy one writes only things that one does not think at all."

---

[24] In England the contribution of the government in 1931–2 amounted to £120,-000,000; in Germany, in 1931, the central and local governments contributed 2233 million Rm.; in France the central government between Apr. 1, 1931, and Aug. 1, 1932, contributed 400,000,000 francs (I.L.O., *Report of the Director: 1933*, p. 23). In Belgium during 1934 the government, the provinces, and the municipalities spent 950,000,000 francs (*New York Herald Tribune*, Dec. 18, 1934).

[25] *Corriere della Sera*, Oct. 22, 1929. Mr. Knickerbocker is enthusiastic over the Italian system: "Students of unemployment relief may be interested in the Italian system: "Students of unemployment relief may be interested in the Italian system of compulsory self-liquidating unemployment insurance. It is particularly interesting to note that the system of collecting premiums during good years gave the fund such a reserve that it has not yet been exhausted even by the crisis of years of unemployment. From 1920 to 1930 a total of about $250,000,000 was paid out in benefits, so large were receipts from premiums and from fund earnings that at the end of 1930 the reserve fund totalled around $450,000,000" (*Boston Evening Transcript*, Sept. 24, 1932).

XIV

The "Battle" Against Unemployment
from 1930 to 1934

ETWEEN the winters of 1926 and 1930 the number of unemployed admitted in official statistics tripled. In the summer of 1930 the position of the unemployed became tragic. Clandestine emigration, in spite of repressive Fascist laws, assumed startling proportions.[1] In order that the reader may judge the extent of this phenomenon, let me give extracts from newspapers of July and August 1930:

1. A group of fugitives, among whom were a woman and a boy twelve years old, lost their way in the Alps on the Groner Glacier, and were rescued with great difficulty by a body of Swiss alpinists (London *Times*, July 9; Paris *Temps*, July 10).

2. At Ponte di Saltrio three men and a woman were surprised in the night by customs officers while attempting to cross the Swiss frontier; in the darkness the guards accidentally shot each other, one man being killed and another seriously wounded; of the fugitives, one man escaped into the night, and the remaining two, with the woman, were arrested and all were subsequently sentenced to a year's imprisonment (*Corriere della Sera*, October 20 and 25, 1931).

3. Fourteen persons escaped to Switzerland through the Jorio Pass (*Libera Stampa*, Lugano, July 12).

4. Six fugitives arrived at Goulaz, one of whom had been injured by a fall (*Paris-Midi*, July 30).

5. Two parties, one of which consisted of 38 persons, made their escape by the St. Teodolo Pass, after having lost a young married couple on the way; one woman arrived seriously injured (*Oeuvre*, August 3).

---

[1] This clandestine emigration is ignored by all Fascist sources. Nevertheless, everyone in Italy is aware of it. The *Corriere Padano*, Aug. 27, 1928, referred to the matter in the following terms: "The emigrants collect in some prearranged spot, and when they are sufficiently numerous, from fifteen to twenty, they start out under the care of a guide, who receives from each of them a sum varying from 200 to 300 lire. The journey across the Alps is both difficult and dangerous. It may last three or four days, for the caravan cannot make rapid progress as it frequently has to hide for hours at a time, crouching behind some rock, in order to escape the vigilance of the Black Shirts on the frontier."

6. Through that same pass no less than 300 persons made their escape in the course of a few weeks (*Libertà*, August 2).

7. Nine men escaped to Corsica in an open boat (*Libertà*, August 9).

8. On July 16, 53 persons, and on the 17th, 61 persons presented themselves without passports at the French police station in Modane (*Libertà*, September 6).

9. On July 22 twelve men, some of whom had succeeded in making their escape to Corsica, while others had been arrested by the police, were sentenced by the Leghorn Court to from six months to two years (*Resto del Carlino*, July 23).

10. A party of monks from the hospice at the Great St. Bernard, who went to the assistance of a woman abandoned in the snow by a group of fugitives, were fired upon by Fascist militiamen (*Libertà*, August 9).

11. Fifteen men escaped to Tunis in small open boats (*Libertà*, August 16).

12. Two fugitives lost their lives in the Cervino Pass (*Libertà*, August 16).

13. Two men with a young woman made their escape across the glacier of the Zwillines Pass, the woman carrying a seven-months-old baby in her arms, and doing the whole journey in thin shoes (Paris *Journal*, August 10).

14. At Selva di Pietro on the Italian-Jugoslav frontier one fugitive was arrested and two others killed (*Foglio d' Ordini* of the Fascist Party, November 8).

15. Two men and two women, one of them a girl nineteen years of age, were sentenced by the Aosta court to terms of imprisonment varying from six months to two years for having attempted to escape into France (*Stampa*, August 17, 1930).

16. Ten persons were arrested at Susa while attempting to expatriate themselves (*Corriere della Sera*, August 2). Another party was arrested there later in the month (*Temps*, August 23).

17. The *Petit Nicois* wrote as follows on August 25: "During the last few weeks the number of Italians arriving without passports in and around Nice has been exceptionally large; they are under the necessity of finding work immediately so as to maintain themselves."

18. On August 28, 1930, the Agenzia Telegrafica Svizzera regretted that "frequently during the last few weeks" the militia on the Italian frontier had crossed over on to Swiss territory in pursuit of clandestine emigrants.

To the cases referred to in the press must be added those that remain unrecorded. In a conversation with a correspondent of the London *Daily Mail* (August 29, 1930) a Swiss guide calculated that in the preceding months from ten to twenty thousand Italians had secretly crossed the Swiss frontier; "If they go on like this, there will be nobody left in Italy after ten years' time." Such assertions were no doubt exaggerated, but they give an idea of the magnitude of the exodus.

This crisis was faced by Mussolini with his usual indomitable courage. First of all, on August 13, 1930, he gave orders that passports were to be granted to any one who wished to emigrate. There was no longer any urgency about creating the Empire. Scarcely had the newspapers published this notice than vast crowds of unhappy people besieged the police stations asking for passports. At Turin men stood all night in a queue. The number of passports issued in Italy for European countries, which in practice meant France, Belgium, and Luxemburg, went up from 11,535 in August 1930 to 42,312 in September and to 50,340 in October.

It was too late. Throughout the year 1929, and even during the first half of 1930, France would have gladly welcomed Italian labour, for the Loucheur Act providing for the construction of 260,000 apartment dwellings in five years, had given a powerful stimulus to work of all kinds. Not being able to import labour from Italy, the French contractors had been compelled to apply to Poland, Czechoslovakia, Rumania, and Austria.[2] But in the summer of 1930 France herself was beginning to feel threatened by the widespread crisis of unemployment.

On the other hand, the Italian police handed out passports to all and sundry, although the labour treaty between Italy and France gave the latter country the right to refuse entry to workers arriving unprovided with a contract from a firm already established in France. During several weeks the French government granted free entry to this stream of immigrants, but in October 1930 it started closing the frontier to the fresh arrivals. The pro-Fascist *Journal de Genève* published the following news from its Basle correspondent:

---

[2] *Regime Fascista*, Aug. 15, 1929, reported: "In view of the resumption of work which during the last months has shown itself in the building trade and in all public works, and which is likely to become even more marked through the realization of the Loucheur Act, the insufficiency of French labour will become still more acute. As the immigration of Italian workmen has been almost completely arrested, the International Federation of the Building Trade has carried out an investigation in various foreign countries, more especially in central Europe, in order to determine the amount of labour available in those regions. It has already been ascertained that the firms which until now had relied mainly on Italian labour will be able to secure an equivalent in the countries referred to above" (Jugoslavia, Hungary, Czechoslovakia, Spain).

Every day a large number of Italian emigrants pours into France, but hardly a dozen out of two hundred are in possession of the labour contract necessary to enter the country. On Friday last two hundred of these unhappy creatures, who in most cases have spent everything they possess to pay for their journey, were driven back over the frontier. Many emigrants are remaining at Basle and many are trying to cross the frontier secretly.

The Fascist militia, instead of shooting down any one caught trying to emigrate secretly, now began to reveal hidden ways of penetrating the barriers to anyone unable to enter openly. Very soon, however, the news that the gates of France were closed permeated throughout Italy, with the result that in November the number of passports issued fell to 31,540, and in December to 13,076.[3] One hundred and sixty-two individuals who had made their way to Australia, found themselves refused admission on arrival.[4]

To this tragic ebb and flow of humanity Mussolini referred as follows in an address to the Senate on December 18, 1930:

The thirteenth of August was the date of a telegram which I sent to the prefects instructing them to relax the rule concerning passports for abroad. Why did I do this? Was it perchance a change in our emigration policy? No. Many people imagined that it was only in Italy that unemployment existed. Well, the measures we took gave 100 per cent results. For the first few days the police bureaus were crowded with persons clamouring for passports. Then the numbers dropped. *Thousands, tens of thousands of individuals are now completely cured* and realize that at the present time life is not easy in any part of the world.

The man boasted that he had deliberately tricked tens of thousands of unfortunate people into misery and ruinous expenditure in order that they might learn that even outside Italy unemployment existed. But in this case he was not as criminal as he made himself out to be. He is simply vain and incapable of admitting that he has made a mistake. Everything that happens must necessarily have happened because he foresaw it and intended it. Rather than confess that he had allowed all these poor people to emigrate in the belief that they would find elsewhere the bread that was lacking in Italy, he boasted of having sent them because he wished and foresaw that they would be turned back.

---

[3] *Bollettino Mensile di Statistica,* June 1931, p. 541; April 1931, p. 353.
[4] *Industrial and Labour Information,* Jan. 19, 1931, p. 82.

While trying to relieve the congestion in the labour market by re-opening the safety valve of emigration, Mussolini organized a spectacular journalistic campaign announcing an avalanche of public works. Here, for example, are the headlines which the Turin *Stampa* carried in August 1930:

On August 3, a four-column headline on the front page: "Imposing plan of public works ordained by the Duce to alleviate seasonal unemployment in the coming winter: an expenditure of hundreds of millions and work for thousands of men." On August 8, first page, headline of last column: "The magnificent scheme of work for next winter." August 9, first page, head-line across two columns: "251 million set aside for the second scheme of winter works." August 17, first page, headline across three columns: "170,000 men will be employed on the public works that will be initiated in the coming autumn." August 19, first page, headline across two columns: "More than 200,000 workmen will be employed in the coming public works." These 200,000 grew to 395,000 in the headlines for October 7.

At the same time Mussolini gave instructions that in the unemploy-ment statistics for agriculture the figures for women were no longer to be included. The reader need not accept my word for this; he can con-sult for himself pp. 1554–8 of the volume *La Provincia di Bologna nell' Anno Decimo*, published by the Provincial Council of Corporative Economy of Bologna for 1932:

Although the figures [for unemployment in the province of Bologna] during 1931 were still notably high, they were, nevertheless, especially in the first part of the year, lower than those for the preceding years. For the later months the figures fell below those of much earlier years, such as 1922. *Such at least is the impression conveyed by the figures. The reality is some-what different.* The figures for 1931 and for a portion of 1930 do not in-clude among the unemployed the considerable mass of female day workers which had been included in previous years. . . . Up to January 1930 the figures had always included a considerable percentage of women, which varied from 40% to 60%.

Mussolini obviously thought that women's duty is to stay at home minding the children and not swell the registers of the labour exchanges.

Finally, in 1931, the labour exchanges in the cities received orders not to put on the registers those who had not been residents in the city before the first of April 1931: [5] another expedient for reducing the number of unemployed—in the statistics.

In spite of all these "battles," the unemployed continued to increase, so that even the official statistics rose from 765,000 in the winter of 1931 [6] to 1,147,000 in the winter of 1932. Happily, Mussolini was there to organize another "battle."

In Italy, as in all other countries, it has always been recognized that people cannot be left to starve to death. This duty is most strongly realized at Christmas-time,[7] especially in years of great distress and in areas hardest hit by depression. With the deepening of the depression in 1930, the work of relief became more than ever necessary. Until the autumn of 1930 relief work was carried on by local government agencies, voluntary organizations, or private persons, without any one dreaming in investing it with a political character. During the winter of 1931 the Fascist Party began to concentrate, here and there, under its own control all the financial means which the municipalities, benevolent societies, and private individuals were in the habit of devoting to the relief of destitution. On December 12, 1931, Mussolini decreed that "the Party and all its dependent institutions are to prepare themselves for political and moral mobilization in order to face the economic crisis and to alleviate the condition of those strata of the population which were suffering the greatest hardships." "Charitable assistance must be given to every one who needs it." All charitable assistance was to be concentrated in the Fascist Party. All the offices of the Fascist branches were to remain open daily from 11 A. M. to 11 P. M. A fresh "battle" then!

---

[5] This fact is to be discovered in the report of a speech delivered by the Secretary of the Fascist Party in the province of Genoa on July 24, 1933: "An appropriate disposition of the law provides that those who have not resided in Genoa since April 1, 1931, cannot be enrolled at the labour exchanges. This regulation permits effective control over local labour and will hence be rigorously observed" (*Lavoro*, July 25, 1933).

[6] In 1931 Marabini, *Le Problème France-Italie*, p. 88, assured his readers that Italy was not suffering from unemployment. In a letter to the *Economist*, Oct. 24, 1931, p. 1031, Signor Villari calmly asserted that "in the pre-Fascist period the Italian unemployment figures were as high as or higher than those of today" and that "unemployment in Italy was greater before 1929 than after that year."

[7] For example, at Christmas, 1914, in the city of Milan 800 packages containing food were distributed to the poor; 800 unemployed workers were invited to the headquarters of the Milanese trade unions; a girls' school organized a Christmas tree for 600 children; etc., etc. (*Corriere della Sera*, Dec. 25–7). On Nov. 28, 1921, the City Council of Turin appropriated a million lire for help to the needy and unemployed (*Stampa*, Nov. 29). The Italian press formerly carried many reports of this sort, especially during the winter months.

Members of all organizations of employers and employees were compelled to contribute to the unemployment fund, the contribution of the
worker usually amounting to one per cent of his wage. The small landowners and farmers, for whom payment in money would be too
onerous, were to give a part of their grain instead. Everyone who lunches
at a restaurant or has a cup of tea at a café pays a tax of five centesimi for
the unemployed. When a workman wins in a dispute with his employer
and the latter is compelled to pay him his due, the secretary of the union
keeps back a portion of the sum in order that it may go into the fund for
the relief of the unemployed.[8] And the credit for the assistance thus given
by the Fascist Party to the unemployed is attributed to Mussolini, as if
the money came out of his own pocket. Christmas in Italy is now known
as "the Christmas of Mussolini," because it is the Duce who sends gifts
to the children and distributes parcels of food to the destitute. The wheat
and flour distributed to starving families are called "Mussolini's wheat"
and "Mussolini's flour."

Thus a new fount of enthusiasm was tapped: Mussolini had not only
conquered unemployment, he had not only refused to demoralize the
unemployed by putting them on a "dole," he had not only provided
work for millions of them, but he even distributed bread, rice, dried
codfish, and tomato paste to all the unemployed—although unemployment had disappeared from Italy now that Mussolini had provided work
for all.

At Christmas 1933 the correspondent of the *New York Times* was so
enraptured by the generosity of Mussolini that he positively envied the
starving Italians and pitied the wealthy classes:

The hard times will be felt chiefly by the wealthy and middle classes, as
the Fascist Party has redoubled its efforts this year to give the poorer classes
a good time during the festive season. It is claimed not a single child will fail
to receive a gift package with articles of clothing, toys and candy.[9]

Needless to say, the distribution of food and clothing is a custom invented by Mussolini.

The method adopted [explains a French journalist, M. Vaucher] presents an original character. The Duce has always shown himself opposed to
the system in vogue in England, which consists in allotting insurance benefit

---

[8] See, for example, the *Corriere della Sera*, Dec. 11, 1933.
[9] Dec. 24, 1933.

to the unemployed, as such a system is likely to encourage idleness. Hence the object of the Italian plan has been to transform works of charity into works of public assistance.[10]

On October 24, 1932, Mussolini himself explained the metamorphosis in official terms:

We have already abandoned the too limited conception of philanthropy, and have reached the greater and deeper idea of relief. We must take another step forward: from relief we must arrive at the complete realization of national solidarity.

Transform all the organizations for direct relief in your country into an instrument of propaganda and political pressure at the service of the party in power, give to your undertaking the name of "national solidarity," and you will always find journalists ready to announce to the world that your method "presents an original character."

In February 1933, Italian official statistics were compelled to admit the existence of 1,229,000 unemployed; and in the ensuing three months the figures continued to rise in comparison with those of the preceding year. At this point another "battle" became necessary. Therefore in June 1933, Mussolini gave instructions that new criteria were to be adopted for the compilation of statistics.[11] What these new criteria were to be remained a mystery. We have learned from a reliable source that the labour exchanges received instructions not to include among the unemployed any person in receipt of an old age pension, regardless of the fact that the pension might not be large enough to enable the beneficiary to live without working; they were also to exclude from their registers all workers of whom *it could be said* that they were registered in other labour exchanges, and workers of whom *it could be said* that they had found work without notifying the exchange to that effect. Finally, the Ministry of Corporations, in "co-ordinating" the figures sent from the provinces, by a mere stroke of the pen transferred 150,000 persons from the category of the totally unemployed to that of the partially unemployed. Even if it be admitted that the new criteria were more correct than the old ones, one fact is obvious—the figures

---

[10] *Le Petit Parisien*, May 17, 1932. M. Vaucher, Rome correspondent of this paper and the *Journal de Genève*, has been decorated with the Order of the Crown of Italy as a reward for his Fascist enthusiasm.

[11] *Bolletino Mensile di Statistica*, Aug. 21, 1933, p. 762, Nos. 1, 2.

from June 1933 onward are no longer comparable with those of the preceding period.

Mussolini's fresh attack upon statistics could not but be successful. The unemployed, during the summer of 1933, became less numerous than in the preceding year:

	1932	1933
June	905,000	883,000
July	931,000	824,000
August	945,000	888,000
September	945,000	907,000

In October, November, and December 1933, the statistics admitted that unemployment was greater than in 1932:

	1932	1933
October	956,000	962,000
November	1,038,000	1,066,000
December	1,129,000	1,132,000

Senator Ricci, speaking in the Senate on January 15, 1934, stated without being contradicted that there was "a perceptible increase of unemployment, especially in the building trades and in public works."

Since at the end of 1933 the official statistics acknowledge that unemployment was much larger than in the winter of 1922—the year in which the "strong man" rescued Italy from anarchy, poverty, bankruptcy, starvation, and the rest—we must conclude either that the situation in the year of grace 1933 was considerably more catastrophic than the official utterances would have us believe, or that the situation in 1922 was considerably less catastrophic than Fascist spokesmen try to make out. At any rate, one is led to ask whether Italy has done very well in destroying the "outmoded" democratic regime and obliging the individual to pay such a tremendous price in terms of liberty and human dignity, when she had to flounder in the same, or an even worse, mire of economic distress than that in which the democratic countries find themselves.

In January 1934 the statistics began again to be obedient to Mussolini's commands:

	1933	*1934*
January	1,225,000	1,158,000
February	1,229,000	1,103,000
March	1,081,000	1,056,000
April	1,025,000	995,000
May	1,000,000	941,000
June	883,000	830,000
July	824,000	886,000
August	888,060	866,000
September	907,000	887,000
October	962,000	905,000

During 1934 imports amounted to 7644 million lire and exports to 5231 million lire, while in 1933 imports had amounted to 7431 million lire and exports to 5990 million lire. These figures show that the depression continued in Italy during 1934.[12]

How, then, was it possible for unemployment to be less in 1934 than in 1933? This is one of the innumerable mysteries encountered by everyone who examines Fascist statistics. In a circular of June 1, 1934, published in Paris by the anti-Fascist paper *Giustizia e Libertà*, September 28, 1934, the Association of Industrial Employees in the province of Milan admitted that from October 1933 onwards the number of workers employed had decreased.

But why bother about such minutiæ in a country where statistics have become "an instrument of governmental action"? [13] It is better to go on with the story of Mussolini's strenuous "battles" against unemployment.

On September 26, 1934, the Associated Press gave the following announcement to the New World:

The government issued definite orders that the number of women admitted to examination for public and semi-public office be sharply reduced.

---

[12] On Sept. 23, 1934, the *New York Times* announced that Italy was "heartened by recovery signs." But if one had not stopped at the headlines, one might have read in the correspondence of the pro-Fascist Signor Arnaldo Cortesi: "The gloomy side of the picture is represented by Italy's export trade, which continues to lose ground every year. The problem of Italian exports has a social as well as an economic side. Italian unemployment is due largely to the decrease in exports. Unemployment is largest in those areas which produce for the export trade."

[13] Mussolini's statement on Dec. 20, 1926.

The Fascist textile organization ordered that 30 per cent of all workers in the weaving branch of the industry should be men, "to meet the demand of male employment." Women now form an estimated 90 per cent of the total number of textile employees. Plans were reported being prepared to extend the percentage system to other industries. The Export Institute ordered all women clerks out and hired young men as clerks and stenographers.

On October 26 the press announced that the two confederations of agricultural employers and employees had agreed that, "wherever conditions made it necessary," the day-labourers should be transformed into share-croppers (*partecipanti*); the employers pledged themselves to employ for a minimum period during the year a number of hands in proportion to the size of their farms; wages should be "revised" as new hands were taken on, and they should be paid "wherever possible" half in money and half in farm products; the employers should open shops and the employees should buy their necessities there. In short, unemployment was to be fought by wage reductions, a share of the wages was to be subjected to the fluctuation of market prices, and the truck system was extended, forcing the worker to give back to his employer the cash which he received. The *Tribuna* for October 26, commented on the agreement in the following terms:

Every farm will have a permanent nucleus of workers, and also a reserve force, which, without adding to the total wage burden which the farm can support, will fraternally share their jobs with the first nucleus. The mass of the peasants will thus acquire a keener sense of responsibility and will gain a closer understanding of the process of production. They will draw their wages from the soil and will assure to the landowner, who stands in a fraternal relation to them, his just share of earnings.

Thus, the employed will, on the one hand, fraternally share with the unemployed their jobs and will, on the other hand, fraternally grant to the employer his just share of earnings.

The *Corriere Padano* of November 10, 1934, explained that "adequate reductions in wages" would make it possible to take on a larger number of hands. Moreover, wages, the fruit of the soil, would return to the soil; payments in kind and the truck system would give the worker "the psychological preparation necessary to strengthen his attachment to the land":

It is to be noted that the practice of paying wages in kind may relieve the strain on the farm budget, inasmuch as the commodities produced on the farm would form, at least in part, actual cash in the hands of the employer.

On October 30 came the turn of the employees in banking and insurance. The managers of these concerns pledged themselves to "take a strong stand in favour of the abolition of overtime work," to eliminate from their employ all clerks receiving pensions exceeding 600 lire and all manual workers getting pensions exceeding 400 lire a month, and to supplant women by men in such a way that within one year women would form not more than twelve per cent of the bank employees and not more than fifteen per cent of the employees in the insurance companies. On November 12 the fate of the commercial employees was regulated by an agreement practically identical with the foregoing.

As a result of such agreements, the official statistics, which for November 30, 1933, had given 1,066,000 unemployed, for November 30, 1934, gave 969,000—an improvement of 100,000! The adult males who took the places of pensioners, women, and children disappeared from the statistics, while those whom they had supplanted also disappeared since they had lost the right to be classified as workers. Not for this had they won the right not to labour from hunger. But another glorious victory in Mussolini's infinite and relentless "battles" was handed down to history. Mussolini had announced this victory in advance in the *New York Times* of September 16, 1934, when, questioned concerning the unemployment situation, he gave the following blunt answer:

Despite the striking increase in our population, Italian industry is absorbing its unemployed without appreciable lowering of wages as measured by their purchasing power.

Italy would be a lucky country indeed if Mussolini utilized one-tenth of his intelligence to bring the facts into harmony with his words, instead of wasting all of it on ingenious attempts to mystify the public.

XV

Public Works, Land Reclamation, and "National Solidarity"

W HAT are the results of Mussolini's "battles" against unemployment?

The policy of relieving unemployment by public works is as old in Italy as the beard of Methuselah. Even without going back farther than thirty years, it might be mentioned that in 1904 the government appointed a commission to study unemployment and propose remedies for those parts of Emilia where the phenomenon was most widespread. The commission suggested a grandiose plan of public works, especially of land reclamation, to be carried on each year during the winter months. This programme came into effect in 1905.[1] In 1918, 3,300,000,000 lire were appropriated for public works intended to minimize unemployment during the post-war transitional period (see above, p. 158). In 1920 and 1921 more sums were set aside for the same purpose.[2] Mussolini has done nothing in the least novel. The only difference is that, the evil of unemployment having reached greater proportions than ever before in Italian history, he has been obliged to increase the doses of the old remedy.

According to official statistics the workers employed on public works reached a daily average of 81,452 in 1926, 99,599 in 1927, and 101,845 in 1928, on an average 94,000 workers a day. After the historic autumn of 1928, when Mussolini discovered the remedy of public works as a cure for unemployment, the average number of workers thus employed rose to 125,224 in 1929; to 153,186 in 1930; to 146,648 in 1931; and to 156,967 in 1932. In 1932 the maximum was reached in January, when for 18 days 184,184 workers were employed, and the minimum in February, when

---

[1] *Bulletin Trimestriel de l'Association Internationale pour la Lutte contre le Chômage*, Ghent, Jan.–March 1913.

[2] Camera dei Deputati, *Disegni di Legge e Relazioni: 1919–20*, No. 583. *Industrial and Labour Information*, May 12, 1922, p. 299. De Stefani, *Documenti sulla Condizione Finanziaria ed Economica dell' Italia*, Dec. 1923, p. 24: "The manner in which unemployment during previous periods of crisis was met is well known: public works, state doles, and social insurance."

for 19.8 days 144,545 workers were employed.[3] Mussolini's "battle" against unemployment is thus reduced to a daily average for the quadrennium 1929–32 of 145,000 as against 94,000 for the triennium 1926–8— an increase of 51,000.

On December 18, 1930, the Duce announced that, thanks to the public works undertaken by the government, 424,000 workers had been able to find employment. As a matter of fact, in 1930 the highest number of workmen employed was 178,000 in September, and 152,000 in October.[4] The Duce flung out the figure of 424,000, knowing very well that no one in Italy was in a position to contradict him.

Unemployment, according to the official statistics, jumped from 438,000 in the winter of 1928 to more than a million in the winters of 1932, 1933, and 1934. When one compares the mass of unemployed, certainly much greater than the official statistics would indicate, with the number of workers employed on public works, which has never reached 200,000, one cannot escape the conclusion that public works and reclamation projects, in which Mussolini is alleged to have discovered the means for combating unemployment, have in reality done very little to relieve the distress of the Italian people.[5]

Those employed in land reclamation schemes count as public works employees.

Land reclamation was started in Italy some thousand years ago. Italy is the classic country of land reclamation. The richest areas in Italy were built up by the intelligence and tenacious labour of man.[6] Signor Pratolongo, an expert in agricultural matters, wrote in 1923: "Italy holds the first place in lands redeemed from unproductivity and sterility."[7] In April 1923 a group of Dutch farmers, when visiting the reclamation projects executed near Ferrara and Chioggia, expressed great admiration for the "Italian Holland" they had discovered.[8] In 1924 the area cul-

---

[3] *Sindacato e Corporazione*, Feb. 1934, pp. 461, 463.

[4] *Sindacato e Corporazione*, Jan. 1933, p. 160.

[5] Cf. Jensen, *Fascism After Ten Years*, p. 149: "According to Fascist statistics, there were 177,770 employed on various public works in Sept. 1930. Yet this is less than three per cent of the working population, certainly a modest proportion in a highly centralized state, in which the national government is responsible for many projects that are elsewhere carried out locally. Forty-two thousand of these were engaged in various projects of land reclamation." See also Rosenstock-Franck, pp. 216 ff.

[6] Valenti, *L'Italia Agricola*, p. xviii.

[7] Porri, *L'Evoluzione Economica Italiana*, pp. 71 ff., 75.

[8] Virgili, *L'Italia Agricola*, p. 200. Cf. De Stefani, *L'Azione dello Stato Italiano*, pp. 120, 132; Henderson and Carpenter, *Report* of Dec. 1922, p. 54.

tivated in the province of Ferrara amounted to 200,000 hectares, of which 100,000 had been reclaimed during the previous fifty years.[9]

During the first years of the Fascist regime, reclamation work was slowed down; the average number employed daily in this type of work dropped from 28,000 in 1922–3 to 14,000 in 1926–7.[10] The act of December 1928 set aside 4.3 billion lire *to be spent in fourteen years,* to provide not only for draining swamps, but also for the reclaiming of land in the mountains, for building country roads, aqueducts, farm buildings, for irrigation, the installation of electricity on farms, etc. It is estimated that the average cost of bringing a hectare of unreclaimed land into cultivation is about 4000 lire.[11] The government was to contribute 3500 lire per hectare, which means that in fourteen years it could effect the reclamation of 1,228,000 hectares, *if the proprietors had been able to raise the capital for their one-eighth of the expense.* But Italian landowners are not in a position to bear this expense. The act of December 1928 caught them midway between the Italian crisis of 1927 and the world crisis of 1929. The government itself has had to reduce its activities because of the deficit in the budget. In 1929–30 the administration was authorized to spend 244,000,000 lire on commencing new works; in 1930–1, 74,000,000 lire were ear-marked for this purpose; and in 1931–2, only 33,000,000.[12] However, the schemes already begun in the previous years were carried forward with greater intensity: expenditures rose to 1,527,000,000 lire (about 500,000,000 lire a year) for the triennium following 1928.[13] The average number of workers employed daily rose to 28,200 in 1928–9, to 35,000 in 1929–30, and to 53,000 in 1931–2.[14] In March 1934, 65,000 workers were engaged in land reclamation, and of these 23,154 were employed in the vicinity of Rome on the Pontine Marshes.[15]

By concentrating a vast expenditure on 26,000 hectares (about 40,-

---

[9] Peglion, *Le Bonifiche in Italia,* p. 5.

[10] Official report published in the *Corriere della Sera,* Oct. 4, 1932.

[11] Estimate made by the president of the National Confederation of Agricultural Employers in the *Giornale d'Italia,* July 4, 1929; Peglion, *Le Bonifiche in Italia,* pp. 22–3.

[12] Serpieri, *La Legge sulla Bonifica Integrale nel Secondo Anno,* p. 73.

[13] Official reports in the *Stampa,* Sept. 29 and Nov. 27, 1932; *Corriere della Sera,* Nov. 3, 4, 1932.

[14] *Corriere della Sera,* Oct. 4, 1932.

[15] *Bollettino Mensile di Statistica,* April 23, 1934, p. 382; official *communiqué* in the press of March 12, 1934.

ooo acres) of the Pontine Marshes without paying any attention to the economic results of the undertaking,[16] it has been possible to stage a spectacular show at the very gates of Rome. Today any foreigner who is not a complete nonentity cannot remain in Rome three days without having some high-placed personage of the regime invite him to go in an automobile, or even an aeroplane, to visit the reclamation works in the Pontine Marshes. Nobody tells the bamboozled foreigner that in order to put up that show at the gates of Rome the government starves the land reclamation works elsewhere in Italy.[17]

In France, between 1928 and 1932 the amount spent on public works in the Department of the Seine (Paris) alone (seven million inhabitants) equalled twelve billion francs, or about 500,000,000 gold dollars. In May 1934 the French government decided to spend within six years ten billion francs on extraordinary public works projects giving work to 100,000 unemployed.[18]

In Great Britain the government spent over £15,500,000 in 1929–30 for unemployment benefit, £12,700,000 for working-class housing, and £5,300,000 as a subsidy to local bodies for road construction.[19] I am unable to say what is the total of public works expenditure—ordinary and extraordinary—in Great Britain, but this much is known: £19,-000,000 were spent *merely to promote the activities of private building societies and local governments,* a sum more than equivalent to the 1,800,000,000 lire spent in Italy during 1929–30 for public works of

---

[16] The Pontine Marshes are divided into two parts: the Pontine Marshes properly so called (26,000 hectares) and the territory of Piscinara (54,000 hectares). The estimated cost of these works is 650,000,000 lire (*Corriere della Sera*, Oct. 28, 1932), or 8,000 lire per hectare. The Fascist review *La Conquista della Terra* for April 1932, after having exalted in most enthusiastic language the work of "resolving 'Fascistly' in the shortest possible time the knotty problem" of the Pontine Marshes, was obliged to explain that "at the present moment, it is not easy to express a reliable opinion on the opportuneness of the work of transforming this area into an agricultural region." In the Senate on May 20, 1931, Senator Ciccotti remarked that a piece of land in the countryside around Rome (*La Campagna Romana*) had formerly produced, when in its state as pasture, 46,000 lire a year, whereas now it was producing not more than 18,000 after having been put to grain: in view of the climate, pasturing is more appropriate for the *Campagna* than is wheat-raising. No one contradicted these statements.

[17] Further information concerning the bluff of Fascist land reclamation is given in the pamphlets entitled *Land Reclamation Under Fascism* and *The Discovery of Italy*, in the series "Italy Today," 1932.

[18] *New York Times*, May 17, 1934.

[19] *Parliamentary Debates: House of Commons*, July 16, 1930, pp. 1273, 1290 ff.

all categories. The *New Statesman* of November 18, 1933, remarked, concerning the road expenses in Italy and in England:

> The total expenditure of the Road Board since 1928 was [in Italy] only £64,000,000. Scarcely an impressive effort for "a new economic system." 670 miles of new roads were completed in four years in Italy. In Great Britain, without Fascism, 1305 miles of Class I roads were completed in the four years ended 1931. And they are much better roads. The total expenditure on public works during the ten years of the Fascist regime is less than the annual loans for local works out of the Local Loans Fund in Great Britain! In fact, when you examine these figures, this "new economic system" is just a gigantic bluff, and the bluff comes off only because the honest Italian critics are in penal settlements.

In 1933 the United States Congress voted to spend $3,166,000,000 for extraordinary public works in two years. In January 1934 the federal government was giving employment to 4,079,474 persons.[20] In the state of New York alone, the federal government was providing work for 240,000 at the end of March 1934.[21] To those employed by the federal government must be added those employed by the state and local governments.

In all fairness one should keep in mind that there is a vast difference in national wealth between France, Great Britain, and the United States on one hand, and Italy on the other. Relatively the Italian expenditure is as great as those of the other countries. The difference is that in Italy the fuss about expenditures is far greater. No one in France, England, or the United States feels the need or duty of shouting from the housetops that the prime minister or the President has won the "battle" against unemployment. The news about the seventeen billion francs spent in the Department of the Seine between 1928 and 1932 was given by the French papers of July 4, 1932, in a few lines and in small type, as of no special importance. In Italy, it is impossible to construct a public wash-house in the smallest village without the newspapers treating it as an unheard-of event. Every year on the twenty-eighth of October, the anniversary of the "March on Rome," the press devotes whole pages to lists of public works completed during the year or in course of execution. This permits them to repeat the latter every year until their completion. "In

---

[20] *New York Times*, Feb. 20, 1934.
[21] *Ibid.*, April 2, 1934.

their zeal to enumerate a large number of public works for reducing unemployment, the local governments go so far as to include ordinary administrative activities and even private undertakings." [22] And, of course, the credit for all these works is given to Mussolini: he decides on the works; he approves the schemes, if, indeed, he does not study them carefully himself; [23] he supervises their execution; he pays the workers out of his own pocket; he sets the emblem of his party on the projects when they are finished—in short, it is he who does everything. If it were not for Mussolini there would be no public works in Italy.

In 1933 the increasing budget deficit obliged the government to limit expenditure on public works. Senator Ricci stated in the Senate on March 25, 1933:

> If we look at the statistics, we shall see that the two most important governmental enterprises show a decrease in the number of workers employed. Land reclamation in June 1932 gave work to 61,000 men; now it takes care of only 43,000. The National Highways Board (*Azienda della Strada*) then employed 43,000; now it employs only 33,000.

In the course of the same discussion, Senator Ancona admitted that the budget did not allow for extraordinary works, remarking that Italy needed "two or three years more of abstinence." This was the result of the method followed by the Italian government during the preceding decade: the multiplication of public works which were paid for, not out of current revenue, but by pledges on the part of the Treasury to pay them by instalments over a period of years. The hidden indebtedness on account of public works had increased to 74.3 billion lire by February 28, 1933, and instalments to the amount of six billion lire came due during the fiscal year 1932–3. Thus no money was left for current expenditure.

---

[22] Statement made by Senator Ricci in the Senate on March 8, 1933, and contradicted by no one. Senator Ricci is one of the few senators left who have the courage to make assertions in the Senate which are unpleasant for the regime.

[23] Cardinal O'Connell, returning from a trip to Italy in the autumn of 1934, felt it his duty to declare that he was "enthusiastic about conditions in Italy under Mussolini's rule," and characterized Mussolini's redemption of the Pontine Marshes as "an illustration of the engineering genius of Mussolini" (*New York Times*, Nov. 2, 1934). No one in Italy, even among Mussolini's basest flatterers, ever gave Mussolini credit for "engineering genius." Cardinal O'Connell's exaggeration was so gross that even Mussolini's press bureau, in "doctoring" the text of the interview before giving it on Nov. 2 to the Italian press, struck out the word "engineering" and left only the "genius."

In January 1934 the Minister of Public Works announced in the Senate that "at the present moment it was necessary to mark time." Senator Ricci on January 15 deplored this announcement, and stated that to the contrary "what was needed was the energetic emulation of Roosevelt's policy in embarking upon a programme of public works." He was interrupted by the Minister of Finance: "But you would withhold your approval from the Ministry of Finance, were it to present a budget with a larger deficit." On May 26, 1934, Mussolini made known his sovereign will. He announced that the fiscal year 1933–4 would end with a deficit of about four billion lire. It was therefore necessary to reduce expenditure: in the budget for 1934–5 there would be no appropriation for extraordinary works. As regards these statements of the Duce, the foreign correspondents entered into a conspiracy of silence. Having in the preceding years extolled Mussolini because he gave work to the unemployed instead of demoralizing them with the "dole," they now found it difficult to glorify him for not giving work to the workers. Silence was obviously the counsel of wisdom.

As for "national solidarity," it functions only during the three winter months. When winter is over, the unemployed are abandoned to their own devices. It functions especially in the large cities, where a mob of hungry people may break out in dangerous riots. Divine Providence alone provides for the unemployed in the small towns and the day-labourers scattered through the countryside.

An official *communiqué* of July 2, 1934, informs us that in the winter of that year "national solidarity" in Italy gave help "almost every day" to 1,750,000 families, made up of 2,884,000 individuals, and that the total cost of relief amounted to 132,649,256 lire. Let us bear in mind that the Italian winter lasts ninety days, then let us multiply by ninety the number of persons receiving relief and divide by the number of beneficiaries the 132,649,256 lire spent on relief: the result is that each person received relief funds to the amount of fifty centesimi (5 cents) a day.

An official *communiqué* of July 5, 1935, states that from November 1934 to April 1935, 3,014,452 needy persons had been assisted "almost daily." "Almost daily" means "during the winter season."

Passing to more detailed figures, we find that according to the French journalist already quoted (see pp. 262–3) the Fascist Party during the winter of 1932 distributed in the city of Rome "more than 20,000 food cards"; the "heads of families without work" could obtain on presentation of these cards, bread, macaroni, milk, and other foodstuffs; the total expense amounted to 1,129,398 lire, "which shows the efficacy of the relief granted." If we divide 1,129,398 lire among 20,000 workless heads of families, it would amount to 55 lire per family, in other words, to less than 20 lire per month for the three winter months. To this sum of 1,129,398 lire we must add: *a*, 50,000 lire for shoes and clothing for the children; *b*, unrevealed sums which were necessary for the maintenance of *one* "Fascist lodging-house" for the housing of homeless men and for eight soup kitchens, which distributed from 2000 to 4000 bowls of soup per day for three months; and *c*, 64,335 lire in grants to needy families among the lower middle class.[24] Rome has over a million inhabitants!

In the province of Genoa (831,000 inhabitants) 1,181,470 lire were spent in January 1934 on relief.[25] According to official statistics, there were 20,890 unemployed in the province of Genoa on December 31, 1933.[26] If the reader divides the above sum by the number of unemployed and then again by 31 (the number of days in January), he will discover that each of the employed included in the official statistics had at his disposal no less than 1.80 lire per day, or 18 cents.

In the province of Milan during the three winter months of 1934 the expenditure for relief amounted to 11,345,000.[27] Remember that according to official statistics the unemployed in that province during those three months averaged 91,000;[28] overlook the fact that official figures are usually much below the mark, and you will conclude that from 11,345,000 lire of relief funds each of the 91,000 unemployed persons in the province of Milan received the large sum of 1.40 lire (14 cents) a day during the ninety days of the winter of 1934. Even if we admit that half of the unemployed had some other source of income and were not in need of relief, we find that the relief allotted to each individual beneficiary rises to only 2.80 lire (28 cents) a day.

---

[24] On June 19, 1932, the secretary of the Fascist Party in Rome published official figures that varied somewhat from those given by the French journalist a month earlier. He affirmed that the Party had collected "nearly five millions," and had spent four million in the relief of 157,000 persons. Each of these persons, therefore, would have received the sum of 25 lire towards his food, clothing, and rent during the three months of the preceding winter, or the equivalent of 8.33 lire per month.

[25] *Lavoro*, Feb. 18, 1934.

[26] *Sindacato e Corporazione*, Jan. 1934, p. 199.

[27] *Corriere della Sera*, Aug. 1, 1934.

[28] *Sindacato e Corporazione*, Feb. 1934, p. 433; March 1934, p. 653; April 1934, p. 888.

While in Italy in the winter of 1934, 2,884,000 persons, i. e., fifteen per cent of the population, were each receiving relief to the average amount of 0.50 centesimi (half a cent) a day, in New York City, throughout the year the average weekly relief check for a family of four persons was fifteen dollars. The schedules for British unemployment benefits in 1934 allowed twenty-five shillings, or five dollars a week for husband and wife, and thirty shillings, or six dollars a week for a family with two children. Note that, if rents in 1934 were higher in New York and in England than in Italy, the cost of foodstuffs was higher in Italy. But who knows how many American and English citizens were comparing relief measures in their countries with the miraculous achievements of Mussolini in his country, as described by their newspapers, and envied the people of Italy for their good fortune in possessing a Mussolini!

In New York City, during the single month of January 1935, public and private agencies together spent $19,886,000 on relief.[29] Thus, New York City alone spent the equivalent of 200 million lire on relief, while in the whole of Italy during the year 1933, according to official statistics, no more than 132 million lire were spent for this purpose. No one contended that the recipients of relief in New York City should be personally grateful to Mayor La Guardia. In Italy everybody is bound to sing the praises and benefits of Mussolini.

---

[29] *New York Times,* March 25, 1935.

From the Eight-Hour Day
to the Forty-Hour Week

In November 1934 the hour struck for the final and decisive "battle" against unemployment.

To understand the importance and the implications of this fresh "battle," we must notice that the great majority of Italian workers won the 8-hour day in 1919 and 1920. In July 1923, in 16,189 factories, employing 1,184,780 workers, 88.1 per cent of the employees worked 48 hours a week; 7.4 per cent from 49 to 54 hours; and 4.5 per cent more than 54 hours. In the metal industry, 94.9 per cent of the workers were on an 8-hour basis, and in the textile industries 89.2 per cent.[1] In October 1922 a bill was ready which, on the model of the Washington Convention, made the 8-hour day compulsory in all economic activities.

By a royal decree of March 15, 1923, Mussolini made the 8-hour day and the 48-hour week compulsory in Italy after August 10 of that year. But, in codifying this general principle, he excepted from the obligation of remaining within the 8-hour limit seamen, employees in public works, even if managed by private individuals, and agricultural labourers on fixed wages, who form the most numerous group of agricultural workers. Besides this, he raised to 12 hours a week the maximum of overtime work, which the Washington Convention had limited to 10 hours; reduced to 10 per cent the measure of compensation for this work, whereas the Washington Convention had set it at 25 per cent; and abolished the penalty of arrest for the person who had violated the law three times. The Socialist leader, Filippo Turati, comparing the Fascist decree with the bill that had preceded it, wrote:

The container is the same, but the contents have evaporated. The headings of the articles are reproduced, but through learned incisions and omissions the virtue and efficacy of the law have taken flight. The body is there; but the soul has gone into exile.[2]

---

[1] MacLean, *Labor, Wages and Unemployment*, p. 7.
[2] *Critica Sociale*, April 1, 1923. Signor Villari, in *The Fascist Experiment*, p. 154,

Thus the bill *for* the 8-hour day was transformed into an act *against* the 8-hour day. The mystification reached its height on December 6, 1923, when another decree listed thirty-three groups of occupations to which the limitation of hours of work to 8 per day did not apply.[3]

In any case, there were occupations subject to the standard of the 8-hour day. But even for these the law remained a scrap of paper. Here is the evidence for this statement:

1. In June 1924, an official of the Fascist unions in Turin wrote: "The law establishing the 8-hour day is often openly and shamelessly violated. Derogations of this law are too readily sanctioned by the authorities. The hours of overtime, often paid at very low percentages of the ordinary wage rate and sometimes not paid for at all, go far beyond the maximum of 12 hours a week granted by the law. This happens, for example, in some sections of the Fiat Works" (Avarna di Gualtieri, *Il Fascismo*, p. 117).

2. On January 17, 1925, Signor Rossoni made the following statement: "In Sicily miners and peasants are working 10 and 12 hours a day for a few lire" (*Stampa*, January 18, 1926).

3. On June 30, 1926, the employers were authorized to prolong the working day from 8 to 9 hours,[4] without increasing wages (see above, p. 184).

4. On January 13, 1927, the working day for the postal employees was raised to 9 hours, without, of course, any increase of salary (*Industrial and Labour Information*, April 4, 1927, p. 13).

5. In the labour agreement of July 1928 concerning employees in commerce, the latter were obliged not to refuse to work overtime within the limit of 12 extra hours a week and 2 extra hours a day (*Industrial and Labour Information*, July 23, 1928, p. 84).

6. In that year there were employers who were not even satisfied with the 10-hour day and demanded 12 hours.[5]

---

after informing his readers that the decree of March 15, 1923 established "the general principle," added: "Certain attenuations of the rule are permitted." Naturally he did not explain wherein the "attenuations" consisted.

[3] *Industrial and Labour Information*, March 3, 1924, pp. 265 ff.

[4] In the July 1926 number of the *Fortnightly Review*, Mr. Heathcote, in his article on *Mussolini's New Conception of the State*, gave Mussolini the credit for having instituted the 8-hour day and, in addition, the minimum wage, the "ceding to representatives of labour of the right to take part in the management of industrial concerns," the stabilization of the currency, etc. In 1925 and 1926 the exchange was subject to violent fluctuations; stabilization took place only in Dec. 1927. Consequently, Mr. Heathcote, by asserting in July 1926 that Mussolini had stabilized the currency, was making a genuine prophecy. His other prophecies have, however, not yet materialized.

[5] Haider, *Capital and Labour*, p. 155. Schneider, in *Making the Fascist State*, p.

7. In October 1929, in the sulphur mines of Sommatino and Riesi, in Sicily, "the 8-hour day was a mere pretence; the men worked from 10 to 14 hours per day; those on piece-work might earn up to 15 lire if they obtained a maximum of output with 14 or 15 hours of consecutive work" (*Lavoro Fascista,* November 2, 1929).

8. In November 1930, an official of the commercial unions lamented that in Turin the law of the 8-hour day was not respected, and that in the province of Alessandria the agricultural labourers had to work 15 hours a day from May to October (Rosenstock-Franck, p. 166).

9. In August 1930, the textile industries were declared to be seasonal and therefore exempted from the 8-hour limit in the busy months (*Industrial and Labour Information,* August 18, 1930, p. 226).

10. The labour agreement of November 1930 between butchers and their employees in the province of Brindisi ruled that the employees were to work 60 hours a week, i. e., 10 hours a day (*Lavoro Fascista,* November 22, 1930).

11. By the labour agreement of January 1931 between agricultural employers and employees in the province of Mantua, the normal working day consisted of 8 hours, but "when the exigencies of production required it," the working day from May 15 to August 15 could be lengthened by two hours without the workers' having a right to extra payment: "In harvest time the labourer must work day and night beyond the limits of the regular working day without extra payment, whenever the crops demand urgent attention. Not counted in the working day are the rest periods and the time of going to and from the field or the place of work, which are settled in accordance with local customs. The employer may arrange the daily work according to the necessities of his farm" (*Lavoro Agricolo Fascista,* February 1, 1931).

12. In the newspaper *La Tribuna* for June 13, 1931, a contributor expressed pleasure that "the 8-hour day in agriculture fortunately still remained a myth," but regretted that "the agricultural labourer was producing less"; "where once ten workers sufficed to perform a given piece of work, we see today fourteen, fifteen, or more." He thus reminded his readers that the work of slaves is less productive than that of free men.

13. In December 1931, 29 per cent of the workers in the shipbuilding

209, writes: "Rossoni had succeeded in getting a decree (Jan. 11, 1927) which permits the nine-hour day (decreed in the summer of 1926 as a temporary emergency measure) only if it is granted by a collective contract made between legally recognized syndicates. This practically restores the eight-hour day, for Rossoni's attitude in its favor is well known, and employers will be unable to force a nine-hour day concession unless in very exceptional circumstances." The decree of Jan. 11, 1927, has never existed save in the imagination of the Fascist from whom Professor Schneider derived his information without checking it.

industry, 12 per cent in the woollen industry, and 14 per cent in the boot and shoe industry, were doing overtime work (Banca Commerciale Italiana, *Movimento Economico: 1932*, p. 255).

14.   On July 28, 1932, the Minister of Corporations conceded that, for four months in the year, employees in the cheese industry could exceed the 48-hour week; on August 12, he extended this concession to the commercial firms selling fruit and vegetables; and on September 22, he consented that the men who work grain-threshing machines should work 60 hours a week (*Bollettino del Lavoro*, September–October 1932, pp. 219–20).

15.   On September 2, 1932, the secretary of the commercial unions in Turin made the following statement: "It would be a good idea to adopt immediately a measure that would produce a noteworthy falling-off in unemployment: that is, to forbid overtime work. It is a well known fact that the 8-hour day is applied in very few cases. The employees work 10 hours a day in shops and commercial firms in general, while in restaurants and hotels they work from 10 to 13 hours a day. Estimating that the number of those dependent upon commercial activities in our province is 35,000, and that at least 25,000 of them do 10 hours of work (we believe that they actually do more), that is, 2 hours more than 8, we shall have 50,000 hours of work to be distributed among the unemployed, who are, in the general category of commerce, more than 5000" (*Stampa*, September 3, 1932).[6]

16.   By a decree of December 5, 1932, the government authorized the electro-chemical industries to exceed the 8-hour day and the 48-hour week during six months of the year (*Industrial and Labour Information*, February 20, 1933, p. 252).

17.   On January 6, 1933, the *Stampa* published the following letter from an "Italian and Fascist" worker: "In an important rayon factory in the province of Aosta the employees are working in shifts from 6 A. M. to 2 P. M. and from 2 to 10 P. M. Many workers, when the shift is finished, are obliged to return to the factory and do 3 or 4 additional hours' work in order to make up for a shortage of hands or to meet the necessity of greater production. These extra hours are not paid as overtime, and sometimes the workers have to walk more than an hour to go back to the factory. Along with this, workers are still being discharged."

18.   On February 15, 1933, in the Chamber, a union official let slip the following admission: "Even now there are workers who are compelled to work 12 or 14 hours a day."

19.   On October 11, 1933, the president of the unions of commercial

---

[6] For Aug. 31, 1932, the official statistics gave scarcely 637 unemployed in commerce for the province of Turin (*Bollettino del Lavoro*, Oct. 1932, p. 289); another proof, if we need one, that the unemployment statistics are falsified.

employees made the following statement, in a speech delivered at Genoa: "The working hours of the personnel employed in hotels and restaurants are undoubtedly much too long. Hotel employees work 13 hours a day, those in restaurants 10 hours; it is therefore necessary to demand a revision of the labour agreement" (*Lavoro*, October 12, 1933).

20. In the labour agreement of February 1934, concerning the employees in the firms that produce and sell vegetables in the province of Savona, the employees were obliged to work 10 hours a day and 60 hours a week for three months out of the year (*Lavoro*, February 10, 1934).

21. In the *Lavoro Fascista* of April 24, 1934, one of the officials of the bank employees' union wrote as follows: "For some time there has been gaining ground slowly but inexorably, like cancer and the mountains that move, a curious manner of paying overtime work in our banks. It is well-known that overtime work by an employee should be paid on a higher scale than the usual hourly rate. However, the managements have thought out an elegant method of avoiding payment for that part of the work done by the staff in addition to the usual schedule. The method consists in 'compensating' the greater length of today's work, not with money, but with a shorter working day tomorrow or any other day. Usually the employee learns of the 'compensation' in place of payment only after the work has been completed."

Meanwhile Signor De Michelis, the head of the Italian delegation at the International Labour Office, wrote in December 1926:

The head of the Italian government has on more than one occasion said that the workers' conquest of the 8-hour day should be inviolable. The Italian government has never broken this engagement.[7]

Still more brazenly than his esquire, Mussolini, on April 29, 1928, gave the following news to the world:

We have been the first to establish by law the 8-hour working day, while richer states which enjoy the name of democracies are still talking about doing it.

In order to give a striking proof of the tenacity with which the Fascist regime was upholding the principle of the 8-hour day, Mussolini in the spring of 1932 introduced into the Senate a bill authorizing the government to ratify the famous Washington Convention without waiting for the cowardly and sluggish democratic countries to do the

---

[7] *Industrial and Labour Information*, Jan. 17, 1927, p. 69.

same. The Senate committee which examined the bill made it clear that such class co-operation was not at all dangerous:

> In all countries, especially in those where unemployment is greatest, there is a tendency to have recourse to a working week of less than 48 hours, as one way of meeting the present economic depression.

As a consequence, the Senate unanimously approved the bill on May 23, 1932, thus enshrining in a new and brilliant form the principle of Fascist class co-operation. Moreover, a law written on paper is not necessarily applied in daily practice; when an employer finds it convenient to make his factory work overtime, nothing prevents him from ignoring the law. Finally, an attentive study of the text reveals that the bill abolished the clause in the act of March 15, 1923, obliging the employer to pay overtime work at a rate 10 per cent higher than the ordinary wage, and it left the function of determining wages for overtime work to the labour agreements; it reduced fines for the violation of the law by 50 per cent; and it allowed the 56-hour week and abolished the weekly day of rest for those firms which demanded a 7-day working week. In short, Mussolini kept up the farce of proclaiming the 8-hour day in the abstract and annulling it in the concrete.

At this point the opportunity for the definitive "battle" presented itself: the "battle" for the 40-hour week.

On July 25, 1932, Signor De Michelis, the Italian representative at the International Labour Office, requested its governing body to call a special session of the International Labour Conference "in order to draw up proposals which could be put in immediate operation as regards hours of work." [8]

Everybody knows how the machinery of the I.L.O. functions. First, they discuss the question of whether discussion is advisable; next they discuss the question of whether a decision is advisable; then they decide to entrust to a commission the task of drawing up a project for an agreement; then, in God's good time, they discuss and approve the project for an agreement; then they send it to all the governments of the earth, the moon, and the other inhabited heavenly bodies; then they wait for the ratification of the agreement by all these governments; and while they wait for universal ratification, they begin to discuss the

---

[8] *Minutes of the Special Meeting of the Governing Body of the International Labour Office, Geneva,* Sept. 1932, p. 56.

problem of the desirability of discussing the project for another agreement. Mussolini thus knew exactly what he was doing when he instructed Signor De Michelis to ask the I.L.O. for a "proposal which could be put into immediate operation." In reality, his sole desire was that the press throughout the world should repeat that Mussolini had taken the initiative towards making the 40-hour week compulsory everywhere, just as he had given the example of making the 8-hour day compulsory in Italy.

During the discussions (January 10–25, 1933), the representatives of the workers demanded that, while the week should be reduced to 40 hours, wages should be left intact; the employers maintained that the working hours could not be cut down unless pay was cut too, and were opposed even to the reduction in hours; the representatives of the government were divided. Of the Italian delegates, the representative of the employers voted with the employers, the representative of the workers with the workers; and the representative of the government, Signor De Michelis, voted with the employers.[9] This fact is highly characteristic of Fascist "class co-operation."

Now that he had made the proposal of the 40-hour week for the workers of the world, Mussolini laid before the Chamber the so-called bill for the 8-hour day, i. e., the 48-hour week, for the Italian worker, which the Senate had passed in May 1932. The bill passed amid general enthusiasm in the session of February 15 and became law on March 16, 1933.[10] "Who defends the 8-hour day?" asked the *Resto del Carlino* on February 17, 1933—"Mussolini, always Mussolini." But the Senate commission that examined the budget estimate for 1933–4, observed that the law of the 8-hour day "under the present conditions of labour, when there was an urge towards reducing the working day to less than 8 hours, had a certain anachronistic character." [11] Anyhow the law of March 16, 1933, on the 8-hour day had not yet come into operation two years afterward, because the list of the industries which would have been authorized to overcome the 48-hour week had not yet been published.[12]

At the June 1934 conference of the I.L.O. Signor De Michelis again

---

[9] *Sindacato e Corporazione,* Jan. 1933, pp. 201 ff.

[10] *Ibid.,* June 1933, p. 995.

[11] Senate, *Documenti,* No. 1515 A, p. 2.

[12] I.L.O., *L'année sociale 1934–35,* I, p. 102.

held out for the 40-hour week. This measure, he maintained, must be permanent and not a mere temporary stop-gap during the present crisis. And those nations that "extract from their workers the maximum amount of labour by imposing upon them unfavourable conditions of work" should not place at a disadvantage those countries "which maintain a high living standard for their workers," among which countries Italy, of course, was to be counted:

The same arguments against the 40-hour week which we hear today were heard during the discussions over the 8-hour day. Yet the 8-hour day has preserved society from a situation even worse than the present one. My government believes, today as it did two years ago, that the reduction in the working week is a measure which is imperative and will become more and more imperative, given the present evolution of industrial life, and that consequently its adoption as an international system is an ineluctable necessity.[13]

Unfortunately, the I.L.O. was a body without power. It was necessary to break down all barriers and set a great example. Fascist Italy would heroically adopt the 40-hour week immediately, without waiting for the sluggish and inefficient democracies.[14] Such heroism was the less difficult in that the cotton industry—one of the most important—had in June adopted the 5-day working week; [15] and in that, in the last week of July 1934, according to official statistics, from 14 to 20 per cent of the workers in the metal industry, 26.9 per cent in the shipbuilding industry, 26.7 per cent in the macaroni industry, and 28.7 per cent in Italian industry as a whole were working part time.[16] In September 1934 the employees of the Fiat motor works, the most important firm in the metal industry, were working only 35 hours a week. In the province of Ferrara "the workers in almost all the factories were working less than 40 hours a week; those in the building trades were employed, on an average, sixty or seventy days in a year." [17] Therefore, the reduction of

---

[13] The Italian press of June 8, 1934.
[14] Jones, *Is Fascism the Answer?*, p. 190, had announced to his readers, a year before the event, that Italy had already adopted the 40-hour week: "The idea of the benefit of shorter hours spread for the benefit of a larger number of workers originated in Italy several years ago with the proposal of a 40-hour week as a relief for unemployment. The idea has been adopted in America and elsewhere."
[15] *Lavoro Fascista*, June 30, 1934.
[16] *Bollettino Mensile di Statistiche*, Sept. 1934, p. 794.
[17] *Corriere Padano*, Nov. 9, 1934.

the working week was, for the majority of Italian industries, like forcing one's way through an open door.

On October 11, 1934, the presidents of the confederations of industrial employers and employees came to an agreement, according to which the employers pledged themselves not to exact more than 40 hours' work a week, but retained the right to require overtime work "in exceptional cases"; "wages were to be proportionate to the lower number of hours," i. e., the workers would lose as many hours' wages as hours' work. The worker, for instance, who had previously worked 48 hours a week would lose 17 per cent of his earnings.[18] Workers with pensions were to be dismissed. The places of women and boys were to be filled by men "wherever possible." [19] Mussolini thus kept punctually the promise made during the preceding May (see above, p. 205) to lead the Italian people toward a nobler life of heroism and of asceticism. This was the rude and decisive ordeal which the *Lavoro Fascista* had then announced.

The agreement went into effect in December. This time the victory was decisive, as is revealed by a comparison of the unemployment statistics for 1933–4 with those for 1934–5.

	1933	*1934*
December	1,132,000	961,000
	1934	*1935*
January	1,158,000	1,011,000
February	1,103,000	955,000

[18] The Rome correspondents of the London *Times* (Dec. 14, 1935) and of the *New York Times* (Jan. 20, 1935), in informing their readers of the agreement, took good care to conceal the fact that the workers were losing as many hours' wages as hours' work. The Italian delegate to the I.L.O., on Jan. 30, 1935, boasted that while working hours had been reduced in Italy, wages "for every hour of work" had not been reduced. He omitted to explain what had happened to the wages for the hours of work which had been abolished, and no one asked him any questions on this point.

[19] The Rome correspondent of the London *Times*, Dec. 14, 1934, declared that these measures for grappling with the unemployment problem had been put forward "by various bodies composing the structure of the Italian Corporative State." In actual fact, they were decided upon by the presidents of the confederations, i. e., by the organs of Fascist syndicalism, without even the expression of an advisory opinion on the part of the National Council of Corporations, the Central Corporative Committee, or the corporations which as yet had not begun to function. The misinformation given by the *Times* formed part of the campaign of propaganda designed to convince the public that "the structure of the Corporative State" was in complete operation.

No official *communiqué* informed the public how many women, boys, or pensioned workers had lost their positions or part of their wages. In compensation, the Under-Secretary for Corporations stated in the Chamber on March 29, 1935, that, as a result of the introduction of the 40-hour week, "more than 200,000 unemployed had found work in the last three months." If this information were correct, we should have to conclude that without the recent measure referred to the unemployed would have risen to 1,250,000 in February 1935, that is, they would have exceeded by 150,000 the number reported for February 1934. But to base conclusions upon Fascist unemployment statistics is to build a house upon sand.

The *Lavoro Fascista* of July 16, 1935, announced that the statistics of the preceding June had presented 200,000 unemployed less than the corresponding month of 1934, and stated triumphantly that this fact "meant a great victory for Fascism on a field in which the other countries were carrying on a forlorn fight." It ignored: 1, that, according to the official statistics, the 40-hour week had procured work for fully 250,000 unemployed; and 2, that in the first six months of 1935 there had been called to arms for the war against Ethiopia and to hold themselves ready to face every surprise in Europe not less than 300,000 men, to whom were to be added the auxiliary workmen from the war industries. Without these facts by how much would not the number of unemployed have been increased? The day Mussolini starts a world war, unemployment will disappear; and this will be Mussolini's most startling victory in his "battle" against unemployment.[20]

---

[20] In April 1935, in Parma, the labour agreement between the owners of barber shops and their employees enacted that the latter from October to March were to work 65½ hours a week, and from April to Sept. 72½ hours a week. In April the papers of the sixteenth announced that in the labour agreement concerning a group of workmen in the textile industry, the hours of weekly work had been fixed at 54. This after so much fuss had been made about the 40-hour week.

XVII

Sunday Rest, Annual Vacations, and Labour Exchanges

THE well-being of the working classes in a given country is not solely a matter of wages, cost of living or employment. It can be greatly improved by social legislation.

Fascist social legislation is hailed as one of Mussolini's great glories. Even the chief editor of the British labour paper, the *Daily Herald*, June 5, 1934, was deeply impressed by Mussolini's merits as a "social reformer":

> The Fascist Government and the Fascist Party have a record in social legislation of which any democratic government might be proud. *Even their bitterest critics and bitterest enemies admit that here Mussolini and his Ministers have done a good piece of work.*

If the chief editor of the *Daily Herald* had been less ignorant of Italian conditions, he would have known that before Mussolini came into power Italian social legislation was one of the most advanced in Europe.

The work of women and children was regulated by the acts of June 19, 1902, and November 10, 1907. Children of both sexes under 12 years old could not be employed in factories; boys under 15 and women under 21 could not be employed in dangerous or unhealthful trades; night work was forbidden for women of any age and for youths under 18; women were prohibited from working during the month following childbirth.

By an act of July 17, 1910, a maternity fund had been created to aid women employed in industry during the month following confinement, when, in accordance with the law of 1902, they had to abstain from work. The fund was made up of the contributions of employers and women workers. The number of women insured rose from 590,555 in

1919 to 643,870 in 1922, and the number of those receiving aid rose from 14,478 in 1919 to 33,791 in 1922.[1]

By an act of January 31, 1904, the workers were obliged to insure against accidents in the course of industrial work. On August 23, 1917, compulsory insurance against accidents had been extended to agriculture.[2]

An act concerning weekly or Sunday rest dated from August 8, 1908.

Labour exchanges had been founded on January 5, 1919. On December 31 of the same year, 4000 labour exchanges were in operation.[3]

Insurance against incapacity and old age had been made compulsory on April 21, 1919, for certain categories of industrial workers. On October 27, 1922—Mussolini became prime minister on October 30—compulsory insurance had been extended to all categories of workers, including the *mezzadri* (*métayers*, share-croppers) and the tenant farmers, provided that their yearly revenue did not exceed 9000 lire. All workers fifteen years old and over were obliged to pay a certain sum in weekly instalments to the insurance company; the employer contributed a quota equal to that of the employee; and the government also contributed to the fund 50 millions yearly. The worker who by the end of his sixty-fifth year had paid in at least 240 weekly contributions, had a right to a minimum pension; one who had paid 480 weekly contributions received the maximum pension; one who had paid at least 120 weekly contributions had a right to a pension at any age if he was certified as unable to work.

Compulsory insurance against involuntary unemployment had been enacted on October 19, 1919.

There was no law compelling the working classes to insure against every form of sickness so as to have a right to a daily subsidy in case of illness. But many mutual-aid societies had arisen throughout Italy. Mazzini and his followers had been active apostles of these institutions during the first decades of the free regime.[4] On December 31, 1904, there were in Italy 6535 mutual-aid societies with 926,026 mem-

---

[1] *Annuario Statistico Italiano:* 1919–21, pp. 419–20; *ibid.:* 1922–25, pp. 311–2.
[2] Cabrini, *La Legislazione sociale,* pp. 110 ff.; Fantini, *La legislazione sociale,* p. 342.
[3] De Michelis, *Relazione sui servizi per il collocamento per la disoccupazione in Italia,* p. 15.
[4] Rosselli, *Mazzini e Bakounine,* pp. 30 ff., and 50 ff.

bers.[5] They paid out to their members benefits for sickness, disability, old age, accidents, and unemployment, relief to dependents and funeral expenses in case of death, and a subsidy if the wife of the member gave birth to a child.[6] In the territories which belonged to the Austro-Hungarian Empire before 1914 and were annexed to Italy as a result of the World War, a law of 1888 had made sickness insurance compulsory for all workers, and there existed in each province flourishing sickness funds, whose administrators were elected by the workers themselves. An official Fascist document of 1932 had to admit that among these funds, administered by Socialists, "several functioned well and some could even be held up as models, with strong organizations, sound finances, regular activity, and the best reputations."[7] In the years immediately following the war—the years of "Bolshevism"!—the labour agreements began to impose upon employers the obligation of giving to their workers, in case of illness, a subsidy proportionate to their length of service in the factories.[8]

In 1919 and 1920 a large number of unions succeeded in forcing the employers to grant an annual paid vacation to their employees.[9] Another right the unions wrested from the employers was the right of the worker in the event of discharge to compensation proportionate to the length of his service.[10]

What has the Fascist Government accomplished in the sphere of social legislation?

The Fascists claim that weekly or Sunday rest, the indemnity upon

---

[5] *Annuario Statistico Italiano: 1930*, p. 406.

[6] *Industrial and Labour Information*, Sept. 28, 1923, pp. 39 ff.

[7] Senate, *Documenti N. 1473A*, Dec. 16, 1932.

[8] *Bollettino dell'Ufficio del Lavoro*, XXXIV, pp. 164, 196.

[9] *Industrial and Labour Information*, May 11, 1923, p. 21 said: "Before the war manual workers in Italy had no paid holidays. Since the war, however, clauses providing for holidays with pay have been inserted in a number of collective agreements for manual workers, and the system of holidays is now in force in most of the main branches of Italian industry. The length of the holiday granted varies from six days (chemical, metal, and textile industries) to twelve or fifteen days (gas and electricity undertakings and printing trades). In most cases workers become entitled to a holiday after one year's service, in one or two instances after six months' service." Agreements may be seen in the *Bollettino dell'Ufficio del Lavoro*, July–Dec. 1920, pp. 182, 190, 196, 212, 393, 401, 407. One of the crimes of which the "anti-Bolshevists" accused the "Bolshevists" before 1922 was the obligation of granting paid holidays to the workers, which the latter's unions imposed upon the employers (Pantaleoni, *Bolscevismo Italiano*, p. xvi).

[10] *Bollettino dell'Ufficio del Lavoro*, July–Dec. 1920, pp. 182, 191, 198, 207, 394, 400, 405, 504.

discharge, and the annual paid vacation are "Fascist innovations." [11] The truth is that the act concerning weekly or Sunday rest, which goes back to 1908, was not observed under the pre-Fascist regime, but neither is it observed today. The *Osservatore Romano* on November 14, 1931, wrote as follows:

Walk of a Sunday through the cities, towns, and rural districts, and everywhere you will find troops of workers applying themselves perhaps a little more strenuously than on weekdays. And by saying *everywhere* we do not exaggerate; he who goes outside his house on a holiday can observe this grievous and deplorable phenomenon for himself. It is a deeply rooted and widespread abuse. And not a soul bestirs himself to put an end to this indecency; the authorities are generally deaf, and the employers in the business firms, the managers of the factories, the official heads connive at the abuse. Most scandalous of all, one sometimes sees groups of labourers working on holidays in the pay of the municipalities. He who has occasion to go outside the city on Sunday—and we are now speaking of Rome—can notice that in the suburbs and in the outlying countryside work goes serenely on, without any scruple, from sunrise to sunset, as if this were the order and duty of the workers. The legal provisions concerning weekly repose are clear, but perhaps are not sufficient to guarantee complete observance of the Christian precept.

An act of June 16, 1932, renewed the prescriptions of 1908 and imposed heavier penalties upon all violators; but on July 16, 1932, the *Osservatore Romano* again deplored that "abuses against the laws prescribing observance of weekly and Sunday rest continued to be perpetuated not only in little shops, but in important industrial concerns as well." In September 1932, the secretary of the unions of commercial employees in the province of Turin stated that the law concerning weekly or Sunday rest commanded but little respect in practice (*Stampa*, September 3, 1932); and in October 1933, the president of the confederation of the unions in Commerce in his turn deplored the fact that the waiters were renouncing the weekly rest to which they were entitled (*Lavoro*, October 1, 1933). Therefore, in the fall of 1933 the government passed through the Senate and the Chamber another law on Sunday and weekly rest, which was promulgated on February 22, 1934. Everybody knows that the more the laws multiply for the enforcement of a

---

[11] Welk, *Fascist Economic Policy*, p. 102.

measure, the greater the indication that the measure is not respected—
corruptissima respublica, plurimae leges.

In September 1934, a national conference of the officials of the industrial unions demanded the abolition of work on holidays, "save in
exceptional cases," as a measure for combating unemployment: [12] this
is evidence that not even the law of February 22, 1934 was observed.
In the text of the agreement of October 30,1934 between the confederations of employers and employees in banking and insurance, we find
that the confederations asked the government "to intervene energetically" to induce the banking institutions connected with the government and the savings banks "to observe the schedule of working hours,
weekly and Sunday rest, and the Saturday-afternoon rest, since, when
they infringe the law on this point, the other concerns are forced to do
the same." Thus we have proof that the prime offender in disregarding
the law is the government itself.

There are employers who, after making their employees work on
Sunday or compelling them to work longer hours than the law permits,
are seized with remorse for having violated the law, and—refuse to pay
wages for the illegal work; but the Supreme Court has ruled that the
employer must pay.[13]

The obligation of the employer to pay his permanent employees an
indemnity upon discharge and to give them an annual paid vacation,
was introduced into all the Fascist labour agreements. But the employers
do everything they can to avoid fulfilling this promise. Out of 4117
disputes in the metal industry in the first ten months of 1930, 2274, i. e.,
more than half, concerned compensation for discharge, which the employers were trying to escape paying.[14]

In the *Lavoro Fascista* of August 31, 1934, a clerk, the father of five
sons, whose earnings after the 7 per cent of 1934 amounted to 500 lire a
month, related that he had asked his manager to pay him for the overtime work which during the last two years he had done "every day,
either at night, or at meal-times, or on Sundays"; the manager replied
that "a clerk ought not to work with his eye on the clock." The same

---

[12] *Corriere della Sera,* Sept. 2, 1934.
[13] *Industrial and Labour Information,* Dec. 4, 1933, pp. 301–2; *Sindicato e Corporazione,* Jan. 1934, p. 53.
[14] Rosenstock-Franck, p. 191.

newspaper, September 19, 1934, published a letter from a laundress almost seventy years old, who had worked continuously for thirty-six years under the same employer in the city of Catania, Sicily: she stated that her weekly wage of 31 lire, i. e., 5.17 lire a day, had been cut 16 per cent in 1930; she had been discharged; had she a right to demand back pay for the holidays which she had not taken? The newspaper replied that "it believed, it sincerely believed and expected that her grievances would soon be removed without fuss and excessive talk."

The same newspaper, November 1, 1934, published a letter from the foreman of a farm in Bitonto (southern Italy), who had worked on that farm since 1902 and whose salary had been cut in 1933 from 300 to 250 lire a month. He was now threatened with discharge. Had he a right, he asked, after working every day in the year during his thirty-two years of service, to demand an indemnity for the holidays which he had not taken? The newspaper replied in the affirmative.

One cannot expect the purification of the whole country through Mussolini's magnetic power alone. But the Fascist propaganda agents claim that such purification has taken place and they conceal all facts that demonstrate the contrary. That is why such facts must be recalled.

The labour exchanges, founded on January 5, 1919, were abolished by the Fascist government in 1923 and re-established in 1929 (see above, pp. 243–4). Of course they are represented as a Fascist invention. According to the official statistics, the labour exchanges provided 8,541,888 men with work in 1932.[15] There is nothing strange about these figures. The Fascist labour exchanges are not institutions placed at the disposal of the workers in order that they may freely have recourse to them if they are unable to find work by themselves. Every unemployed worker is obliged to register with them if he wishes to secure employment.

Formerly, the workers who migrated from one province to another during the weeks when the wheat was being reaped or the rice fields weeded or the olives picked, did not register at any labour exchange. They knew where work was to be found, and they went there without asking permission from any one. Today, the official statistics announce that the labour exchanges have given work during the year to 200,000 rice-weeders, 500,000 reapers, and 60,000 olive-pickers. Formerly, a

---

[15] Statement of the Under-Secretary of Corporations before the Chamber on March 10, 1933.

worker could move with his family from one town to another without asking permission from any one. Today, one cannot move a step without obtaining authorization from a "commission for domestic emigration" (law of April 9, 1931, Article 7). Heaven alone knows how much time is lost and how much harm is done to the poor people by this bureaucratic machine; but the official statistics announce that from 1929 to 1933 the commission has "withdrawn from unemployment the impressive number of 1,711,222 workers," [16] not one more and not one less.

[16] Official *communiqué* of April 25, 1934.

XVIII

Social Insurance

B Y A royal decree of February 11, 1923, the Fascist government excluded from the obligation of insurance against accident in the course of work, boys from 9 to 12 years old and men from 65 to 75, and deprived of their right to indemnity all workers suffering from slight partial disabilities, even if permanent, and small freeholders, leaseholders, and hired labourers suffering from temporary illnesses.[1] In 1922 the family of a worker who died as the result of an industrial accident received an average indemnity of 24,435 lire; by 1933 the indemnity had fallen to 20,654 lire. On the other hand, the life of an agricultural labourer increased in pecuniary value—from 6856 lire in 1922 to 7176 lire in 1932.[2]

In October 1929, a group of journalists visited Sicily, travelling, eating, drinking, and sleeping, not, of course, at their own expense; and from Sicily they sent to the newspapers of which they were correspondents statistics on the prosperity and happiness of the Sicilian people, particularly of the workers in the sulphur mines. The secretary of the union of these workers dispatched a protest to the *Lavoro Fascista*, November 2, 1929:

> The journalists said that the pit mouth was served by a lift which carried the miners 400 metres down into the mine. But the men are not allowed the use of this convenience; they can only reach the underground galleries by a descent with 2800 steps, making 5600 going and coming morning and evening. Thus, bearing in mind the four kilometres of road to the various villages, it is easy to see that the workers arrive at their task in a state of exhaustion. The journalists declared further that for the last two years there had been no accidents in the mines. The very day before the arrival of the party (October 16) a poor young victim had been crushed by falling material. And who has forgotten the victims of February 15, 1928? Seven dead and twelve seriously injured in one day. And three more killed this

---

[1] Villari, *Fascist Experiment*, p. 155, states that the law of 1917 was "revised and improved" in 1923; but he fails to explain wherein the improvements consisted.

[2] *Annuario Statistico Italiano:* 1922–5, pp. 314–6; *ibid.*, 1933, pp. 391–2; *Sindacato e Corporazione*, Sept. 1933, p. 356.

year? And all those who die in silence, poisoned by the fumes and the fire-damp? These disasters will continue until the mines are provided with the technical apparatus necessary to guarantee the safety of the workers. At present, no precautions are taken.

In the issue of November 14 the same newspaper published another letter, addressed to it by a group of workers in the mine which the journalists had visited. The workers stated that the information which the journalists had circulated had been given to them by one of the worst exploiters of the miners. In the mine, which employed 1200 opera-tives, there was not a single emergency station; in case of accident it was necessary to go about a mile for help.

In the sitting of the Senate on May 20, 1931, Senator Ciccotti observed that an official Fascist publication admitted that the number of accidents that actually happened was twelve times as great as the number reported, and lamented that the number of industrial accidents was mounting in Italy, while it was decreasing in France and in Germany:

> Any one who walks through the streets of Rome can see on the tops of high ladders men who have taken no precautions, although merely a safety belt would suffice to prevent an accident; lack of elementary precautions of this sort is found on an even wider scale in the provinces.

Even in agriculture, the number of accidents grows from year to year (*Sindacato e Corporazione*, September 1933, p. 356). Since the workers are not given any protection by their unions, their employers succeed more easily in economizing on the expenses involved in prevention of accidents: when the accident occurs, it is not the employer who pays, but the insurance company.

The *Lavoro Fascista*, June 8, 1934, stated that in 234 days of work the 300 street-cleaners of Milan had suffered accidents in the course of their work to the extent of one dead, 20 permanently injured, and 305 with temporary injuries. In one year and a half 633 accidents and 834 cases of illness had occurred: that is, each worker had had on an average two accidents and three illnesses a year.

In 1933 there were 394,759 accidents in labour; in 1934 the number of the cases rose to 490,800. The indemnities paid for such accidents rose from 176 million lire in 1933 to 228 million lire in 1934. Greater negligence on the part of employers in taking precautions to avoid accidents and greater fatigue of the workmen explain the increase.

In the sphere of insurance against unemployment, we have seen that the Fascist dictatorship can claim only the following merits: 1, it has limited the insurance to industrial labourers; 2, it has suppressed the annual governmental contribution of 50 million lire to the unemployment fund; and 3, instead of mitigating the distress of the unemployed by helping them with the money they contributed to the unemployment fund, it borrows from that fund in order to stop holes in the budget and to aid capitalistic undertakings (see above, pp. 241, 255).

The act of October 27, 1922, extending to all workers compulsory insurance against incapacity and old age, was reformed, after Mussolini seized power, by an Act of December 30, 1923, excluding share-croppers and tenant farmers from insurance.[3] Moreover, beginning with the fiscal year 1927-8, the government withdrew from the fund the annual contribution of fifty million lire which, according to the law of foundation, it was obliged to make.[4]

The authors of the law of 1919 built up the financial plan so carefully that between 1919 and 1928 a capital of 4.5 billion lire accummulated in the treasury of the Insurance Institute. In the fall of 1928, the government recognized that it was possible to increase the amount of the pensions, which the original financial plan had fixed too low.[5] The official Stefani agency communicated to the newspapers a little summary which announced that "according to the provisions of the democratic governments" old-age pensions ranged from a minimum of 574 lire to a maximum of 2015 lire, while "according to Fascist provisions" they had leapt to a minimum of 1035 lire and a maximum of 2548 lire:

> The Fascist Government from the time of its inception has always busied itself with plans for giving to the worker on the threshold of old age a pension that will enable him to face his declining years more calmly. Mussolini's government, which is the true protector of the working people, has effected a notable increase in the amount of workers' pensions.

To do otherwise, Mussolini would have had to abolish the laws of

---

[3] Villari, *Fascist Experiment*, p. 155, writes that "the provisions concerning old-age pensions and obligatory insurance against disability were modified and coordinated by the decree of December 30, 1923"; but refrains from explaining in what sense they were modified. Fantini, *La Legislazione Sociale*, p. 358, is still more audacious; he ignores the acts of 1919 and 1922 and assigns to the act of Dec. 29, 1923, the merit of "having dealt with the problem wisely and comprehensively."

[4] *Stato di Previsione della Spesa del Ministero delle Corporazioni: 1930–1*, p. 19.

[5] *Corriere della Sera*, Oct. 26, Dec. 11, 1928.

1919 and 1922 and to pocket the 4.5 billion lire which had been accumulating during the nine preceding years.

In January 1930, the president of the Confederation of Employers in Agriculture ordered that the peasants who had reached their sixty-fifth year, and were therefore eligible for a pension, should solemnly receive the certificate of their pension on April 21 "in order to celebrate Labor Day (which the Fascists celebrate on April 21 and not on May 1) as a tangible sign of the benefits guaranteed to the workers by the Fascist government." [6]

What a difference [commented *Lavoro Fascista* on January 25, 1930] between the ardent solicitude of a Government which is truly of the people, and the selfish indifference of the democratic administrations of the past.

The idea of using a pre-Fascist institution for the glorification of Mussolini was so brilliant that from 1931 onwards the certificates of the pensions for disability or old age have been delivered on April 21 amid great pomp to all the workers entitled to them, whether agricultural or industrial, as a gift from Mussolini.

When discussing this subject, the Fascists never fail to make it known that at the end of 1922 there were only 5482 pensioners, while on April 21, 1934 no less than 80,000 workers were receiving pensions on the ground of old age or incapacity: [7]

Not only have the talkative and deceptive democracies done nothing which even resembles the reforms accomplished in Italy, but they never will be able to do anything, because they lack the unity of direction and the national discipline which only the Mussolinian state can give to a people.[8]

The truth is that until the end of 1922 pensions could be obtained only by those who had voluntarily registered with an insurance institution for workers that had been functioning since 1898.[9] The laws of 1919 and 1922 provided that insured persons should not be eligible for benefit until they had reached the age of sixty-five and had paid contributions for a minimum of ten years in respect of old-age pensions; and they would be eligible for benefit in respect of disability only after paying contributions for at least five years. The years which have since

---

[6] *Lavoro Fascista*, Jan. 22, 1930.
[7] Article by Signor Biagi in the *Corriere della Sera*, Aug. 31, 1934.
[8] *Resto del Carlino*, April 21–2, 1934.
[9] Cabrini, *La Legislazione Sociale*, p. 126.

elapsed have seen a steady rise in the number of men or women who have fulfilled the required conditions, and consequently the number of pensioners has automatically increased. The Mussolinian state in this respect reaps what "talkative and deceptive" democracy had sown.[10]

During the years of the Fascist "conquest," many mutual-aid societies, managed by Socialists (see above, p. 288) had their headquarters and registers looted, and departed this life. On December 31, 1924, there still survived 5734 societies with 992,970 members, of whom 85,224 were women, and with property valued at 120 million lire.[11]

In 1926 the 2705 societies which had been "Fascistized," i. e., had accepted members of the Fascist Party as their managers, formed a "National Fascist Federation of Mutual-Aid Societies," with 700,000 members.[12] We may guess the fate of the other less docile societies. Many of the "Fascistized" societies were so well managed by the Fascists that they too disappeared.

A royal decree of May 6, 1928, ordained that labour agreements should contain definite provisions for the protection of workers in case of sickness.[13] This legislative measure, which generalized the custom already formed in the last years of the pre-Fascist regime, led the employers to promote the rise of mutual-aid societies in their factories. According to official statistics, the spread of these institutions among the employees in industry during recent years is portrayed by the following figures:

	Number of Societies	Membership
December 31, 1931	1453	1,049,537
December 31, 1932	1879	1,350,375
November 30, 1933	1672	1,104,935 [14]

[10] Schneider and Clough, *Making Fascists*, p. 9, discovered that "previous to the Fascist Revolution, Italy had obligatory insurance laws, but they did not function very well. Fascism has endeavored to enforce these laws and has passed new ones making old-age and unemployment insurance obligatory." It would be interesting to know in what country of the world the two authors have found laws which function "very well" enough to satisfy them.

[11] *Annuario Statistico Italiano: 1930*, p. 466; article by Signor Biagi in the *Corriere della Sera*, July 17, 1930.

[12] Figures given by Signor Biagi in the article cited above.

[13] *Industrial and Labour Information*, Jan. 23, 1933, p. 123.

[14] *Industrial and Labour Information*, Jan. 23, 1933, p. 123; *Annuario Statistico Italiano: 1933*, p. 185; *Sindacato e Corporazione*, Jan. 1934, p. 130. We give these figures, as usual, without guaranteeing that they are not invented either wholly or in part. Signor Bottai, in the review *Il Diritto del Lavoro*, for Sept.–Oct. 1932, p. 507,

The commercial employees possessed a single national association, whose membership was as follows:

December 31, 1931	199,335
December 31, 1932	218,609
November 30, 1933	220,000

Those employed in inland transport had, in December 1932, 14 societies with 38,370 members, a membership that increased to 56,000 in November 1933. The societies had a limited extension among the agricultural employees, who provided scarcely 87,565 members in December 1931; but the number had increased to 400,000 by November 1933.

The press of August 8, 1933, published an official *communiqué* in which the mutual-aid societies were represented as "one of the most important contributions of the regime." The *Corriere della Sera*, commenting upon this *communiqué* in the issue of August 9, 1933, admitted that there were institutions of this sort in Italy before the "march on Rome," but said that they had had a "limited and unsystematized activity." In this sphere as in others Fascism had manifested its "creative" power:

> Provision for the future and charitable assistance are not mere words under the Fascist regime: hundreds of thousands of men in their hour of trouble have known and still know to whom they may appeal for relief. This is the real Fascism, which infuses new blood into the veins of citizens, organizations, and institutions.

As regards most of these institutions, the Fascists can claim only the merit of not having destroyed them by violence or brought about their failure by bad administration. They are the remnants of a broader system that the Fascist cyclone has not completely swept away. Some of them —we do not know how many—have grown up in recent years through

---

stated that there were 1486 mutual-aid societies in Italy with a membership of 1,372,000; apparently he was thinking only of the workers in industry. If Bottai's figures and those in the *Annuario Statistico* of 1933 were correct, it would follow that between the time that Bottai wrote and Dec. 31, 1932, the number of societies increased while the number of members dropped. According to official statistics published in the review *Sindacato e Corporazione*, Jan. 1933, p. 60, there were 1254 societies with 1,043,439 members on Sept. 30, 1932, and 1447 societies with 1,195,592 members on Dec. 31, 1932. In a report presented to the Senate in Jan. 1935, Signor De Michelis stated that on Dec. 3, 1933, these societies numbered 1974 with 1,317,895 members (*Lavoro*, Jan. 15, 1935). Will it ever be possible to find two sets of Fascist statistics which agree?

the initiative of the industrial employers. These men see in the mutual-aid societies, controlled by the Fascist Party, an instrument whereby the workers may be rendered more docile: the worker who risks the loss of his right to a subsidy in case of illness, if he is put on the black list of the ruling party, will probably be much more submissive than the worker of the old regime, who kept his right regardless of his political attitude. The credit for this new state of things should undoubtedly go to Fascism.

On May 13, 1929, Italian industrial employers were obliged by law to insure their workers against disease contracted in the course of work, just as they had previously been insuring them against accident. The sick workers were on their part obliged to follow the treatment prescribed for them by the Insurance Institute. The regulation for the execution of the law of 1929 was not promulgated until four years later, in May 1933, and only in July 1934 were the workers able for the first time to secure the indemnities decreed by the law (*Lavoro*, May 18, 1934). Concerning the results of the institution it is not therefore possible to formulate a definite judgment at the present time. Anyhow here, at least, we find a new departure.

The law has already had some beneficial effects. In 1929 in Rome, the Association of Industrial Employers of the province founded a Labour Polyclinic on the model of a similar institution which had existed in Milan since 1910. Moreover, on May 31, 1931, a convalescent home was opened in the vicinity of Milan for the care of workers treated in the labour clinic of that city. The home had accommodation for ninety patients (*Corriere della Sera*, June 23, 1931). This institution owed its existence to Professor Devoto who, after founding the labour clinic in 1910, continued with the faith and tenacity of an apostle to collect for many years funds for the workers' home, and finally achieved his end, thanks to the generosity of the Milan Savings Bank. Since the Association of Industrial Employers in the province of Rome is a Fascist institution, and since the Savings Bank of Milan, after a century's existence, is now administered by the Fascists, it is only just to give the credit for the new institutions to Fascism, i. e., to Mussolini. On June 30, 1929, the president of the Confederation of Industrial Unions said in connexion with these institutions:

We know the industrial employers like to display these institutions as examples of their generosity. But the cost of these welfare institutions is met by the workers: the workers pay for them directly by the reduction of their wages.

In 1935 a new form of insurance was created as a result of the agreement arrived at in October 1934 by the confederations of employers and employees in industry (see above, p. 285). The workers, numbering about half a million, who have two or more sons under fourteen years of age and whose hours of work and wages have been reduced, will receive a supplement to their wages amounting to four lire (forty cents) a week for each son. When the worker loses his job, he will receive neither wages nor supplement. The supplement is paid from a fund which is formed by retaining one per cent of the wages of those workers whose hours of work do not exceed forty a week, and five per cent of the wages paid on hours exceeding forty hours a week. The employers contribute an equal amount to the fund. There is no danger that this supplement of forty cents a week will cause the workers' young sons to suffer from overeating. But the propaganda agents of Fascism now feel themselves in a position to announce to the world that another social problem has been solved in Italy by Mussolini's genius: the problem of assuring a wage supplement to the workers who are blessed with large families.[15]

---

[15] The correspondent of the *New York Times*, Jan. 20, 1935, did not fail to inform his readers that workmen with sons would get a supplement to their wages, but carefully refrained from adding that the supplement consisted of only forty cents a week for each son.

XIX

Housing

THE first associations for the construction of working-class dwellings arose at Florence and Verona in 1885. They were philanthropic bodies, not subsidized by either the central or the local government. In 1903 the central government began to encourage, by subsidies and tax exemption, municipalities and associations engaged in the construction of low-rent dwellings for the working classes or for public servants. As a result of these measures, by December 31, 1914, 528 co-operative building societies, 91 housing bodies connected with municipalities (*enti autonomi*), and 22 mutual-benefit societies were engaged in the construction of cheap dwellings, and by that date had provided 111,158 rooms.[1] The Milan "Institute for Cheap and Working-Class Dwellings," founded in 1908, had erected dwellings with an aggregate of 6507 rooms by December 31, 1915; the buildings were supplied with hot water, showers and baths, and seven kindergartens for 834 children to whom the municipality supplied school lunches. They also included day nurseries for babies, both weaned and unweaned; schools of cooking, sewing, embroidery, and laundry work for girls; five popular libraries; and, as a measure against tuberculosis, tenants were visited at regular intervals by doctors.[2]

The war paralysed this movement. But as soon as the war was over, the government energetically resumed its policy of encouraging building.[3] Under acts of 1919, 1920, and 1921, municipalities and other institutions interested in housing borrowed up to May 1922, 1,700,000,000 lire, with which to build dwellings aggregating approximately one hundred thousand rooms. Of this sum more than half was absorbed by Rome.[4]

On December 31, 1922, the Milan Institute was landlord of 12,400

---

[1] International Labour Office, *European Housing Problems*, p. 203.
[2] *L'Istituto di Milano per le Case Popolari*, p. 10.
[3] *Commerce Reports*, March 24, May 19, Dec. 6, 1919; Jan. 29, March 24, Aug. 11, 1920.
[4] Schiavi, *Come si è cercato di risolvere la crisi degli alloggi in Italia*, p. 463.

rooms with about 80,000 square metres of floor space.[5] In Rome the Institute for Popular Housing had under construction 3976 rooms in 1920–1, and at the end of 1922 possessed 17,304 completed rooms.[6] The Railwaymen's Co-operative, a national institution, owned 4395 rooms; its completed building programme was to have comprised 38,385 rooms.[7]

In Naples during 1920–1 dwellings aggregating 4387 rooms were either already built, or under construction, or projected; the city of Venice had provided 1755 rooms in 1921 and had 590 more under construction. The city of Turin had 2232 rooms either finished or under construction. In 1922 the city of Genoa was carrying out a five-year programme for the construction of 8729 houses.[8]

Would this movement have been arrested had Mussolini not seized power in October 1922? Would the houses under construction have been abandoned? Would those already completed have fallen into decay? Everything is possible. One fact, at any rate, is certain: according to a statement made in the Chamber by the Minister of Public Works on March 2, 1933, the municipalities and all the other bodies engaged in attacking the housing problem for the working classes built 193,000 rooms during the decade between November 1922 and October 1932. As during the period between 1903 and 1914 the same organs built 111,000 rooms, and as the tempo of the movement became much faster between 1919 and 1922, it is obvious that the results of the Fascist decade are anything but miraculous.

But the tourist who visits Rome and Milan is unaware of ancient history. He is conducted by the guide to inspect some recently constructed group of workers' houses, just as in the eighteenth century Prince Potemkin took Catherine II to the Crimea to admire some villages—which disappeared as soon as the Empress had seen them. The workers' dwellings in Rome and Milan do not disappear, but the tourist is told that popular housing in Italy was invented by Mussolini:

All over Italy, especially in the south, were communities living in fetid slums (as they still do in many cities in England) under conditions in which no human being should be allowed to live—as though the national health were not the supreme national asset. . . . The State remained essentially

---

[5] Schiavi, *op. cit.*, p. 478; *I provvedimenti adottati dal Comune di Milano*, p. 5.
[6] Schiavi, *op. cit.*, p. 472; *Tribuna*, Feb. 9, 1929.
[7] International Labour Office, *European Housing Problems*, pp. 214–5.
[8] Schiavi, *op. cit.*, p. 472 ff.

neutral, unmoral, and agnostic. . . . Against the neutral, non-interfering, unmoral and agnostic State, Fascism sets up the contrary theory. . . . Italy is a mother. . . . The cities are cleaning up and rebuilding their poorer quarters, erecting thousands of up-to-date model workmen's dwellings. . . . Foreigners do not always realize that these works are done in no boastful spirit, but from a new sense of public dignity and order, in response to a new public demand.[9] In ten years we have in a large measure solved the problem to which attention is least called, but which is nonetheless fundamental to Italian social development—the housing problem.[10]

How can the poor bamboozled tourist fail to gape in wonder and thank God for Mussolini? Here are a few ejaculations of this sort:

New domestic dwellings attest by their profusion the higher standard of comfort attained by the lower and lower middle classes.[11]

When I was in Rome, I saw some workmen's dwellings not to be matched in London. Since then the new working-class dwellings in Rome, to judge by the pictures, surpass those I saw, their architecture being superior to that of the flats built in Park Lane[!] for swells.[12]

The most impressive things for me personally in modern Italy are the new houses for the workmen: airy, roomy apartment buildings with modern conveniences, to which the workers have been transferred from crowded quarters in the slums.[13]

From an article published by Sir Leo Chiozza-Money in *The English Review* of May 1933 (p. 531) we learn that Sir Leo discovered the Italian Building Societies in 1926. In Milan he visited a group of workers' dwellings called the "Villaggio di Campo dei Fiori," and became ecstatic over the beauty of the ground-plan and the buildings. No one told him that these buildings had been built in 1919 by a Socialist municipality,[14] against which Mussolini was in 1919 pouring out torrents of abuse every day.

There was that English gentleman who upon landing at Hamburg was met by a one-eyed porter, and thereupon wrote to his wife that all German porters were one-eyed. Those who are taken to see working-

[9] Goad, *The Making of the Corporate State*, pp. 132–42.

[10] Statement made in the Chamber of Deputies on November 23, 1932, by Signor Olivetti, secretary of the Confederation of Industrial Employers.

[11] Marriott, *The Makers of Modern Italy*, p. 204.

[12] Sir Leo Chiozza-Money in *The New Leader*, Sept. 30, 1932.

[13] Miss Blankner in *New York Herald Tribune*, Oct. 10, 1933.

[14] Comune di Milano, *Annuario Storico-Statistico: 1919*, p. ccxxxxvii.

class dwellings in Rome and Milan imagine that all Italian workers, thanks to the generosity of Mussolini, have been provided with living quarters like those of Rome and Milan. Unfortunately the reality is quite otherwise. In 1926, when Sir Leo discovered that Mussolini had invented working-class housing for Italy and admired the "Village of the Field of Flowers" in Milan, attributing its creation to Mussolini, no one took him to see the sections of Milan where conditions were quite different. There still existed around the edge of Milan 526 horrible shacks of wood, straw, or sticks, in which 3000 persons lived thrown together in the most frightful squalor.[15] These shacks began to be demolished during the summer of 1928. And shacks still existed in January 1932 (*Lavoro*, February 26, 1932).

If one considers as excessively crowded the apartments in which there live on the average more than two persons in each room, one finds that in the city of Milan, one of the richest in Italy, in 1931, 50.67 per cent of the houses were excessively crowded out of a total number of 273,062 houses; 16,994 dwellings lodged more than three persons in each room (*Corriere della Sera*, July 10, 1935).

In the city of Genoa, "hidden by a sumptuous screen of palaces," there was in 1932, and there still is today, "a cluster of huts that seemed like a refuse dump" and in which "are crowded poverty-stricken people who lack too many things: space, air, light, water, furniture and sometimes even bread; nothing abounds but children"; "one must enter the dwellings, and if one is not horrified, it means that one is insensible to filth and the misery of one's fellow beings" (*Lavoro*, October 15, 1932). In one part of the city 25.5 per cent of the dwellings in April 1933 were in bad hygienic conditions. In these houses the number of those suffering from tuberculosis was nine times as great as in the houses in good hygienic conditions (*Lavoro*, April 14, 1933).

There were in Bologna during November 1933, 3500 homeless persons lodged in temporary barracks. This collection of people was described in the following words by the provincial secretary of the Party in a report of December 16, 1933:

It is one of the most melancholy sights one can imagine. There are 3500 persons, men and women, adults and children, living in shacks; eight, sometimes twelve of them living together in a single improvised room under con-

---

[15] *Corriere della Sera*, July 25, 1928.

ditions of infinite economic wretchedness, and what is more serious, of
infinite moral wretchedness.[16]

The French journalist, Monsieur Lachin, in the winter of 1935, after
having been conducted to visit some beautiful houses for workers of
Rome—that is, those houses which serve to bamboozle foreign visitors—
wished to visit also the village of Sette Chiese.

I ask a woman if this is really the village which I am seeking. "Yes, sir, it
is just that, a veritable cemetery." Two hundred little houses of bricks. More
than a thousand persons live in them. . . . Human beings live here. The
State has built this village for unemployed. Indeed, these lodgings are entirely gratuitous. An old woman says to me: "What have we done to the
Lord? My son was employed in the railway company. He is out of work
now. We have come to live here. We shall never get out of here again." An
old man seventy years of age weeps before me: "In the morning, when we
get up, we have a heavy head. The village is built alongside of pestilential
maremmas. I am old. I walk with difficulty. Nevertheless, every morning,
I am obliged to drag myself up as far as the summit so as to breathe the air,
for otherwise it would seem to me that I was suffocating. Happily, they
will soon transfer us from here to a new village. We do not live any more,
we are already condemned to death.[17]

In Rome, in July 1935, a little girl two years of age was crushed and
killed by a stone which had become detached from the walls of a grotto
in which her family lived (*Lavoro Fascista*, July 7, 1935). Those foreign
correspondents who from Rome describe in their newspapers Mussolini's housing policy and achievements, methodically ignore this kind
of fact.

Milan, Bologna, Genoa, and Rome are among the richest cities in
Italy. What the conditions must be in the poorer cities can be inferred
from what was said in the Chamber on March 1, 1933, by a Fascist
Deputy, Signor Catalani:

About a fifth of the population of Potenza lives in underground habitations called *sottani*, or dugouts, from two to five metres below the street
level; damp and miserable huts, unhealthy and dark rooms, beyond repair,
where death is easier than birth, where the most intimate aspects of life take
place in a dreadful *milieu* of sexual promiscuity; tombs where men, women,

[16] *Resto del Carlino*, Dec. 17, 1933.
[17] *La IVe Italie*, pp. 99–100,

and children live like beasts. These underground rooms get light only through their doors. There are a good 575 of them, of which 275 lack a chimney and 101 have no means for the disposal of refuse. In these dens languish 600 children, 1200 women, and 1200 men.

In the city of Matera, which Mussolini has made into the capital of a province, the working population, almost exclusively agricultural labourers, "is housed in caverns dug into the rock, row upon row like the cells of a bee-hive. These caves receive light and air only through the doors. The inhabitants, whether because of poverty or for some other reason, rarely make use of artificial illumination. The single room serves as kitchen and bedroom." [18]

According to a report (May 1933) of the mayor of Catanzaro, Calabria, the capital city of a province, like Matera, there are in that city 5566 dwellings, of which 1444 (i. e., 20.5 per cent) are below street-level. In these basements, or dugouts (*bassi* or *catoi*), there is usually no stove, and the food is cooked in the street in front of the door of the house; there are no latrines, and the house has nothing but a dirt floor; on an average, each of these underground dens is inhabited by 3.85 persons; but some have as many as thirteen inmates.

In October 1928 a party of journalists went to discover Sicily and found that everyone was rich and happy ever since Mussolini had taken the destinies of Italy into his keeping. The description which these journalists wrote of the life of the workers in the sulphur mines was so alluring that it inspires the reader with a longing to rush off to Sicily and become a sulphur worker. But the falsehoods were so startling and the workers protested with so much energy, that the secretary of the Fascist union of Sommatino and Riesi was obliged to address a letter to the *Lavoro Fascista*, in Rome (November 2, 1929), describing things as they really are. From this letter we quote the following passage:

It is not true that the company has commenced the construction of houses for the mine workers. The men have to go home on foot every evening to their respective villages, often four kilometres distant. Those who live on the spot are a few foreigners and the salaried officials, engineers, clerks, etc. It is they who occupy the "charming little cottages" which the journalists were led to suppose were occupied by the miners.

---

[18] *Lavoro Agricolo Fascista*, Nov. 30, 1930; Zanotti-Bianco, *La Basilicata*, p. 375 ff.

The farmhouses scattered over the countryside are often in no better condition hygienically than are the crowded habitations of the cities. In March 1931 in the village of Roncello, almost at the gates of Milan, a room collapsed in which nine people of all ages and both sexes were sleeping, killing the head of the family and two children, one of them 13 months old. The *Lavoro Agricolo Fascista* of March 15, 1931, commented on this accident in the following words:

The fate of that poor family might tomorrow become the fate of many other families; for years and years the majority of the farmhouses have not been inspected by a building expert, nor even by a humble mason, to make the most elementary repairs.[19] The catastrophe of Roncello has brought to light not only the bad state of disrepair prevalent among rural dwellings, but also the deplorable hygienic and moral conditions under which the peasant families are obliged to live, even within a few kilometres of Milan. Let not the case of this Roncello family be regarded as an exception: it represents the situation of, one may say, all of the numerous rural families in the northern section of the province.

A year later the same newspaper described the dwellings of the Lombard peasants in the following terms:

Three or four beds are lined up side by side without any passageway between them and here sleep the parents and the children of both sexes. Beside and under the beds are the provisions along with the *nécessaire* for night use. These hovels are frequently without air and light, the floors are rough-paved or earthen, and the plaster has fallen from the walls, permitting every sort of vermin to nest in them.[20]

An investigation made in 1933 showed that out of a total of 3,390,336 rural dwellings in Italy there were 142,298 which should be completely demolished; 475,122 which, to become fit for human habitation, required major repairs; and 930,000 requiring minor repairs.[21]

In the province of Genoa, 60.4 per cent of the houses need repairs, the water in most cases is drawn from suspicious sources and badly constructed cisterns, the drainage is very primitive, and abdominal typhoid and pulmonary tuberculosis are very wide-spread diseases. (*Lavoro*, September 7, 1935).

---

[19] Goad, *Making of the Corporate State*, p. 95: "No landlord may allow habitable houses to fall into disrepair."

[20] *Lavoro*, May 14, 1932, quoting the *Lavoro Agricolo Fascista*.

[21] *Corriere della Sera*, Aug. 17, 1934.

The pre-Fascist governments concerned themselves little with the rural areas because the peasants were less politically awakened than the great urban agglomerations. To this reason for neglect, there is to be added, as far as the Fascist regime is concerned, the fact that any beneficial action by the government in the country districts would not serve to glorify the Duce in the eyes of the tourists, who flock almost exclusively to the cities. The Italian government is today, above all, a publicity agency, and anything that fails to help publicity does not interest it. A Fascist deputy, Signor Caldieri, said to the Chamber on March 2, 1932:

We note with regret that it is more difficult for the Minister of Agriculture to find a few millions to subsidize, to the paltry extent of 25 per cent, the construction of rural habitations in the countryside, than it is for the Minister of Public Works to erect costly urban structures. The large construction enterprises succeed better than the small farmers in obtaining grants for large works.

In his speech of March 19, 1934, Mussolini revealed that "it is now time to concern ourselves with the peasants, if we want to keep them in the countryside; there are at least thirty years of work to be done in this sector; within a few decades all the rural inhabitants must have large and healthful houses, where generations of peasants can live and endure down the centuries as the secure and immutable foundation of the race."

According to the estimates of an expert in agriculture, Signor Mazzocchi-Alemanni, it would be necessary to allow from 4.5 to 6 billion lire for the tearing-down and rebuilding of the 142,000 houses which are totally unfit for habitation; from 5 to 7.5 billions for the repair of the 475,000 houses which are in bad condition; and from 4 to 8 billions for the 930,000 which are in need of lesser repairs.[22] A visit to Italy a few decades hence will enable us to see how much of this promise has been fulfilled. Meanwhile another propaganda campaign has been started all over the world, praising Mussolini for what he *intends* to do in order to supply the Italian peasantry with fine houses.

The rural home-building programme [writes the *Corriere della Sera*, August 27, 1934] will take about thirty years to carry out. Mere talk will not accomplish our rural policy. It is too gigantic a task, even if the work is

---

[22] *Corriere della Sera*, Aug. 17, 1934.

spread over a period of thirty years. We must wait until the plan outlined by the head of the government has been worked out in concrete detail and until its financial aspects have been fully considered. Fascism refuses to be visionary and unpractical when it fights and wins its battles.

Naturally, the news of Mussolini's latest triumph was rapidly carried to America. *Il Giornalino*, a periodical published by the Casa Italiana of Columbia University with the purpose of helping American students to learn Italian, made the following announcement in its issue of November 15, 1934: "The aim of the project is to improve the living conditions of the Italian peasant. It is estimated that the execution of the project will take thirty years. *The work will begin soon.*" No Italian newspaper had said that the work would begin soon. Information concerning Fascist activities and achievements swells as it crosses the ocean.

The reader must not infer that we blame Mussolini for not having accomplished in twelve years what a regime of liberty failed to accomplish in sixty. When the liberals assumed the government of a united Italy in 1860, the conditions of the rural population were abominable. There were provinces, for example that of Potenza, in which cemeteries were practically unknown: the dead were thrown into tombs in the churches to poison the air with their decay, or they were left unburied in some field among the nettles where the dogs went scavenging after them, dragging bones and half-gnawed skulls out into the roads.[23] Between 1860 and 1900 the most urgent problems were attended to as well as circumstances permitted. Between 1900 and 1922 problems began to be tackled which had hitherto been ignored. The work was carried forward after 1922, in some fields with greater and in others with less effort and results. There is still much slack to be caught up. No one can perform miracles. Neither Mussolini nor the men who governed Italy during its half century of free rule could solve in an instant all the problems which had been handed down for centuries from one generation to another. The objectionable point in Fascist propaganda is that it claims that nothing had been accomplished before Mussolini and that since his advent all problems have been speedily solved.

---

[23] Zanotti-Bianco, *La Basilicata*, p. 40.

XX

The "Battles" Against Tuberculosis
and Malaria

THE first centre of specialized research in tuberculosis arose at
Genoa in 1889. By 1921, it had developed to such a point as to
assume the name of "Institute for the Scientific Study and Treatment
of Tuberculosis." [1] In the decade before the World War, sanatoria arose
in many other cities of northern Italy, while in this sphere of civic
activity as in all others southern Italy lagged behind. In 1910, the
municipality of Milan built two sanatoria with a joint capacity of 233
beds.[2] In Bologna there arose in 1913 an "Association for the Prevention
of Tuberculosis," which in 1914 opened a dispensary and in 1915 founded
a home for the care of poor children. From 1914 to December 31, 1929,
the day on which these institutions became part of the Fascist system,
the dispensary examined 4512 adults and 2822 children, and treated 419
children in their homes.[3]

The war, which brought about an alarming increase in the number
of cases of tuberculosis, necessitated a more intense activity on the part
of both public and private associations. A law of 1917 offered financial
assistance to those local governments which built centres for the treatment of tuberculosis cases. In 1919 the city of Milan possessed, in addition to the sanatoria dating from 1910, a newer one containing 172
beds; it also began the building of a tuberculosis hospital for 500 patients; it treated 278 persons in its sanatoria, besides sending 440 patients
to the mountains and 483 to the seaside for treatment; 11,335 persons
were examined at the municipal anti-tubercular dispensary during that
year, and 1299 dwellings were inspected and disinfected.[4] In Florence,
in 1920, there were six institutions for the care of children threatened
with tuberculosis.[5] The Red Cross collaborated in this work; it maintained at Fara Sabina, province of Rome, a sanatorium which could

---

[1] *Lavoro,* June 2, 1931.

[2] Comune di Milano, *Annuario Storico-Statistico: 1919,* p. 117.

[3] *Resto del Carlino,* Sept. 6, 1930.

[4] Comune di Milano, *Annuario Storico-Statistico: 1919,* pp. civ, cxc, 117,
128–9.

[5] Sarfatti, *Guida della Assistenza,* p. 53.

accommodate 80 little boys and 30 little girls all the year round and an additional hundred children for about 45 days during the summer. In 1920 the Southern Italy Society opened a home for children threatened with tuberculosis at San Stefano d'Aspromonte, in the mountains of Calabria.[6]

The Fascist regime dedicated to the "battle" against tuberculosis a law of October 27, 1927, and another of May 20, 1928. All persons insured against sickness and old age (see above, pp. 296–8) must be insured against tuberculosis; tuberculosis cases must be isolated and cared for in special sanatoria; families of patients, when these are wage-earners, receive an indemnity of 6 lire a day for a period of six months; all persons belonging to the sick man's family must undergo medical examination and be isolated if found to be infected; in each province there must be a committee for the fight against tuberculosis; all the committees form a national federation; provincial committees and national federation supervise the medical service and each year organize weeks of health propaganda, during which money is collected. The National Insurance Institute, which receives the premiums of the insured workers, looks after the building and upkeep of the sanatoria. A special clinic for the study and treatment of tuberculosis was founded in Rome in 1928, and on December 1, 1934 a huge sanatorium for 1400 patients was inaugurated in one of the suburbs of Rome and dedicated to Mussolini.

Official *communiqués* in 1933 stated that institutions dedicated to the fight against tuberculosis could accommodate 7000 patients in 1922.[7] In a report of December 1, 1934, Signor Bottai stated that by 1937 there would be in Italy fifty-eight sanatoria with 18,686 beds.[8] In October 1934, a Fascist hygienist, Signor Morelli, in discussing this subject before the National Confederation of Italian Scientists, broke into the following pæan:

Before the fight against tuberculosis was organized, the death-rate from this disease in Italy was 30,000, and the number of tuberculosis cases reached 400,000. The head of the government, who devotes his life to the welfare of the Italian people and the improvement of the race, could not be indifferent to these figures. As a result of the methods employed by the regime, the

---

[6] Zanotti-Bianco, *La Basilicata*, plates facing pp. xvi and xxii.
[7] *Corriere della Sera*, April 23, 1933; official *communiqué* of Oct. 19, 1933.
[8] *Stampa*, Dec. 2, 1934.

tuberculosis death-rate has greatly decreased. The miracle of the resurrection began under Fascist auspices; in this sphere as in others the gratitude of the nation goes out to its great leader.[9]

On April 1, 1935, the president of the national federation stated in the presence of Mussolini that the death-rate for tuberculosis had dropped from 60,000 in 1924 to 35,000 in 1934; "in a little less than ten years, much has been accomplished in a sphere in which no progress at all had been made before the advent of Fascism."

The truth is that during the three years from 1887 to 1889 there were in Italy per million inhabitants 2128 deaths from tuberculosis; in the two-year period 1912–3 the number of deaths from this cause had declined to 1567 per million inhabitants. As a result of the war, in 1918 the deaths were 2090 per million, i. e., almost a reversion to the death-rate of 1887–9. But after the close of the war, conditions began to improve; by 1922 the tuberculosis death-rate had fallen to 1399, and the decline continued in the years that followed. In 1928 the deaths numbered 1240 per million inhabitants.[10] It was then that Mussolini discovered tuberculosis and initiated this new "battle." In 1929 the deaths per million inhabitants fell to 1240; in 1930 to 1120; in 1931 to 1080.[11] In the four years 1919–22, when the mortality from tuberculosis dropped by 33 per cent, no one thought of giving the credit for this decline to the prime ministers of the time. Mussolini receives all the credit for the decline which has taken place since 1922.

The fight against malaria is another ground on which the Fascist regime attributes to itself great achievements.

Deaths from malaria were very numerous in Italy in the nineteenth century. In 1887, 21,033 persons, that is, 7.1 per 10,000 inhabitants, died of this disease. In 1914, on the eve of the war, the number of deaths had declined to 2045, that is, 0.6 per 10,000 inhabitants. During the war, life in the muddy trenches and in the malarial zones of Macedonia and Albania produced a violent recrudescence of the disease. In 1918 the number of deaths from malaria in the civil population was 11,487, i. e., 3.2 per 10,000 inhabitants; these figures do not include those of the army and of the territories invaded by the Austrians at the end of 1917. At the close of the war, the struggle against malaria was vigorously re-

---

[9] *Corriere della Sera,* Oct. 13, 1934.
[10] *Annuario Statistico Italiano: 1930,* p. 67.
[11] *Ibid.: 1933,* p. 66.

sumed and the situation rapidly improved, although the improvement was accompanied by the oscillations customary in this phenomenon.

The following table shows the recorded malaria deaths from 1919 to 1923:

            1919 .... 6760, i. e., 1.8 per 10,000 inhabitants
            1920 .... 4223, "   1.1   "   "   "
            1921 .... 4848, "   1.3   "   "   "
            1922 .... 4085, "   1.1   "   "   "
            1923 .... 3307, "   0.8   "   "   "

From 1924 onwards, the statistics cannot be compared with those of the preceding years, because included within them is the population of the territories annexed to Italy as a result of the peace treaties. But if we take the figures of 1924 as a new point of departure, we reach the following results:

            1924 .... 4036, i. e., 1.0 per 10,000 inhabitants
            1925 .... 3588, "   0.9   "   "   "
            1926 .... 2683, "   0.6   "   "   "
            1927 .... 2582, "   0.6   "   "   "
            1928 .... 2925, "   0.7   "   "   "
            1929 .... 2705, "   0.6   "   "   "
            1930 .... 2781, "   0.6   "   "   "
            1931 .... 3101, "   0.7   "   "   "

One cannot see what achievements in this realm are to be attributed to Mussolini.

But in February 1932, when the *Official Gazette* published a *communiqué* declaring four little towns with a total population of 3000 to be exempt from malaria—one of the numerous announcements of similar tenor that have been issued during the last thirty years, as malaria has gradually been obliterated from Italian territory—the newspapers received the command to sing triumphal odes to Fascism:

> Four more Italian municipalities are exempt once and forever from the humiliating epithet, "malarial zone." Today's victory is perhaps modest in itself, but nevertheless it is another victory to add to the long list of those already won in the gigantic struggle initiated by the regime with the aim of freeing every section of Italy from the scourge of malaria.[12]

---

[12] *Stampa*, Feb. 1, 1932.

The struggle against malaria was, therefore, not continued, but initiated by the Fascist regime!

For the province of Rome, the statistics for deaths from malaria are as follows:

Pre-Fascist era: average	1912–14	111
	1918	831
	1919	426
	1920	165
	1921	188
	1922	131
Fascist era:	1923	128
	1924	336
	1925	367 [13]

We do not possess the figures for the years following 1925. We only know that the number of deaths from malignant fever increased from eight in 1929 to seventeen in 1930.[14] But a professor at the University of Rome and Fascist senator, Signor Umberto Gabbi, writing in the *Popolo d'Italia* on August 5, 1928, burst forth into the following dithyramb:

Within five years the Roman Campagna has been almost completely redeemed for the purposes of economic production and has been made a potential centre of healthful habitation. This great abandoned district is no longer the kingdom of the goddess Fever. Malaria is in large part conquered.

In September 1930, the official Stefani agency adduced as a proof of the continued decrease in malaria in the Roman Campagna the fact that the number of malarial patients in the hospitals of Rome had fallen from 2180 in 1925 to 1049 in 1926, 910 in 1927, 982 in 1928, and 957 in 1929. A year later, the *Annuario Statistico* for 1931, p. 59, contained the information that the cases of malaria reported in the province of Rome had increased from 8689 in 1929 to 11,377 in 1930. While the cases of malaria reported by the medical profession were increasing, the hospitals of Rome were reducing the number of their malarial patients. In this way, malaria was on the decline . . . in the hospitals and in the

---

[13] These figures are taken from the following sources: Lutrario, *La Malaria in Italia; Annuari Statistici* from 1914 onwards; and Direzione Generale della Statistica, *Statistica delle Cause di Morte*, 1919–23, and later volumes.

[14] *Osservatore Romano*, Feb. 20, 1931.

official statistics. He who looks in the *Annuario* for 1933, p. 57, for the cases of malaria reported in 1931, will be agreeably surprised to find that the relevant figures are not quoted in the statistics. That year was the year in which the work of reclaiming the Pontine Marshes began. In Italy it is generally known that in their desire to have things done, that is, to have things done in a hurry, the reclaimers of the soil neglected to take serious precautions against malarial infection. Consequently, malaria spread at an alarming rate among the workers imported to this unhealthful region from other parts of Italy. This explains the failure of the statistics to record the cases of malaria notified by the medical men.[15] Naturally, these matters are not mentioned to distinguished foreigners who are taken to see the places which were formerly the Pontine Marshes and are today the scene of one of Mussolini's most advertised "victories."

The Italian newspapers of July 10, 1935, gave the news of a visit made by a group of Russian, German, Roumanian, South American, etc., doctors to the Eastman Institute of odontology of Rome, and they let it be known that the visitors had admired that "achievement of the regime." No one had explained to those visitors that many other cities of Europe possessed analogous institutes, and that all these institutes had been built and donated through the generosity of an American philanthropist. All the merit of the Fascist regime in the "achievement" of the Eastman Institute in Rome is reduced to not having impeded its erection.

Mussolini's glories are epitomized in the figures showing that under

---

[15] We had just written the above words, when we read in the *Corriere della Sera* of July 13 and 15, 1934 two articles by Professor Coletti, a Fascist "expert," explaining "how malaria had been conquered in the Pontine Marshes." By rescuing the facts from the flood of verbiage in which Professor Coletti has immersed them, we learn that deaths from malaria increased from 0.9 per one thousand inhabitants in 1930 to 1.8 in 1932, then fell to 0.073 in 1933; and that the number of persons infected for the first time with this disease increased from 29% of the total number of cases in 1930 to 41.7% in 1932, then fell to 11.5% in 1933. It should be borne in mind that the cases in 1930 occurred among a population of 6000 persons, while by Jan. 1933 the population had grown to 30,000 (*Corriere della Sera*, Aug. 11, 1934). Thus there were 54 deaths in 1930 and 540 in 1932. These figures show that the reclamation of the Pontine Marshes was initiated in 1931 without adequate precaution against infection; only in 1933 did the government become conscious of its duty to protect the health of the workers. The figures for 1933 contain a shocking revelation of the negligence of 1931 and 1932. No one thought of building an aqueduct for the new centres of habitation. Consequently, during 1932 and 1933 water had to be brought from Rome in tanks.

him the Italian death-rate has declined. Under Secretary Biagi, in an article published in the *Corriere della Sera*, August 11, 1934, was made the following triumphant announcement:

Health institutions have been established in Italy, thanks to the Fascists, and have been extended and intensified. As a result of such activities, the conditions of life of the Italian people have enormously improved.

And to prove "how true this was," he pointed to the fact that the death-rate had declined from 14.8 per thousand in 1931, to 14.6 in 1932, and to 13.5 in 1933. He found it advisable to ignore the fact that the death-rate in Italy had been declining since 1872, when it was 30.5 for 1000 inhabitants. It stood at 19.1 during the quadrennium 1911-4. The figures went up tremendously, of course, during the World War. In 1919 the death-rate was 18.7, but by 1922 it had already gone down to 17.6. This means that the death-rate declined by 1.1 points in the course of the three years 1920-2, and that it has declined by 4.1 points during the twelve years 1923-34. If the proportion of the pre-Fascist triennium 1920-2 had been maintained, the decline during the twelve years of Fascist rule would have to be represented by the figures 4.4 and not by the figures 4.1. Note that in the years immediately following the war deaths from wounds, from diseases (tuberculosis and malaria) spread by the war, and from privations suffered during those years, must have been very numerous. Even the figures for the death-rate, when examined honestly, do not extol the glories of Mussolini.

XXI

The Protection of Mothers and Infants

U NDER the pre-Fascist regime there existed not only the maternity
fund to aid women employed in industry during the month following confinement; in addition, local governments, private associations, and charitable individuals maintained institutions that assisted
mothers before and immediately after child-birth, protected the infants during their earliest years; took care of illegitimate children, or-
phans, weak, rickety, undernourished, or tubercular children; sent the
weak children to the seaside or the mountains or kept them in permanent colonies until they became strong.

In Milan in 1919 midwives paid by the city made 13,793 home calls
and handled 1048 deliveries. The municipality maintained an emergency
station which rendered service to 7481 women. There was a hospital for
expectant mothers. An institute took care of suckling as well as weaned
babies during the hours when the mothers were at work outside their
homes, or gave aid to indigent mothers who nursed their own babies at
home. Another institute chose and placed wet-nurses, arranged for visits
to nurslings, and distributed milk to babies whose mothers were unable
to nurse them. Another institute spent large sums for nursing service. In
1919 the local branch of the National Association for the Protection of
Foundlings took care of 268 children, of whom 78 were under 5 years of
age. A provincial foundling home had under its tutelage 4928 children
of unknown parents. An orphan asylum kept 828 boys and girls. Other
institutes took care of abandoned minors and wayward children. Twelve
doctors regularly examined the children of the elementary schools and
sent away 2861 children afflicted with tuberculosis, conjunctivitis, otitis,
etc. A large corps of lady inspectors, one for each group of 1000 pupils,
aided the doctors. Each school was provided with a room fully equipped
for emergency cases. There were special schools for abnormal children.
For frail and weak children there were "colonies" in the mountains and
at the seaside.[1] Venice was also well known for its many fine institutions

---

[1] Comune di Milano, *Annuario Storico-Statistico*, 1919, pp. 118, 223, 232, 247,
250–4, 325, 329, cxii, cxvii, cclxxvi; *Sei Anni di Amministrazione Socialista*, pp. 83 ff.

for the protection of mothers and children. Altogether the cities of northern and central Italy were well equipped with beneficent institutions. The rural population, however, received less attention than that of the cities.

In September 1923 the Fascist government extended the application of the law for the maternity fund to many groups of industrial women workers who had not been provided for in the act of 1910. Consequently the number of insured women workers rose from 643,870 in 1922 to 822,385 in 1925, out of about 1,100,000 women workers employed in industry. In January 1929, the law was broadened to include women workers engaged in commerce. Thus in 1931, 1,220,000 out of about 1,500,000 women employed in industry and commerce, were insured. But there was not a proportionate increase in the births, which, after rising to 37,791 in 1925 and reaching the maximum of 44,030 in 1930, fell to 35,839 in 1931.[2] In view of the fact that the number of insured women doubled, while the births remained almost stationary, it was possible from 1929 on to increase the benefit from 100 to 150 lire and to compel women to abstain from work during the month before childbirth. Moreover the two months of rest are considered a period of involuntary unemployment and the woman worker receives also an unemployment benefit of 250 lire.[3] Four hundred paper lire in this day of devalued currency would be equal in purchasing power to a little more than the 100 gold lire provided by the act of 1910.

All the other institutions, both public and private, which at one time took care of mothers and infants, were by an act of December 10, 1925, placed under the supervision of a national organization for the protection of mothers and infants (Opera Nazionale per la Protezione della Maternità e dell'Infanzia) which began to function in 1927. It was a huge bureaucratic machine composed of a national council in Rome, a provincial council in each province, and one or more committees of patrons in each city. This machinery was so cumbersome that in 1933 it became necessary to simplify it by abolishing all committees and substituting commissioners in their place.[4]

Naturally the directors and the officers of the national organization

---

[2] *Annuario Statistico Italiano: 1933*, p. 388. These are absolute and not relative figures.
[3] Fantini, *La Legislazione Sociale*, p. 389.
[4] *Corriere della Sera*, May 30, 1933.

must belong to the Fascist Party and enjoy the confidence of the party leaders. Assistance to mothers and children has become an instrument of political pressure in the hands of the party in power.[5]

The organization has a large income of its own, made up of 100,000,-000 lire yearly from the tax on bachelors and a yearly contribution of about 12,000,000 lire from the legal organizations of employers and employees. With this income it should be able to take care of those needy cases which the existing local organizations cannot reach and this work should benefit especially southern Italy where local initiative is less efficient.

What have been the achievements of the new national organization? An official report of June 27, 1933, stated that the number of institutions dependent on the national organization had risen from 5914 on December 31, 1932, to 7429 on March 31, 1933.[6] But another official report of October 18, 1933, stated that "about 6000 institutions" existed in December 1925. Evidently these are the 5914 institutions referred to in the report of June 27, which were assigned to the latter part of 1932. Therefore, the increase from 5914 to 7429, boasted about in the last report, took place in seven years, not in four months. Of the 1515 new institutions which came into being between December 1925 and March 1932, we do not know how many were due to the efforts of the national organization and how many were due to the initiative of private organizations and individuals, which had nothing to do with governmental measures and which had manifested itself before Fascism and will continue to do so even after Fascism.[7] According to an official *communiqué*

---

[5] The press of July 12, 1932, published an official *communiqué* under the following headline: "Even boys not enrolled in the Balilla (the Fascist national organization composed of boys from 8 to 14 years of age) will be admitted to the summer colonies." The text of the *communiqué* said: "Even the boys not enrolled in the national Balilla organization are now admitted to the mountain and seaside summer colonies. But on admission membership cards will be given to them gratis and they will join the ranks of the Balilla without expense and without formality. The aim of the measure is not to round up members. The organization has no need of it. The purpose is rather to give to a greater number of families the advantages of various kinds which the membership card brings to the holder." The *communiqué* did not explain what would happen to the child whose parents refused the membership card.

[6] *Industrial and Labour Information,* July 31, 1933, p. 187.

[7] While the report given to the public on June 27, 1933, had stated that in March 1933 the existing institutions numbered 7429, another official *communiqué,* of Oct. 26, 1934, whose author had certainly forgotten the preceding figures, announced that the institutions in question numbered 6661 in Oct. 1933 and that 900 new institutions had been created between Oct. 1933 and the same month in 1934. God alone knows which is the truth.

of December 20, 1934, the institutions "created or in existence" from 1926 to 1934 numbered 7500. This would mean that only 70 new institutions had come into existence from March 31, 1933, to December 1934.

The national organization publishes a flood of statistics, and to increase the effect of its statistics it adds the figures of one year to all those of preceding years, so that it has been possible to read in the newspapers of February 11, 1934 that the national organization and all the institutions dependent on it had given assistance to 1,200,000 mothers and 3,500,000 children from 1926 to the end of 1933. By December 1934 the total number of mothers and children assisted had increased to six millions.[8]

In order to judge the value of these figures one should be able to differentiate the institutions that arose in the Fascist era from those of the period before 1923. Unfortunately, the pre-Fascist institutions did not as a rule publish statistics because their charitable activity was not a matter of "propaganda." Nevertheless one fact should be noted: in Fascist statistics we find no distinction made between what the national organization does in northern Italy and what it does in southern Italy, where the need is greater. This silence leads to the suspicion that the funds of the organization are diverted principally to northern Italy, as the practice has been for seventy years, with all activities centralized at Rome.

If one inquires into some field of activity concerning which we have statistics for the pre-Fascist period, it becomes possible to reduce to their true proportions the miracles wrought by Mussolini.

An official report published in the press of May 19, 1933, stated—and this is repeated by the propaganda agents of Fascism abroad [9]—that of the 1621 seaside and mountain "colonies" existing in Italy in 1932 for the children who were weak, lymphatic, or threatened with tuberculosis, etc., hardly 60 existed at the end of 1925, before the new national organization began to function. But from the report on Lombardy made by Signora Garzanti-Ravasi in 1929 (Vol. II, p. 150 ff.) it appears that before 1926 there were 164 colonies in Lombardy alone, of which 127

---

[8] *Stampa*, Dec. 21, 1934.

[9] Report of D. M. Fraschini to the Tomarkin summer school at St. Moritz, Switzerland, in the *Corriere della Sera*, Aug. 17, 1933.

existed before 1923. Since Fascist statistics for the period before 1926 are false, it is natural that they should appear suspicious even when they would have us believe that the number of colonies rose from 1621 in 1932 to about 2000 in 1934 and that the number of children taken care of by the colonies rose from 100,000 in 1923 to 225,000 in 1931 and to 506,635 in 1934.[10] But another official *communiqué*, whose compiler had forgotten the preceding figures, announced on July 5, 1935, that 506,655 children were expected during the following summer to enjoy health resorts, as against 405,142 who had received this advantage in 1934.

If we are to believe the review *Le Vie d'Italia* for August 1935, p. 630, the 60 colonies which the women's Fascist organizations ran in 1925 had risen by 1935 to 3000, of which 2000 were helio-therapeutic, 5 thermal, 350 at the seashore, 280 in the mountains, 33 on the rivers, 3 on the lakes. Even granted that these figures are correct, one should ask how many of those 2940 colonies, which have joined the 60 colonies of 1925, had been created before 1925 by other beneficent organizations.

According to Fascist propaganda, it is due to the national organization that the number of women who died in childbirth fell from 3111 in 1925 to 2900 in 1930 and that the number of still-births, which were 48,-117 in 1925, fell to 35,000 in 1933.[11] But examination of statistics for the years prior to 1925 discloses that deaths connected with child-bearing were 2982 in 1921 and 2810 in 1922, that they rose to 3632 in 1924 and fell again to 3111 in 1925, and that in the five successive years there was a gain of only 200. The number of still-births fell from 56,768 in 1923 to 48,078 in 1925; that is, there was an improvement of 8000 in two years, while after 1925 there was an improvement of 7000 in eight years. In this field, therefore, the national organization counts for nothing.

With reference to the mortality of children who have not yet reached the age of one year, Under-Secretary Signor Guidi-Buffarini stated in the Chamber on March 14, 1935, that during the three years 1920–2 the average annual death-rate of infants in this category was 127.4 per 1000, while in the three years 1931–3 this mortality had fallen to 111.7, with a gain of almost 16 per thousand; and credit for this should go to Mussolini. If he had compared the last pre-Fascist triennium 1920–2, not

[10] *Enciclopedia Italiana*, XIV, 880; *Corriere della Sera*, Sept. 27, 1934.
[11] *Corriere della Sera*, April 7, 1933; *Resto del Carlino*, April 6, 1933.

only with the triennium 1931–3, but also with the triennium 1909–11, he would have discovered that in the last eleven years of the pre-Fascist era the average had declined from 150.8 [12] to 127.4, i. e., there had been an improvement of 23 per thousand, a gain considerably higher than that accomplished by Mussolini during eleven years of the Fascist regime.

Tourists visiting Rome, after being conducted about to admire the work of reclamation in the Pontine Marshes, the low-cost dwellings for the working class, the clinic for industrial diseases, and the clinic for tubercular diseases, are also taken to admire the maternity dispensaries, the clinics for convalescing mothers, the *crèches* for infants, and the kindergartens where the Montessori method is used. The institutions that are visited are always those that are maintained with the greatest care. Rome, on which the government spends an enormous sum of money, lends itself better than any other city to this kind of display. But even in other Italian cities there are not lacking old and recent institutions that have no reason to envy those in Rome and the finest in the rest of the world. The Fascists and those Fascist propaganda agents who introduce themselves to tourists as anti-Fascists [13] explain that when Mussolini came into power Italy was in a state of "complete decay and deplorable abandonment"; it was necessary "to start all over again"; [14] "only the Fascist government has been able to solve the problem completely." [15]

In these matters the tourist follows the method of false generalization; that is, basing his judgments on what he is shown and made to see and not on what he does not see, he bursts into enthusiasm and writes home that "in every town and indeed in many villages, institutions have been founded to help and advise mothers of every class." [16] Some even discover that "the small boys and girls that you see in school and street are cleaner, sturdier, a finer little race than they were but a few years

---

[12] *Annuario Statistico Italiano: 1913*, p. 36.

[13] "About the children's services in particular I have heard *strong anti-Fascists enthusiastic in praise.* Every school child is entitled to free medical attention and free dentistry. They are sent, if the doctor declares it necessary, to holiday-camps in the hills or by the sea. If they are in need of it, they get food and clothing and boots free of charge" (Chief editor of the London *Daily Herald*, June 5, 1935).

[14] *Corriere della Sera*, Feb. 1, 1928.

[15] Speech of Signor Fioretti in the Chamber of Deputies, May 18, 1934.

[16] Mrs. Bywater, *Saving Italy's Babies*, in the London *Daily Telegraph*, May 9, 1934.

ago," [17] that is, Italian children have become finer because of Mussolini.

There is not an international congress where the question of the welfare of mothers and children is discussed that does not see one or more Fascist "experts" taking the floor to point out how many litres of milk were distributed in one year in Italy to mothers, children, and the sick; for example, 4,813,945.35 litres in 1931—not even the fraction .35 is omitted. They describe the health and hygiene institutions of Milan and for them they give credit to the Duce and the Duce only. They conceal the fact that those organizations were almost all established during the sixty years that preceded Fascism. They withhold the information that the Milanese institute for low-cost and working-class dwellings, which in 1921 allotted 27.23 per cent of its expenditures to hygienic and cultural purposes, had by 1929 reduced the expenditures to 1.89 per cent.[18] The delegates stand agape before so many marvels and the chairman of the congress "pays homage to Fascist civilization" and exclaims:

The achievements of Milan on the field of health institutions required two factors: the inspirer and the executor. The city of Milan was the executor and succeeded in fulfilling the dream of modern hygienists. But the inspirer was indispensable, and as you know who was the inspirer I need not name him. It is to him that we are indebted for strong modern Italy.

These words were uttered by a Swiss hygienist, Professor Flessinge, at the Tomarkin international summer school of advanced medicine at St. Moritz, after two Italian professors had expatiated on the litres of milk distributed all over Italy in 1931 and on the health institutions of Milan.[19]

---

[17] Hamilton, *Modern Italy*, p. 25. Everywhere there is a dictatorship, be it Communist or Fascist, be it in Italy, Germany, or Austria, Mrs. Hamilton rushes there, finds out that all is right, and publishes a book in which she sings the praises and benefits of the dictatorship.

[18] Schiavi, *Come si è Cercato di Risolvere il Problema degli Alloggi in Italia*, p. 471; *Corriere della Sera*, March 13, 1929.

[19] *Ibid.*, Aug. 19 and 23, 1932.

XXII

Women and Boys in Factories and the "Battle" Against Illiteracy

T HE best way to protect mothers and the rising generations would be to keep them away from arduous and unhealthful occupations and to create enough schools to meet the needs of the entire youthful population. In the pre-Fascist era, the laws on the work of women and children in factories remained a dead letter in those parts of Italy where there were no labour unions strong enough to compel their enforcement. Nor have conditions improved in the Fascist era. In October 1929, the newly mined material in the sulphur mines of the province of Caltanisetta was being transported on the shoulders of young boys (*carusi*), who toiled up and down thousands of stairs:

It would be idle to speak of hygienic and humanitarian provisions for the work of boys under fifteen. When the journalists arrived, the boys from eleven to fourteen years old were sent away from the mine by the foremen according to orders received from the local management. This happens every time that the employers wish to make a good appearance and receive congratulations. As for hours of work, the eight-hour day, decreed by Article 4 of the labour agreement, is only a fiction. The miners work from ten to fourteen hours a day.[1]

A union official, writing in the *Lavoro Fascista* on November 6, 1929, confirmed these statements, adding that "sometimes local conditions were worse than those which had been described."

A lady who in 1929 made a careful investigation into the conditions of the children in Lombardy—one of the richest and most progressive regions in Italy—wrote the following in regard to the mountainous zone of that region:

Born amid great privations, these children, *even before they are six years old*, are set to work. At school and even in kindergarten the children are already tired when they arrive, having been wakened in the early hours of

---

[1] *Lavoro Fascista*, Nov. 2, 1929.

the morning to help their mothers in the fields and to lead the flocks to pasture. School is regularly attended, but the children are too worn out to receive any real benefit from their instruction.[2]

The work of boys, forbidden by the written law but permitted by the unwritten law, allows employers to cut the wages of adult workers by threatening to give their places to boys. The following words were written in the *Corriere della Sera*, September 10 and 24, 1931, by Signor Biagi, who was then a high official in the industrial unions and who in 1932 became Under-Secretary of Corporations:

In moments of crisis, the employer is inclined to reduce wages, cutting them to their legal minimum. . . . The managements find it convenient to substitute boys for men, since the latter have reached a higher wage level, while boys can be hired at the minimum rates provided for in the agreements. Thus, men who are still vigorous and who almost always have families dependent upon them, are discharged. The employer very often tells them that he can no longer afford to hire them. Occasionally he re-employs them, not on the old terms but as new employees at the minimum wage.[3]

In the *Lavoro Fascista*, July 22, 1933, we read:

In the factories boys are assigned the most miscellaneous types of work: from the humble task of cleaning the buildings to the transport of material, from the function of the specialized workers to that of carriers of tools.

Another union official lamented, in the *Lavoro Fascista*, August 2, 1933, that in the brick-making industry the employers demanded from the women and boys the same production as had previously been furnished by adult men workers and thus saved about fifty per cent on the wages of their employees: [4]

In the brick-making factories, a woman employed at a machine for the manufacture of common bricks transports, in 8 hours of work, 3000 raw bricks, weighing altogether 1.5 tons. The transport is effected by means of wheelbarrows along an average distance of 170 yards in a period of 4

---

[2] Garzanti Ravasi, *Inchiesta*, p. 45.

[3] This phenomenon has received in Italy the name of "rejuvenation" ("svecchiamento"). "The fortieth year," wrote the *Lavoro Fascista* of Aug. 4, 1931, "is the critical period which, according to the employers, marks the limit beyond which they cannot guarantee permanent employment to the workers in their factories"; and it demanded that at least the ex-service men should be protected against this menace.

[4] Goad and Currey, *The Working of a Corporate State*, p. 29, have made the discovery that "women must receive equal pay for equal work."

minutes, so that the woman covers 14 miles in a day. Each machine turns out between 17,000 and 18,000 bricks a day. The weight of the material for each machine is 2½ tons. This is transported on carriers borne by five women, who carry as much as 43 tons of material in 8 hours of work. In the factories where cement blocks are manufactured, the weight of the mould, usually operated by women, is 135 pounds. This mould has to be carried about 2 yards and placed at a height of 1½ yards by a single woman. This operation is repeated about 700 times a day, so that the total force required is equivalent to that used in lifting 3.5 tons. The facts which we have enumerated can be verified in different establishments. From 1929 to 1931, among 20,000 workers in the trade 22% were ill for an average period of a fortnight. Among the women workers the percentage of illness was 30%, with an average period of 40 days. It is interesting to point out that 57.4% of the cases of sickness occurred among women between 18 and 25 years old; 19.2% among those between 25 and 30 years old; 16.2% among those between 30 and 40; and 7.1% among women over 40. This shows that young working women especially are subject to sickness.

In a national conference of the officials of the industrial unions, held in Rome on July 13, 1934, one of the officials deplored that "the habit was spreading of giving to women and young boys work suitable only for grown men. This was doing great harm to the adult male workers." [5] From the *Lavoro Fascista*, September 1, 1934, we derive the following information:

At Sesto [province of Milan] there is a factory which makes electric batteries. The work among acids and leads is done by women employees, who are compelled to wear trousers, leggings, and masks.

In the old era local governments, private associations, and public-minded individuals maintained kindergartens and furnished the children of poor families who attended the elementary schools with lunches, clothing, books, and school supplies. The central government encouraged these enterprises by subsidizing them. In 1915 there were in Italy 4587 kindergartens which by 1922 reached 5902. At least 25,000 kindergartens would have been needed to provide for the 2,500,000 children from three to six years of age. The existing kindergartens took care of scarcely 397,610 children. Moreover, many kindergartens were located in ill-suited or absolutely unhealthy buildings, were entrusted to teachers who were unfit and led a precarious existence with an uncer-

---

[5] *Lavoro Fascista*, July 14, 1934.

tain income.[6] It was a state of affairs of which everyone felt ashamed. Finally the new era came into being in the fateful October of 1922. By the school year 1924–5 the number of kindergartens had been reduced to 5828. The reduction was in reality greater since for the first time there were included, in the statistics of 1924–5, 413 kindergartens in the territories formerly belonging to the Austro-Hungarian Empire which were annexed to Italy as a result of the World War.[7] Even in the city of Milan, so proud of the number and good maintenance of its kindergartens, these fell from 69 in 1919 to 56 in 1925.[8]

In the official statistics for the school year 1926–7 we find that the number of kindergartens suddenly rose to 17,076 with an attendance of 607,891.[9] But according to the *Enciclopedia Italiana*, there were no more than 9546 kindergartens in 1930;[10] and in the school year 1931–2 the official figures gave 9321 kindergartens with an attendance of 750,553.[11]

These figures would seem to show that kindergartens decreased in the first two years of the new era, then increased rapidly from 1926 to 1930, and then decreased again in 1931. In that year, according to the government commissioner who was at the head of the national organization, the latter was subsidizing 3300 kindergartens.[12] But according to another official *communiqué*, of February 1935, the kindergartens subsidized by the national organization numbered only 1452 in 1933, and rose to 3534 in 1934.[13] Let us hope that some day at least a semblance of order will be brought to these statistics, so that they will be less inconsistent.

However all information that comes to us from trustworthy sources attests to the fact that there has been considerable progress in this field. The Fascist Party seeks to make itself master of the new generations by imbuing them in their earliest years with its propaganda. Therefore it pays much attention to kindergartens. In the former Austrian territories, kindergartens are used to "Italianize" the German and Slavic children and they have increased from 413 to 596 in a few years.[14] Nevertheless

---

[6] Lombardo-Radice, p. 94; Garzanti-Ravasi, II, p. 13.
[7] *Annuario Statistico Italiano: 1927*, p. 69.
[8] Comune di Milano, *Annuario Storico-Statistico: 1924–5*, pp. 503–5.
[9] *Annuario Statistico: 1933*, p. 74.
[10] Vol. XIV, p. 879.
[11] *Annuario Statistico Italiano: 1933*, p. 74.
[12] *Popolo d'Italia*, Oct. 28, 1932.
[13] *Resto del Carlino*, Feb. 17, 1935.
[14] *Enciclopedia Italiana*, IV, p. 944.

the problem of kindergartens is far from being solved. Any one reading the important report made by Signora Garzanti-Ravasi on conditions in Lombardy in 1930 (II, p. 17 ff.) will find that the number of kindergartens leading a precarious existence for lack of funds and located in unfit and unhealthy quarters, with uncompetent teachers, is still very high. And Lombardy is the richest part of Italy, where kindergartens were first established on a large scale. Conditions in southern Italy continue to be frightful. But today no one is any longer ashamed of this because every one is under a duty to repeat that Mussolini has solved this problem with his magic wand.[15]

A report of February 9, 1934 announced that in the preceding year, 1933, there had been distributed all over Italy 3,364,544 school lunches at a total cost of 2,881,507.43 lire.[16] But according to a report of February 1935 the lunches distributed in 1933 had been 6,020,700 at a total cost of 2,167,452 lire; and the lunches distributed in 1934 numbered 11,956,802 at a total cost of 4,418,566 lire.[17] It is obvious that when the author of the second report invented the figures for 1933, he was ignorant or forgetful of the figures which had been invented a year earlier. Anyhow, even if one admits that these statistics were not invented, one should remember that in 1919 Milan alone distributed to the children of its schools 2,907,407 free lunches at a cost of 889,696.36 lire.[18]

Mrs. Hamilton, in *Modern Italy*, p. 27, informs us that she was assured "by those in a position to know" that "no discrimination is made in the schools between children who join the Balilla and the children who remain unenrolled." Unfortunately, there is in Italy a review, *Problemi del Lavoro*, written by former Socialists, now converted to Fascism,

---

[15] At the congress of the Fascist institutes of culture, Nov. 21, 1931, an orator asked the central Board of Directors to publish a handbook which would indicate what Fascists should say on certain subjects. He, for example, wanted to know what he should have said in a lecture on the "famous southern problem on which no definite word has as yet been uttered." He was right; the problem of improving economic, social, and moral conditions in southern Italy, on which there exists a whole library, has taxed many minds of Italy for half a century. A voice interrupted him: "That problem no longer exists!" Another voice continued: "The Duce has solved it!" (*Educazione Fascista*, Dec. 20, 1931, p. 1122.) Signor Gentile, a university professor, presided at this congress, and several other university professors attended.

[16] *Resto del Carlino*, Feb. 10, 1934.

[17] *Ibid.*, Feb. 17, 1935.

[18] Comune di Milano, *Annuario Storico-Statistico: 1919*, p. 328.

who are allowed now and then to publish some mild criticism so that it can be said that there is freedom of the press in Italy. A contributor to the review wrote the following in the issue of December 1930:

At the beginning of this school year, parents were again requested to enroll their children in the Balilla. An unfavourable decision by parents may be prejudiced to the granting of aid to indigent students. It is tantamount to forcing the entire school population into the Balilla organization, since the parents have no real freedom of decision and cannot refuse to enroll their children without exposing themselves to the suspicion of being anti-nationals and seeing their children deprived of aid.

The Fascist law of June 26, 1923, made school attendance compulsory up to the age of fourteen, and thus by implication raised the minimum age for admission to work from twelve to fourteen years; but the law remains a dead letter. In 1932, 9933 certificates of admission to work in Italian industry were issued for boys of ten and 13,895 for girls of twelve; 9823 for boys and 9464 for girls of thirteen; and 9581 for boys and 711 for girls of fourteen.[19] According to the law of 1923, all these boys and girls should have been going to school. In the spring of 1933, there was talk of raising the minimum age for admission to work to fourteen years for ordinary employments and to fifteen years for the mines. It was hoped that in this way unemployment among adult workers would be reduced (*Lavoro*, April 1, 1933). But the new law concerning the work of women and children, which the Fascists promulgated in January 1934, allowed the minimum age to remain unchanged at twelve years.[20] Miss Currey, however, is certain that in Italy there is no child labour and writes: "In Italy the age is fixed by law at 15. *These are matters of fact, not of opinion*" (*International Affairs*, Sept. 1935, p. 748).

One of the indications of economic and social progress in Italy during the half century preceding the advent of Fascism was the decrease of illiteracy. In 1872, after the crisis which had wiped out all the despotic governments from Italy, scarcely 31% of the population knew how to read and write. The number of persons knowing how to read and write went up to 38% in 1882; to 52% in 1901; to 62% in 1911; to 73% in 1921. The last figure drops to 72%, if the territories formerly subject to

---

[19] *Sindacato e Corporazione*, Feb. 1934, p. 394.
[20] *Bollettino del Lavoro e della Previdenza*, Nov. 1931, p. 650 ff.; *Sindacato e Corporazione*, Jan. 1934, p. 123.

Austria and annexed to Italy as a result of the World War are eliminated from the reckoning; these regions were in a better condition than the rest of Italy and therefore raised the general average by one point.[21] On the eve of the "march on Rome," illiteracy had practically disappeared among the rising generation of northern Italy, and had been sharply reduced among the youth of southern Italy. Of the young people who attained their twentieth year in 1927, and therefore had gone to school before the war, 87% knew how to read and write.[22]

In the spring of 1929, Deputy De Francisci, who in 1932 became Minister of Justice, published a table showing that the number of illiterate persons had decreased from 27% of the population in 1921 to 21% in 1927.[23] The last datum was invented, because the census of illiteracy is taken in Italy every ten years, together with a general census of the population, and no such census was taken in 1927. But the figures invented by that future Minister of Justice continue to circulate in the newspapers,[24] and have penetrated into the school text-books.[25]

The census was taken in April 1931. In the previous censuses, a person who could read any sort of printed matter, for example a newspaper, was considered as literate. Consequently, many boys who had reached their sixth year and were attending school, were counted as still illiterate. In 1931 the Central Institute of Statistics changed the rule, and decided that all children from six years upwards who had begun to ink their fingers and maltreat their spelling-books in an ele-

---

[21] *Annuario Statistico Italiano: 1922–5*, p. 71.

[22] *Annuario Statistico: 1931*, p. 79.

[23] *Camera dei Deputati, Legislazione, XVIII, Disegni di Legge e Relazioni*, 14A e 14 bisA, p. 18.

[24] The *Giornale d'Italia* gave them first in the issue of May 30 and then again in the issue of July 4, 1929. Dr. Marraro, in *Current History*, Feb. 1933, p. 572, did not content himself with reproducing the statistics that were circulated in Italy, but put into circulation others, still more magnificent, on his own account: "While between 1921 and 1923 the Kingdom reduced illiteracy from 69 per cent of the population to 27 per cent, 10,800,000 individuals over six years of age in 1923 were unable to read or write. Careful estimates made in 1927 showed that the percentage had been reduced to about 21 per cent. This means that during the first four years of the Fascist regime, a total of 2,400,000 Italians had been taught to read and write."

[25] Crinò, *Imago Mundi*, pp. 43 and 193: "According to the census of 1871, 71 out of 100 persons could neither read nor write. According to the last census [1921], 27 per cent of the population were illiterates. But, thanks to the watchful foresight of the national government, this percentage has diminished during recent years. . . . The percentage of illiterates, which in 1921 was 40 per cent [!] had in 1928 fallen to 25 per cent, and continues to decrease all the time." The author, who is a professor of geography at the University of Messina, gives these figures without realizing their inconsistency.

mentary school, should be considered as knowing how to read and write.[26] Everybody in Italy knows that many small children are registered at a school, but give it up during the year and soon forget the little they have learned.[27] For the Central Institute of Statistics the new rule had the merit of swelling the figures of the literate, so that the Fascist regime could claim the merit of having combated illiteracy more efficiently than had the pre-Fascist regime.

Yet the census of April 1931 revealed that the number of persons knowing how to read and write had gone up during the last decade only from 73% to 79%; that is, illiteracy had declined at a slower rate than between 1901 and 1921. If, instead of considering as literate all the six-year-olds who were enrolled in schools, whether they attended them or not, the census had considered as literate only those who could read a newspaper, what results would have been obtained?

It is worthy of note that the Central Institute of Statistics, in publishing the new data in the *Compendio Statistico Italiano: 1932*, p. 96, suppressed the figures for 1911 and 1921 and contrasted the figures for 1931 with those for 1871 and 1901, thereby concealing the slackening that had taken place during the decade from 1921 to 1931. When the King of Italy opened the session of the Chamber of Deputies on April 28, 1934, he rejoiced that "illiteracy was on the wane and in many parts of Italy had disappeared entirely." An achievement, it was understood, to be attributed to Mussolini.

---

[26] The fact was revealed by Professor Coletti in the *Corriere della Sera*, Feb. 10, 1933.

[27] Lombardo-Radice, *Scuole, Maestri e Libri*, p. 64; Zanotti-Bianco, *Basilicata*, p. 259.

XXIII

The "Dopolavoro"

ANOTHER national welfare organization which the Fascists make much of is the "Dopolavoro" ("Afterwork"). This organization takes care of the recreation of Italian workers during their leisure hours. In glorifying the achievements of this institution as of others, Fascist propaganda attributes to Mussolini not only what has been accomplished in Italy since October 1922, but everything that had been accomplished there from the beginning of the world to the fateful "march on Rome."

The Italian Alpine Club was founded in 1863. In 1880 it had 4000 members; in 1914, 10,000; and after the war, 40,000. The first cycling club in Italy was founded in 1870. A national organization was formed in 1885. In 1886 an Italian, Verri, won the international track championship. The first open-road race across Italy was held in 1909. In 1893 the first soccer club was founded by Italians and Englishmen at Genoa. In 1894 was founded the Italian Touring Club, which soon became popular all over the country. As early as the first decade of this century its publications were held in high esteem for their scientific and practical value, and for their typographical excellence. In 1910 the club had a membership of 83,603, which by 1920 had risen to 162,336. In 1910 the Italian Cross-Country Union was formed. Another club whose popularity quickly spread was the Italian Workers' Excursion Society, with headquarters in Monza, Province of Milan, and branches in the principal centres of northern Italy.[1]

Musical bands were a special passion with the people, especially in southern Italy. Little towns, crushed under a burden of debts and taxes, somehow managed to maintain good bands. Well known as early as the 'nineties were the bands of Chieti, Pratola Peligna, Pianella, and Lanciano, in the Abruzzi; and those of Acquaviva delle Fonti and Sansevero, in Apulia.

In the post-war years, sports spread rapidly over Italy, as over all the

---

[1] *Enciclopedia Italiana*, II, p. 658; VIII, p. 340; X, p. 208; XI, p. 503; XIV, p. 307.

other countries of continental Europe. In 1920 Italian contestants participated in practically all kinds of sports in the Olympic Games held at Antwerp, and made a respectable showing. A correspondent of the London *Times*, on July 10, 1929, acknowledged that "sport was widely practised in Italy before Fascism":

In mountaineering, cycling, and fencing the Italians have long excelled, and some of the climbing feats performed by the Alpini during the War made a great impression upon their colleagues of the Allied Armies. From the very outset bicycles were received in Italy with an enthusiasm that has never died down. Since the War, sport, and more particularly games, have developed remarkably. In Italy, as elsewhere, the greatest increase in popularity has been won by football. The small clubs founded by foreigners resident in Genoa, Turin, and Milan between 1893 and 1899 have spread all over Italy. Italy was already in line with other countries in devoting more and more attention to sports of all kinds.

The article was written, however, to emphasize the merits of Fascism even in this field, and so the correspondent could not help adding that, thanks to Fascism, "the old type of habitual loafer in the café or wine-shop is gradually passing away." The *New York Times*, also, on October 30, 1932, had this to say:

Italians, as a whole, are endowed by nature with excellent physique, but in past years they did little to exercise their bodies. The idea of perfect bliss of most of them was to sit in cafés ogling the girls, and the few who actively took up sport were rather contemptuously regarded by the majority. Now, the juvenile organizations of the Fascist Party give every boy an opportunity to indulge in sports, and this has led to a general awakening of interest.

In other words, before the "advent of the saviour" Italy was full of loafers, drunkards, and dandies. Then came Mussolini, and there was light.

It is impossible to ascertain how many associations in the pre-Fascist era were devoted to athletics, sports, cultural training, workers' amusements, etc., for at that time there was no idea of placing these institutions under the control of a single political party and making a statistical survey of them.

In 1925 all athletic and sports societies, choral societies, bands, university extension groups, night schools, circulating libraries, pleasure clubs, etc., were "Fascistized," or, as they say in Germany today, *gleichgeschaltet*, that is, they were compelled to join a national organization consisting of a government commissioner, a dozen or so national committees, and an infinity of provincial and local committees, directorates, inspectors, etc.[2] The finest buildings of the old Socialist organizations, like the Spreti Palace in Ravenna[3] and the People's House in Rome,[4] after being confiscated were donated by the government to the Dopolavoro.

On December 5, 1926, the following declaration appeared in the press:

> The Secretary-General of the Fascist Party has ordained that the Italian National Olympic Committee shall be considered a dependent organ of the Party, which will supervise all activities concerning physical education and sport.

This decision created surprise in Italy and protests abroad, for it had always been supposed that sport was neither Fascist nor anti-Fascist. In order to dispel these "diverse and alarmist comments," the Secretary-General of the Party announced in the press on December 19, 1926, that this measure "should absolutely not be interpreted as putting restraints upon the federations, the clubs, or the individual athletes"; but he added:

> The youth of Italy is now entirely Fascist. Since everything which is Italian is placed under the nation's flag, it was only logical that the sporting world should likewise be ranged under its shadow. We must not forget that sport not only develops the race physically, but gives rise to moral and political phenomena which must be followed and watched.

This signified that those sport clubs which refused to submit to Fascist supervision, would be dissolved forthwith.[5]

---

[2] Fantini, *La Legislazione Sociale*, pp. 430 ff.

[3] The ownership of the Spreti Palace was vested in a group of leading Socialists, as political parties were not entitled to hold property. When the Prefect of Ravenna transferred the palace to the Fascists, the Socialist *Avanti*, August 26, 1926, made the following comment: "The decree of the Prefect of Ravenna establishes the principle, new indeed in Italy, that private property—for the People's House of Ravenna was, legally speaking, private property belonging to certain citizens—can be expropriated without indemnity and handed over to another entity at the discretion of the government. This means that private property is no longer sacred in Italy. This measure may have incalculable consequences in the whole domain of the law. We shall not complain of that."

[4] Royal Decree, Jan. 24, 1929, n. 124.

[5] The newspapers of Sept. 14, 1933, reported that the Secretary-General of the Party, in his capacity as president of the National Olympic Committee, had ap-

Many privately owned dance halls were closed "for reasons of morality," and anyone who wishes to dance must enrol in the Dopolavoro and dance under the shadow of the lictoral fasces.

Needless to say, a flood of statistics has been let loose purporting to show how many workers during a given year have gone mountain-climbing, taken part in athletic games, attended literary and scientific lectures, visited museums, etc. In the old era no one knew how many individuals in Italy rent the slumber of their neighbours with strumming of mandolins. In 1928 it was possible to learn that Italy had been afflicted in 1927 with 49 societies of mandolin-players, and that in 1928 the scourge had risen to 225 societies (*Tribuna*, May 8, 1928). The latter figure does not show that between 1927 and 1928 there arose through Mussolini's efforts 176 new societies, but rather that 176 old societies were discovered and forced to become "Fascistized" during this period. The Fascists have not yet come to the point of publishing statistics on the number of kisses exchanged under the auspices of the Dopolavoro, but these will soon be counted, and the staggering total will be attributed to the genius of Mussolini. For the time being the *Compendio Statistico 1934*, p. 259, informs us that in 1933 the members of the Dopolavoro had participated in precisely 1,155,365 excursions, musical performances, cinema performances, sports exercises, etc. In the summer of 1934 the musical band of Chieti, clad in black shirts, was sent on a tour through the United States to display its excellence and to show that, if it had not been for Mussolini, even the arts of blowing the trombone and beating the drum

---

pointed the presidents of the various Italian sport associations, all of which are under the supervision of the Olympic Committee. Even the Italian Chess Association must be presided over by a Fascist appointed by the Secretary-General of the Party. The English weekly, *The Observer*, which has always been enthusiastic about Mussolini, announced on April 15, 1934, that in the Italian Golf Federation all club presidents, secretaries, and committees must now be Italians; "all clubs must obtain the consent of the Commissione Federale del Golf (an organization subordinate to the Federazione) before arranging inter-club matches; they must advise the Federazione in advance whenever they intend to hold a committee meeting; they must obtain its consent before engaging or dismissing members of the club staff or making structural alterations; all players competing for cups must pay a special fee to the Federazione; in addition all non-Italian players must pay a special daily tax to this organisation and obtain a tessera (identity card) in order to use an Italian course." Golf is a sport in which the English tourists to Italy frequently join when on their holidays; which explains why the English paper did not look favourably upon the regulations and asked the following question: "Will Italian golf survive the innovations?" As long as this sort of restriction had been applied to other sports, the English journal had had nothing to object to; for it was natural that Italians should not be allowed to play even a game of chess without being supervised by the party in power.

would have vanished from Italy. The Chieti band had been famous for half a century.

The worker who seeks recreation must register in one of the institutions subordinate to the national Dopolavoro. In order even to fish or bowl it is necessary to belong to a club controlled by the Dopolavoro, and to pay dues (of five lire yearly up to August 1930, and two and one-half lire since then) to the national institute, as well as local dues. In return, a member enjoys special privileges: reductions in the prices of theatre, cinema, and railway tickets, etc. The members of the unions are all in duty bound to join the Dopolavoro. Anyone not attracted by the privileges will soon find himself enrolled by order of the higher authorities,[6] and let him try to protest if he dare!

One of the activities of the Dopolavoro deserves particular mention because it is really new and good: the "cart of Thespis." One musical and three theatrical companies tour Italy, transporting in trucks actors, choruses, musicians, and the equipment necessary for the erection of temporary open-air theatres in places without regular ones. According to the official statistics, in 1933 the three theatrical companies visited 114 towns, and the musical troupe, 49.[7]

An Italian Fascist told the Rev. H. W. Fox of a serious weakness in Italian life before the advent of Fascism:

> What was wrong with our working-people before the War was that they used to think and talk too much about politics. They were all right when they were working, for then their minds were on their work; they were all right when they were asleep, for then they didn't think at all, at least consciously. Their leisure hours were a danger-spot for the whole nation.[8]

To remove such a "danger-spot" was the main purpose for which the Dopolavoro was founded. And that worthy servant of God, the Reverend Fox, gave the foregoing words his whole-hearted approval, even though suspecting that such a system "might not be applicable to other

---

[6] This is what the president of the Dopolavoro in the Fiat factories at Turin had to say in the presence of the provincial secretary of the Fascist Party on May 12, 1934: "Last year the number of employees in the Fiat voluntarily joining the Dopolavoro reached 75 per cent; as a consequence the provincial secretary of the Party was able to acknowledge the fitness of our organization, *making enrolment compulsory*" (*Stampa*, May 13, 1934).

[7] *Resto del Carlino*, Feb. 2, 1934.

[8] The London *Spectator*, Feb. 6, 1932.

countries." In a country like Italy, "where private or local initiative was lacking, it was probably inevitable that the state should step in with a centralized scheme; perhaps post-war Italy needed a paternal government in order to re-create the nation." In any event the Dopolavoro did not serve merely to keep the Italian workers from the dangerous practice of thinking; it was also "a means of keeping the workers from wasting their money and fuddling their heads in the wine shop when they come back from the fields or the factories at the end of the day." The propaganda method is always the same: the more they depreciate the Italian people, the more reason for the dictatorship. "In order to exalt a regime, they do not hesitate to dishonour a people." [9]

Not all Fascists are in agreement with the Reverend Mr. Fox. Some of them admit that in the beginning "there were not lacking shrewd ones who saw nothing in the Dopolavoro but a trick to tame the proletariat," but insist that these were mistaken:

Let us be frank. The idea has prevailed for a long time among a part of the old ruling class that those creations of Fascism which aim at conquering the masses are nothing more than red herrings to make the masses forget their inferior position. We must destroy the idea that such work is motivated by tactical and opportunist considerations. If we accepted it, the Revolution would amount to an imposture foisted on the Italian people, giving them idols in whom we do not believe. This sort of farce is not conceivable in the Italy of Mussolini. If anyone still entertains these ideas, the real facts would be enough to contradict him. [10]

Thus far, however, there has been no evidence to show that the "shrewd ones" were mistaken. The Dopolavoro serves not only to "tame" the workers but also to spy on them. In the beginning of 1932, a certain Testa, director of the Dopolavoro in the Miani and Silvestri factories of Milan, had the following notice affixed to the entrances of all the factories:

Obeying my orders, four of our comrades and a woman have succeeded in discovering the plot of a radical organization. We have given over the members of the plot to the courts. Those comrades have received the well-earned reward of 150 lire each. (Signed) Lieutenant Testa. [11]

---

[9] Sforza, *L'Âme Italienne*, pp. 154, 159.
[10] *Corriere della Sera*, July 5, Oct. 22, 1932.
[11] This document was published at Paris in the anti-Fascist weekly *L'Operaio Italiano*, Feb. 27, 1932, and its authenticity was never denied.

Sports have been systematically turned into an instrument for nationalist and militarist propaganda. One of the highest personages of the regime, Signor Maraviglia, wrote:

Sport is not an end in itself. It is no longer a matter of personal choice. Organizations are not built up in accordance with personal tastes, but along military lines. In this transformation of sports, we see one of the most interesting and important phases of Fascism. Fascism avails itself of the various forms of sports, especially those requiring large groups of participants, as a means of military preparation and spiritual development, that is, as a school for the national training of Italian youth. By popularizing and militarizing sports requiring large groups, Fascism accomplishes perhaps its greatest governmental work. All Italian youths placed under the same discipline will begin to feel themselves soldiers. In this way there is built up in spirit a formidable militant organism which is already a potential army.[12]

To sports, thus distorted in purpose, the Fascist government has given all possible encouragement. Italian champions, trained and maintained at government expense, have in recent years been among the first in many international contests. In the Olympiad at Los Angeles in 1932, Italy came second only to the United States and held first place in certain categories of sport, namely, fencing, cycling, pentathlon, gymnastics, and shooting. Yet, in precisely the same categories in which she distinguished herself in 1932, precedents can be found in 1920. For example, in 1932 she took the seventh place among the competing nations in track and field sports;[13] in 1920 she had stood sixth.[14] One-fifth of her points in 1932 were due to her prowess in fencing;[15] in 1920 the London *Times* (Aug. 20) contained the following comment:

Italy gained a great victory over France in the foils team matches. Both teams were represented by their most expert foil fencers, and no more brilliant display of foil fencing has been seen in modern times.

In the Olympiad of 1932 Italy won the title for shooting;[16] in March 1920 an Italian was proclaimed world champion in the international shooting contest at Monte Carlo.[17] Still another achievement of Italian

---

[12] *Tribuna*, July 5, 1929.
[13] *New York Times*, Aug. 9, 1932, p. 15.
[14] *Ibid.*, Aug. 24, 1920, p. 1.
[15] 53½ points out of a total of 262½ points, according to the unofficial point tabulation of the *New York Times*, Aug. 15, 1932, p. 17.
[16] *New York Times*, Aug. 13, 1932, p. 11.
[17] *Ibid.*, March 28, 1920, p. 18.

sportsmen in 1920—the year of "Italian bolshevism"(!)—was the winning of the Schneider Cup by an Italian aviator, a victory that was repeated by Italy in 1922.

There is, however, this difference between the victories of 1920 and those of 1932. Those of 1920 were the victories of private individuals or organizations. The Fascist government now provides organization, money, and publicity. The champions of 1932 were selected, supported, and subsidized by the home government to an extent unknown twelve years before. It is perhaps characteristic of the changed governmental attitude towards sports that in 1932 the *Lavoro Fascista* in all seriousness proposed that a life pension or a life job should be conferred upon Signor Beccali, who won the 1500-metre run at Los Angeles, establishing a new Olympic record.[18] The achievements of private individuals and organizations are not comparable with those of institutions lavishly subsidized and strictly regimented by the government.

In conclusion, no more than a few fresh initiatives can be accredited to the Fascist dictatorship in the so greatly glorified field of social legislation, besides the bureaucratic centralization of all those institutions which once battled against tuberculosis, assisted maternity and infancy, and aimed at promoting the recreation, education, and sports of the workmen. To maintain those institutions wages are subjected to deductions which amount to 4.5 per cent of the wage.[19] Furthermore there has been a notable increase in the number and in the activities of these institutions under the impulse of the new bureaucracy. Would the increase have been greater, lesser, or equal, if the dictatorship had left at least in these fields a free hand to private initiative? To this question the Fascists reply concealing all that which the Italian people had done through free co-operation prior to October 1922 and affirming that the iron hand of "the man of destiny" has created all there is of good existing in Italy. Even one who does not accept this doctrine can recognize that in this field not all the merits which the dictatorship attributes to itself are imaginary. Only, in appraising those merits, one must not forget that sports and assistance to children have become vehicles of partisan propaganda, of nationalistic exaltation, and of warlike drill. In striking the final balance one must take into account negative as well as positive factors.

---

[18] *New York Times*, Aug. 20, 1932, p. 4.
[19] *The Economic and Financial Situation of Italy*, p. 43.

XXIV

Professional Classes and Public Officials

THERE are no statistics illustrating the economic conditions of the professional class. No one therefore is in a position to say how many Italians of this class are unemployed and even suffering the pangs of hunger.

If we are to believe the statement made on April 18, 1935, by Signor Pavolini, the president of the Confederation of Professional Classes, ten per cent of these classes are unemployed. But in view of the Fascist habit of always softening the gravity of unpleasant facts, it is probable that the unemployed are far in excess of this figure. I learned from a reliable source that an inquiry aimed at ascertaining the numbers of university graduates who were out of work gave the figure of 150,000. The figure was so disheartening that it was never given to the press.

In 1913, on the eve of the World War, the Italian universities turned out 4271 graduates trained for the liberal professions. There was a general opinion at that time that the legal profession was overcrowded, but, on the whole, it cannot be said that there was an alarming degree of unemployment among the intellectual classes in Italy. The fifteen years preceding the war were for Italy as for the rest of the world a period of great economic progress and of uninterrupted development of the public services. The young men who emerged year after year from the institutions of higher learning were practically all absorbed without difficulty by private business and by the service of the national and local governments.

After the war, the number of young people graduated from the universities increased to 6697 in 1919; 9102 in 1920; 9365 in 1921; 9046 in 1922; 11,140 in 1923. But this increase did not bring about any perceptible measure of unemployment. During the war, 60,000 officers had been killed, a third of whom may be safely put down as having come from the liberal professions, and the epidemic of influenza in the winter of 1918 also carried off many intellectuals. The newcomers took the place of those who had disappeared. Moreover, during the decade 1913–23, the population of Italy increased from 35 millions to 39.5 millions, and it was natural that the growth of the population should have been accompanied by a corresponding growth of the intellectual classes.

Under the Fascist regime, thanks to the raising of the school fees with the avowed purpose of "disencumbering" the universities, the number of those completing their professional training has diminished slightly, but it is still very much higher than it was during the pre-war period: 8237 in 1924; 7495 in 1925; 7400 in 1926; 7033 in 1927; 8702 in 1930; 8606 in 1931; 8651 in 1932. While from 1913 to 1931 the population increased from 35 millions to 41 millions, that is to say, 18 per cent, the number of professional men turned out by the universities increased, roughly, 100 per cent.

In the early years of Fascist rule, this exuberance of the university population did not disturb the social equilibrium, for then the posts rendered vacant in the public administrations by the dismissal of "anti-nationals," could be filled by the young men who could present the membership card of the Fascist Party. There were, moreover, new offices, created by thousands, in the organizations created and con-trolled by the Party—legal organizations of employers and employees, authorized associations of public officials, associations of the profes-sional classes, youth organizations, Dopolavoro, etc. The holders of such offices were not members of the bureaucracy strictly speaking, but were invariably remunerated at the expense of the country. During the first five years of its existence, the dictatorship created employment for not less than 150,000 persons. It had something to offer to each batch of young intellectuals when they arrived on the scene year by year.

But the economic crisis brought about by the revaluation of the lira, and then the world depression, changed the situation. The economic enterprises under private initiative no longer absorbed but discharged workers both manual and intellectual. On March 21, 1928, a Fascist deputy, Signor Perna, stated in a speech before the Chamber that there were about a thousand pharmacists and as many physicians unemployed in Italy. In August 1928, out of 15,000 engineers 3000 had no work, and many of those who were employed had to be content with salaries of from 800 to 1000 lire a month.[1] The *Corriere della Sera* of February 20, 1929, informed its readers that among the stage supers of the Scala Theatre at Milan "lawyers and physicians were not lacking"; "the want

---

[1] *Lavoro d'Italia*, Aug. 24 and 30, 1928.

is so great today, that for ten lire a man becomes for an hour a Roman senator or an Egyptian priest." A Fascist deputy, Signor Zangara, writing in the *Resto del Carlino* on July 5, 1929, observed that "serious harm might be done to their own future and to that of the ruling class which the Fascist Revolution had the right and the duty of setting up, by allowing young graduates to remain unemployed for two or three years; they ought to be utilized in the diplomatic service, in the legal organizations, in the public administrations, in the Party offices."

In 1930, at a competitive examination for 150 police apprenticeships, "about a thousand candidates presented themselves, many of them with university diplomas." [2] Among the 1300 persons engaged in distributing the census papers in Milan in the spring of 1931, "many gave evidence of superior education and culture":

There is nothing surprising about this when one learns that many among them could boast of college diplomas and doctors' degrees: bookkeepers, accountants in large numbers, engineers, and even doctors of law; all of them persons temporarily unemployed, to whom a month's work represented a little stop-gap until they could get something better.[3]

In April 1932, a thousand persons, among whom were engineers and lawyers, sent in applications for one hundred and fifty posts as prison warders. The Minister of Justice decreed that all those with qualifications higher than those required should be excluded from the competition.

In the review *Pegaso* for May 1932, p. 331, a university professor wrote:

The number of intellectuals unemployed is growing at an alarming rate; this unemployment is no less disturbing than unemployment in industry and agriculture; for it creates confusion in the realm of social values.

In a speech before the Senate on March 30, 1933, Senator Sanmartino discussed the conditions obtaining among the professional musicians.

The situation of men in these professions is serious. Few of them have steady employment. National barriers have increased the painfulness of their position by preventing them from emigrating. The "talkies" have taken

---

[2] *Relazione della Giunta Generale del Bilancio sul Preventivo degli Interni;* Documenti, XXVIII Leg., N. 802A, p. 21.
[3] *Corriere della Sera,* May 1, 1931.

work away from many thousands of persons. It is imprudent to encourage the growth of this class; it would be wiser to reduce its numbers.

An official *communiqué* of January 29, 1935, stated that 1500 actors were without employment.

In the *Lavoro* of August 4, 1934, a physician complained that young physicians were obliged to serve for many years without salary in hospitals; when they began to draw a salary, this amounted to no more than 5000 lire a year, and often they had to be content with food, lodging, and 3600 lire a year minus income tax and other subtractions amounting to 12 per cent of their meagre salaries.

As for graduates in chemistry, it has become virtually impossible for them to find work.

The lawyers, who numbered 21,488 in 1913, that is, 61.97 for every 100,000 of the population, had increased by 1927 to 26,679, that is, to 68.85 for every 100,000 of the population, notwithstanding that a "purge" of 2000 "anti-nationals" occurred in the last-named year. A law of March 25, 1926, effected a veritable "lockout" in favour of lawyers who were already established in the profession: a newcomer cannot exercise his profession until he has had five years' practice; in order to be inscribed in the register, he is obliged to take a competitive examination, and the number of positions competed for in this way is always much lower than that of the lawyers who die: each year only ten new lawyers, on an average, are inscribed for the whole of Italy, although there are about 200 vacancies.[4] Consequently, in 1929, the number of lawyers fell to 25,353, that is, 64.21 for every 100,000 of the population, and a gradual diminution was foreseen for the future. But this diminution, although satisfactory to those who took the precaution to be born thirty years ago, is not calculated to infuse joy into those of less mature years. In 1913, the various faculties of law turned out 1812 graduates: in 1927 they graduated 1762; 1918 in 1928; 2240 in 1929; 2197 in 1930; 2204 in 1931; 2246 in 1932. In view of the increase in the population which occurred between 1913 and 1932, one can say that the production of lawyers has not increased; to the contrary, it has rather diminished. But what benefit do the newcomers draw from this fact, if, among them, only one out of two hundred can succeed in entering the paradise of the privileged? In the sitting of the Chamber that took

---

[4] Information given by the president of the Court of Cassation, in the *Corriere della Sera*, Jan. 26, 1932.

place on April 13, 1932, a deputy asked that "the roads should not be closed to the young men who ask only to be admitted in order to work," and he deplored "the selfishness shown by the older lawyers towards the younger generation, many of whose members had real Fascist virtues." But on the following day, the Minister of Justice stated that, in view of "the economic crisis, the effects of which were felt much more severely among the lawyers, and the increasing number of young lawyers each year," the system of limited admissions to the bar was necessary: let families choose other openings for their sons! Italian families had not waited for the minister's advice before seeking other openings. Many young people turned towards the schools of political science, economics, and business administration. The latter awarded a bare 238 diplomas in 1913; they gave 789 in 1928; 904 in 1929; 1180 in 1930; 1020 in 1931; 1332 in 1932. These graduates are just so many more persons who are hungry for work.

Most graduates in law or political science should be absorbed by the state bureaucracy or other public institutions. But after so many "purges," there are no longer any "anti-national" officials to dismiss. The budgets of the state, the provinces, the municipalities, the legal associations, the Party organizations, do not permit the creation of new positions unless taxes are increased also—a difficult thing to do in the present economic crisis. Still worse: the positions taken from the "anti-nationals" have been given to young men; formerly a certain number of the older men in the various bureaux retired or died each year, and newcomers took their places. Now they don't die. Unless a bureaucratic murrain intervenes, many positions will remain in a state of blockade for an indefinite period to come.

In all countries, of course, there is at present widespread unemployment among intellectuals. This evil, like the others which today prey upon Italy as upon the rest of the world, one should not attribute to Mussolini, as his admirers attribute to him every possible and imaginable good. The point which must be made clear is that Fascism has not found any way out of a *malaise* from which the whole civilized world is suffering, and that those who affirm that Mussolini has "put Italy on the map" either deceive themselves or hope to deceive others.

According to Mussolini (speech of May 26, 1934), the public officials, both civil and military, have not suffered any cut in salary. The total of their salaries was increased by 250,000,000 lire in 1923 and by 650,-

000,000 lire in 1926; it was decreased by 380,000,000 lire in 1927; in 1929 it was again increased by 670,000,000, but was diminished by 640,000,000 in 1930 and by 410,000,000 in 1934. There remains in 1934 a net gain of 90,000,000 lire per year as compared with 1922. Consequently, the drop in the cost of living that has taken place during the last few years represents a bonus for the public officials. But as usual, the official figures do not tell the whole truth. The salary increases granted between 1923 and 1929 were not equitably distributed among the various strata of the hierarchy; in the highest ranks salaries were doubled between 1923 and 1930, whereas in the intermediate and lowest grades the increases were much more modest;[5] on the other hand, the 1930 cuts amounted to twelve per cent for everyone, and those of 1934, while not affecting those officials whose monthly salary was less than 500 lire, varied from six per cent to twelve per cent for the higher grades. The results may be gauged from the following:

FLUCTUATION OF FIVE PUBLIC SALARIES (IN LIRE)

	SALARY A	SALARY B	SALARY C	SALARY D	SALARY E
In 1922	42,480	14,080	9,860	8,120	6,820
In 1930	74,000	25,200	14,580	10,920	7,520
After the 12% cut of 1930	65,000	22,176	12,829	9,612	6,620
After the 12% cut of 1934	55,308	—	—	—	—
After the 10% cut of 1934	—	19,959	—	—	—
After the 8% cut of 1934	—	—	11,805	—	—
After the 6% cut of 1934	—	—	—	9,036	—
Difference between 1922 and 1934	+ 12,828	+ 5,879	+ 1,945	+ 916	− 200

If officialdom today costs 90 million lire more than in 1922, this sum has been absorbed in part by the intermediate and higher grades of the hierarchy and in part by the increased number of officials. In the lower grades the increases are imperceptible, or there has been a reduction.

[5] *Il Bilancio dello Stato*, p. 33 ff.

An elementary-school teacher who in 1926 received a yearly salary of 7600 lire after four years of service, now receives 7100 lire.

There are 250,000 public officials who earn less than 500 lire a month, and 245,000 who earn less than 1000 lire a month.[6]

In the *Lavoro* of July 10, 1934, may be read a letter from a postman, who stated that at sixty-five years of age he had a monthly salary of 240 lire.

The Provincial Economic Council of Bologna estimated in 1932 the weekly cost of living for a typical family of five persons (two adults and three children under 10) in December 1931.[7] Let it be noted that among the larger Italian cities, Bologna is one of the cheapest in which to live:

1. Expenditures on food .... 118.52 lire weekly [8]
2.   "   " clothing .... 14.75 "   "
3.   "   " shelter .... 39.56 "   "   9
4.   "   " light and heating .... 11.92 "   "
5. Miscellaneous expenses .... 23.97 "   "

       Weekly total .... 208.72 lire

The *Lavoro* of October 24, 1933, after examining wages in Genoa, came to the conclusion that the "typical family" taken in the official statistics as the norm for determining the cost of living "is not of the working class but of the lower middle class: public officials, clerks, professional men, etc., who have a monthly income of from 1000 to 1200 lire"; on an average a worker earns only 605 lire per month of 25 working days; so if the worker were to eat what the "typical family" of the official statistics eats, he would have to spend 475 lire a month on

---

[6] Mussolini's statement in the Chamber on May 26, 1934.

[7] *La Provincia di Bologna nell'Anno Decimo*, p. 1151.

[8] The cost of bread was 1.56 lire a kilogram. The Fascist Ambassador to the United States, Signor de Martino, asserted in Oct. 1930 that bread cost 40 centesimi a kilogram (*Il Grido della Stirpe*, Oct. 18, 1930). An ambassador is sometimes defined as a gentleman sent abroad to lie for his government.

[9] The American correspondent, Mr. Knickerbocker, reported (*Boston Evening Transcript*, Sept. 24, 1932) finding on the Peninsula of Sorrento an American couple who had leased a house: "It was all done over, renovated, modernized, cracks mortared, and the whole whitewashed; it dazzled like the dwelling of a California millionaire; there were seven rooms, four overlooking the gulf . . . for this they paid $50—but $50 a year! And their Italian friends complained they had been robbed by an unscrupulous realtor." If he had not already won the Pulitzer Prize in 1930, Mr. Knickerbocker would have merited it in 1932 for this epoch-making discovery.

food alone, or nearly 52 per cent of his monthly expenditure: that is to say, "the working-class family must give up almost entirely the rest of its budget: rent, clothing, heat, light, and miscellaneous; or else it must reduce its food item considerably." It is probable that the families of those 250,000 public officials who earned less than 500 lire a month also had to reduce their food item "considerably."

The *Corriere della Sera*, May 30, 1928, published the following item:

Giuseppe Mariani and Giovanni Cattaneo, both postmen at Codogno, appeared before the local court on a charge of theft of postal orders and forgery while on public duty, for having receipted the said postal orders with false signatures; a serious offense for which the maximum punishment is ten years' imprisonment. But the Court sentenced them to only one year's imprisonment in consideration of the extenuating fact that both postmen have wives and large families to support and receive wages of only 270 lire per month.

From an article published in the review *Diritti della Scuola* for May 27, 1934, we learn that if an elementary school teacher falls ill, he loses 100 lire a month:

As is well known, it is not possible for us, even when we enjoy the best of health, to put aside a modest sum against unforeseen necessities. That is the reason why we see those pitiful cases of teachers going to school with a fever or otherwise in poor health, or of others who regardless of the doctor's opinion insist that they are convalescing if not completely cured, in order to return to school.

On the whole, however, the public servants, even those in the lower categories, are better off than manual labourers and the white-collar employees in private employ, because not only have they profited since 1930 by the decline in the cost of living, which has been greater than the decline in their salaries, but above all they are not threatened by the scourge of unemployment.

XXV

"There Are No Longer Any Beggars"

THE degradation which has taken place in the standard of living of the Italian people during the Fascist decade is revealed by the official statistics themselves.

The *Annuario Statistico Italiano* for 1922–25, p. 198, and that for 1933, p. 219, give the following statistics for the consumption of certain products, including both luxuries and necessities, in 1922 and in 1932:

Year	1922	1932
Population	38,800,000	41,400,000
Consumption of		
Tobacco	279,000 quintals	245,000 quintals
Coffee	472,000 "	407,000 "
Salt	2,646,000 "	2,606,000 "
Wheat	73,237,000 "	69,204,000 "
Maize	27,213,000 "	26,739,000 "

In regard to tobacco it is to be noted that not only has the quantity diminished, but also the quality, inferior grades now being used in much larger proportion.[1] And in regard to wheat one must bear in mind that the official crop statistics are purposely exaggerated.[2]

For meat consumption, from an article published in the *Tribuna* of May 1, 1935, we learn that "the annual consumption of meat, which in 1928 was 22 kilograms [48.4 pounds] per each member of the population, had by 1932 declined to 18 kilograms [39.6 pounds]."

In the city of Milan the average annual consumption of meat per capita was 38.8 kilograms in 1914; it went down to 23 in 1918; went up to 38.9 in 1922; continued to rise until it was 45.8 in 1928; but fell to 27.0 kilograms by 1932.[3] The consumption of wine in Turin went

---

[1] This fact was admitted by the Minister of Finance in the Chamber of Deputies on Jan. 4, 1934.

[2] Salvemini, *Mussolini's Battle of Wheat*. In the *Political Science Quarterly* for Dec. 1931, Mortara contested only a few of the details in this study, none of them concerning the central thesis. He thereby implicitly admitted that the figures given in the study and the inductions based on them were incontrovertible.

[3] *Relazione della Commissione di Finanza del Senato sul Preventivo del Ministero*

down from 712,682 hectolitres in 1929 to 656,788 hectolitres in 1930; even water consumption dropped from 42,435,000 cubic metres in 1929 to 41,123,000 cubic metres in 1930, and during the first months of 1931 the consumption of water was 150,000 cubic metres less than for the corresponding months of the preceding year.[4] From the *Gazzetta del Popolo* of Turin, June 12, 1934, we learn that in 1933 the average consumption of meat in the city was 36.45 kilograms per head; and that of wine, 120 hectolitres. In 1912–4 the consumption of meat had been 47.77 kilograms and that of wine 158.53 hectolitres per head.

The consumption of sugar which in Italy had risen from the average of 4.95 kilograms per person in 1913 to 7.5 kilograms in 1922, continued to rise slowly up to 9.2 kilograms in 1930, but dropped to 7.5 in 1931 and 6.9 in 1932.[5] In England the annual consumption is 40 kilograms; in France, 25; in Germany, 23; and in Spain, 13.[6] The parliamentary committee on the budget estimates for 1931–2 reported:

On a rough estimate the Italian consumer pays for sugar [in taxation and protective duty] around two billion lire for a production which is worth roughly two hundred million. It is therefore not surprising that the individual consumption of sugar in Italy is among the lowest of all the countries.[7]

The *Bollettino di Statistica*, July 1935, p. 556, stated that the retail sale of foodstuffs had gone down in Italy by 13 per cent between March 1934 and June 1935. According to the Milanese federation of retail traders the retail sales in the city of Milan dropped from the index number 100 in January 1934 to 95.88 in January 1935 (*Corriere della Sera*, March 25, 1935) and to 64.3 in August 1935.[8]

"Beggars are no longer to be seen in the streets of Italy": Who has not

---

di Agricultura: 1933–4, Senato, Documenti, No. 1515A, p. 6. Mr. Knickerbocker related in the *Boston Evening Transcript* of Sept. 24, 1932, that "the statistics of consumption in this country [Italy] show that the population during the economic crisis not only has more to eat than it ever had before, but is eating a higher quality of food than it ever did before." Mr. Goad, *The Corporate State*, p. 788, states that "the consumption of meat and bread by the Italian peasant is *out of all comparison* with that in the pre-war days."

[4] *Stampa*, May 29, 1931.

[5] *Annuario Statistico Italiano*, 1927, p. 158; *Compendio Statistico Italiano*, 1932, p. 180; *Annuario Statistico Italiano*, 1933, p. 214. Cf. *Il Sole*, March 9, 1932: "The consumption of sugar presents a persistent shrinkage of no slight amount. The figures tend to indicate that the phenomenon cannot be considered a transitory one."

[6] Figures given by the review *L'Industria Saccarifera Italiana*, April 4, 1933.

[7] *Commissione del Bilancio della Camera: Relazione sull'Esercizio 1931–2*, p. 81.

[8] Quoted from the Paris anti-Fascist paper *Giustizia e Libertà*, Nov. 2, 1935.

heard this litany repeated many times? This statement can mean one of two quite different things: 1, that the beggar class has disappeared from Italy as a result of the prosperity created by the Fascist regime; or 2, that the beggars are gathered up by the police and put in jail. The tourist who does not wish to be annoyed by mendicants and wants to enjoy his vacation in peace naturally prefers to accept the first implication. Anyone living in Italy knows that neither of these explanations is correct. The truth is that the police persecute the beggars mercilessly at the places where ships land passengers, in the railway stations of the big cities, and in the vicinity of the great hotels, churches, and monuments most frequently visited by tourists. But this does not mean that the population has become wealthy or that beggars have everywhere disappeared.

Some tourists of course do not let themselves be deceived by appearances. For instance, the former Belgian Minister of Foreign Affairs, Monsieur Vandervelde, after a trip to Italy, wrote in the *Peuple* of Brussels, April 19, 1932, that he had found "perhaps more beggars than ten years before; and not only the professional mendicants, but also the unemployed who extend the hand with an air of humiliation." I have before me a letter sent from Naples in the fall of 1932 by an American writer, Miss Caroline Singer, to some friends of hers in New York:

We dived into a narrow lane, running parallel to the very prosperous-looking shopping streets but having no direct communication with them. This was another world. And what a world! The lane, which we were unable to leave for more than a mile except to turn into more dangerous-looking lanes, was not more than twelve feet wide at its widest. The buildings went up and up, magnificent old stone skyscrapers with huge inner courtyards and fine carved doorways. But the people . . . Where shops had been, were bedroom living-rooms, so many beds open to the street that there was room for nothing else but a cookstove; miserable women sewing by lamps everywhere, miserable old men crunching bread, young toughs sitting outside, puny children, odor of dirt, odors of sickness and congestion everywhere, shabby young harlots coming out with sailors, with soldiers. It was a great shock since all this lay so close to an apparent prosperity. The whole walk was a prolonged nightmare. It was unreal, like a dream. And the street was so silent. Nowhere was there conversation or the noise that one associates with Italians. It was an utterly silent quarter and yet filled with human life.

But how many tourists travel with their eyes open?

Here are documents which will help some of these tourists to obtain a faint suggestion of the real situation:

1. The *Regime Fascista* of Cremona, July 3, 1928: "A few days ago this paper deplored the fact that begging had become a regular profession, invading even the principal streets with a crowd of ragamuffins and persistent wailers, and thereby creating before the eyes of everyone a spectacle little edifying and little decorous. The police have intervened without delay. The first day has had excellent results. The prisoners, after having served their terms, will be sent back to their native villages and those belonging to Cremona will be placed in a poor-house."

2. The *Impero* of Rome, October 31, 1930: "Professional beggars, wandering organ-grinders, fortune-tellers in the streets and squares of the great cities, especially at Rome and Naples, employ every means to move the passers-by to pity to obtain alms. Ragged and dirty, they place themselves at the entrances to churches, and there with shrill lamentations annoy those who pass. There are some astute women who go from house to house asking charity. Others lie in ambush inside churches and cemeteries. Certain women of the lower classes with babies in their arms ask alms with the excuse that their husbands are ill or have been out of work for many months. Is it possible in the Year VII of Italian Redemption to tolerate these pseudo-paupers, astute professional beggers, and most vulgar trouble-makers?"

3. The *Corriere Padano* of Ferrara, July 6, 1929: "Yesterday the police arrested six men, and four boys under the age of 12, taken in the act of begging."

4. The *Corriere della Sera*, November 2, 1929. Circular of the Minister of the Interior, inciting the prefects to more energetic action against professional begging: "Too often it happens, expecially in the more populous centres, that clever persons succeed in imposing upon the good faith of others by pretending to have physical disabilities which in reality they do not have. There is another form of beggary, that which makes use of children in order to touch the public's pity. The professional beggars, in order to escape the attention of the police, abstain from putting out their hands in the street and squares, but enter houses and ask alms, sometimes even in a brusque manner with threats more or less masked, when they find at home only women, children, or elderly people."

5. The *Libertà*, an anti-Fascist weekly published in Paris, on May 3, 1930, reproduced a circular of March 28, 1930, from the secretary of the Fascio of Jesi (Central Italy, province of Ancona) inviting citizens to send contributions "for the upkeep of the charitable kitchens rendered necessary

by unemployment and by the fact that professional begging has assumed alarming proportions during the last few days."

6.   The *Corriere della Sera,* August 5, 1931, published an article on the professional beggars who, banished from the large climatic resorts, have gone to the mountains.

7.   The *Corriere della Sera,* February 5, 1932, contained an article in which there is described a building in Milan where "the population of the shipwrecked" found food and lodging; "it is thus that those nocturnal mendicants who slept on the steps of churches, in doorways, everywhere where there was a little space set apart and protected from the weather, have almost completely disappeared from the city streets."

8.   The *Corriere della Sera,* August 28, 1932. In a single day at Mantua thirty "importunate mendicants" were "picked up" and condemned to from seven to ten days in jail.

9.   The *Corriere della Sera,* April 2, 1933. The police of Milan have discovered that a group of mendicants had appointed "their trusted cashier," who passed continually from one to another in order to collect from time to time the money received; thus those who were arrested were always with empty pockets, and the police could not confiscate the money; at the end of the day the "trusted cashier" gave each one his earnings, keeping for himself an honest percentage.

10.   The *Lavoro* of Genoa, June 6, 1933, carried an article concerning the professional beggars who go from house to house.

11.   The *Resto del Carlino,* June 24, 1933: "It seems incredible, but professional begging is acquiring ever-increasing proportions and the work of diminishing it is neither easy nor expeditious. Along with the real pauper there ask alms the drunken professional, the malingerer, the accumulator of capital, in a word, all those simulators of poverty, of infirmities, and even of deformities."

12.   The *Resto del Carlino,* January 21, 1934. A man is condemned to eight months imprisonment for having maltreated his wife and obliged his three children to go from house to house and beg for charity.

As far as the professional beggars are concerned, some of them may be anything but poor. But the existence of genuine poverty is attested by the large number of persons whom the Fascists boast of feeding at Christmas. At Christmas 1930 in the city of Milan food, clothes, etc., were distributed to 15,000 indigent families; at Parma in a single section of the city 300 families were benefited (*Corriere della Sera,* December 25, 1930); in Ferrara 2800 poor families obtained 8527 lire worth of meat, flour, etc., that is, less than four lire, or 20 gold cents, per family (*Corriere della Sera*, January 3, 1931). They certainly did not have much to waste! In the town of Jolanda di Savoia (population 3017) in the province of Ferrara it was necessary to succour 100 families, and a like number in Formignana (population 3715). In Argenta (population 5335) 114 families were aided (*Corriere Padano*, December 29, 1930); at Padua (population 83,281), 3000; at Reggio Emilia (population 43,695), over 3000; at Voghera (population 25,174), 1300 (*Corriere della Sera*, December 27, 1930); at Bologna (population 214,955), more than 4200 families (*Resto del Carlino*, December 25, 1930); at Medicina (population 4264), 340 families (*Resto del Carlino*, December 30, 1930).

At Christmas 1933 it was necessary in Genoa and its province (population 831,000) to assist 13,162 families (*Lavoro*, December 27, 1933), 2800 persons were fed by the free public kitchens (*Lavoro*, December 31, 1933); in Milan and province (population 1,000,000) the families aided numbered 40,992 (*Corriere della Sera*, December 30, 1933). In Bologna and province (population 683,000) 19,598 families composed of 120,000 persons were benefited (*Resto del Carlino*, January 13, 1934).

The poor, it would appear, have the habit of eating on every "feast" day. We therefore have from time to time reports of dinners to which the poor are invited in order to celebrate some happy occasion, which unfortunately does not occur every day in the year. In the city of Modena it is the custom to give a supper to the poor on Maundy Thursday. The city comprises about 13,000 families. "In 1922," I read in a letter sent me in this regard by Signor Ferrari, author of the excellent work *Le Régime Fasciste Italien* (Paris, Editions Spes, 1928) and a citizen of Modena, "there would not have been found, not merely in the city but in the whole commune, four hundred poor to feed." On February 27, 1930, the poor invited to partake of food numbered eight hundred (*Regime Fascista*, February 28, 1930), and on February 1931 the number had increased to fifteen hundred (*Resto del Carlino*, February 18, 1931). At Pavia a custom similar to that of Modena is observed at Mid-Lent. In 1932 five kitchens set up in a public square distributed gratuitously *polenta*, codfish, and cheese to "whoever wanted any."

The work [stated the "Popolo d'Italia" on March 5, 1932] continued all the morning and afternoon amid the perpetual going to and fro of the men serving at the "guns," almost as if the cauldrons were mortars unable to vomit bombardments of *polenta* fast enough to placate the *multitude of requests*. Ten thousand rations were distributed to 2300 families. *A fifth of the population of Pavia was fed.*

By way of celebrating the visit of the Secretary-General of the Party to Perugia in May 1932, a meal was given to 1000 of the city's poor, while in the province "9000 needy received rations" (*Corriere della Sera*, March 6, 1932). At Cremona on October 28, 1932, a thousand destitute received *polenta* and codfish in order to commemorate the tenth anniversary of the "march on Rome." [9]

In July 1934, the Pope had 3000 pounds of bread distributed among the poor of the town of Loreto. If we calculate that each needy person received two pounds of bread, we find that 1500 persons were fed. The town of Loreto has 3000 inhabitants.

Speaking in the Senate on December 15, 1933, Senator Marcello, a 100 per cent Fascist, stated that in the city of Venice from 1929 to 1933 the consumption of electric power for lighting purposes had declined by 22 per cent, unrented apartments numbered 4000, and 25,000 out of 59,000 taxpayers were in arrears in their payments; moreover, the amount of movable property sequestrated for non-payment of taxes was so great that "all available storehouses were full of it, and the municipality was continually under the necessity of providing new places for storage"; in order not to increase still further the amount of sequestrated property, the tax collector was refraining from prosecuting in 4000 cases of non-payment. Senator Marcello ended his speech by expressing his gratitude to Mussolini, who "was saving the world from anarchy and want." It is clear that, as far as want was concerned, the senator did not regard the city of Venice as part of the world.

A sports correspondent of the *Echo de Paris*, who assisted at a bicycle race across Italy, sent, as is the custom, to his paper some "picturesque" impressions of the country traversed. In the issue of June 13, 1935, we read that in the Abruzzi he found "deplorable streets

---

[9] One of the most pitiful spectacles to be seen in Italy today is that of the hungry men, women, and children gathered at noontime around the entrances of the barracks. They are waiting for the well-to-do soldiers who are able to supply their own food and who therefore take their military rations and give them to the crowds instead of throwing them away. Even this scene was a source of enthusiasm for Mr. Knickerbocker: "Here in Milan we passed the War Memorial. Across the street was the canteen of the military barracks. In a park near by sat several dozen ragged men, all above middle age, all eating happily out of tin buckets. From the canteen came a fragrance of spaghetti" (*Boston Evening Transcript*, Sept. 24, 1932).

where asphalt is unknown, *streets which are the opposite of the magnifi-cent automobile streets and of those of large circulation.*" He "saw at close range the misery of the peasants"; "the children covered with rags and barefoot; the women also barefoot, aged before their time; the men seem in a very bad mood. Here, an Italian told me, 'We feed ourselves with bread and oil.' " Let it be noted that the *Echo de Paris* is a conserva-tive paper which has always elevated to the skies the prosperity miracu-lously bestowed upon Italy by Mussolini. Its correspondent, there-fore, could not have been biased against Mussolini. Tourists have not the habit of going off from the "magnificent automobile streets."

XXVI

The Prosperity of the Italian People

THE number of homeless people who have to be sheltered in public lodging houses is distressingly high.

In the city of Milan, during the exceptionally cold weather of February 1929, "shelters against the cold" were opened. They were always crowded with homeless persons, principally unemployed men, who spent their days living from hand to mouth and their nights in the public dormitories (*Corriere della Sera*, February 19, 1929). In October 1933, Mussolini "was pleased to assign 250,000 lire to the relief of those families rendered homeless by their inability to pay their rent," and the press bureau of the Milanese Fascist branch announced that "hundreds of families would enjoy the benefit of this" (*Corriere della Sera*, October 14, 1933). In the same month the municipality of Milan decided to construct dwellings, consisting of one room, a kitchenette, and the sanitary conveniences, for 1000 of these homeless families: 500 dwellings would be ready in May 1934; in November the necessity of building lodgings for 1500 families was recognized.[1] During the last two months of 1933, it was necessary to lodge 37,350 men, 13,650 women and 8735 children, making a total of 59,735 persons, or a daily average of around 1000 (*Corriere della Sera*, December 30, 1933). From January 1 to February 17, 1934, 41,715 men, 11,372 women, and 7414 children were accommodated, making a daily average of more than 1200 persons (*Corriere della Sera*, February 18, 1934).

In the city of Genoa between October 29, 1932, and June 30, 1933, there were lodged in these establishments 16,378 "homeless and unemployed men" and 4728 women (*Lavoro*, July 25, 1933). During the last week of 1933 those sheltered numbered 1042, among whom were 304 women (*Lavoro*, December 31, 1933). During the last two months of 1933, 4535 were accommodated (*Lavoro*, January 17, 1933).

Let the reader keep in mind that these examples have been chosen from the wealthiest *cities* in northern Italy, where the relief of the poor is better organized, because the population of the cities might other-

---

[1] *Corriere della Sera*, Oct. 20, 21; Nov. 1, 25, 1933.

wise break out into riots. Poverty remains unsuccoured in the country districts of northern Italy, and in southern Italy, where the population is almost wholly agricultural. Yet, if the official statistics are to be believed, from November 1932 to October 1933 it was necessary to lodge in the public night shelters throughout Italy 295,574 persons.[2]

According to the same statistics, the Fascist Party during the year 1933 daily aided an average of 2,328,924 needy persons with money, clothing, food, lodging, etc.[3] There were, then, in Italy nearly two and a half million people who, to keep from starving or freezing, had to go each morning to the local Fascio to obtain a bowl of soup or permission to sleep indoors. It is with this army of 2,328,924 famished that Mussolini is creating his new Roman Empire. Having broken the record for propagating beggars, he may justly boast of having won a new victory in doling out so many bowls of soup to so many beggars. But if you read the London *Saturday Review* for February 4, 1934, you will admire a glamorous picture of Mussolini and under it the following words: "He dragged Italy out of the mire of Socialism and in a few years has made it the most successful and prosperous country in Europe."

Some will no doubt be inclined to remark that very likely the Fascist papers multiply the numbers of persons fed by the Party, in order to throw into higher relief its welfare activities. Let us therefore examine other indications, in which it is difficult to imagine there is any tendency to exaggerate.

In Italy the pawnshops (*Monti di Pietà*) are under the supervision of the municipalities. The rise and fall in the number of articles in pawn is regarded as an index of the increased or diminished economic distress among the working classes. The statistics of articles in pawn on the thirty-first of December during eight years appear on the opposite page.

Beginning with 1927, the year of the crisis induced by the revaluation of the lira, the Central Institute for Statistics felt the need of chang-

---

[2] Official *communiqué* of Dec. 30, 1933. Sir Leo Chiozza-Money wrote in the Glasgow *Forward* of Aug. 9, 1930: "Let me call attention to the case of a Scotsman, Mr. James McMillan, who has just been sent to prison for refusing to vacate his house after it had been condemned. This amazing tyranny is exercised although no alternative accommodation has been offered to Mr. McMillan. Does any Scotsman believe that Mussolini would tolerate such treatment of a hard-working man?" He did not explain to his Scotsmen that the alternative accommodation that Mr. James McMillan would have found in Italy would have been a public lodging-house.

[3] *Sindacato e Corporazione*, Jan. 1934, p. 133.

ARTICLES IN PAWN

Pre-Fascist era	1919	1,168,000
	1920	1,007,000
	1921	1,174,000
	1922	1,177,000
Fascist era	1923	1,363,000
	1924	1,429,000
	1925	1,512,000
	1926	1,704,000

ing the criteria governing the collection of these figures. Another change was made in 1929.[4] Hence, the figures from 1927 onward are not comparable with those of the previous years. In any case, here is the new series:

1927	1,688,000		1930	2,004,000
1928	1,566,000		1931	2,190,000
1929	1,822,000			

Thus, in spite of Fascist statistical manipulation, the number of objects pawned almost doubled between 1922 and 1931.

What happened to the statistics after December 31, 1931, we do not know. Only this is certain, that the 2,190,000 pawns reported for that date in the *Compendio Statistico* for 1932, p. 240, dropped *for the same date* to 1,662,000 in the *Annuario Statistico* for 1933, p. 375.

In February 1929 a charitable lady of Milan, moved to compassion for the poor folk whose sufferings were especially severe owing to the exceptionally cold season, gave to the municipal pawnshop the sum of money necessary to get all winter clothing and woollen blankets out of pawn free of charge. For two days the employees of the pawnshop had to work from 8 : 30 A. M. to 6 P. M. to return 2528 pawned articles valued at 52,907 lire, or an average of 21 lire (a little more than a gold dollar) per article, to people who had been unable to ransom their clothes while the temperature was at 16 degrees below zero Centigrade (*Corriere della Sera*, February 21, 1929). At Reggio Emilia in June 1930, there were persons who had articles in pawn valued at 5 lire, or 26 cents at par (*Solco Fascista*, June 24, 1930)—what could a poor wretch have pawned for 26 cents?

---

[4] *Annuario Statistico*, *1927*, p. 58; *idem*, *1929*, p. 348; *Compendio Statistico*, *1932*, p. 240; *Bollettino Mensile di Statistica*, April 1929, p. 382.

Here are the figures of the families entered by municipalities on the registers for poor relief in five of Italy's largest cities in 1933:

	Population	No. of Families Registered	No. of Persons in Families Registered
Rome	1,045,000	29,040	116,160
Milan	1,017,000	25,693	102,693
Genoa	620,000	11,488	45,954
Florence	320,000	14,345	43,750
Venice	266,000	11,146	44,586

The proportion, therefore, varies between the sixteen per cent of Venice and the seven per cent of Genoa.[5]

In a speech on January 17, 1926, Rossoni said:

During a recent visit to Sicily I ascertained that at 300 metres below the ground, the miners, half naked and in almost total darkness, work like beasts; all they have to satisfy their hunger is a little black bread and a few olives.[6]

And Mussolini, during the sitting of the Senate on June 22, 1929, let fall the remark that "there are places in Sardinia and southern Italy where for months the inhabitants have had to live on wild plants." What were the consequences to these unfortunate people of the depression that manifested itself after 1929?

In the weekly review *Cantiere*, September 29, 1934, one reads:

The worker in the Sicilian sulphur mines has fallen upon hardship after hardship, especially during recent years. It suffices to recall that while in 1923 the worker earned an average daily wage of 16 lire, in 1929, when the first labour agreement was made, wages dropped to about 12 lire; and today wages are still lower, since the labour agreement has never been completely observed. Moreover, the number of workers, formerly 13,000, has been reduced to 7,000, and work, which was once continuous, is now no longer so.

In 1928 Professor Milone, an expert in economics, wrote concerning the peasants in the province of Padua:

---

[5] These figures, taken from the official publications of the various cities, were published in the anti-Fascist weekly of Paris, *Libertà*, on Nov. 2, 1933. The official register of the poor for the city of Genoa contained in 1932 the names of 41,803 persons (*Lavoro*, April 5, 1932); the number had, therefore, increased by 4000 in one year.

[6] *Stampa*, Jan. 18, 1926.

A few of the more intelligent sanitation officials, like some of the *podestàs* [mayors of municipalities appointed by the central government from among the faithful Fascists], recognize *courageously* that in this vicinity for the past two years, that is, since the end of 1926, there has begun an appreciable deterioration in the nourishment of the peasants. One year of drought and a fall in the price of wheat would be enough to annul the betterment in the life of so many of our poor people, who during the last ten years and after the economic changes due to the war had succeeded in attaining a level of nutrition which not all the local doctors describe as sufficient.

In 1929 Milone added: "Unfortunately, conditions today are still worse." [7]

The *Lavoro Fascista* of October 23, 1934, stated that in the district of Forli, from January 1 to August 31, 1934, the average day-labourer had become able to find only sixty-five days' work and earn 397 lire; public works—the famous public works about which the newspapers make so much stir—took only seventeen days out of the sixty-five. From September 1 to December 31, thirty days' work and earnings totalling 360 lire were expected. Thus, working 95 days out of 365, the day-labourer in 1934 earned 1297 lire; i. e., 3.55 lire a day.

Can a worker with a family to support live on these wages? Be it noted that the estimate has been based upon conditions in a town offering the greatest opportunities for work. In the majority of the towns in the province, it is only with difficulty that a day-labourer succeeds in earning 1000 lire in a year. The only ones who escape positive hardship are the families in which there are two or more wage-earners. But in the families made up of young couples with small children there is only one wage-earner, and only in a few cases can the wife be of substantial economic assistance to her husband. The mass of the day-labourers in the province live in actual want, especially in the hilly and mountainous zone.

According to the *Corriere Padano*, November 19 and 20, 1934, in the province of Ferrara a family of day-labourers composed of five or six persons "had to provide for all its necessities throughout the year" with sums varying from 1925 lire (about $200) to 3300 lire (a little over $300): "The situation, to say the least, could be called tragic."

Professor Bizozzero, an agricultural expert, advised the Italian

---

[7] *La Provincia di Padova*, p. 43 ff.

peasantry in June 1931 to return to the use of the stiff mush made from maize (*polenta*) as a staple food:

> The agrarian crisis will be overcome by producing more and at lower prices, and at the same time by living, at least for several years, very parsimoniously, that is, by spending as little as possible on food and clothing. *Polenta* must again return to its pristine honour. If to maize we add beans, we will have the two principal foods, which will be supplemented by potatoes and vegetables. Little bread and less meat. I see no other way out of the present difficult situation.[8]

Polenta, when not supplemented with other foods, produces pellagra. Professor Coletti, an expert in rural economics and a 100 per cent Fascist, wrote in 1922:

> Southern Italy, where maize is not an article of diet, remains immune from pellagra; pellagra is connected with a diet of maize.[9]

Doubtless it is to prevent the Italian peasantry from waxing fat through overeating *polenta* that the "corporative state" on August 21, 1931, raised the tariff on maize from 4.50 to 30 lire per quintal (at par, about 4 cents on every five pounds). And lest they put too much salt in their *polenta*, the price of salt, which in Italy is a state monopoly, was raised on September 24, 1928, from 100 to 250 lire per quintal (at par, about 12 cents per pound).

An Italian Fascist professor writes:

> Among animals only the herbivorous have need of salt, not the carnivorous. For the carnivorous rich, salt is a luxury; for the herbivorous proletariat of Italy it is a necessity.[10]

By the beginning of this century pellagra had become practically extinct in Italy. Deaths from this disease had dropped from 4292 in 1892 to 2376 in 1902, to 985 in 1912, and to 198 in 1922. In 1925 the number

---

[8] Article published in the review *L'Avvenire Agricolo* and reproduced in the daily *Corriere Padano* of June 14, 1931, from which we took it. Even in the advice given to the Italian peasants by Professor Bizozzero arguments were found by Signor Villari to prove that Italy enjoyed prosperity thanks to Mussolini: Signor Villari's mouth watered at the thought of *polenta*, which he described as "wholesome" and "nourishing as well as extremely appetizing *when it is varied, as it is now*, with other kinds of food" (*Economist*, Oct. 24, 1931).

[9] *La Popolazione Rurale in Italia*, p. 170.

[10] Flora, *Scienza delle Finanze*, p. 572.

had dropped to 108 and in 1926 to 81.[11] In a speech of May 26, 1927, Mussolini announced, as if it had been entirely due to him, that "the Italian nation has definitely won this battle." In the succeeding years deaths from pellagra continued to decrease in number until there were only 61 in 1931.[12] However, in 1930 a 100 per cent Fascist, Signor Messedaglia, drew attention to the fact that three new cases of pellagra had occurred during the previous three years in a zone of the province of Verona from which the disease had disappeared. The statement of Signor Messedaglia was officially confirmed in March 1933 by the Finance Commission of the Senate, which recognized that among the 81 pellagra deaths in each of the years 1929 and 1930 there were "a few new cases." [13] The words of Signor Messedaglia, minus the indispensable adulatory remarks apropos of the regime, are worth quoting:

Towards the end of the nineteenth and in the early part of the twentieth century the condition of the working classes was improving. Not only the industrial, but also the agricultural workers made notable advances in their wage scales and were able to attain higher standards of living and to render their food more varied. A fine and encouraging advance in civilization, to which was put the characteristic seal: the rapid decrease of pellagra. The rural population, as everyone knows, felt less than the middle classes the effects of the war on food-stuffs. And after the war? Whoever is acquainted with country life knows that the peasants continued after the war to live better than formerly, and that their food continued quite good. Our peasant learned, while continuing to use maize, to consume good wheat bread, eggs, milk, and dairy products, sugar and meat. His diet remained frugal, but meat was no more what it had once been, a purely luxury food, reserved for some rare feast day. The peasant ate better, and pellagra disappeared almost entirely. . . . But this phenomenon, being quite recent, could not possess the characteristics of absolute stability. It was a state of equilibrium, for obvious reasons unstable. . . . Malnutrition, by many held to have gone forever, returns in wide areas to the disadvantage of the peasant. . . . Wherever the peasant has to go back to the poor, monotonous diet of former times based on nothing, or almost nothing, but maize, it is certain that he will again fall victim to pellagra. Those who are in the places of command will do well to keep their eyes open.[14]

[11] *Annuario Statistico Italiano: 1904*, p. 131; idem: *1914*, p. 77; idem: *1922–5*, p. 35.
[12] *Ibid.: 1933*, p. 61.
[13] *Senato, Legislatura XXVIII, Documento 1575A*, March 30, 1933, p. 17.
[14] *L'alimentazione dei contadini e la pellagra nel Veronese*, pp. 22, 23, 27, 31, 53.

Yet, in spite of the reductions in real wages and increasing unemployment, the Italians manage to keep alive. The secrets of their resistance are group solidarity and sobriety, in both of which there is something of the miraculous. The father, in order to make ends meet, works overtime, and brings home everything he earns. The mother works in the day-time among the well-to-do families as maid, cook, dressmaker, etc., receiving as a part of her pay, her lunch, which she takes home. The spirit of sacrifice among Italian women is limitless. The father has first claim on the food, because he is the bread-winner; if he should fall ill, the family would be reduced to begging. Then come the children, who must eat because "they must grow up." If anything is left, the mother may have it. Beautiful girls of twenty are decrepit by the time they are thirty-five. As soon as the boys and girls have reached the age when they can earn, they are set to work, and they too bring home their small earnings. The neighbours help as best they can when the children of poorer families go hungry. An unemployed man's credit is always good, because as soon as he finds work, he starts paying his debts by instalments, with meticulous punctuality. During the first two decades of this century the habits of the people rose rapidly above the wretchedness that had previously prevailed. They ate more bread, bought meat once a week, and no longer went barefooted or wore patched clothing. Today they are little by little cutting down on things that are not indispensable. They are sinking back into the sub-human existence of previous generations. But the vitality of the race is marvellous. They will forget their poverty and enjoy life on practically nothing.

In a speech on December 18, 1930, Mussolini said that it was one of Italy's blessings that "the Italian people has not yet become accustomed to eating four meals a day." He might have added that during the first twenty years of this century the Italian people had begun to acquire the bad habit of eating its fill, and that he, Mussolini, had undertaken to "put the door back on its hinges."

A few days later, in an interview with *Il Sole* on January 1, 1931, Signor Bottai pointed out that the methods of Mussolini and Ford in dealing with the depression were diametrically opposed. Ford was trying to overcome the depression by a rise in the standard of living. Mussolini had "boldly but deliberately adopted the method of reducing incomes and wages." This shrinking of income, among many other beneficial effects, "would have valuable psychological and moral consequences by enforcing a more rigorous way of living."

As long as he can assert that Italy is riding the crest of prosperity, the Fascist glorifies Mussolini for raising the Italian people's standard of living. But as soon as he is compelled to admit a lowering in that standard of living, he changes front and eulogizes Mussolini for enforcing a more rigorous way of living. He finds it convenient to forget that the Italian people has long been one of the most frugal in the world, and scarcely needed to be taught to live more rigorously!

He who wishes to sleep with his eyes open, can very well hope that under Fascism agrobiologists can obtain a free rein to render humanity rich and happy much more effectively than under a regime of economic liberty:

> Like all other major branches of Italian industry, agriculture has been "integrated" and made capable of action as a unit, with a central body recruited from its own ranks to co-ordinate and guide its activity in directions that best appear to coincide with the broad national interest. In other words, Fascismo has fashioned, *at least on paper*, an instrument to its hand whereby a programme of abundance can be initiated and controlled without disturbing the general economic harmony, because the intention is that all units of the industrial body politic shall function together. The Fascist chiefs have only to will that every Italian shall have his standard of living doubled, and it then remains only to materialize their planned social-economic machinery for effectuating the purpose.[15]

He who is not content with what is written on paper but wishes to know what is going on in reality, must recognize that until the summer of 1935 no one had become aware in Italy that the Fascist chiefs were going to double the standard of living of the Italian people.

---

[15] Willcox, *Can Nations Live at Home?*, p. 201.

XXVII

Fascist Social Peace

THE Fascist mechanism is quiet, silent, and obedient. "Strikers,"
Mr. A. P. Dennis, formerly American commercial attaché at
Rome, wrote in 1929, "are promptly jailed. *The labour problem in Italy
no longer exists.*" [1] "Italy," wrote Mr. Isaac F. Marcosson in the *Saturday Evening Post*, March 15, 1930, "became a commonwealth of industrial peace. Between 1926 and the closing months of last year there was
not a single ripple on the labour surface." A year later, at the close of
1932, Dr. Einzig found the same social idyll in Italy: "In no country
was it so easy as in Italy to obtain the consent of employees to a reduction of wages." [2] Signor Scotti, industrialist and deputy to the parliament, on March 7, 1933, expressed to the Chamber his satisfaction that
"the corporative system" had functioned "as an effective means of
regulating the reduction of wages." [3]

This, according to Mussolini, is the basic difference between the Fascist economic system and Mr. Roosevelt's New Deal, and constitutes the
essential superiority of the Italian system over the American system:

> Why are there strikes in America? They are not necessary. Here in Italy
> we have done away with strikes and lockouts; we do not waste our time in
> brawls. I believe the New Deal basically sound. If it doesn't function it is
> because the methods of application are at fault. America must work toward
> closer co-operation between capital and labour. [4]

When on April 15, 1934, the salaries of public servants were reduced,

---

[1] *World's Work*, Aug. 1929, p. 48.
[2] *The Economic Foundations of Fascism*, p. 31.
[3] In June 1933, at the International Labour Office, one of the high Fascist officials
who are supposed to represent Italian labour there, made the following statements:
"Our corporative regime has demonstrated that only by means of an effective co-
operation *can the standard of living of the working class be protected or raised*. If we
are meeting the crisis more easily than elsewhere, *if the normal tenor of our lives is
maintained*, if the appearance of our country is being transformed by extensive works
of land redemption and improvement, by systematic building, and by progress in
technique, this is due to our corporative method and to the efficacy of the unified action
of our associations and unions" (*Corriere della Sera*, June 23, 1933).
[4] *New York Times*, Sept. 16, 1934.

the Rome correspondent of the *Petit Parisien* noted that the measure had "produced a considerable impression on public opinion":

The public bought up the successive editions of the paper with more avidity than has been seen in a long time, and everyone in the cafés, on the buses, in the street cars, on the streets, and on the park benches, is carefully studying the numerous new dispositions of the government. Nevertheless, this lively interest does not give rise to any sort of critical discussion on the street or in public buildings, or to any manifestation.

In other words Italian "social peace" is the passivity with which manual workers and clerks endure wage-cuts, unemployment, and want. It is used by Fascist apologists to prove that in Italy the "corporative man" already exists and functions, and will function still better when the corporations have descended from heaven to earth to perform miracles.

This "social peace" is doubtless satisfactory to the employers and the government. But is it equally satisfactory to the working classes, and is it equally advantageous for the community as a whole? Permit us to reproduce the remarks which Professor Lindsay Rogers of Columbia University—a writer not content with repeating equivocal formulæ and abstract words—published in *Current History*, May 1931, p. 165:

Is it legitimate to assume, as all defenders of the Fascist regime do, that industrial peace is a supreme good? That strikes are costly and that their apparent waste is great, cannot be denied. But it by no means follows that a body politic without strikes is healthier than a body politic with strikes. One must know what kind of strikes have been avoided and what have been the terms of the "peaceful settlements." It may well be that a settlement of an industrial dispute by the machinery of state works more injustice and causes greater economic waste than would have resulted from a strike. In other words, the mere absence of labor troubles in a state means little. One must know the terms on which trouble has been avoided.

Aside from this problem, another question remains to be discussed: Is Italian social peace due to the virtues of the "corporative man," or rather to that atmosphere of repression within which the said corporative man lives and has his being? There are no longer any strikes in Italy. But there are two different explanations for this fact: one is that the Italian working people are happy with repeatedly reduced wages and therefore do not wish to strike.[5] The other is that strikes are punished by imprisonment. Would the workers approve the labour agreements concluded by the officials of their unions if they were allowed to discuss them freely? If they were permitted freely to elect the secretaries, directors, and presidents of their local, provincial, and national organizations, would they re-elect the present incumbents or would they dismiss them?

In July 1926, the peasants who were protesting against the nine-hour day were arrested and then sentenced to four or five years in prison (see above, p. 185). In January 1932, when the salaries of the bank clerks were cut, employees made noisy demonstrations in the banks at Milan, Brescia, Turin, Genoa, and Rome; much furniture and window glass was broken, and several union officials were beaten, among them Signor Marcello Diaz, the son of Marshal Diaz who inherited from his father the title of "Duke of Victory." But the police intervened, made several arrests, and order was restored. The Rome correspondent of the London *Daily Telegraph*, on May 1, 1934, informed his readers that "the publicity given in the Italian press to a small riot which took place in the province of Aquila a few days ago, when one man was killed and several wounded by the police, was meant as a timely warning that the law against public meetings will be rigorously enforced." As Mr. Finer points out, "not a new spirit, but *force majeure*, has achieved a victory; and the victory has been won over overt acts and not over the state of mind or the justification of such acts" (*Mussolini's Italy*, p. 505).

There are in Italy today two sets of institutions: those of the "corporative state" and those of the *Polizei-Staat*. Speaking in the Chamber on May 26, 1927, Mussolini stated that to keep public peace he had at his disposal 60,000 *carabinieri;* 15,000 policemen, besides 5000 guards for Rome alone; 10,000 militiamen engaged in guarding the railroads, ports, roads, and postal services. The police were equipped with 774 automobiles, 290 trucks, 198 motorcycles, 48 motorboats, and 12,000 bicycles. Add the 3600 men of the frontier militia, the 40,000 men of the regular

---

[5] Jones, *Is Fascism the Answer?*, pp. 71 and 84: "Workmen in Italy today, when they read of the strikes in other countries, have been heard to remark, 'How could we have been such fools?' The continuation of the deplorable policy of striking becomes only necessary when workmen have no assurance that they will get a fair deal. *Having established a system of conferences* with a fair court at the top, they know that they will obtain equitable terms."

militia on duty, and the 260,000 reserve militiamen, and you can form a fair estimate of the power of the *Polizei-Staat*.

There exists in Italy a "Special Tribunal for the defence of the state," consisting not of regular judges but of officers of the Fascist militia, which from February 1927 to June 1932 sentenced nine persons to death, one to penal servitude for life, and 1902 to an aggregate of 10,157 years in prison.[6] There is no survey covering the period from June 1932 to January 1934. From January 10 to March 21, 1934, twenty-nine persons were sentenced to an aggregate of 270 years' imprisonment. From July 1934 to April 5, 1935, 315 persons were sentenced to terms ranging from one to twenty-two years.

From 1927 to 1934 three thousand persons who escaped the benevolent attentions of the Special Tribunal were interned by the police, without a preliminary trial or even an interrogation, on small penal islands, there to meditate on the "corporative state." In 1931 the police in all of Italy "stopped" (*fermó*) 78,004 persons,[7] that is to say, they did not put them under arrest, but kept them in prison until they were satisfied that the "stopped" persons had committed no crime. It is impossible to ascertain how many were put under special police surveillance; that is to say, were compelled to go home in the evening at a given hour and were not allowed to leave the city of their domicile without obtaining permission from the police.

While the "corporative state" is paring down wages, the *Polizei-Staat* is repressing every sign of unrest. Probably the credit for Italian "social peace" should be awarded to the *Polizei-Staat* and not to the "corporative man." "They make a desert and call it peace."[8]

---

[6] A systematic statement of the condemnations pronounced from Feb. 1927 to May 1931 was published in the collection *Italy Today*, in the number for July-Aug., 1932, entitled *The Special Tribunal for the Defence of the State*. To the figures given in that pamphlet we have added those of the sentences pronounced from June 1931 to June 1932.

[7] Camera dei Deputati, *Relazione della Giunta Generale del Bilancio sul bilancio preventivo del Ministero di Grazia e* 1933–4, *Documenti 1586A*, p. 31.

[8] Mr. Goad, in the *English Review* for Mar. 1933, advises whoever wishes to make himself an expert in Fascistology not to concern himself with the national militia, nor the Special Tribunal for the Defence of the State, not the "so-called censorship or control of the Press," for these are "emergency institutions" not essential to the Fascist regime. One should study "the permanent constitutional machinery" of the corporative state. When associated with Miss Currey, in writing the book *The Working of the Corporative State*, pp. 18 and 20, he stated not only that "it cannot be too often pointed out that the Corporate State does not involve dictatorship," but also that from 1922 to 1929 there were in Italy "seven years of gradually diminishing dictatorship during

the growth of the new institutions of the Corporate State," and that as a consequence of this abatement in the dictatorship "the Corporate State is a new form of Constitutional Democracy." There are in Italy many left-wing Fascists, especially among the lower officials of the unions, who hail the Fascist economic organizations as the cornerstone of a new social order, but do not like to see the political dictatorship in their background and maintain that the dictatorship is no more than a transitory phase and will be discarded as soon as the Italian people has been imbued with the spirit of Fascism. On the other hand, many employers think that the dictatorship is the only valuable part of the Fascist machine and they would be happy if some fine day the unions were wholly and definitely discarded, since at least on minor issues their officials are not seldom restive and troublesome. Mr. Goad and Miss Currey have on their own account solved the problem by making out that no dictatorship is to be found in Italy. Finer, *Mussolini's Italy*, p. 499, did perfectly understand that "the Dictatorship is the necessary rack and screw of the Corporate system; all the rest is subordinate machinery." According to Dr. Einzig, *Economic Foundations*, p. 94, Italy has a dictatorship, and the system has this advantage among others that "Italian banks are better safeguarded against panic than the banks of democratic countries; in Fascist Italy anyone who attempted to undermine confidence in the banks would soon find himself on the Lipari Islands or in an even worse place." But "dictatorship, as it has existed in Italy during the last ten years, is only a transition period: the trend of evolution is towards the creation of a new democracy as a permanent basis of the Corporate State; already the heavy hand of dictatorship is used much less than in the earlier stage" (p. 26). A man can say anything that he wishes, provided that he completely ignores the facts.

IS FASCISM
A CAPITALIST
DICTATORSHIP?

I

Sorel and Mussolini

T HOSE who seek to understand what is happening in present-day Italy, often chance to meet someone who is convinced that "Mussolini in his heart of hearts has remained a Socialist" [1] and that one fine day, when the world least expects it, he will "go to the left." In 1928, Mr. Edward Corsi returned to the United States from Italy, convinced that the Fascists would "ultimately transform Italy as the Bolshevists have transformed Russia." [2] In 1932, Professor H. E. Jensen of Duke University was present at an informal gathering of Fascists in Rome:

The older Fascists were speaking of the Regime in glowing terms, but the younger ones had little to say. Afterwards, a member of the younger group remarked, "These older people are in favor of the Regime because they think it is taking Italy to the Right. We know it is leading cautiously to the Left." Similar views are frequently encountered. [3]

Signor Biagi, from 1932 to 1934 under-secretary at the Ministry of Corporations, admits that from the ideas and philosophy of Georges Sorel the Fascist doctrine "differs profoundly, as it repudiates the concept of the class war and direct action, and hence the myth of the general strike, reconciling instead the syndicate with the state." But he maintains that Fascism has preserved "several precious legacies" from "that noble mind": for example, his idea that "syndicalism is the pivot of social life" and his "ardent revolutionism." [4]

No wonder, therefore, if the chief editor of the London *Daily Herald* related in his paper on June 6, 1934, after visiting Italy, that he had found there a Fascist Left Wing, which saw in the corporation "a definitely revolutionary instrument, a weapon for the abolition of Capitalism":

The corporation is to be the means whereby the workers' organizations secure, not only a right to bargain over hours and wages, but also a right to share in the control and management of industry: ultimately to divide

---

[1] Einzig, *Economic Foundations*, p. 59.
[2] New York *World*, Oct. 28, 1928.
[3] "Fascism After Ten Years" in *South Atlantic Quarterly*, Apr. 1933, p. 159.
[4] *Gerarchia*, May 1933, p. 357.

control with the technicians, eliminating capitalist management altogether. The ownership of the "means of production, distribution and exchange" is to be taken out of private hands and vested in the corporations themselves.

Mussolini, with his exceptional demagogic perspicacity, does not discourage this kind of speculation. The Russian Bolshevists did away with capitalism and democracy at one and the same time. Mussolini has begun with democracy. The turn of capitalism will come next. A Fascist dictatorship which might crumble in a communist dictatorship, is a good theme for journalists in search of "good stories."

But neither does Mussolini discourage speculations of precisely the opposite tenor. The chief editor of the *Daily Herald* found in Italy, therefore, a Fascist right wing too:

On the other hand, the Conservative Fascists, and, of course, the industrialists, are determined that there shall be no nonsense. They hope to find in the corporation an instrument by which they can keep the workers more effectively under control, and by which they can free themselves from much of the governmental and party interference of which they complain bitterly today. The one side hopes that inside the corporation the employers will get the upper hand and effectively rule the rest. The other side hopes that the workers will get the upper hand.

"There has taken place no expropriation in industry," the secretary of the confederation of employers in industry declared to Monsieur Lachin during the winter of 1935. Also the secretary of the confederation of employers in agriculture stated that the principle of expropriation had never been applied in agriculture:

In only about twenty cases the direction of an enterprise has been taken from the hands of landowners who had insufficiently cultivated their holdings, and has been confided to the provincial association of employers in agriculture. That does not mean that the right of ownership has been violated.

As to the corporations, the industrialists do not fear lest they become the owners of the instruments of production and distribution, as certain left-wing Fascists hope:

Never has this thesis been officially upheld. Such a tendency never was sanctioned by our Duce. On the contrary, Mussolini has always affirmed that he did not want a proprietary state and he has always defended private property and individual initiative. . . . The day when the corporation transcends these boundaries, discussion will arise and we shall have our say. We will not let ourselves be deprived of our ownership.

The bankers also made light of the have-nots who pretend to participate actively in the running of the banks. "Those are aspirations which will remain in the state of aspirations," declared a "very exalted financial personage." "We have not in any way decided to allow ourselves to be expropriated. We are convinced that the head of the government will not take such a course." [5]

But at the opportune moment the right-wing Fascists disappear and the left-wing Fascists come to the front. In the spring of 1935 a group of French revolutionary syndicalists came down into Italy to discover Fascism as guests of the Italian government. Rossoni told them that "Fascism had begun as a political revolution but was on its way to a social revolution; capitalism was finished; whosoever defends capitalism cannot be other than an imbecile or riff-raff." Naturally, several French revolutionary syndicalists were filled with a great enthusiasm, and one of them, at a banquet, after having eaten and drunk at the expense of the Italian taxpayer, exclaimed: "I do not drink to Rossoni the minister, but to Rossoni the comrade." [6] But when the French revolutionary syndicalists had passed over the frontier, there came forward a high Fascist personage, Signor Farinacci, and speaking in Florence on June 21, 1935, taught that in the Fascist regime there no longer exists a parasitic bourgeoisie; there exists only the bourgeoisie "which works and which creates and which deserves the respect of the Fascists"; Mussolini, in June 1921, had announced that the Fascists would oppose "with all their strength any attempts at socialization"; in 1923 he had eulogized private initiative and declared himself hostile to every form of managed economy; the economic policy of Fascism remained in 1935 faithful to the principles of 1921 and 1923.

What is the reality behind these conflicting opinions?

He who knows the social and political structure of Fascist Italy and the powerlessness to which the working classes are reduced by the *Polizei-Staat*, can foresee with absolute certainty that, *as long as the present Polizei-Staat lasts*, these classes will never gain the predominance in the corporative state.

---

[5] *La IVe Italie*, pp. 204, 205, 206, 222, 245.
[6] *Notre Temps*, June 7, 1935, p. 87.

Fascist revolutionary syndicalism is mere humbug. The Fascist "syndicates" are actually the direct opposite of those "syndicates" to which Georges Sorel in his clouded imagination entrusted the duty of destroying capitalist society and of laying the foundations of a new society of labour.

According to Sorel the class struggle—not the mild class conflict of the reformist Socialists, but the violent class war—must be the method of attack of the workers' "syndicates." These syndicates must be created by the working class without any participation by intellectuals and politicians, following the exigencies of the daily struggle, outside the administrative framework of the capitalist state, through a spontaneous, unconscious, instinctive process of creation and development. They must wage war on all the institutions of the capitalist state, whose functions and powers they must without truce try to eliminate, arrogating to themselves the right to legislate, to collect taxes, to possess armed forces, courts, and schools. In this truceless struggle they are to make constant use of the strike, and of that most effective of all weapons, the general strike, with the final objective of expropriating the capitalist class. The "syndicates" of all trades must unite in each city to form Chambers of Labour (*bourses du travail*), which, when the social revolution takes place will take over all the powers of the old bourgeois municipalities, and govern the cities and their adjacent areas with sovereign authority. The national confederation of all the "syndicates" and all the chambers of labour will supplant the old bourgeois central government.[7]

The Fascist "syndicates" were created at a stroke by a legislative act through what Taine would have called *la raison raisonnante;* they are administered by officials whose authority emanates not from the workers but from the government and from the leaders of the party in power; they are closely watched by the political authorities and by the upper ranks of the dominant party's hierarchy. The Fascist syndicates must abstain from class war and must obey the moral law of class cooperation. The Fascists have destroyed the old General Confederation of Labour, which tried to unite into a national body all the working-class organizations of Italy; and they prohibit any grouping of unions on a communal basis. In place of the old Confederation of Labour they

---

[7] Guy-Grand, *La Philosophie Syndicaliste.*

have created four different workers' confederations, none of which may have anything to do with any of the others. The buildings in the hearts of the large cities once occupied by the "chambers of workers," the meeting place of the great mass of the working people, were "conquered" between 1924 and 1926 by the Fascists and became their headquarters. The headquarters of the unions of today are scattered in outlying districts of the cities, so that a rapid massing of their membership is impossible if danger should arise of popular movements against the regime. The only gatherings allowed are those in which the crowd is classified into small units, each under a Fascist leader responsible to the Party for the behaviour of his fellows. The unity of local and national organization among the working class is systematically denied by the Fascist regime.

Thanks to the legal unions that have control over wages; thanks to labour exchanges to which application must be made by the workers seeking employment; thanks to the many insurance institutions on which the worker is dependent in case of accident, sickness, or old age; thanks to the National Organization for the Protection of Mothers and Infants, on which depend the women and children of the working classes; and thanks to the Dopolavoro, which exercises control over the leisure hours of the worker, the trusted men of the party in power keep a check at all times on the actions—and one might say even the thoughts —of the workers. There is not a single corner of the worker's life that is free from the control of the Party. Agricultural labourers, spread over farms, can more easily escape the grip of the Fascist institutions. But they are not considered to be as dangerous politically as the industrial workers who live in the cities. The government reserves for the latter its chief measures of "protection."

M. Rosenstock-Franck has described in the following terms the difference between the dictatorships of former times and the dictatorships of today:

The dictatorships of former times, of which the Napoleonic regime is a typical example, had only to struggle against liberty in all its forms: liberty of the press, liberty of association, liberty of assembly. The authorities knew precisely where to apply police surveillance: at the office of such and such a newspaper, in the environs of such and such a music hall transformed into a club, in the neighbourhood of the home of such and such a citizen who was suspected and watched. Economic development had not yet given rise to the temporary assembly of those enormous groups of human beings who are massed together in the most important factories. The social consequences of industrial progress imposed new necessities and new tactics upon dictatorships. What good does it do to struggle against the right of assembly, to shackle the press, to prohibit manifestations in the streets, if one tolerates the development of revolutionary centres within the factories? What good does it do to prevent the workmen from engaging in any kind of political activity outside of the plant, if one must resign oneself to the recrudescence of this activity within the plant itself, on the numerous occasions when the workmen come together apart from their work, as they go in and out of the shop? There was every necessity that the new government should adopt an attitude of strict surveillance towards the groups of workmen.[8]

What connexion can a man of common sense discover between the syndicalism of Sorel and the elephantine bureaucratic machine with which the Fascist Party controls Italian labour?

What Fascist doctrine has in common with Sorel is not syndicalism, but the dislike of parliamentary institutions, the advocacy of violent direct action as a means of political action and the method of exciting the emotions of the mob through myths in order to be able to exploit those emotions for ends anything but mythical. But these doctrines were not invented by Sorel and they have no essential connexion with the real syndicalist doctrine. Aversion to parliamentary institutions is present in innumerable writers of the nineteenth century—Catholics, Protestant reactionaries, anarchists, etc. And since the beginning of time there has been an infinity of politicians who have deceived the crowd with myths and who have had recourse to violence when they thought they could do so with impunity. Sorel associated the doctrine of the myths and of violence with that of anti-parliamentary syndicalism, just as he took fragments from the philosophies of Bergson and James and others, none of which had anything to do with genuine syndicalism. The anti-parliamentary animus and the daily use of the myth and of violence, detached from syndicalist doctrines, have been employed by Mussolini, as a means of placing under the control of the Fascist Party and at the service of the employers those very syndicates which according to Sorel were, independently of all parties, to destroy capitalist society.

---

[8] *L'Economie Corporative*, pp. 50–1.

Signor Razza, President of the Confederation of Agricultural Unions and a former revolutionary syndicalist, in an address delivered September 27, 1931, put matters in their true light:

> We Sorelians of yesterday proclaim that our Fascist syndical movement has nothing in common with Sorel and his theories. The Sorelian dogmas of the general strike and violence aimed at creating the myth that at a certain moment the best prepared and equipped technical syndicates would dominate all the categories and would control the whole economic process. Fascism repudiates this theory, and asserts that the syndicates are at the service of the nation, the unitary organization of the fatherland. The unitary conception of our movement raises itself above the selfish interests of the strongest and the myopia of the smallest.[9]

Even clearer is another Fascist "thinker," Signor Costamagna:

> Strictly speaking, the terms syndicalism and syndicate might be struck out of the Fascist dictionary. The syndicate, which no longer controls the activities of the individual and of other groups, let alone the activities of the state, but is itself rigorously controlled by the state, which no longer operates with its own means to particular ends but moves according to the rules and standards of public law, and strives to attain ends alien to its members but proper to the state; the Fascist syndicate as defined by the law of April 3, 1926 and as it obtains in Italy, is no longer a syndicate, but actually the anti-syndicate.[10]

Signor Rocco, who as Minister of Justice prepared the law and the regulation of 1926, and to whom more than to any other Fascist "doctor" is to be credited the paternity of Fascist institutions and doctrines, when questioned by Monsieur Rosenstock-Franck as to whether Sorelian syndicalism had exercised any influence over the elaboration of the law of 1926, replied abruptly: "None." [11]

Mussolini and his followers continue to make use of the old word "syndicalism" to signify the reverse of the old idea, because that word arouses vague notions of a proletarian and revolutionary movement, and causes many innocent souls to believe that the Fascist dictatorship has created in Italy a new syndicalist state after having heroically swept away the old capitalist state.

---

[9] *Informations Corporatives*, Sept. 10–5, 1931, p. 509.
[10] Quoted by Elwin, *Fascism at Work*, p. 181.
[11] Rosenstock-Franck, *L'Economie Corporative*, p. 21.

II

The End of Laissez-Faire

THOSE who believe that Mussolini is leading Italy towards the left, cite the fact that the Fascist "corporative state" has done away with the doctrine and practices of *laissez-faire*. The Fascist corporative state not only cuts wages—although this fact is seldom mentioned—but it grants tariff protection to many industrial and agricultural products, gives subsidies to banks on the verge of failure and to industries about to collapse, obliges capitalistic concerns desirous of governmental aid to merge with other similar concerns, forbids the opening of new factories, etc. Mussolini and his followers in Italy, as well as his admirers abroad, never touch upon economic topics without proclaiming that the policy of *laissez-faire* is dead forever. And, since the abolition of economic *laissez-faire* has been associated in Italy with the abolition of personal rights, political liberties, and representative institutions, whoever rejects the doctrine and practices of *laissez-faire* is termed a Fascist, and state intervention in economic life is called Fascism. Therefore, President Roosevelt becomes a disciple of Mussolini—though not so big as his master.[1]

This is a gross misconception. The sun rises daily in both Italy and the United States. This does not make Italy and the United States one and the same country. Mussolini and Roosevelt both intervene in the economic life of their respective nations. This does not put Mussolini and Roosevelt in the same category as statesmen. While they have in common the policy of economic intervention, they differ in this: that Mussolini has repudiated not only economic *laissez-faire*, but has also suppressed personal rights, political liberties, and representative institutions. Roosevelt leaves those rights, liberties, and institutions intact. Fascism is political dictatorship. Economic intervention is not Fascism.

The Colbertists and Mercantilists who opposed the Physiocrats in the eighteenth century, and the "utopian" Socialists, "scientific" Socialists,

---

[1] Mussolini, interviewed in the *New York Times* of Sept. 16, 1934, said: "America appropriated one of the Fascist principles when the new regime delegated more power to the executive head of the government."

State Socialists, Christian Socialists, Protectionists, and Nationalists who attacked *laissez-faire* in the nineteenth century, would have been much surprised to learn that in the twentieth century a Mussolini would be born who would claim to have discovered, for the first time, a way of killing the doctrine of *laissez-faire*.

As for the practice of *laissez-faire*, no government has ever confined itself to playing the policeman of private initiative, as the *laissez-faire* school recommended. Free trade, which is the application of *laissez-faire* to international commercial relations, was the exception and not the rule in the nineteenth century. The English government, while it practised free trade in the nineteenth century, gave at the same time the earliest examples of social legislation; i. e., it intervened in economic life to protect the workers against the abuse of private initiative. During the World War the economic life of all countries was controlled by their governments, although the "*Homo corporativus*" of the Fascist "thinkers" was as yet unborn.

Under the pre-Fascist regime in Italy, the Government intervened so often in the economic life of the country that, when it rained, the people amused themselves by throwing the blame upon the "robber government." The government built the railroads, not as revenue-bearing investments, but as an instrument of political unification. Marsh reclamation at the expense of the government was half a century old in Italy when Mussolini discovered it in 1928. Education in all its grades was either directly imparted or supervised by the government. Italian tariff policy from 1878 onwards became ever more intensely protectionist. The shipping companies were always obtaining subsidies of all kinds from the government for building, equipping, and sending out their vessels. Interventions multiplied during the World War. They diminished during the period between the end of the war and 1926, i. e., during the last four years of the pre-Fascist regime and the first four years of the Fascist regime. They began to multiply again during the crisis provoked by the revaluation of the lira; and during the world depression have assumed proportions reminiscent of the state capitalism of the war years.

The policy of intervention in economic life is characteristic neither of free, nor of despotic, nor of oligarchical, nor of democratic governments. All governments in all periods have intervened, more or less thoroughly, in the economic life of their countries, if by no other fact than that they have built roads, imposed taxes, and issued currency. Whether capitalists or proletarians, men are not favourable in an absolute sense either to *laissez-faire* or state intervention. They invoke such intervention when they expect to profit by it, and they repulse it when they foresee no advantage or fear a positive injury from its action. Signor De Stefani has judiciously remarked that the price of goods is always and everywhere the result of two factors: the private initiative of the producer and the environment which the politics of the government have created for production. Private initiative always is planned after taking into account pre-existing legislation. Private initiative independent of the government does not exist. And if "corporative" initiative is that which is developed by adapting oneself to rules imposed by law, it is clear that all private initiatives are "corporative," and all states are "corporative" (*Corriere della Sera*, July 14, 1935). From these affirmations the conclusion can be deduced that Mussolini could have saved himself the trouble of inventing the corporative state.

The world nowadays teems with people who have fits of enthusiasm whenever they hear of state intervention, planned economy, five-year plans, and the end of *laissez-faire*. They do not care to ask who are the social groups in whose interests the state, i. e., bureaucracy and the party in power, is to intervene and plan. It is for them a matter of indifference whether the *laissez-faire* of big business is limited in order to protect the little fellow and the worker, or whether the *laissez-faire* of the little fellow and the worker is sacrificed to the interests of big business. What matters is that private initiative should be shackled by some one and in some way. Yet the first question which should be asked when invoking the end of *laissez-faire* is precisely this: in the interests of whom should such abolition take place?

If one wants to answer this question in connexion with the Italian Fascist regime, one must take into account the following facts:

1.   Italy has never seen anything similar to the type of planning exhibited by the government of Soviet Russia.[2] When an important branch of the banking system, or a large-scale industry which could

---

[2] *Resto del Carlino*, Nov. 7, 1933: "If Fascism does not believe in economic liberty, it has always favoured and assisted the most powerful spring, the most creative force, of human activity: individual initiative. It is evident, therefore, that Fascist economic policy will not allow the corporations of category to become organs of a planned economy."

be confused with the "higher interests of the nation," has threatened to collapse, the government has stepped into the breach and prevented the breakdown by emergency measures. If there is a field in which planning is necessary and can be done without notable obstacles, it is that of public works; but even a Fascist expert is obliged to recognize that "they are begun as required without a general plan in the region where the depression is most severe." [3] The policy of the Italian dictatorship during these years of world crisis has been no different in its aims, methods, and results from the policy of all the governments of the capitalistic countries. The Charter of Labour says that private enterprise is responsible to the state. In actual fact, it is the state, i. e., the taxpayer, who has become responsible to private enterprise. In Fascist Italy the state pays for the blunders of private enterprise. As long as business was good, profit remained to private initiative. When the depression came, the government added the loss to the taxpayer's burden. Profit is private and individual. Loss is public and social. In December 1932 a Fascist financial expert, Signor Mazuchelli, estimated that more than 8.5 billion lire had been paid out by the government from 1923 to 1932 in order to help depressed industries (*Rivista Bancaria*, December 15, 1932, p. 1007). From December 1932 to 1935 the outlay must have doubled.

2.   The intervention of the government has invariably favoured big business. As writes a correspondent of the *Economist*, July 27, 1935:

So far, the new Corporative State only amounts to the establishment of a new and costly bureaucracy from which those industrialists who can spend the necessary amount, can obtain almost anything they want, and put into practice the worst kind of monopolistic practices at the expense of the little fellow who is squeezed out in the process.

The small and medium-sized firms have been left to take care of themselves and have had to sink or swim without external assistance. On March 26, 1934, Mussolini stated that "three-quarters of the Italian economic system, both industrial and agricultural," had been in need and had been helped by the government. This was an exaggeration. He should have said three-quarters of the *big* firms engaged in banking, industry, shipping, etc.[4]

---

[3] Marcelletti, *Aspects of Planned Economy*, p. 334.
[4] Signor Pirelli, in his address of Oct. 15, 1934, said: "Beyond the frontiers there has been a misunderstanding of the meaning of one of Mussolini's phrases to the effect

3. In order to avert the bankruptcy of the big concerns that were on the verge of ruin, the government created certain public institutes to take over the shares of the rescued companies and to supervise the companies in question until they were again in a healthy condition. Mussolini described these institutes as "convalescent homes, where organs which have more or less deteriorated come under observation and receive appropriate treatment" (January 13, 1934). These institutes have been hailed as instruments of a managed economy. As a matter of fact, in none of the firms for whose rescue the government has imposed heavy sacrifices upon the taxpayers has the government introduced direct management. The governmental institutes merely keep in their coffers the shares of the firms which they have saved, and await the day when the market shows signs of recovery; when this occurs, the shares will again become private capital. To the big business men the government is what the Moor is in Schiller's tragedy, *Fiesco:* when the Moor has committed the assassination, he has to disappear. After rendering the services asked by big business, the government must retire into the background and leave a free field to private initiative. The Charter of Labour says that state intervention in economic life, when private initiative proves insufficient, may assume the form of encouragement, supervision, or direct management. But it also says clearly that private initiative is the most useful and efficient instrument for furthering the interest of the nation. Private initiative must be respected. Therefore, direct management remains embalmed in the Charter of Labour together with the principle that labour is a social duty.[5]

The act of May 15, 1933, which empowered the Central Corporative Committee to forbid the creation of new factories or the development of existing plants, may be regarded as the *ne plus ultra* of government

---

that three-quarters of the Italian economic system, both industrial and agricultural, is under the supervision of the state. Almost all the medium-sized and little firms and the great majority of slightly larger firms, with the exception of a few categories, are completely outside the sphere of the state's healing activity."

[5] Excellent surveys of the economic policies of the Fascist dictatorship since 1926 have been made by Perroud, in the *Revue d'Economie Politique,* Sept.-Oct. 1933, and by Rosenstock-Franck, *L'Economie Corporative,* pp. 331 ff. This phase of Fascist action has developed completely outside the so-called syndical institutions created by the dictatorship, and also outside the National Council of Corporations and the corporations themselves. The history of the relations between capital and labour under the Fascist dictatorship is only one chapter in the history of the intervention of the dictatorship in the economic life of the country; it is not the whole history. It has been our purpose to write that one chapter alone.

intervention in business. Official *communiqués* announce from time to time that a certain number of permits have been granted or refused. But they never explain which kind of factories has been allowed or forbidden to be created or developed. Neither do they give the reasons why permits have been granted or refused. The great industrial magnates can be assured that a permit will never be granted to a company which wishes to build a new type of motor-car, to new sugar, hydro-electrical, or rayon concerns, or to new chemical plants, unless they give their consent. As a well-informed contributor remarked in the *Economist*, January 5, 1935, each time that the corporative system has functioned, "it has turned out to be nothing more than the most ordinary protectionism."

But if one takes seriously Signor Bottai's statements, in *Corporate State and N.R.A.*, p. 623, one is led to believe that in the United States the result of the labour codes "seems to be the triumph of the interest of the individual industrial group rather than the triumph of the interest of the community," whereas in Italy the corporations "are in a much better position than is any one isolated industrial group to regulate not only particular group interest but also the interests of the community as a whole." In the United States "a corporate regulation of production in the Italian sense could only be achieved *if, in the present codes substantial changes were made by permitting a much broader participation of labour.*"

III

Fascism, Capitalism, and Bureaucracy

M UST we conclude from these facts that Fascism is a capitalist dictatorship?

Under the heel of the Fascist dictatorship in Italy today are found not only the working classes, but the great majority of the middle and lower middle classes as well, although the latter groups stand a grade higher in the social scale than the working classes proper. On the other hand, the oligarchy of which Mussolini is the supreme chieftain consists not only of capitalists, but of other groups who can be called capitalists only by an arbitrary use of this term. The capitalists proper—big business men, big landowners, and the upper professional classes—would not be able to survive in Italy, if the masses of the middle, lower middle, and working classes were not kept in obedience by no less than three bureaucracies: the officers of the regular army, the civil service, and the officials of the Fascist Party. The members of these three bureaucracies amount to about a million out of about twelve million adult males in Italy. The chiefs of the three bureaucracies also form part of the Fascist oligarchy.

In this oligarchy the big capitalists are far from exercising an uncontested sway. When a big business man goes to ask governmental aid in his difficulties, he has to reckon with one or another of the high civil servants who prepare the text of the law or regulation which is to rescue the business man from disaster. Now the civil servant looks enviously at the big landowner who enjoys vast revenues and the captain of industry who juggles daily with millions, while he, the civil servant, has applied himself to his profession precisely because he was not too highly endowed with the spirit of initiative and lives on a salary which, although fairly safe and sure, will never equal the profits of a business man or the revenues of a big landowner. The civil servant, therefore, when he has to prepare the legislative or administrative measures in question, tends to set conditions to the exercise of state intervention. Money is granted with strings attached to it. It is given only upon certain conditions, such as measuring up to certain standards and submitting to governmental inspection. The state will rescue the business man at the expense of the taxpayer, but the former must submit to the supervision of the state, i. e., of the high civil servant who is its living embodiment.

In this attempt, the high civil servant finds himself as a rule in agreement with the Fascist leaders. The latter, almost without exception, come from the intellectual lower middle classes, and live on salaries which will never equal the gains of those who in Italy are called "sharks." They no longer depend, as they did from 1921 to 1926, on the money of private capitalists. In Italy today everyone who wishes to live an untroubled life must become a member of the Party and pay it a yearly contribution in proportion to his means. The officials of the Party have, therefore, their own revenues. Even the Fascist militia is no longer maintained, like the Fascist bands of the early times, by the subsidies of the bankers, big landowners, and big business men. It is supported by the taxpayers. The capitalists have lost financial control of the machine. The Fascist Party is no longer an organization of mercenaries in the service of capitalism, but has become an independent force. Nay more, the Fascist unions have put into the hands of the Fascist leaders a formidable instrument, which has hitherto been used to bring pressure to bear upon the employees, but which could also be used against the employers if they ever dared to come in conflict with the Fascist chieftains. If the capitalists stopped playing the policies of the Party, the Party could easily steer to the left. Thus, although the employers are protected, they are intimidated at the same time. It is not the first time in history that mercenaries have become their masters' masters.

Fortunately for them, the big business men have many strings in their bow. The majority of the newspapers could not exist without their subsidies. A man who holds an important newspaper in the palm of his hand and can destroy it by simply abandoning it to its own resources, can exercise a great influence over a government that is unable to dispense with the most spectacular publicity.

Moreover, a high civil servant can always supplement his normal salary with additional emoluments as soon as a big business man has shown him where his *true* duty lies. There is a continual interchange of personnel between the high civil service and private business.[1]

---

[1] An "expert" of the regime, ex-Minister Signor Belluzzo, wrote in Sept. 1933: "Men of great ability and experience, the best elements of the Italian bureaucracy, have long since passed into the framework of the confederation of employers. *It is the con-*

The army chiefs also have links with big business analogous to those of the high civil servants.[2] Basic industries (iron, hydro-electric, chemical, shipping, etc.) are necessary to the "national defence," and with "national defence" the army chiefs are very much concerned.

One must also take into account the fact that army chiefs, high civil servants, big business men, and Party leaders do not form four compact masses each one of which behaves as though it were a walking regiment. Legitimate conflicts of opinions, and mean personal incompatibilities and rivalries, play their role as much in Fascist high quarters as in all human gatherings. Last but not least one also must take into account the personal idiosyncrasies of Mussolini, even though the thing may seem absurd to those Marxists of strict observance for whom history is made only by "masses." In a despotic regime the will, the caprice, the self-love, the uncontrollable impulses of the despot have a wider field of action than the personal initiatives of a prime minister in a free regime.

The Lateran agreements of February 1929 were secretly negotiated between Pius XI and his Secretary of State on the one hand and Mussolini and no more than two advisers on the other. Nobody else knew anything about what was going on behind the scenes. Mussolini, owing to his absolute ignorance in such matters as the relations between state and church, committed enormous blunders and made concessions to which no other sensible Italian politician would have agreed. Therefore when the texts of the agreements were made public there was great discontent among the high civil servants and the leaders of the Party. But they had been confronted with the *fait accompli* and they could not give vent to their misgivings.

When a disagreement arises between a big business man and a high

---

federations and not the state, who control the national economic system, and who have created a state within the state to serve private interests which are not always in harmony with the general interests of the nation" (quoted by *Libertà*, Sept. 21, 1933).

[2] For instance, Signor Ciano, one of Mussolini's most trusted advisers, was an officer in the Royal Navy before and during the war; when the war was over, he joined the Orlando Shipbuilding Company; in Oct. 1922, he entered Mussolini's cabinet, and the subsidies for naval construction and the merchant marine came under the control of his department. General Cavallero, at the close of the war, left the army and entered the Pirelli Rubber Company as an employee; in 1925 he became under-secretary at the Ministry of War; in 1930 he left the Ministry of War, and entered the service of the Ansaldo armament firm. Among the directors of the big capitalistic companies in Italy, retired generals and generals on active service became very numerous after the advent of Fascism.

civil servant, Mussolini's spontaneous inclination is to favour the high civil servant. The person who repeats to him that the state must "discipline" private initiative is sure of awakening a sympathetic echo in his soul. For what is the state if not Mussolini himself? To give new powers to the state is to testify to the glory of Mussolini, just as the heavens bear witness to the glory of God. But his natural inclination is restrained by the knowledge that he cannot treat a big business man as if he were a mere "anti-national," for whom a place on a penal island is always ready. And when the army chiefs, worried about "national defence," align themselves with the big business men, as often happens, Mussolini knows that to resist would be folly. The army chiefs could disband the Fascist militia in a single night and substitute their own dictatorship for Mussolini's. Military expenses have gone up from two and a half billion lire in 1922 to five billions in 1934, and a large part of this money reposes in the coffers of big business.

Among these groups, therefore, it behoves Mussolini to move warily and watchfully, now sacrificing the big business man to the high civil servant, now the civil servant to the big business man, conciliating them whenever he can with convenient compromises, never sacrificing the military chiefs, taking no unnecessary risks, and always yielding to the strongest pressure or to necessity.

The revaluation of the lira was desired in the second half of 1926 and in 1927, not by the big capitalists, but by the high civil servants. Their salaries had been cruelly diminished by inflation. By obtaining the revaluation of the lira, they benefited not only themselves, but also the entire civil service, the army officers, the officials of the Fascist Party, and the holders of government securities. As a compensation for the losses which they suffered through the revaluation of the lira, the big business men obtained wage cuts. These wage cuts benefited employers of the middle class also, but they did not quite make up for the losses. After 1929, big business men were obliged to seek other ways, if not of salvation, at least of relief. One way would have been a reduction in taxes. It was absurd that in 1934 the country should continue to pay to the central government, the local governments, and to the Fascist Party and its dependent organizations, taxes which collectively amounted to twenty-five billion lire a year, that is, as much as it paid in 1926 before the revaluation of the lira and before the world depression. Therefore, each year from 1929 on, the committees appointed by the Chamber and the

Senate to examine the budget, proclaimed that all was well in the best of all possible worlds, but exhorted the Duce to render his own glory still more brilliant by ordering a stringent curtailment of public expenditure. Which expenditures should be cut? Military expenses were sacrosanct. It was necessary to restrict other expenditures. This entailed a reduction in the salaries of the civil servants. The salaries of the civil servants, after having been raised in 1923 and 1926, were cut in 1927, were increased again in 1929, and were cut again in 1930 and 1934 (see above, p. 345 f.). But the high civil servants and the army chiefs succeeded in preserving in their salaries part of the acquisitions made from 1923 to 1929. Those who have lost all the ground are the men in the lower and intermediate ranks of the civil and military bureaucracies.

The act founding the corporations was a victory of the high civil servants over "private initiative." In 1934, when that law was launched, Italian business men were demoralized by eight years of an acute economic crisis, and were knocking at the doors of the "state" as suppliants for aid.[3] The middle, lower, and working classes will have no influence in the corporations. But in the corporations the men who represent big business will be in a minority. The majority will consist of high civil servants and experts appointed by the government, so-called union delegates, and members of the Fascist Party. The only defence remain-

---

[3] A document illustrative of this demoralization is found in a speech delivered at Turin on Nov. 20, 1933, by Signor Olivetti, secretary of the Confederation of Industrial Employers, the best representative of the Italian big business men. The speech was made before an audience of steel men: "In these moments, each man is inclined to think that others are getting along better than he is. But if you talk with the heads of a big firm, they lament the competition of the medium-sized and the small firms. If you talk with the heads of small or medium-sized firms, you will encounter the point of view which someone in the back of the room voiced just a moment ago. It is my personal belief that at present the large firms, with a few exceptions, are worse off than the small ones. You must remember that there are some big firms today which are working at twenty per cent of their productive capacity. Do you think that they can keep this up very long? . . . Among the industrialists, or rather among certain i.idustrialists, an attitude is gaining ground against which it is well that the live forces of industry should react. Some people are thinking: let us only go ahead; when our firm can no longer carry on, we shall ask the state to help us. I know very well that, in this period of difficulties and obstacles, many manufacturers would gladly exchange their position as heads of their firms for that of mere officials placed in charge of given factories, so that they would not be exposed to the risk of failure and could invoke external help in a crisis. But the day which witnesses the triumph of this attitude will see the end of private business; and the industrialists will no longer have anything to do. Those among you who have technical proficiency, will become good technical directors; those among you who have had good administrative training will become good administrators: but industrialists you will no longer be!"

ing a big business against that majority will be Mussolini, since the corporations will not be able to move a step without his permission.

This tutelage on the part of Mussolini cannot fail to be irksome to persons who are accustomed to exercising authority themselves, not to submitting to the authority of others. When discussing the bill on corporations in the Senate on January 13, 1934, Senator Corbino managed to insinuate this feeling of fatigue and worry into the adulations with which, in accordance with the obligatory ceremonial, he overwhelmed the Duce:

Italians of today are more and more convinced of the exceptional qualities of the Chief. But they are also getting out of the habit of solving their economic problems unaided. They find it simple and convenient to turn to Signor Mussolini for their solution. All doubts and obstacles are eliminated if one can say that one is following the path traced by the Duce. Let me deplore the spread of such a tendency, which might give rise to a generation of individuals averse, either through laziness or fear, from assuming necessary responsibilities. The fact that the Duce's statesmanship becomes greater every day, does not justify Italians in becoming every day less and less active as citizens.

Mussolini saw the asp which was concealed under the flowers and had these words deleted from the report of the session as communicated to the daily press.

The resentment of the big business men towards governmental interference in their affairs is illustrated by the history of the iron trust. Between 1929 and 1931 the iron industrialists attempted to form a trust among all the iron manufacturers in order to dominate the domestic market behind a high protective tariff. The trust was not called a trust—this word is not allowed in the corporative state—but a "consortium." Since some of the manufacturers refused to join the trust, the government came to the aid of the great industrialists with a royal decree of January 16, 1932, authorizing the Ministry of Corporations to encourage compulsory trusts among the concerns in the different branches of the iron industry with a view to "disciplining the manufacture and sale of the products." Following the example of the iron manufacturers, many other important industrialists hastened to demand the aid of the government in the formation of compulsory trusts: concerns on the point of failure demanded to be associated with concerns that were strong and robust; large industrialists demanded to be associated with small ones, so that they could engulf them more easily. It was a "race to form trusts."[4] To protect itself against so much pressure, the ministry introduced into parliament a bill obliging those trusts which asked government aid in passing from the voluntary to the compulsory form, to subject themselves to the supervision of the National Council of Corporations. The latter would at last have had something to do. But those who represented industrial interests in the Chamber and the Senate were opposed to such supervision even if it took the form of mere advisory opinions on which Mussolini had the last word. The big industrialists—the only ones who really wanted trusts—invoked the aid of the government in subjecting their recalcitrant colleagues to their own will but had no intention of subjecting themselves to any supervision whatsoever. The bill passed just as the ministry had prepared it. It would have created too great a scandal if the government had renounced all right of supervision over the trusts after it had helped them to get a stranglehold upon the country. But the result of the law was that no obligatory trust was formed. In September 1933 the iron trust itself was dissolved. Rather than accept supervision, the big industrialists renounced government aid in forming compulsory trusts.[5]

Today the great industrialists, bankers, great landowners, and shipping companies are imploring the government to save them from ruin. Their *laissez-faire* is temporarily in abeyance because they are weak. As soon as they are again able to carry on their affairs without government aid, they will hoist the flag of private initiative and *laissez-faire*, that is, their *laissez-faire*. Speaking on November 20, 1933, Signor Olivetti defined the attitude of Italian capitalists towards the Corporations:

> The Corporations *will not suppress private initiative*. In speaking of the discipline of production, no one has ever dreamed of making this phrase synonymous with ending the attempts of each employer to preserve the life or increase the productivity of his plant.

On the contrary, Mussolini has stated that the measures taken to meet the crisis are not mere emergency measures. When the present depres-

---

[4] *Stampa*, Feb. 25, 1932. In a speech before the Chamber on Feb. 24, 1932, Signor Bottai, the Minister of Corporations, said: "It has become fashionable to ask for a trust as soon as it is felt that things are not going well in a given branch of industry."

[5] Rosenstock-Franck, pp. 374–83. The *Corriere della Sera*, Sept. 3, 1933, announced the end of the iron trust as evidence of the fact that "the corporative consciousness was rapidly developing among the members of the various branches of economic activity"!

sion has been overcome, "discipline will be even more necessary, because men, who are prone to forget, would be prone to commit the same errors, to repeat the same follies" (January 13, 1934). The corporations are to create the rules governing such discipline. Who will get the upper hand?

The Ethiopian war, as far as one gathers from all reliable sources, was willed neither by the army chiefs nor by big business. Most of the army chiefs knew that Ethiopia would be a very hard bone to pick, but they had obtained from Mussolini his consent to raise military expenses from two and a half to five billion lire, they had made him repeat so many times in his speeches that Italy had become a military giant, and they could not now confess to the Duce that this giant with difficulty would be able to subdue a barbarous and badly armed people. Among them De Bono was one of the few to assure Mussolini that a military triumph was a matter of a few months. In the six weeks that he directed the military operations he gave such proofs of senile imbecility that Mussolini was obliged to recall him. Even many among the big business men did not feel any enthusiasm for so costly an undertaking. The producers of war materials foresaw many profits, and thus they too contributed to encourage Mussolini. But the war was willed primarily by Mussolini and by the leaders of the Party, especially by those who sprang from the ancient Nationalist Party, because something had to be done to restore the prestige of the Fascist regime in Italy. This prestige had begun to waver at the end of 1926 as the result of the economic crisis produced by the revaluation of the lira. It had steadily declined during the six years of world depression. An increasing number of people in Italy were asking themselves what was the good of a dictatorship that was no better able to solve their economic difficulties than any democracy. During 1934 a deadly and unconquerable inertia had become apparent all over Italy among the bulk of the population. The people having been deprived of any right to express themselves, reacted by this terrible indifference to any external stimulus. At the same time among the Fascists—the only persons in Italy who are to a certain extent allowed to give vent to their grievances, on the condition they start and stop talking by singing the praises and benefits of Mussolini—a deeper and deeper restlessness was spreading. At the end of 1934 and the beginning of 1935, an able French journalist, Monsieur Lachin, in making an inquiry in Italy, was struck by the fact that everywhere there existed a

Fascist left wing which had taken seriously the "social revolution" which Mussolini had promised to bring about through the corporations, were tired of waiting and demanded that Mussolini put an end to capitalism. They had waited for the corporations to give them the much-heralded revolution, but revolution was as far away as ever. "The true enemy of Fascism," they said, "is neither socialism nor communism, it is capitalism." Monsieur Lachin concluded: "This cannot continue longer. A new revolution is inevitable with, without or even against Mussolini." [6] The Ethiopian war was the way out of domestic stagnation. The Ethiopian war is called in Italy by the Fascist leaders a "revolution." Mussolini hoped it would give the people military glory instead of their daily bread. The war also had to serve to dispose of many of those left-wing Fascists who had become restive. The latter were called one by one to the local Fascist headquarters, were told to their astonishment that they had signed a petition as volunteers to Africa and that the Duce had done them the honour of accepting their request, and were sent to East Africa to make the "revolution" in Ethiopia. The Ethiopian war was a purge like the one in Germany on June 30, 1934, but on a larger scale. Mussolini being considerably more intelligent and less brutal than Hitler, called his purge a war. The Ethiopian war is waged by Mussolini and by the leaders of his Party not only against the Ethiopians, but also against the left-wing Fascists of Italy.

One who takes this condition of affairs into account, will understand a fact that would be incomprehensible if Italy were really subject to a dictatorship of capitalists who did not have to reckon with any other social group. The fact is that in Italy today not only the owners of small businesses, who with the workers form the *servum pecus*, but also most big capitalists are at heart dissatisfied with the present and worried about the future.

Why?

Certainly not because Mussolini did not try to compensate the big business men for the losses they suffered through the revaluation of the lira, and to help them to battle the world depression. The reason is that they feel they are no longer the masters of the government as they were in the early years of the regime. A machine has been formed which eludes their control: a machine composed of the bureaucracy, the Fas-

---

[6] *La IVᵉ Italie*, pp. 21, 23, 25, 34, 182, 196, 202, 242, 244.

cist Party, and the organizations subsidiary to the Party. This machine can use its massed forces "like a powder magazine, to persuade refractory employers into accepting its social policy." [7] With this machine they now have to reckon, just as they once had to reckon with the Socialist and Christian-Democratic unions. Will the high civil servants, acting in agreement with the supreme chieftains of the Party and of the unions, succeed in "disciplining" so-called "private initiative"? After suppressing the *laissez-faire* of the little fellow and the worker through the institutions of the corporative state and of the *Polizei-Staat*, will the Italian big business men be able to protect their own *laissez-faire* against the expansion of bureaucratic control? The future is in the lap of the gods.

For the time being one may gladly admit that Fascism has solved the problem of the relations between capital and labour by suppressing the *laissez-faire* of labour. To forbid strikes, to outlaw autonomous unions and create nation-wide "company unions"— this is such a brilliant solution of the problem, that one wonders why it is not adopted in every country. It has the powerful logic of that commandment which, according to Anatole France, would forbid both rich and poor to steal bread or to sleep in the open air. But is this really a solution? Italian big business men would of course answer in the affirmative. He who would think with his own brain, and not with that of the big business men, has more than one reason for affirming that the Fascist experiment indicates how the problem must *not* be solved, not only out of an elementary respect for human dignity, but because it is no solution at all.

---

[7] Finer, *Mussolini's Italy*, p. 508.

Index and Bibliography

Bibliographical entries give the titles of the works or reviews or newspapers to which references are made in the text, and the pages where such references occur.